Thomas H Benton

GREAT DEBATES IN AMERICAN HISTORY

*From the Debates in the British Parliament on the
Colonial Stamp Act (1764–1765) to the Debates
in Congress at the Close of the Taft
Administration (1912–1913)*

EDITED BY

MARION MILLS MILLER, LITT.D. (PRINCETON)

Editor of "The Life and Works of Abraham Lincoln," etc.

IN FOURTEEN VOLUMES

EACH DEALING WITH A SPECIFIC SUBJECT, AND CONTAINING A SPECIAL INTRODUC-
TION BY A DISTINGUISHED AMERICAN STATESMAN OR PUBLICIST

VOLUME TEN

ECONOMIC AND SOCIAL QUESTIONS: PART ONE

With an Introduction by ARTHUR TWINING HADLEY, LL.D.
President of Yale University

CURRENT LITERATURE PUBLISHING COMPANY
NEW YORK

CONTENTS OF VOLUME TEN

ILLUSTRATIONS IN VOLUME TEN

INTRODUCTION

Our Physical Bonds of Union: the Public Domain and Interstate Commerce

THE problem which lay before the United States in 1789 was in many respects a unique one. The federal governments of earlier times—in Greece and in Switzerland, for instance—had been charged with the duty of making nations out of elements that already existed. The statesmen of America had to create the elements as well as to unite them.

The territory of which the United States found itself in possession at that time was underpopulated to an extraordinary degree. Never, perhaps, in the recent history of the world has so large and fertile an area supported so small a population as was the case in North America under the dominion of the Indian tribes. These peoples were so backward in industry that they could neither multiply their own numbers nor amalgamate with higher races, while at the same time they were so forward in the arts of war that they had contrived to exterminate all the higher civilizations with which they had come in contact until the advent of the white men from Europe. The men who settled the United States found much land but little labor or capital. The country presented a clean sheet on which the statesman gifted with industrial knowledge and industrial vision might write what he pleased.

Other nations have always been face to face with the question how they should make their land support their population. The United States during the first century

1

of its existence was dealing with the opposite question: how to get a population which should occupy and utilize the land. Natural resources were abundant; labor was scarce. How should we get this labor? We might, of course, have trusted to the natural increase of our own numbers. But this policy would have involved private loss and public danger; private loss, by preventing the development of trade and trade centers; public danger, by leaving the Western land so long unoccupied that it would have tempted the English to send colonies up the St. Lawrence and the Spaniards or French to send them up the Mississippi. Under such circumstances the United States would have found the back country taken out of their hands before they knew it, and the most fertile parts of the continent occupied by alien, if not hostile, powers. It was necessary for us to attract the labor of Europe by the offer of free lands, abundant business opportunities, and an early participation in the rights of American citizenship; it was almost equally necessary to give the population which settled the new territory access to markets on the seacoast and in Europe by a proper system of internal communications.

Dominant in the financial policy of the Administration at the beginning of the history of the United States was Alexander Hamilton; and Hamilton, more than any of his contemporaries, saw the possibility of using industrial policy to make a nation great. He laid down the principle, which was accepted at the time and never has been abandoned, that the public domain should be used, not primarily for the profit of the Government, but with a view to the settlement and sound development of the country as a whole.

In pursuance of this policy the United States gave direct encouragement to the settler by a series of preemption, homestead, and timber culture acts; and it gave indirect encouragement to the development of the country by grants of land in favor of schools and colleges on the one hand and of canals and railroads on the other.

It was the railroad land grants which, for good and for ill, furnished the most distinctive feature in the commercial policy of the United States. More important to our country than its foreign trade, or indeed than any other part of its industrial development, was the growth of its internal commerce. Our large extent of territory and our sparse population gave this matter of domestic trade and exchange an importance which it probably possessed nowhere else. Without facilities for internal commerce the country was bound to remain a nation of clans, very slightly advanced in economic civilization; prosperous, indeed, to this extent, that the people would have plenty of land and abundant supplies of food, but unprosperous when measured by the range of comforts that they could enjoy or the opportunities for progress for themselves and their children. Politically, also, the development of internal trade was as necessary as it was industrially. Without it the United States would remain a number of disconnected provinces, bound to fall apart by their own weight as soon as occasion should arise. A good system of internal communication would bind these separate units together as nothing else could do.

Under these circumstances the leading American statesmen of all parties, whatever their theories of government, favored practical measures for the development of internal trade. George Washington foresaw the importance of canal communication in the development of the United States. DeWitt Clinton devoted his public life to this development, and by so doing placed on a secure basis his own reputation as a statesman and the industrial prosperity of his State. Albert Gallatin and John C. Calhoun, though differing in many of their constitutional theories, were united in their wish that the Government should establish an efficient system of post roads, and have left their views on record in two of the most masterly documents in the whole series of American state papers.[1]

When railroads were invented the matter became even more vital and urgent. To other countries the railroad was in some sense a luxury. It enabled communities which were already well developed to exchange their

[1] American State Papers, XX, 724; XXI, 533.

surplus products with other communities. To the United States the railroad was a necessity. It ministered to the opening of new regions which, without railroad communication, could have had neither commerce nor civilization for many years. Nor was it from the industrial standpoint alone that railroads were of vital importance to the United States. They were a political necessity if we were to remain one nation instead of several.

This necessity was sharply felt at the time of the Civil War, when the secession of the Southern States brought closely home to men's minds the danger of a similar movement in the extreme West. California indeed held to the Union, sending men and money to the support of the North in the contest with the South. But California was a State apart. She had come into the possession of the United States only a few years prior to the war; and, in order to cement the adhesion of California more firmly to the Union, Congress was ready to do everything to open railroad communication across the continent, wholly apart from the industrial return promised. The Central Pacific line to San Francisco, begun in the early part of the war and completed not long after its end, received, in addition to its land grant, a use of Government credit which amounted to a money subsidy of many thousands of dollars a mile. The Northern Pacific, a little later, was unsuccessful in its application for a money subsidy, but it received a double grant of land in lieu thereof.

The work of these Pacific railroad builders, crossing thousands of miles of desert and mountain, did for the United States on the industrial side what the Civil War did for it on the political side. It made us for the first time a single nation, whose parts were so bound together that secession was not only indefensible in theory but improbable in practice. It was a matter of more than ordinary significance that Charles Carroll, last surviving signer of the Declaration of Independence, laid the first rail of the Baltimore and Ohio Railroad. The Declaration of Independence initiated the making of a nation; the development of a railroad system completed it.

In the earliest days, when we had much land and little capital, every possible means was used to attract the capitalist. We were concerned with getting the country developed; that the powers which we invoked to develop the country might become unduly strong, or that they might waste its resources instead of utilizing them, did not enter our minds for many years afterward. A few clear-sighted men saw signs of danger before the Civil War, but it was not until the year 1870 that public attention was aroused to these dangers on a large scale. The Granger movement, in spite of all its political and economic blunders, was significant as being the first organized protest of the legislature against the abuses of corporate power. Since that day the country has witnessed a succession of movements, both in the State legislatures and in Congress, to restrain railroad corporations and other corporations from dangerous extensions of their authority. The debates on these movements possessed exceptional interest on account of the constant necessity of appeal to fact. There is no field of discussion in which the incautious use of rhetoric or the attempt to analyze a situation from one side only leads a speaker to graver practical blunders and his followers to surer discredit than the domain of railroad regulation.

The significance and importance of the debates on railroads are not bounded by the limits of their immediate theme. The success or failure of our experiments in railroad regulation will probably determine the lines of action which the Government pursues in regulating industry of many other kinds. For the railroad is not a thing which stands apart from other industrial agencies, as people thought a generation ago. It is simply the foremost example of tendencies which are making themselves felt in the organization of industry as a whole. Thirty years ago we said that, while other industries were subject to competition, railroads tended to become a monopoly. To-day we see that the same tendency toward monopoly which was felt in connection with railroads is being manifested in every industry involving large fixed capital. Thirty years ago we said that railroads differed from other industries because their schedules of rates and wages were matters of public concern. To-day we see that to a greater or less degree all schedules of rates and wages are becoming matters of public concern. The railroad problem of 1880 and the trust problem of 1910 were not two different questions. They were two different phases of the same question.

All this adds enormously to the interest of a collection of debates on railroads. What was said in the discussions on the Interstate Commerce Law from 1879 to 1887 may be mere matter of past history as far as interstate commerce is concerned. It is a matter of present-day politics in its relation to a dozen problems of production and distribution, of rates and wages, which are coming up in connection with the consolidated manufacturing and commercial enterprises of this generation. If we take the lessons derived from our experience with railroad regulation at their full value and make effective use of them we may perhaps be spared the expense and delay and the political tumult of learning the same lessons over again in other fields.

Arthur Twining Hadley

CHAPTER I

The Land Question

[THE HOMESTEAD LAW]

Senator Thomas H. Benton [Mo.] Advocates Donations of Public Lands to Settlers: His Speech on "Free Land the Cure for Poverty"—Samuel A. Foot [Conn.] Introduces Resolution in the Senate to Suspend Sales of Public Land; Debate: In Favor of Donations to Settlers, Robert Y. Hayne [S. C.]; In Favor of Sales, Daniel Webster [Mass.]—Andrew Johnson [Tenn.] Introduces in the House Bill for Free Grants of Land to Settlers—Debate: In Favor, William C. Dawson [Ga.], Joseph Cable [O.], Charles Skelton [N. J.], Cyrus L. Dunham [Ind.], Galusha A. Grow [Pa.], Joseph R. Chandler [Pa.], Mr. Johnson; Opposed, Thomas J. D. Fuller [Me.], Richard I. Bowie [Md.]—Final Passage of the Bill.

THOMAS HART BENTON was elected to the Senate from Missouri in 1820. In the earlier years of his long service in that body he specially devoted himself to the policy of having the public lands sold at fixed graduated prices with outright donations to actual settlers instead of the system which prevailed of selling them at auction to the highest bidders, with an arbitrary minimum price. From 1824 almost annually he presented bills to this effect, which, though defeated, had an effect in modifying the public land system in respect to recognizing preëmption rights of so-called "squatters" upon the lands.

On April 8, 1828, he spoke as follows:

Free Land the Cure of Poverty

Senator Benton

I know it to be written in that book which is the epitome of all knowledge, "that the rich ruleth the poor, and the borrower is the servant of the lender." I know, too, that it is said

7

by my venerable and venerated friend from North Carolina [Nathaniel Macon] that governments are not made for the poor, but against them; that the rich get the benefits and the poor get the burdens of government; and I know that this severe remark has much foundation in the history of mankind, yet it has not always been so. There have been exceptions, and especially in that great republic, whose name, after the lapse of two thousand years, still shines as a leading star in the firmament of nations. It was not so among the ancient Romans. With that heroic people, although the government was chiefly in the hands of the Patricians, yet the poor had an interest in their country, and that interest was founded in their share of the public lands. When a conquest was made, half the lands were immediately set aside for gratuitous distribution among the poor; the other half was put up to sale for the benefit of the public treasury. Besides this fundamental law, we read in the history of that great people of occasional donations of land to 20,000 poor families at a time. Many laws were made for the protection of their lands—as the Licinian law, which secured their possessions for several hundred years, and for the enforcement of which the Gracchi lost their lives. It was this interest in the soil of their country which made the love of that country so strong a passion in the breast of the Roman citizen. It was this which made every Roman glory in the name, and hold himself forever ready to fight and die for his country. And cannot the same cause produce the same effect with us? Congress is charged with providing for "the common defence" of the nation, and she expends millions upon the fortifications of the seacoast, and upon the equipment of ships for the sea. And may she not give land for the defence of the Western frontier? Great Britain is now filling upper Canada with freeholders, at a great expense to the Crown. One hundred and fifty acres of choice land to each emigrant—expenses of removal—provisions for one year—seed grains for the first crop —farming tools, and household utensils, a cow, at the cost of £4 10s. sterling: such are the inducements which England holds out for the settlement of upper Canada. And why? For the obvious purpose of strengthening herself against us in that quarter: and shall we not strengthen ourselves against her in the opposite quarter? And by the same means? The defence furnished by patriotism and valor has been called "the cheap defence of nations," and so in fact it is. A brave people, devoted to their country, is its cheapest, as well as its surest, defence. Of this defence, it is in the power of this Government

to avail itself to any degree. It may have as many warriors
as it pleases on its frontier. It has hundreds of millions of
acres of vacant land in the frontier States and Territories, and
some hundred thousand citizens without freeholds. Let it give
them land; let it give them an interest in their country; a home
for their wives and their little ones; and they will never be
found without a horse and a rifle; without a willing mind, a
courageous heart, and a strong arm, when that country demands their service.

Poverty is not always the effect of vice or laziness. Many
are born poor, and remain so; many are born rich, and become
poor through misfortune; and, to all, the change of condition
from tenant to freeholder is the most difficult part of their
lives. Let the Federal Government make that change for them.
It can do it for hundreds of thousands, and be none the weaker
or poorer, but richer and stronger on account of it. Great and
meritorious are the services of the poor. They are soldiers in
the time of war, and cultivators both in war and peace. Their
daily labor is the perennial source of food to man and beast.
Daily do they moisten the earth with the sweat of their brow.
Shall that sweat continue to fall upon ground which is not their
own? Shall they remain without land under a government
abounding with land? Shall they be compelled to choose between the hard alternatives of being trespassers or tenants all
their lives? Shall they see forever this Federal Government,
after constituting itself sole purchaser of land from Indians,
resolve itself into the hard character of speculator and monopo-
lizer, and make "merchandise" out of God's first and greatest
gift to man?

WEBSTER-HAYNE DEBATE

This question of the proper disposition of the wild
lands belonging to the Government was brought forward
in the Senate on January 19, 1830, by a resolution of
Samuel A. Foot [Conn.] inquiring into the expediency of
a temporary suspension of the sale of such lands. On
this subject Robert Y. Hayne [S. C.] and Daniel Webster [Mass.] were the chief speakers, Hayne being in
favor of a free grant of the lands to actual settlers, and
Webster advocating a continuance of the old policy of
sale to the highest bidder.

The discussion, like many side issues in this period,

was soon drawn into the main current of political thought: the increase of Federal powers to the weakening of those of the States, and this debate has therefore been reported elsewhere in this work [see Volume V, chapter ii].

During the session of 1849-50, Andrew Johnson [Tenn.] introduced in the House of Representatives a bill to grant to every head of a family a homestead of 160 acres out of the public domain, conditioned only on its occupancy and cultivation. It was referred to the Committee on Agriculture, who reported it to the House, whereupon it was referred to the Committee of the Whole, where, said one of the speakers on the bill— Joseph Cable [O.]—"it took the infidel's eternal sleep," Mr. Johnson brought it up again in 1850-51, when it was again smothered. Finally, on March 3, 1852, it succeeded in getting before the House. It remained a subject of discussion throughout the session. Among those who spoke in its favor were William C. Dawson [Ga.], Joseph Cable [O.], Charles Skelton [N. J.], Cyrus L. Dunham [Ind.], Galusha A. Grow [Pa.], and Joseph R. Chandler [Pa.]. Among those opposed were Thomas J. D. Fuller [Me.] and Richard I. Bowie [Md.].

The Homestead Law

House of Representatives, Beginning March 3, 1852

MR. DAWSON.—This Government was founded by the people for the good of the people. Its great basis is popular affection. It possesses an immense property which it cannot sell but by a process equal in time to a period of centuries. Compare the number of acres sold up to this date, and the length of time (sixty-four years) that has been consumed in making the sales, with the number of acres now undisposed of, and it will be seen that it will require, at the same pace, nine hundred years to dispose of the same. The progressive spirit of the age is impatient of the delay, and demands a quickened step. Vast forests and prairies separate our Atlantic and Pacific regions, which every consideration of security and of intercourse require should be settled. Its settlement would place upon a distant frontier a force able and willing to defend us against hostile savages, and thus spare us much of the expense we are now required to defray. It would be justice to the new States in which portions of the public lands are situated, by converting them into private property—subjecting them to taxation—and thus requiring them to bear their legitimate proportion of the burdens of State government.

With all of our unexampled prosperity, Mr. Chairman, in the arts and sciences, in the progress of improvement, in the extent of our commerce, in the growth and success of our manufactures, in wealth and in power, it is nevertheless true that there is great inequality in the condition of life, and that much can be done to ameliorate that condition without doing injustice or violence to the rights of any. There is no government that has so much to spare as ours, and none where the gift would be productive alike of mutual benefit. It would be the exhibition of a union of philanthropy and national interest, consummating a measure by which worthy citizens would be made comfortable, not by wasting the property of the State, not by exactions from the property of others, but by moderate grants of wild land, the cultivation of which would swell the productive property of the country, and thus contribute its proportion to the common necessities, in peace and in war.

A large portion of our population is desirous, yet unable, for the want of means, to push forward to the frontier, and there form settlements. It is difficult enough for them to reach the country and provide for their support until the land, improved by their labor, becomes productive. To require them to pay beyond that for the land amounts to prohibition against their going there. The preëmption system stimulated emigration and settlement; but experience has shown that inability to pay the Government for the title after a period of severe trials incident to such new settlement gave the land, in many instances, into the clutch of the speculator, and drove the hardy pioneer again to the forest.

Certainty and *reliability* are words full of import and value in the American language. The certainty of being secure in a small possession—a *home*—even on the extreme confines of civilization would nerve the heart of many an honest man of limited means to make the effort to secure it. Pass this bill, and it will provide homes, and happy ones, for a vast number of meritorious persons, and teach them the value of a government which desires to fulfill the first of its duties: that of promoting the happiness and prosperity of its citizens.

What a useful lesson would such a plan prove to the governments of Europe, and what an example would it furnish of republican care for the good of all, thus promoted by our happy institutions. It would present a spectacle at which the patriot, in the full exultation of his heart, might rejoice—at which the honorable gentleman from Tennessee [Mr. Johnson] might rejoice—as Lycurgus did when returning through the fields just reaped, after the generous provision that he had made for the citizens of Sparta and Laconia; and, seeing the shocks standing parallel and equal, he smiled, and said to some that were by: "How like is Laconia to an estate newly divided among many brothers."

MR. CABLE.—The history of mankind proves the fact that the *monopoly of the soil* has been a more fruitful source of wars and bloodshed—of oppression and cruelty—of poverty and misery—of debauchery and crime, than all other causes; and they are legion. For a single instance, look now at the tears, groans —dying groans, misery, wretchedness, famine, destitution, squalid poverty, and prostration of brave, generous, industrious, and faithful Ireland? What is the great, the leading, the *only* cause of all her calamity? Why does now, *seemingly,* a curse rest upon the once joyous "land of song"? *Monopoly of the soil*—nothing else!

The fee simple of the "Green Isle" is held by perhaps less than thirty thousand persons who abstract from *labor* its whole reward, except so much only as may be deemed necessary to keep the laborer's "soul and body together"; and often those who labor are reduced to starvation, while those in whom the fee simple is vested roll in wealth and luxury, pride and pomp, dissipation and crime, thus pampered and luxuriating upon the hard earnings of those in poverty and want. The identical year in which we, as a people, were sending over our vessels loaded with the necessaries of life to relieve the people of Ireland from starvation there were raised in Ireland and shipped to the landlords in England (the seat of the worst government, because of its power to do more evil than any other on earth), *one million's* worth of good and wholesome provisions. Thus did the monopolist of the soil in Ireland abstract from the then *eight* (now *six*) millions of Irish people so much of the reward of their labor as to leave, in that year, *one-half million* of their number the victims of disease and awful famine—died for want of food! What heart can contemplate such scenes of human misery, agony, and death, even in that one year, without realizing that the tongue can be robbed of utterance other than to invoke God's mercy upon the sufferers and his judgments upon their oppressors? So it has ever been, and so it ever will be, in all countries where the *monopoly of the soil* is tolerated. So, too, it would have been in this country, had not the foresight of our heroic fathers, in connection with our immense domain, prevented it.

Had the boundaries of our own beloved country been confined to the limits of the "original thirteen States," this people, too, would have been, ere this, trodden down by the iron heel of usurpation, fraud, and tyranny. The Shylocks, bankers, with their paper issues, stock jobbers, speculators, and their auxiliaries, would have *monopolized* the entire soil of this country long ago and put the people under contributions. But, thanks to an allwise Providence who has guided the star of these States to a more glorious destiny, our widely extended domain has thrown an insurmountable barrier in the way of usurpation and oppression based upon the *monopoly* of the soil.

In reference to the fee simple of our *public domain,* it is held by some that these wild lands *belong* to the Government. Under our form, under the science of free government, this is a gross absurdity. The title rests with the *source* of sovereignty, and not with the representative agency thereof.

The title, the proprietorship of the unsold lands (the public domain) is in the whole people; and "the Congress" has the disposition thereof *in trust,* and so delegated constitutionally. It then follows that the fee simple is in *man,* not of this nor the other generation, but of the whole people in all time to come.

My friend from Tennessee, on a former occasion, quoted, as authority on this point, from Moses, Vattel, and Jackson, but he might have gone still further, and *proven the original title in man from his creation, bestowed by God himself upon the whole human family—not the few!* After his creation man was directed to *"fill the earth and subdue it."* "And the Lord God sent him out of the Paradise of pleasure—the Garden of Eden —*to till the earth from which he was taken."* The Lord said: "In the sweat of thy face shalt thou eat bread, till thou return unto the ground; for out of it thou wast taken: for dust thou art and unto dust thou shalt return."

By these quotations two things are proven.

First: that man (speaking alone of his mortality) is of the earth, belongs to the earth—and, by God's decree, the earth belongs to him—while he lives, and when he dies his body *returns to the earth of which it is formed.* Man cannot live in the air *above* the earth, nor *under* the earth; but if he lives at all he must live *on* the earth, and sustain life by feeding upon its production.

Then withhold not from thy brother what God had bestowed upon him before "thou wast."

Secondly. The foregoing quotations, with their contextures, prove man's *inalienable* connection with the earth. Consequently there is no retreating from the fact that man has an inalienable right to so much of the earth, at least, as will yield him and his household all the necessaries and comforts of life, by industry and application; just as man has a right to life, to the air, the rays of the sun, or the water from the earth. It would be insolent mockery to say to a man live, while you deny him the means of life; to say to him pursue happiness, while you bind him hand and foot, and put a gag in his mouth. And a government, a congress, an administration that withholds this right to the soil—a right conferred by God himself on *all*, "high and low, rich and poor"—from any portion of the people, is guilty of usurpation, tyranny, and fraud.

Moses prophetically declares that "the land shall not always be sold"; and this prophecy will be fulfilled on this continent sooner or later.

There was an excuse, an apology for our venerable sages and heroes of our Revolution in selling the lands. They had involved themselves in a debt of many millions; the people were destitute of everything except patriotism, honor, and virtue. The general Congress could devise no means by which that ponderous debt could be paid. The people of the States—the proprietors of the unappropriated lands, ever true to themselves, came to the rescue, and ceded *their* lands to the general Government, *in trust,* for the purpose of paying *that* debt. In other words: they gave to the creditors, through "the Congress," a mortgage—a lien—upon the domain, as a guaranty that the debt should be paid—that the creditors might be easy. The last dollar of that debt was paid off under the wise administration of the heroic Jackson, and the mortgage lifted. The lands being thus released from incumbrances, the whole system should then have been changed, as the patriot Jackson recommended. But, *no!*—the *demon*—usurpation, fraud, speculation, and ignorance—held dominion in these halls, to stifle justice and insult humanity.

Jefferson, the immortal Jefferson, and his compatriots—that *August Council of Rebels,* on the 4th of July, 1776, declared that "*all* just powers of government are derived from the consent of the governed.'' The people, from whom emanate all just powers of this Government, ask the recognition of their right to "life, liberty, and the pursuit of happiness," in a grant of homes and independence upon *their own soil*—soil upon which they had given only a lien to secure a debt—no more!

The science of free government teaches that *there is no acquired or incidental right of any stability or virtue that is not based upon or does not flow upon a natural right*. Hence, if it be claimed that the people have not a natural right to the soil, then, indeed, they could not bestow or confer, through their agent, the government, any title to the purchase of land. To repeat, if you destroy man's natural, inalienable right to the soil, you also destroy the virtue and stability of your land titles. This is an important point that should not be overlooked or be treated lightly; especially by those of large estates. For, when you strike a blow at the natural, the inalienable right of the people to the public domain, you destroy the basis and virtue of the tenure by which you hold title thereto; and strike a more deadly blow at your *acquired* rights to your own possessions. The one follows or flows from the other; and, as the former is denied, the latter is weakened. But when you admit the plain fact of the one you make secure the other. Thus have we quoted and referred to authority, which must be conclusive to many, from the *Father of all* to Adam, Moses, Vattel, Jefferson, Adams, and Jackson. Who can war against all this authority, with Blackstone and a cloud of other witnesses corroborating?

Notwithstanding the people's right to the soil is unquestionable—notwithstanding they have paid for these lands *once, twice,* or *thrice*—yet sage statesmen gravely tell us the people must pay again; the Government must not lose the price; as though *government* was something separate and apart from the people! —above the people!—or that there is an ever-continuing strife between the people and the Government! Nothing could be more absurdly ridiculous than an attempt to separate the people and their government. Such statesmen have only mistaken one thing in their philosophy; and that is—like Jeshurun who "waxed fat and kicked"—they have forgotten the God who made them, and remind me of Milton's fallen angels, fighting against the power that made them all they were while in a state of innocence and virtue.

The only objection to the freedom of the public lands to actual settlers, which has come to my ear, is, that "we have paid for our lands, and others should be required to do the

same." To this envious objection it is only deemed necessary
to remark that if you have oppressed our fathers to pay off a
heavy national debt, which they did pay, *cease* unjustly to oppress their sons. Besides, there is a great deal too much money
annually collected and paid into the treasury. If there was no
more than half the amount of revenue collected, there would be
less corruption, less peculation and speculation, while the administration of the Government might be reduced to one-half
of its present expenditures, and those who do the labor and
drudgery thereof could be better paid, and still have funds on
hand.

Having said thus much of the right of *labor* to fell the
forest and tame the wild lands, it may be proper to offer a
few thoughts upon the utility and beneficial results flowing
from the passage of this bill. How many young men and maid-
ens are there in this country, who have been raised to farming
—whose parents, with their aid, have felled your forests,
reaped your fields—who have been burdened so as to be "kept
back" by opening up the country and paying the enormous
expenses of governments, and who are unable to give each of
their children a farm at speculator's prices "to begin the world
upon"—would be benefited by the privilege of locating and cultivating one hundred and sixty acres—*acres*, too, which are
their natural birthright, and thereby add to the general welfare.
It would relieve them from the necessity of wearing out their
best days to feed up the luxurious banquets of the wine-bibber
and the taskmaster, while their own children go barefooted,
unclad, and upon scanty food. For it is now understood that
he who rents or crops a farm only realizes *twenty-five per cent.*
of what he earns. One-half goes to the landlord, a moiety of
the other half in the way of taxes, tariffs, and for charitable
purposes—all this, too, while you rob him of his natural right
to the soil.

By the passage of this bill, how many would be drawn away
from your cities, towns, and villages, whose children have continually before them every allurement to vice and temptation
to folly, intemperance, and crime, and who, by a removal to a
forest life, would be "snatched as brands from eternal burn-
ings!" How many, I ask, of such would be led "to green
pastures, the quiet waters by," and become ornaments to society, the bulwark of government, and finally take their places,
with the patriarchs of old, in a world of happified and glorified
spirits?

Pass this bill, and by the close of the present generation the destitution, misery, groans, and starvation of your *"Bonus Courts"*—the pollution, crimes, and prostitution of your *"Dandy Halls,"* of your large cities, would almost entirely disappear; for it is want, oppression, despair, and imposition in consequence thereof that "feed up" these caldrons of human dissolution.

Pass this bill, and you bring millions of acres of land annually on the tax list, and thousands of dollars to the treasuries of the States and Territories, from that which is now aiding no one. Would it not open up new and increasing demands for iron, steel, and all kinds of utensils for felling the forest and cultivating the soil? Would it not increase the demand for cotton and woolen goods, with every species of merchandise? It most certainly would; and give encouragement to every kind of mechanism and manufactures. While you all admit that when the agriculture of the country flourishes all other branches of industry prosper, yet you obstruct the agricultural prosperity by denying to it the fertile soil.

The fact should ever be kept in view that there are but two sources of wealth in this country—the hand of *labor* and the *bowels* of the earth. The child of toil and mother earth produce *all* the wealth of this vast country; and, consequently, they pay *all* the expenses of government, State and national. From these two sources, the Shylock, the stock jobber, the banker, the speculator draw all their profits and dividends. From these two sources, much as some men seem to despise them, your army, your navy, the Congress, the Executive, the judiciary, throughout all their various departments, are supported, and all your cities are built up. Yes, from these sources supplies are furnished *indirectly* to the general, and *directly* to the State treasury, whence all officers are paid for their services. How important it is, then, that you withdraw the *clogs* from the mechanical and agricultural interests of the country. While other classes are asking, are invoking the power of this Government to enable *them,* under the plea of protection and tariffs, to *abstract* still more and more from the *reward of labor,* the mechanics, artisans, laborers, and farmers only ask you to remove your *clogs,* which hang upon their rights like an incubus upon the slumbers of an irregular system. They only ask the recognition of their unquestionable rights, that they may be the better *enabled to produce the wealth* of which this Government is so lavish. To ask the producers to raise these vast sums of money, which keep the non-producers in pomp and luxury, to meet all the expenditures of

X—2

government, proper and improper, necessary and unnecessary, while you withhold from them the very means—*the soil*—necessary to enable them to produce the money, is both unjust and tyrannical; it is gross usurpation.

We ask not the derangement of society or its organizations. We would deprecate anything tending to disorder or anarchy. For, in any such events, it is the producers under free government that suffer most. We seek not to strike down the exalted, but to exalt the lowly. We only ask the recognition of our rights—rights with which God and nature have endowed all; and that, too, only in the way secured by the Constitution of our common country; and alone in the way it prescribes. And why shall we be denied? Again—I insist upon it—while you demand such heavy amounts of revenue to keep the wheels of government in motion, and support "the *dignity* of official station," withhold not from us the only means by which we can be enabled *to dig it up!* Turn out all your "loose floating population" upon the wild lands, and soon they will become virtuous, industrious, independent, and a bulwark to the country. A forest life is free from the contaminating influences of cities; inspires virtue; and will restore the fallen to usefulness, if not to innocence. And while you complain of poor taxes and almshouses—of jails and penitentiaries—you contribute greatly to the number of inmates by usurping their rights, and by denying to them the very means of life—"Thou shalt till the earth until thou return to it."

The Eternal Fiat has gone forth that *this* country shall be the *redemption of labor*. Here, labor must be redeemed from that thralldom which now drags it down and robs the toiling millions of their just reward, while they are burdened with heavy taxes, tariffs, and denied, *by their servants*, the means to produce the money they demand of them. Then, sir, let us unite our aid, our votes, and all our energies to accomplish this great event—*homes and independence for all!* Let us not lose our golden hours, but aid the ushering in of that day—that glorious dawn of an immortal day (Oh, the happifying thought!), *"when every man shall sit under his own vine and fig tree, where no one dare molest nor make afraid."*

MR. FULLER.—I regard the bill as *unconstitutional, partial,* and *unjust* in its provisions. I deny that this Government holds the public domain by such a *tenure* as that it is susceptible of any such severance and partition as is prayed for by the bill. I ask by what right—by what warrant—by what title deeds— a certain class of persons, aliens and foreigners, or citizens of a limited age—of a particular condition in their domestic relations—of a particular condition in their pecunary affairs—as they chanced to be, on the 1st day of January, 1852, appear here and claim that all, or any portion of the public lands—the common property of the whole people of the United States—shall gratuitously be set off to them, by metes and bounds, and thereafter be held and owned in severalty, to the exclusion of a much greater portion of the people, possessing equal rights and equal privileges.

Sir, in support of the position that our present land system is better than any other, I wish to read an abstract from a report made by Lord Durham, in the year 1839, to the British Parliament. It seems a commission was sent out by the home Government to examine into the Crown-land system, existing in the British North American provinces. I presume it is well known to the members of this House that *Crown lands* are donated to actual settlers, for a mere nominal sum, barely paying the expense of survey. These lands are as fine and productive soil as can be found on this continent in the same latitude. Within a year past I have had occasion to travel through such a settlement, and observed its condition—contrasting it with other sections in the same region. The settlement upon which the Government bestowed its patronage appeared to be struck with blight and mildew, compared with other settlements, whose inhabitants relied upon their own unaided energies. The idea is an erroneous one, and proceeds from false notions, that the Government, by any system of bounties, can build up a substantial and independent yeomanry. Men must rely upon their own resources, and when they do so success crowns their efforts.

It was a matter of great surprise to the British Government that the better portion of the emigrants, particularly the English and Scotch, as they passed up the St. Lawrence to Canada West, where fine choice settling lands can be had for the mere expense of survey, should prefer to pass into the United States and pay $1.25 per acre for land not in any way superior to that upon the north side of the great lakes. Some have ascribed the cause to be a preference for our institutions; but I think not. The Scotch and English are very loyal in their attachment to their own institutions. And nowhere do the burdens of government rest lighter upon the shoulders of the subject than in the colonies.

Comparing the colonial crown-land office system with ours, Lord Durham remarks:

"The system of the United States appears to combine all the chief requisites of the greatest efficiency. It is uniform throughout the vast confederation; it is unchangeable save by Congress, and never has been materially altered; it renders the acquisition of new land easy, and yet, by means of a price, restricts appropriation to the actual wants of the settlers; it is so simple as to be easily understood; it provides for accurate surveys, and against needless delays; it gives an instant and secure title; and it admits of no favoritism, but distributes the public property among all classes and persons upon precisely equal terms. That system has promoted an amount of immigration and settlement of which the history of the world affords no other example, and it has produced to the United States a revenue which has averaged about half a million sterling per annum, and has amounted in one twelvemonth to about £4,000,000, or more than the whole expenditure of the Government."

This is the opinion of one who ought not to be considered as possessing any partiality for our system over that of his own government.

Now, sir, I come to the main subject of my argument, and I affirm these three positions as applicable to our public lands:

1. That the public lands shall be *disposed of* for the use and common benefit of all the people of the United States, as a whole.

2. That each State shall participate in that common benefit, according to its respective and proper proportion in the general charge and expenditure.

3. That they shall not be disposed of for any other use or purpose whatsoever.

Now, sir, this bill proposes to divert these lands from the *general charge and expenditure,* and to bestow them, not upon all the people, but upon a *select favored few.* Is this honestly executing the trust? The seven States from whom the United States derived its title, and all its claim, are now represented upon this floor by eighty-seven Representatives. I ask you if you can sit quietly by and witness so gross and palpable a violation of the objects and purposes for which these grants were made—yea, more—be instrumental in thus violating the sacred compact? From the perusal of these deeds of cessions it will be noticed that four of them, New York, Massachusetts, Connecticut, and South Carolina, contain the language that the cessions were made.

The deeds of Virginia, North Carolina, and Georgia contain not only the same language, but go further, and prescribe how the common benefit is to be realized, and *in what proportion* each State shall share in this common fund, *viz.:* according "to *the respective and usual proportion in the general charge and expenditure."* What is this general charge? Has it ceased to exist? Your common treasury has a continual drain and charge upon it—increasing most fearfully within the past few years. And yet you propose to divert from it a portion of its accustomed supply.

These conveyances are in terms perpetual; no change in the destination of the funds, arising from their *disposal,* is contemplated. It is for the payment of no particular debt, to which they stand pledged, but for the *"common benefit"*— *"common use"* of the United States, so long as a charge remains upon the treasury. These donors or grantors, for the purpose of preventing themselves at any future day from being deprived of their *"share,"* or *proportion,* and to clinch the nail, so far as confidence could be reposed in the integrity of man, added the words, *"to be faithfully and bona fide applied for that purpose, and for no other use or purpose whatsoever."* Such, sir, is the language of the deeds under which you hold your title in trust, which trust appears on their face; and I submit whether, from these deeds, I have not made good my three propositions.

But, it may be said, the deeds from the seven old States cover but a small portion of the territory of the United States. Now, the fact is that a consideration in money was actually paid by the United States in each of the three treaties made with France, Spain, and Mexico—thirty-five millions in the aggregate—besides the accumulating interest, and the yielding up of Texas to Spain, and the expense of two wars, which formed only a part of the consideration for the acquisition of the remaining territory. Can the Government do that *indirectly* which it cannot constitutionally do *directly?* This territory represents money to the extent it has been paid for it— the land cannot be appropriated to any other object than the money could have been before it was turned into land. If this reasoning be incorrect, the Government is without limitation as to the purposes for which it may appropriate money. All it has to do is to turn money into *"stocks"* or *"lands,"* and then it may make appropriations for any conceivable object, and thus accomplish by indirect means what it cannot and ought not to accomplish by direct means. If the land States, by reason of the public domain being within their exterior limits, have superior rights to, or claims over, this *"common property,"* so have the old States to the custom houses, forts, arsenals, and other public property situated within *their* limits. Where is the distinction? In the latter case the old States *ceded* their jurisdiction—in the former case the new States, in quite as solemn and formal a manner, pledged their faith not to assert property or jurisdiction over the public domain.

I will not deny that, by giving away land to actual settlers, it may serve, in some degree, to check the tide of emigration from these new land States; and I really felt, upon reading these remarks of the honorable Senator, that I could sympathize with him at the state of things in Michigan. How is it, sir, in my own State, in reference to emigration? Maine is almost reeling by the depletory effect of constant emigration. Her stalwart sons march away by scores and hundreds to the "piny forests" of the Northwest or to the Pacific shore; and though we who remain regret to part with them, if they must and will go, let prosperity attend them. And all I can say is, most fortunate is that State or Territory which shall receive the largest accession of them; for, like the renowned men of the olden time, *"they are famous for lifting up the axes upon the thick trees."*

Our present system is, in my opinion, just and equal toward all sections and interests of the country. I seek no change —I desire none. I ask nothing for my own section of country that I am unwilling to extend to every other section. I disclaim all sectional feeling. I believe our past growth has been greatly promoted by the existing policy. If it shall be materially changed, it cannot fail to produce gloomy apprehensions for the future growth and prosperity of the people. Our present land system operates like a great balance wheel upon our political institutions. It regulates the value of real property; it controls the wages of labor; and so long as one day's work will purchase an acre of productive land, and secure a certain and sure title, directly from the Government—Eastern manufacturers can never control the wages of labor. The value of real property in the agricultural regions of the older States is adjusted, in a great measure, by this system. As our population increases and becomes more dense, they will emigrate to this broad domain, occupy and cultivate the soil, establish schools and churches, and form settlements, and thereby avoid those evils incident to a more dense and thickly settled country. But offering extraordinary and unusual inducements for settlement will not increase the number of good and reliable settlers. Such settlers multiply only by time and the natural course of events. I trust, sir, that our public domain may be long so held, and that our children, and our children's children, may always have the privilege of resorting to it for settlement and support, and at an unvarying price, with a certainty of title, until the almost countless acres of our unoccupied domain shall be covered with a virtuous, industrious, and happy people.

MR. SKELTON.—The great difficulty under which laborers suffer in our part of the country is that there is too much competition. They enter into our market and underbid each other, and reduce the remuneration of labor, until they are compelled to work for a pittance which is not sufficient to sustain nature in the condition in which it ought to be sustained. But what will be the effect of throwing open these public lands upon this excess of labor in the Eastern States, and upon the men there who are bowed down in the dust, and who, by competition with each other, have reduced the price of their labor to the lowest possible point? I say that, by throwing open these public lands, you not only fertilize and improve the West, but you relieve us of the Eastern States of an evil that is pressing us into the earth. I ask you how a man getting fifty cents a day can support a wife and six children and pay a heavy rent? And yet that is the pay that many of the laboring men get in my part of the country. I appeal to any honorable gentleman here if it is possible for such a man ever to acquire sufficient to purchase a farm in the West, and take his family out there?

When men are compelled to work sixteen or seventeen hours per day for a mere pittance, how it is to be expected that any attention should be paid to the culture of the mind? It is true that in the East we have done something to provide for this class of our citizens. It is true that we have recently levied a direct tax upon all the property holders in the State for the purpose of supporting schools and providing the means of education to every child, whether poor or rich. I recollect hearing it said that some one in passing through one of the Eastern States, and seeing the barren and stony hills of Massachusetts, said, "What do you raise here?" The Yankee, with that acuteness which is peculiar to the well-educated and well-trained citizens of that State, replied, "We raise men, sir." Sir, we raise men in New Jersey; and we have a few of them to spare occasionally to people the great West. And now, is it not best that we should throw open this great West to our citizens, and place the means in their power to educate their children, rather than to force them into our crowded cities? Is it not best that our farmers' sons and mechanics' sons, who cannot again divide their fathers' farms, because they are already perhaps too much divided, should be enabled to provide themselves homes in the great West, rather than that they should be driven into the closely confined and illy ventilated workshops of our cities, there to remain until their energies are broken down, until they become debilitated and prostrated by want of exercise and wholesome air and sunshine? This is a question which involves not only the increase of the wealth and happiness of the nation, but also involves the morals of the rising generation. Talk about dollars and cents! Let us take care of the human energy of our country. Now, shall we build up our large cities—sink-holes of licentiousness—or shall we enable our citizens to become worthy, intelligent freemen, qualified to defend our country from foreign invasion? Talk about hoarding up dollars and cents at the expense of human sacrifice! Why, I saw a statement not long since that twenty thousand females in the city of New York were earning their living by their needles— toiling on, day after day, and not receiving more than a quarter of a dollar per day. Why is this? Is there not something wrong in our social condition?

A Member.—Why not give the land to them?

Mr. Skelton.—I tell the gentleman that, had we given the land to their fathers and grandfathers, they would not have been found there.

In my professional avocation in the city of Philadelphia I have attended many cases where the person was physically and intellectually prostrated by extreme application and want of air and sunshine.

I recollect some time since visiting one of these cases. He had a package of medicine by his side. I said to him, "Do not touch it. What you want is air and sunshine. This will restore you." "But, sir," said he, "my family must be fed and clothed. I cannot work out of doors, because my health is so much impaired. I can work at my light avocation—that of making shoes." "But," said I, "if you continue to do so, you will go down a martyr to the grave." Said he, "I have no other remedy."

Let the Christian blush when he hears of it from the halls of the nation, that America is a nation where human sacrifices are offered to the god of mammon. I call upon every honorable member here to-day to remedy these evils. Is it possible that a nation can exist for any series of ages where labor is degraded and the laborer trodden down to the earth? Our great prosperity consists in elevating labor to the highest standard.

But, sir, I am not one of those levelers that wish to pull down elevated men. I honor and respect the man who has accumulated property by his energy and industry. I would not pull one farthing from his pocket; but this I would do: I would elevate the laborer to the same standard of intelligence, if I could not elevate him to the same position in wealth. I would like to see him receive a just compensation for his labor, and placed in a position where he could maintain his family in respectability—supply all their wants, and feed, clothe, and educate his children, as they rise up around him.

The gentleman from Maine [Mr. Fuller] tells us that he protests against this scheme as illegal in the first place, and in the next unjust. How, sir, is it illegal? The public lands are placed in the hands of the representatives of this country, to be disposed of to the best advantage of the citizens of the nation. So far, then, for the illegality of this scheme. Then, for the injustice: How are these lands situated, and who are the owners of them? I contend, sir, that the people of this country own those lands—those vacant lands. The people, the whole people, hold those lands, and every man has an inherent right, as an American citizen, to those lands. And how much of those lands have we got, sir? Why, there is enough there to supply, three times over, every citizen of the United States, after you have given all you propose to give; hence, the individual who takes possession of one hundred and sixty acres does not get his full share of the public lands of the country. Is there any injustice in that?

The gentleman from Maine says that men must rely upon their own resources; let them take their money and go there and cultivate the lands. Now, I would like to ask the gentleman if the man who goes into the Western wilderness, that wild, uncultivated forest, where there is no habitation, no cultivation, no fences, and faces not only the savages and the savage beasts, but the inclement seasons and storms, and takes his axe upon his shoulder, and fells the forest trees, and digs the ground to plant his cornfield, and prepare his potato patch, whether he does not rely upon his own energies? Yes, sir, that is a noble reliance; it is what I want. I want to give every man a chance to rely upon his own energies. But can a man, in a crowded State, where he is compelled to beg leave to toil, depend upon his own energies? No, sir, there is no field of labor for him. There is no employment. I have myself, as a mechanic, gone for three months around the streets of Philadelphia, when not a dollar's worth of work could be obtained. Is that a place for a man to depend upon his own resources? Place him where he can get no labor, no land to cultivate, shut him off from the public domain, and then insult him by telling him, "Sir, depend upon your own resources." What sort of resources are these? The only resource is beggary, theft, or starvation.

The gentleman from Maine further states that we prefer to see the proceeds of these lands devoted to the promotion of commercial purposes. Now, look at this proposition. We vote the proceeds of these lands to the encouragement of commerce. Now, what is commerce? It is merely an interchange of commodities between one nation and another; and if we have no industry—and I place industry, agricultural, mechanical, and the manufacturing arts before commerce, because commerce is based upon them, and is stimulated and kept in existence by them—I say, if we have no industry, what will be our commerce? But look at the patronage commerce has received. What are we doing for commerce? We are spending for our navy some $7,000,000 or $8,000,000 annually. Is not this sufficient for the support of commerce? How much do you spend for the promotion of agricultural pursuits? Not one cent. And yet honorable gentlemen come here to say they want not only the revenues derived from the duties on imported goods devoted to the promotion of commerce, but they want the proceeds of the sales of the public lands devoted to the same object. I would like the honorable gentleman to say, in the name of common sense, whether commerce is not already sufficiently patronized.

Let us turn our attention to the true wants of civilized life, and commerce will take care of itself. If we have commodities to exchange with foreign nations for their productions, we will readily find avenues by which to conduct those exchanges. If we have not these commodities to exchange, commerce fails of course, and we cannot sustain it. Hence the most effectual way to sustain commerce is to sustain and patronize agriculture, manufactures and the mechanic arts. This is the true system upon which commerce is to be based, and made a source from whence we derive our revenue.

The honorable gentleman observed that these lands are the balance wheel that regulates the labor of our country. Now, if this is the balance wheel which regulates the liberty of our country—if this is the asylum to which the oppressed are to flee for refuge—if this is the place where the intelligent, the industrious, and worthy may go to get themselves homes, I would like to know why every man, a citizen of this country, should not have a plat of ground which he may call his home? We have given our public domain to our soldiers who have nobly breasted our enemy on the battlefield, which meets my hearty concurrence. But who has built up the prosperity of this country? We have another class of soldiers—the laborers. If a man goes to the Western frontier of our country, fells the forest, makes the wilderness blossom like a rose, and by his courage and address repels the savages without charging the Government one cent, is not he equally entitled to the land of our country as the soldier who only for three or four months, and that for hire, stands up and faces the common foe?

MR. DUNHAM.—It seems to me, Mr. Chairman, that, of all the propositions which have been made here for the disposition of the public lands, this is certainly the best. Grant the lands to actual settlers—encourage population—stimulate enterprise in your new States, and the surplus productions that will follow will create a necessity for railroads as an outlet to your markets, as well as ability to build them, and, at the same time, the same necessity will exist in your commercial towns to dispose of their commercial materials in exchange for that surplus, so that a double interest will be brought to bear that will carry through these works of improvement.

But there is another point of view in which, as a great question of political economy, I wish to present this subject. It is this: These lands are a portion of the capital of the country. When I speak of capital, I do not use the word in that limited and technical sense in which it is used in the books merely, but I use it rather in the sense of material; for there is no real capital in the country except its natural material. What is technically called capital—the money of the country—is but the medium through which the labor is applied to the real capital, the material; and there is no way of increasing the wealth of a country except by the application of the labor of it to that material. There can be no other way. There is no man, however ingenious, under the broad canopy of heaven, who can devise any other way for producing wealth but by bringing labor to act upon material. These public lands are a part of the material of the country. Here is, then, a part of the capital of the country lying in a state of unproductiveness because uncultivated. Now, sir, go into your older and more thickly populated States, and you will find a surplus of labor which, if not absolutely idle, is but partially employed, or, at least, not as profitably employed as it would be if it had the material to work upon. In the West is the material—these lands lying unemployed and unproductive. If this labor, then, was employed upon this material, it would not only be itself more profitably employed, but that profit would be increased by the use or income of this material beneficially used and developed by it.

The difference is precisely this: One mechanic starts out in the world to make his fortune by his own unaided toil; another starts out with a capital or material of his own to work upon. The one receives the income derived from his labor alone, while the other receives the income derived from his labor and capital combined. I submit, then, to the committee, whether it would not be better that the unemployed, or the unprofitably employed, labor of the country should be applied to this unemployed material, and it developed, improved, and made to yield, than that it should remain unproductive, and the labor but partially occupied, and partially remunerated? As a question of political economy, would it not be better that this capital of the country should be brought into a state of productiveness? Here are millions upon millions of capital lying idle, while you have the labor to make it productive, and which, if applied to it, would add to the wealth, the comfort, and the happiness of the people of the nation. But you say you will not allow this labor to be applied to this material unless the laborer will pay you for the privilege of thus adding to the wealth and welfare of your country. And this you call statesmanship; and this policy of mine, which would bring the toil of the country to add to its wealth and happiness, you call demagogism! Yours is statesmanship, though you are deriving no benefit from the immense amount of material. Mine is demagogism, because I desire to employ the means to improve that material—to develop it and make it productive to the country and to the world. Judge ye between the two! I repeat, this land is capital. Yet it is only when labor is applied to it that it becomes productive—that it becomes valuable. It is only when you bring the toil of the husbandman to bear upon it, to stir its turbid bosom, and open it up to the sun and the dews of heaven, that it begins to yield something for the support, the comfort, and the happiness of man, and to add to the wealth of the country and of the world. But you will not allow your citizens to toil to add to your wealth, your power, and your greatness, unless they pay you tribute. You are like the miser, who, if he cannot get ten per cent. for his money, hoards it up, and gloats over it, day after day and year after year, and it yields him nothing, when he could, perhaps, have profitably and safely invested it at a smaller per cent., to the benefit alike of himself and his fellow men. It seems to me that there is little or no difference between the policy of hoarding money and hoarding land. In the one case, as in the other, you add nothing to either individual or national wealth; it pays no taxes, and yields no revenue to the State or nation. The capital, in both cases, lies idle, waste, and useless; it seems to me in violation of every maxim of good policy and sound sense.

But it is said that this measure of granting public lands is entirely selfish, and that the measure is exclusively for the benefit of the new States. But is this so? I undertake to say, sir, that so far as legislation removes restraint from the free labor of the country, or from the free enjoyment of the natural material of the country, just so far you add not only to the wealth of the country, but you benefit all classes of citizens of every section. Now, I will illustrate it by the question of the tariff, which we have been discussing for so many years. When you reduce the tariff, you add to the common welfare of all classes of community equally. Why? Because you remove the unnatural restraint from the enjoyment of the labor and the materials of the country, and allow your citizens to seek the best market for the disposal of their surplus and for the supply of their wants. Apply the same principle to your public lands. Just so far as you remove the restraints, you add to the wealth and to the welfare of every portion of this nation. But place the poor and humble man who now, by unremitting toil, is able to make enough to support his family, and barely make the ends meet at the close of the year—place him upon one of these farms of the West, now lying idle, and he will be thenceforth adding to the capital of the country. He increases his wealth, sends his produce to market, and receives its return. That return is the comforts of life, which are manufactured goods. The manufacturer is benefited by having the farmer in a position where he can furnish something for commerce and is able to buy and consume his manufactures.

MR. FULLER [Maine] (interrupting).—My own little town consumes seventy thousand bushels of corn, twenty thousand bushels of wheat, and ten thousand barrels of pork. If all our population should remove to the West, where will the growers of the West find a market?

MR. DUNHAM.—If there was any objection on that score, it ought not to come from gentlemen from New England. It ought to come from Western men. And I tell that gentleman that we are not afraid of a competition in this respect. Even if you will send out all the surplus population of New England, and settle them upon our uncultivated land, and bring them into immediate competition with us, we fear not that competition. We feel, at least, that your people, when they are planted upon the virgin soil of the great West, cultivated under the nourishing dews of heaven, are supplying themselves and their families with plenty. That, at least, is something. Nor do I think, sir, that any portion of the gentleman's constituents will go to the West, unless they are convinced it will be for their interest. Surely, then, the gentleman, as a faithful Representative, ought not to oppose a measure so well calculated to secure the welfare and happiness of any portion of those whom he represents.

There is another class that will reap the benefits of this measure. It is the commercial class. Your ships find their employ in transporting the agricultural products of the West, and by importing such articles as are received in exchange for them. It cannot, then, be otherwise than as you increase those products you increase that commerce, and, in increasing it, you furnish these abundant supplies to the starving nations of Europe, taking in return the productions of their labor, to minister to the comforts and pleasures of our own people. It is like the circling wave, which spreads broader and broader until it loses itself upon the most distant shore.

I need not speak more of what such a system would add to the national wealth of this country. I need not tell intelligent men that a quarter section of land in cultivation, with its buildings and improvements upon it, is worth much more to the nation than in its uncultivated state. I need not say that a man will save more of the proceeds of his labor when he is located upon that land, and can constantly lay out that labor, or its earnings, in its improvement, than if he were living with no fixed home and no fixed purpose. You, therefore, in thus bestowing land upon those who will occupy and improve it, add more to the individual and national wealth of the country than by any other disposition of it.

But another objection to this bill, and it is one to which I have perhaps already incidentally alluded, is: that it takes the proceeds of the sales of these lands from the public revenues, and it is alleged that we shall thereby decrease these revenues; but I think not; for, if it be true (and no one will controvert it) that, by giving these lands, as this bill proposes, to men of limited means, you augment the income of their labor, you increase their ability to purchase, and consequently their desire to consume those articles of commerce upon which a tariff is levied, and from which our revenues are derived; this will increase the importation of them, and, as a matter of course, the resulting revenue; and this increase, I doubt not, will equal, if not exceed, the revenue now derived from the sales of these lands. If it should not, the deficiency will be supplied by the tariff; and, as the articles upon which that is imposed are mostly consumed by our agricultural population, those who enjoy the benefits of the provisions of this bill will also bear the increased burdens resulting therefrom—for, as the people of the West are mainly engaged in agricultural pursuits, and can reap little or no benefit from the tariff, and being the largest consumers of those articles taxed through our custom houses, it is, as a necessary consequence, they who must make up, as consumers of imports, any deficiency in the revenue which may be occasioned by this bill.

But, sir, I had like to have forgotten the question of the gentleman from Maine [Mr. Fuller]. He asks me if the individual who emigrates from the New England States and settles in the West consumes anything more than he did before he removed from the East? I answer yes, because he betters his condition, adds to his wealth, and hence to his ability to indulge in the gratification of his taste and comfort—and ability always begets desire to enjoy—and this increased gratification increases consumption. And if the consumers of New England shall emigrate to and settle upon these lands, others will take their places —the annual increase of her own citizens and the many coming every year from the various parts of Europe, which is sending us not its pauper population, as we are often told, but its thriving and industrious laborers.

Another of the objections urged to this bill is that it grants land to foreigners. I must confess that if the proposition be true, that labor properly applied increases wealth, and is an advantage to the country, and that this land unemployed yields nothing to increase that wealth, I cannot see how it should be injurious to us that the honest, industrious, and hard-working German should come here and settle upon a quarter section of this unemployed land, and make that which is now worthless valuable and productive—that which is a wilderness to blossom as the rose. I cannot see how the nation has lost anything by it. I cannot see how humanity has lost anything by it. I know something of the German and Irish who come to settle upon our soil. There is not a better, a more industrious, nor a more loyal population anywhere. They may come here with a little exuberance of republicanism, if you please, just as they have escaped from the shackles of tyranny, which have fettered their spirits and restrained their energies; but give them land to cultivate, and labor will soon sober down their judgments, and teach them the important lesson that that only is true liberty which is regulated by law.

But suppose gentlemen differ with me, and consider that this immigration of foreigners is an evil? Yet, evil or no evil, its increased momentum every year is a fixed fact, and cannot be prevented. We cannot, if we would, adopt the Chinese policy of national isolation. No one, at this day, will think of preventing the oppressed victims of the tyranny of the Old World from seeking an asylum upon our shores. No one can be so selfish as to desire to prevent others from partaking of these blessings of liberty which have been showered upon us with so bountiful a hand, and especially when their enjoyment cannot diminish our own. So long, then, as your country maintains its superiority, so long as your institutions are worth enjoying —in short, so long as your liberties remain, this immigration will continue. It were better, then, to cease to inveigh against it, and endeavor to make it useful; to consider how we shall diminish its evils and augment its benefits. You can in no way so well accomplish this as by holding out such inducements as shall prevent these people from congregating in your towns and cities, as shall take them out upon your soil, where their labor can be profitably employed, and where, at the same time, they can obtain a permanent interest in that soil. There is something in the nature of man which makes him cling to the spot of earth he can call his own, and to the government that protects him in its enjoyment.

From whence came we? Your fathers and mine were of those very foreigners who heretofore came to this country, whose glory and prosperity you have so much at heart. Did they ruin it when they came? No, sir; our liberties, as you all know, and as our history will demonstrate, were won by emigrants, or the immediate descendants of emigrants. With no example before them, they established this Government and its institutions; and shall we, at this day, fear to trust a similar people, who have fled from the same oppressions of the Old World, to enjoy the liberties of the New—when, too, they have these institutions and their glorious results before them, as also the example of the millions who have been born beneath them, and who understand and have enjoyed them? Let us not, sir, by a narrow policy, in effect say that the countries from whence sprung the progenitors of the Washingtons, Jeffersons, Lafayettes, Montgomeries, and DeKalbs have exhausted "the breed of noble bloods"; and that henceforth nothing distinguished by talent, or exalted in patriotism, can spring from the countries of our own ancestors.

I cannot, Mr. Chairman, abide the narrow-minded, cold-hearted policy that wraps itself in the cloak of its own selfishness, and says, It is well with me, let others take care of themselves. Nor can I appreciate this vaunting philanthropy, which talks of going forth to right the wrongs of other lands,[1] yet would refuse a home to the oppressed in our own; would refuse to allow them to occupy what we cannot use or enjoy; and especially when by doing so they add to our wealth and greatness, and help us to bear our burdens. If we take too much of your population from the old States, supply yourselves from those daily seeking homes upon our shores; and, in doing this, we shall be accomplishing the great mission for which we were sent—to relieve mankind, and restore to them liberty and happiness. I believe, Mr. Chairman, that we were placed here for wise and glorious purposes—to restore poor, downtrodden humanity to its long-lost dignity; to overthrow despots, and shed abroad the genial influence of freedom; to break the bonds of the oppressed, and bid the captive go free; to liberate, to elevate, and restore—not by going abroad, sword in hand, conquering and to conquer, as did Mahomet—but our destiny is to be accomplished by peaceful means, by the sword of the spirit, by the genius of our institutions. And this very bill will do more to extend the influence of those institutions and make them popular; more to break the chains of tyranny, and give an impetus to freedom, than anything else you possibly could do. What has given the people of Europe the ideas they possess of our system of popular government? Is it the mere right of your citizen to go to the ballot box and vote? Why, sir, the late example in France shows us that the most downtrodden wretch under the iron heel of tyranny has been permitted to do the same. No! it is not that; it is something more. It is the spirit of our institutions; it is the fact that, wherever the American flag has been borne, the people have been taught that here men enjoy the rights of men; that they stand up in the image of their God, responsible to none but Him for their action, not only morally and physically, but politically. It is this that has given *éclat* to the Government of our country; and, in no way can you add to that *éclat* more effectually than to let the world see that your citizens are in the enjoyment of the greatest blessings and benefits under it. I am sometimes reproached here

[1] Intervention in behalf of Hungarian and Irish patriots was a question of the hour. See Volume II, chapter X.

X—3

for my refusal to vote for appropriations for your magnificent public buildings and your other public works; that I am penurious in regard to appropriations of public money. I will acknowledge the charge to a certain extent, and I will give my motive for it. We are frequently pointed to the public buildings and the public works of the nations of Europe as examples, and it is said that we must, like them, have magnificent public buildings; a magnificent army, and a magnificent navy. I tell you that we never can rival her in matters of this kind, nor do I desire that we should.

It is not these which strike the attention of the European traveler when he visits our shores and passes among our people; but it is your home firesides scattered all over the land; the fact that, wherever he finds a hearthstone, it is almost always the happy consolation of him who rests by it that the little roof that shelters him and his family, protecting them from the storms of heaven, belongs to himself, and not to some mercenary landlord, and that it has been improved and beautified by his own honest industry.

Our public works I would make convenient but plain, simple, and unostentatious. The Government I would administer on principles of the strictest economy. I can never forget that every dollar uselessly expended has been earned by the labor of the citizen, and takes so much for empty show of what would otherwise be employed to add to the pleasures and comforts of a home. I can never forget that we are but the servants and agents of the people, clothed with their power and dispensing their means, and that we should exercise that power and dispense those means only for their good. I can never forget that these magnificent public works are like the bright and brilliant blaze of some burning city that flashes upward to the *skies*, but which consumes and destroys. I much prefer to light the many cheerful blazes upon the home hearthstones, which, like the stars above us, speak of hope, of happiness, of heaven.

I have spoken of this measure merely as one of political economy. I want now to speak of it as a great question of moral right. I am no red republican. I do not desire to take a man's home from him, because he may have a little more land than he needs or can properly cultivate; but this Government of ours is a peculiar one—a very peculiar one. It is a government of the people. It has not one single dollar in its public treasury; it has not one single dollar invested in its public works; it has not one single dollar invested in its public lands, but what has been paid from the earnings of the people, and which does not belong to the people. It can, then, *give* nothing to them. It may restore that which they have contributed, and which belongs to them, as it ought, when their interests will thereby be better subserved. I, then, submit this question to the committee and to the country: Is it right for such a government to hoard up what belongs to the people, so that it cannot be used by them, especially when its use would be for the common benefit of all—to let these lands lie waste when your citizens need them for their support and sustenance? I do not believe it is. I do not believe that we are accomplishing the purposes for which this Government was ordained. I do not believe that we are faithful to the trust of our citizens in keeping in idleness these immense resources of wealth and happiness, doing no good to the people or to the country. I have often admired that lofty expression of the great Tecumseh—for he was great, though a savage; he was one of Nature's great men, made in God's own image, he spoke God's own language—the voice of nature—who, when General Harrison was negotiating a treaty with him and the Indians under his command, ordered his interpreter to set the great chief a chair, and to tell him that his father desired him to take a seat. He drew himself up, only as can he who feels the dignity of a man, and replied: "My father! The Great Spirit is *my* father, the earth is my mother, and upon her bosom will I repose." And he stretched himself upon the bosom of our common mother. But you, in your wisdom—in your statesmanship—as intelligent American legislators, refuse to allow your fellow men to repose upon that bosom, and to draw sustenance therefrom.

Sir, if this measure will add to the revenues of the Government, to the wealth of the country, to the happiness of our citizens, shall we not do more by adopting it to diffuse the spirit of liberty throughout the world than by going forth, sword in hand, to accomplish such a result? Our mission is one of peace. The principles of liberty must be disseminated in the still small voice of moral and peaceful influences; not proclaimed by the roar of cannon and the clangor of arms. War is anti-republican in its tendencies. It concentrates power in the hands of those who administer the government. It destroys the people, and consumes their substance. If we would keep the fires of liberty burning brightly upon her altars, we must cultivate the arts of peace, we must add to the prosperity, the virtue, the intelligence, and the happiness of the people. You will thus give an influence to the cause of freedom that armies and navies cannot restrain. Tyrants may attempt to beat it back, but it will overleap their embattled walls, and break the serried hosts of their steel-clad soldiers, and find its way to the hearts of their oppressed people. It will kindle a love, a burning love, of liberty which cannot be restrained until oppression shall be swept away as with the bosom of destruction.

MR. GROW.—It is neither just nor sound policy to hold the public lands for revenue. As long ago as 1832, General Jackson, whose sympathies were ever with the sons of toil, and whose heart was as warm as his will was stern or his intellect penetrating, said in his annual message to Congress on this subject:

"It cannot be doubted that the speedy settlement of these lands constitutes the true interest of the Republic. The wealth and strength of a country are its population, and the best part of the population are the cultivators of the soil. Independent farmers are everywhere the basis of society, and true friends of liberty." . . . "To put an end forever to all partial and interested legislation on this subject, and to afford to every American citizen of enterprise the opportunity of securing an independent freehold, it seems to me, therefore, best to abandon the idea of raising a future revenue out of the public lands."

But, aside from the question of sound policy, the Government has no right founded in reason and the nature of things to make the public lands a source of revenue.

It is well sometimes to go back of the authority of books and treatises—composed by men reared and educated under monarchical institutions, whose opinions and habits of thought consequently were more or less shaped and molded by their influence—and examine, by the light of reason and of nature, the true foundation of government and the inherent rights of men.

The fundamental rights of man may be summed up in two words, life and happiness. The first is the gift of the Creator, and may be bestowed at his pleasure; but it is not consistent with his character for benevolence that it should be bestowed for any other purpose than to be enjoyed, and that we call happiness. Therefore, whatever nature has provided for preserving the one, or promoting the other, belongs alike to the whole race, and each may, of right, appropriate to his own use so much as is necessary to supply his rational wants. And, as the means of sustaining life are derived almost entirely from the soil, every person has a right to so much of the earth's surface as is necessary for his support. To whatever unoccupied portion of it, therefore, he shall apply his labor for that purpose, from that time forth it becomes appropriated to his own exclusive use; and whatever improvements he may make by his industry become his property and subject to his disposal. For the only true foundation of any right to property is man's labor. That is property, and that alone which the labor of man has made such. What rights, then, can the Government have in the soil of a wild and uncultivated wilderness? Or what right has one man more than another to an acre of uncultivated land to which not a day nor hour's labor has been applied, to make it more productive, and answer the end for which it was created, the support and happiness of the race?

It is said by the great expounder of the common law [Blackstone] in his "Commentaries" that "there is no foundation in nature or natural law why a set of words upon parchment should convey the dominion of land." The use and occupancy alone give to man, in the language of the "Commentaries," "an exclusive right to retain, in a permanent manner, that specific land which before belonged generally to everybody but particularly to nobody."

As property is the only proper subject of taxation, nor should the Government look to aught else for its support, it has no right to hold the public lands as a source of revenue. It may be said, True, such would be man's right to the soil in a state of nature; but when he entered into society he gave up a part of his natural rights, in order to enjoy the advantages of an organized community.

This is a doctrine, I am aware, of the books and treatises on society and government; but it is a doctrine of despotism, and belongs not to enlightened statesmen in a liberal age. It is the excuse of the despot in encroaching upon the rights of the subject. He admits the encroachment, but claims that the citizen gave up part of his natural rights when he entered into society; and who is to judge what ones he relinquished but the ruling power? It was not necessary that any of man's natural rights should be yielded to the state in the formation of society. He yielded no right but the right to do wrong, and that he never had by nature. All he yielded in entering into society was a portion of his unrestrained liberty, and that was that he would submit his conduct, that before was subject to the control of no living being, to the tribunals to be established by the state, and with the tacit consent that society, or the Government, might regulate the mode and manner of the exercise of his rights; but why should he consent to be deprived of them? It is upon this ground that we justify resistance to tyrants. And, whenever the ruling power so far encroaches upon the natural rights of men that an appeal to arms becomes preferable to submission, they appeal from human to divine laws, and plead the natural rights of man in their justification. That government, and that alone, is just which enforces and defends all of man's natural rights, and protects him against the wrongs of his fellow man.

But, it may be said, although such might be the rights of men, yet the Government has a right to these lands, and may use them as a source of revenue, under the doctrine of eminent domain. This claim by government had its origin in the maxim that whatever was capable of ownership must have a legal and determinate owner. Therefore, whatever was not appropriated by individuals, as it belonged in common to the whole state, was vested in the king as its head. Not only was this true of forests, waste grounds, and wrecks, but he was also the sole proprietor of the soil of his empire, and he might deal it out in manors to the favorites of his court. But it is not necessary for me to spend time in noticing the origin of this doctrine of eminent domain, or the wrongs inflicted on man under it; for the claim of this Government, so far as this point is concerned, is embraced in the right of discovery. This is a claim, also, upon which the books vest a right to the soil in the king, or ruling power, under whose patronage land is discovered not before known to civilized man. It might be proper that a nation that has sent forth a fleet, and discovered land, should have the direction of the legislation for the government of the men who should settle it—have jurisdiction of the laws of the territory; but how can it acquire rights which man himself cannot acquire by the same process? It is a reasonable supposition that a man is attached to the government and institutions of his fatherland; and, if the men who first discover a country were to settle in it and enact a system of laws, the presumption is that they would be similar to those of the land of their kindred. Therefore, there is a propriety in giving to nations jurisdiction over the men and property of the country they may discover, but not a proprietorship to its soil.

France, England, and Spain claimed by right of discovery various parts of the North American continent; and by conquest and parchment this Government has taken their title to the territory now composing the United States. We became vested, it is true, with all their rights, but they had nothing to convey, save that a subject of theirs was the first to discover land never before, in their own quaint language, "looked upon by Christian eyes." What kind of a foundation is that upon which to base a right affecting the happiness of man and the destiny of the race? What is there in the constitution of things giving to one individual the sole and exclusive right to any of the bounties provided by nature for the benefit and support of the whole race, because, perchance, he was the first to look upon a mere fragment of the creation? By the same process of reasoning, he who should first discover the source or mouth of a river would be entitled to a monopoly of the waters that flow in its channel. Or he who should first look upon one of the rills or fountains of the earth might prevent fainting man from quenching there his thirst, unless his right was first secured by parchment. Why has this claim of man to monopolize any of the gifts of God to man been confined, by legal codes, to the soil alone? Is there any other reason than that it is a right which, having its origin in feudal times—under a system that regarded man but as an appendage of the soil that he tilled, and whose life, liberty, and happiness were but means of increasing the pleasures, pampering the passions and appetites of his liege lord—and, having once found a place in the books, it has been retained by the reverence which man is wont to pay to the past and to time-honored precedents. The human mind is so constituted that it is prone to regard as right what has come down to us approved by long usage and hallowed by gray age. It is a claim that had its origin with the kindred idea that royal blood flows only in the veins of an exclusive few, whose souls are more ethereal, because born amid the glitter of court, and cradled amid the pomp of lords and courtiers; and therefore they are to be installed as rulers and lawgivers of the race. Most of the evils that afflict society have had their origin in violence and wrong enacted into law by the experience of the past and retained by the prejudices of the present.

Is it not time you swept from your statute book its still lingering relics of feudalism, wiped out the principles ingrafted upon it by the narrow-minded policy of other times, and adapted the legislation of the country to the spirit of the age, and to the true ideas of man's rights and relations to his government?

For if a man has a right on earth he has a right to land enough to rear a habitation on. If he has a right to live, he has a right to the free use of whatever nature has provided for his sustenance—air to breathe, water to drink, and land enough to cultivate for his subsistence. For these are the necessary and indispensable means for the enjoyment of his inalienable rights, of "life, liberty, and the pursuit of happiness." And is it for a government that claims to dispense equal and exact justice to all classes of men, and that has laid down correct principles in its great chart of human rights, to violate those principles and its solemn declarations in its legislative enactments?

The struggle between capital and labor is an unequal one at best. It is a struggle between the bones and sinews of men and dollars and cents, and in that struggle it needs no prophet's ken to foretell the issue. And, in that struggle, is it for this Government to stretch forth its arm to aid the strong against the weak? Shall it continue, by its legislation, to elevate and enrich idleness on the wail and the woe of industry?

For if the rule be correct, as applied to governments as well as individuals, that whatever a person permits another to do, having the right and means to prevent it, he does himself, then indeed is the Government responsible for all the evils that may result from speculation and land monopoly in your public domain. For it is not denied that Congress has the power to make any regulations for the disposal of these lands not injurious to the general welfare. Now, when a new tract is surveyed, and you open your land office and expose it to sale, the man with the most money is the largest purchaser. The most desirable and available locations are seized upon by the capitalists of the country who seek that kind of investment. Your settler who chances not to have a preëmption right, or to be there at the time of sale, when he comes to seek a home for himself and his family, must pay the speculator three or four hundred per cent. on his investment, or encounter the trials and hardships of a still more remote border life. And thus, under the operation of laws that you call equal and just, you take from the settler three or four dollars per acre, and put it in the pocket of the speculator. But not upon the capitalist or the speculator alone is it proper that the blame should fall? The laws and the lawmakers are responsible for whatever evils necessarily grow out of their enactments.

While the public lands are exposed to indiscriminate sale, as they have been since the organization of the Government, it opens the door to the wildest system of land monopoly— one of the direst, deadliest curses that ever paralyzed the energies of a nation, or palsied the arm of industry. It needs no lengthy dissertation to portray its evils. Its history in the Old World is written in sighs and tears. Under its influence, you behold, in England, the proudest and most splendid aristocracy, side by side with the most abject and debased people; vast manors hemmed in by hedges as a sporting-ground for her

nobility, while men are dying beside the inclosure for the want
of land to till. Thirty thousand proprietors hold the title-
deeds to the soil of Great Britain, while in Ireland alone there
are two and a half millions of tenants that own no part of

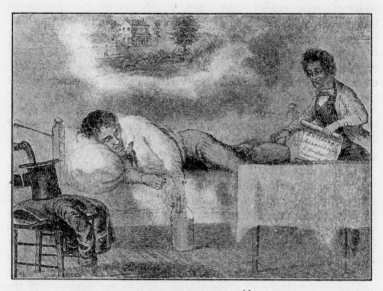

BUILDING ASSOCIATIONS!!

The slumbering mechanic while dreaming of a homestead loses
his last loaf

From the collection of the New York Historical Society

the land they cultivate, nor can they ever acquire a title to
a foot of it; yet they pay annually from their hard earnings
$20,000,000 to absentee landlords for the privilege of dying
on their soil. Under its blighting influence you behold industry
in rags, and patience in despair. Such are some of the fruits
of land monopoly in the Old World; and shall we plant its
seeds in the virgin soil of the New? Our system is subject
to like evils, not so great in magnitude, perhaps, but similar
in kind. Let the public domain, then, be set apart as the
patrimony of labor, by preventing its being absorbed by capital,
and thus, instead of blessing the race, becoming its curse.

If you would raise fallen man from his degradation, elevate
the servile from their groveling pursuits to the rights and dignity of men, you must first place within their reach the means
for supplying their pressing physical wants so that religion may

exert its influence on the soul and soothe the weary pilgrim in his pathway to the tomb. For it is in vain you talk of the goodness and benevolence of an Omniscient Ruler to him whose life, from the cradle to the grave, is but one continued scene of pain, misery, and want. Talk not of free agency to him whose only freedom is to choose his own method to die. In vain you entreat him to cultivate the intellect and purify the heart whose days are dragged out in procuring a morsel to sustain life, and whose last prayer, as he falls broken-hearted into his kennel of straw, is that he may never behold the light of another day.

Riches, it is true, are not necessary to man's enjoyment, but the means to prevent starvation are. Nor is a splendid palace necessary to his real happiness, but a shelter against the storm and winter's blast is.

If you would lead the erring back from the paths of vice and crime to virtue and to honor, give him a home—give him a hearthstone, and he will surround it with household gods. If you would make men wiser and better, relieve your alms-houses, close the doors of your penitentiaries, and break in pieces your gallows—purify the influences of the domestic fire-side. For purifying the sentiments, elevating the thoughts, and developing the noblest impulses of man's nature, the influences of a rural fireside and agricultural life are the noblest and the best. In the obscurity of the cottage, far removed from the seductive influences of rank and affluence, are nourished the virtues that counteract the decay of human institutions—the courage that defends the national independence, and the industry that supports all classes of the state.

It was said by Lord Chatham, in his appeal to the House of Commons in 1775, to withdraw the British troops from Boston, that "trade, indeed, increases the glory and wealth of a country, but its true strength and stamina are to be looked for in the cultivators of the land. In the simplicity of their lives are found the simpleness of virtue, the integrity and courage of freedom. These true, genuine sons of the soil are invincible."

The history of American prowess has recorded these words as prophetic. Man, in defence of his hearthstone and fireside, is invincible against a world of mercenaries. In battling for his home, and all that is dear to him on earth, he never was conquered save with his life. In such a struggle every pass becomes a Thermopylæ, every plain a Marathon. With an independent yeomanry scattered over your vast domain, the "young eagle" may bid defiance to the world in arms. And, even though the foe should devastate your seaboard, lay in ashes its cities, they have made not one single advance toward conquering the country. For, from the interior come up your hardy yeomanry, and, with their hearts of oak and their nerves of steel, they expel the invader. Their arms are the citadel of a nation's power, their hearts are the bulwarks of liberty.

You grant bounties to the soldier of the tented field. It is well. But there are soldiers of peace as well as of war, and, though no waving plume or floating ensign beckons them on to glory or to death, their dying scene is oft a crimson one. They fall, leading the van of civilization along untrodden paths, and are buried in the dust of its advancing columns. No clarion's note wafts the expiring spirit from earth to heaven; no monument marks the scene of deadly strife; and no stone their resting-place. The winds, sighing through the branches of the forest, alone sing their requiem. Yet they are the meritorious men of the Republic; the men who give it strength in war, and glory in peace. From the backwoods, the workshop, and the plow, came the men who gave victory to your arms in the struggles of the Revolution; that upheld your standard amid the canebrakes of Marion, and on the bayou of New Orleans; and that have borne it in triumph over the battlefields of your frontiers. The achievements of your pioneer army, from the day they first drove back the Indian tribes from your Atlantic seaboard to the present hour, have been the achievements of science and civilization over the elements, the wilderness, and the savage. All the settler asks of his country and his Government is to protect him against the cupidity of soulless capital and the iron grasp of the speculator. Upon his wild battlefield these are the only foes that his own stern heart and right arm cannot vanquish. While, then, the shield of this Government is thrown over the moneyed interests of the country, fostering, by your protective laws, its associated capital, withhold not justice from the men who go forth, single-handed and alone, to subdue the forest, tame the savage and the wild beast, and prepare, in the wilderness, a home for science and a pathway for civilization.

MR. BOWIE.—The public lands are a patrimony sufficient, for centuries to come, to combine and sustain the Union against foreign aggression and domestic dissension. While they remain common property, disposed of for the common welfare, they constitute capital, to strengthen public credit; they create a sinking fund to extinguish the public debt; they furnish means whereby the Federal Government, exercising a wise discrimination, may promote the mutual and reciprocal prosperity of the East and West by extending means of communication, transportation, and population.

It is an unenviable and ungracious duty to oppose any proposition for the amelioration of the condition of those who feel "poverty's unconquerable bar," "the proud man's contumely," and "the oppressor's scorn"; but the general Government cannot act as the grand almoner of the States. Each State, each county, and each city must alleviate the sufferings of its unfortunate population.

The present bill is legislation, in my judgment, based entirely upon a new principle. It is legislation calculated to sap the foundations of our Government, and, if persevered in, must result in the most deplorable consequences.

Mr. Chairman, upon what principle is this bill based? Upon the principle of gratuity—a principle not ingrafted as a system before in our laws. This, if nothing else, is enough to wake up this Congress to the consequences of the bill. This, if nothing else, is sufficient to make us inquire, if we grant this boon, when and where are we to stop? What treasury will be ample enough to relieve the wants of the indigent who will crowd around us?

The bill is a direct appeal to the venality of voters. It assails the citadel of suffrage—the purity of the ballot box. It is calculated to divide society into two parties—those who are in favor of voting the public lands to the indigent, and those who are opposed to it; and who can doubt, when a motto of that kind is engraven upon their banners, which party will prevail? It constitutes a privileged class, to be pensioned on the Government.

I regret to say, Mr. Chairman, that the only precedent to be found for this legislation is to be found in the decay of the Roman Republic, and there we find it staring us in the face in its most formidable and revolting features. Yes, this bill is in principle but a repetition of that agrarian law which was reënacted by Caius Gracchus, but not carried to the same extent. Gracchus, after requiring there should be an annual distribution, also required that granaries should be established and the poor supplied with corn below the market price. He also obtained a decree by which the revenue of the estate bequeathed by the King of Pergamus to the Roman people should be allotted for the maintenance of the poorer citizens.

This, for a time, lifted the tribune above the Senate, and above the government. He won golden opinions of all sorts of men. These signs were portentous, Mr. Chairman. They preceded and foreshadowed that decline of the republic and that decay which ultimately resulted in the most formidable of empires, and the most odious despotism. Let us not fail to be instructed by history, though it be the history of the schools.

MR. CHANDLER.—I am indifferent about any remarks upon myself, but I ask that my old school friend, Tiberius Gracchus, may not be misrepresented. It will be found, if gentlemen will examine a little more carefully, that the Gracchi were not so censurable as they have been considered. When the aristocracy write history, woe to the plebeians. Tiberius Gracchus, if I remember correctly (and I am taken a little by surprise in this matter), never attempted any wrong upon the citizens of Rome. Tiberius Gracchus, sir, was a member of the House of Representatives of Rome. He found that horrible abuse had crept into the practices of the aristocracy, who, during the absence of the plebeians in the war, got possession of the public lands, of which, by law, no man could hold more than three hundred and thirty-three acres, and for that must pay a *usury*, or ground rent. But, in the absence of the soldiers, these grasping landholders refused to pay the rents, and Tiberius Gracchus, to prevent the civil and servile wars, sought to revive the Licinian law. He sought to prevent the accumulation of the public lands in the hands of those who could not plead preëmption rights, and would not pay for the use of them. And, sir, this attempt of Gracchus to restore the public land to public use would have gone on very well, but the aristocracy bribed one Octavius, one of the tribunes, to take part against the measure which he had approved, and this led to a disturbance. And, let me add, that the very consul (Opimus) who, under pretence of great purity and patriotism, made such a rumpus in Rome on account of the reforming influence of Gracchus, and of his homestead land bill exertions, was subsequently convicted of sacrificing the interests of his country for the gold of Jugurtha! Sir, let me say that this cry of "agrarian laws" and the Gracchi are inapposite. By agrarian laws, people are led to understand a legislative attempt forcibly to equalize the possession of lands. Sir, no such attempt is made in this bill—none, as far as I know, ever was made in Rome. Rome never had a law, I believe, that limited the individual possession of land—certainly she had none at the time of the Gracchi. Every citizen might own as much as he could pay for, and might occupy besides that three hundred and thirty-three acres if he would pay the small rent. To this Tiberius Gracchus limited the operation of his law, and Caius Gracchus only undertook to divide the *public* lands among the soldiers and others who had aided to conquer them—bounty lands, sir, which the aristocracy were laying their hands on for their foreign slaves to cultivate, while they (the rich occupants) were holding in fee simple any amount of lands which they could purchase.

The honorable gentleman speaks of his schoolbook authority. Sir, authorities are to be found later and better than those he seems to have read. The honorable gentleman speaks of these attempts of Gracchus to correct the rapacity of the aristocracy as occurring in "the decay of Rome." Does my honorable friend think that Rome owed her decline and fall to the attempt of patriotic citizens to check the civil wars of the country, lessen the corruption of the nobles, and extend the comforts of the great mass of the people? Or was it the failure of the Gracchi to effect the remedial objects they proposed that hastened the catastrophe they foresaw and dreaded? Spare the Gracchi, and read Niebuhr.

MR. BOWIE.—I have no doubt the gentleman is accurate in his recollection, but I quote Plutarch and Ferguson for what I have said. The original law upon this subject was not proposed by either of the Gracchi. It was a law proposed by Licinius.

MR. CHANDLER.—That was a very old law, brought back by Tiberius Gracchus.

MR. BOWIE.—Yes, soon after the destruction of Rome by the Gauls, Licinius proposed a law which prohibited any citizen from holding more than a certain number of acres of land, and a certain number of cattle. But two hundred and fifty years after that, Tiberius Gracchus having disgraced himself in some measure in the wars, and subjected himself to the rebuke of the senate, returned to Rome and attempted to revive the law of Licinius, in order to reëstablish himself in favor of the people. I have taken care to provide myself with a report of the speech made before the people—not in the senate—by Tiberius Gracchus, and I propose to read it, to show the remarkable coincidence in the thoughts and expressions of two gentlemen—one living before the Christian era, Plutarch, and the other in the nineteenth century, my honorable friend [Mr. Chandler] from Pennsylvania. Since the honorable gen-

tleman has corrected my memory of history, I recite from
Plutarch the remarks of Tiberius Gracchus:

"Every wild beast in this happy land has a cover and place of retreat,
but many valiant and respectable citizens, who have exposed their lives
and who have shed their blood in the service of their country, have not a
home to which they may retire. They wander with their wives and children, stripped of every possession but that of light and air. To such men
the common exhortation to fight for their tombs and their altars is a
mockery and a lie. They have no altars or monuments."

This is the language of Tiberius Gracchus. Now refer to
the language of the honorable gentleman from Pennsylvania:

"If we deny it (a home) to them, we deny what God has given to us;
we deny what our fathers fought and bled for. We deny what your ancestors achieved, and sought to distribute among all men."

Much as I respect my learned friend, and highly as I
regard his theology, I ask him to show any divine right for
our lands in this country. I think it would puzzle him, as
he said, not irreverently, "the earth is the Lord's, and all
that therein is," or "the fullness thereof," according to another version. But we are bidden to earn all that we have by
the sweat of our brow, and this is the only title sanctioned
by divine authority that I know of to property of any kind.
I ask the honorable gentleman to review the sentiments which
he has offered in his speech, and I think in his calm and more
deliberate moments he will acknowledge that he could have
uttered nothing which would have a more direct tendency to
weaken the bonds of society and shake the title of property
throughout the world. Sir, we must guard against small things
—"obsta principiis." We must arrest the flood at the commencement, or not arrest it at all. Arrest it now, or the barriers
which the Constitution and law designed to throw around this
invaluable property will be swept away.

Ours is a government which lives and acts by public opinion.
The honorable gentleman from Pennsylvania [Mr. Chandler]
has gone so far as to intimate that the tenure of our lands has
changed with public opinion; that legal rights and constitutional rights are dependent upon public opinion. I defy any
man to assign a rational foundation for such an argument. It
is the argument, not of one who has examined into the legal
claims of the United States, but of a generous heart, borne
away by superserviceable zeal. Ay, the milk of human kindness, which flowed so abundantly in his bosom, has drowned

his judgment. The tenure of the public lands can never change as long as there is any obligation in our oaths to support the Constitution, and as long as there is any force in the deeds which ceded them to the United States; if the hour shall ever come when these solemn sanctions are not to be observed, it is better that they be blotted out, for then there will be no ghost to rise up and remind us of their violation. It would be better, not that black lines be drawn around them, but that by common consent they be annulled. I would rather witness a solemn convention of the people of the United States absolving each and every man from his oath of allegiance to the Constitution than to see the principle adopted that the tenure of public property held under the Constitution should change with public opinion, for then *might* would be *right*.

MR. JOHNSON.—The opponents of this bill seemingly think that they have erected a rampart that is impregnable, and over which none can pass. This rampart, thus erected, seems to be sustained by three main barriers, or columns; on the center one they have written *"unconstitutional"*; on the right-hand column they have inscribed *"diminution of the revenue"*; on the left-hand one, *"rank demagogism and agrarianism."*

Well, now, it is more in compliance with my nature than perhaps with my better judgment and discretion always to meet an enemy and fight him upon his own ground; and with their own weapons, therefore, instead of attacking the enemies of this bill in their weak points, I purpose to attack them in their strong ones.

The first column—the constitutional one—stands out in bold relief.

We find, when we turn to the Constitution of the United States, that there are certain powers contained in it. For instance, in article first, section eight, we find it is provided "that the Congress shall have power to lay and collect taxes, duties, imposts, and excises." Well, we will stop there. This is the vitalizing principle of the Constitution, for, without the exercise of the revenue, or taxing power, all other parts of the Constitution become torpid, and, I might say, dead. When this power is exercised, and revenue is collected, it passes into the treasury, and, being there, the Constitution points out the mode and manner of its application. After the revenue is collected, what then does the Constitution say in regard to it? It is, to "pay the debts, provide for the common defence and the general welfare of the United States." I shall not attempt here to enumerate all the objects to which Congress can appropriate money, but shall content myself with making this distinction: that there are some objects to which Congress cannot appropriate money, but to which Congress can appropriate land. The power of Congress over territory is one thing, and that over taxes and money another thing.

Well, there is another provision in the Constitution, and although no lawyer, and not in the habit of public speaking, I want to address myself, as humble as I am, to the intellect and thinking powers of this House in relation to it. And what is that power? "The President, by and with the advice and consent of the Senate, can make treaties." By the exercise of the treaty-making power, territory can be acquired, and that without the payment of a dollar. Suppose that, in the acquisition of the Territory of California, we had acquired it without the payment of a single dollar. What was the object of the acquisition? It was for settlement and cultivation. It is one of the highest objects of government, whether democratic or monarchical, in the acquisition of territory, to have it peopled. This Territory was acquired for the purpose of settlement and cultivation. Now, we have the territory acquired by the treaty-making power. Then there comes another provision of the Constitution which bears immediately upon such an acquisition. What is it? "That Congress shall have power to dispose of and make all needful rules and regulations respecting the territory or other property of the United States." Is not the passage of a law to induce settlement and cultivation carrying out one of the highest objects contemplated by the Constitution in regard to the acquisition of territory? Certainly. Is there any encroachment, any infringement in this? Is it not in strict compliance with the objects of the Constitution—the settlement and cultivation of the territory?

Well, we will now pass on from this constitutional point; and I think I may safely say that this column, placed at the center of the rampart, has been made to give way. It has fallen at the very touch of truth and sound reason.

Then let us go to the right-hand column: "Diminution of the treasury, diminution of the revenue," and see how they stand there. How does this proposition stand when you come to examine it? I say it is a revenue measure. I say it will increase the receipts into the treasury. And how increase the receipts? By the enhancement of the value of the remainder of your public domain. Let us take a case to illustrate: Take the laborer in society that has no profession, no trade, that has no sort of work of his own, and how much tax does he pay to the support of your Government under the present system? How much? Scarcely anything. But take one of these men, transplant him in the West, upon one hundred and sixty acres of its fat, virgin soil, and in a few years, when he clears a few acres around him, gets a horse and a mule or two, and some fat, thrifty hogs, which come grunting up to his log cabin, through the bushes, and a few milch cows, lowing at the barnyard, with their udders distended with rich milk, at once, you have increased his ability—to do what? To purchase a considerable amount of foreign imports or goods of domestic manufacture, when previously he could have bought little or nothing. I could show how much the Government will lose under the present system, and the length of time it will require to bring this public domain into cultivation, considering the time it has already been in market. It would be some seven hundred years at the present rate of disposition. I could show, upon the principle of time operating upon value, what a great advantage it would be to the Government to give the land away, and thereby induce its settlement and cultivation.

Well, then, Mr. Chairman, I think it is pretty near time to pull down from this right-hand column those words, that you would have "a diminution of the revenue."

Now, what comes next upon the left, the weakest, and based upon the least principle, but upon broad and presumptuous assertion? You have up there "agrarianism and rank demagogism." Is it demagogism to comply with the requirements of the Constitution? Is it agrarianism to permit a man to take that which is his own? They say, when you come to the principle of agrarianism, you take that which belongs to one man to give it to another. Such is not the principle of this bill. We have 9,000,000 quarter sections, and 3,000,000 qualified voters. Suppose we were going to make a *pro rata* distribution; there would be three quarter sections for each qualified voter in the United States.

Now, the bill provides for everybody, rich or poor, high or low, to come forward and take a quarter section. By permitting one man to take part of what belongs to him, it does no one else injustice. We see there is no agrarianism in that. What does agrarianism mean? Property which had been accumulated by the labor, industry—by the sweat of the brow of you, me, or anybody else, taken and divided with some one who had not made use of a corresponding industry, I would call agrarianism. Agrarianism is the division of property among those who did not participate in or contribute to its accumulation. This proposition does no such thing. By permitting a man to come forward and take one-third of his own, is anything taken away from you? Does it diminish your estate? Does it make you worth one cent less than you were before? Not at all. Then where is the agrarianism? Where is the demagogism—the injustice? It pulls none down, but elevates all. It takes the poor by the hand and lifts them up—taking nothing from the rich. What now becomes of the left-hand column of the rampart? It topples and falls to the ground with the other two. It is time for the enemy to make an unconditional surrender.

While the Homestead Law was not enacted for many years, a bill was passed in the session of 1853-4, and approved by President Pierce on August 4, 1854, by which the price of public lands was fixed in accordance with the number of years which they had already been in the market, and with a sliding scale down to twelve and one-half cents per acre.

Mr. Grow then became the chief advocate of the original measure, introducing it in varied forms at each session. It gradually assumed the aspect of a party measure, the Republicans being its advocates and the Democrats opposing it, ostensibly on the ground that the Graduating Act had settled the land question, but really because the act would augment the preponderance of the free States over the slave States.

Andrew Johnson, advanced to the Senate, introduced the bill in that Chamber in 1857. It was passed by the Senate and the House, but vetoed by President Buchanan upon the ground that, by a strange oversight, persons of foreign birth might enter lands without being the heads of families, though this was a condition of entries by native citizens.

The same bill, with this defect remedied, was introduced in the next Congress and passed the House by 107 votes to 16, and the Senate by 33 votes to 7, and was approved by President Lincoln on May 20, 1862.

CHAPTER II

LAND-VALUE TAXATION

[THE SINGLE TAX]

Herbert Spencer and Patrick Edward Dove (1850) Deny Rightfulness of
Property in Land—Edwin Burgess [Wis.], in 1859, Proposes to Restore
the Land to the People by Limiting All Taxation to That on the Value
of Land Exclusive of Improvements: His Letters to the Racine *Advocate* on the Subject, Including a Controversy with "S. S."—Henry
George [Cal.] Arrives Independently at Burgess's Theory: His
"Progress and Poverty" and Other Books upon the Doctrine: His
Career—Tom L. Johnson [O.] and Other Representatives "Frank"
George's "Protection and Free Trade" Throughout the Union—Speech
of Johnson in the House: "Free Trade and the Single Tax", Quoting
from "Protection and Free Trade" on "Restoration of the Land to
the People"—Charles E. Belknap [Mich.], in Reply, Quotes from
"Progress from Poverty" by Giles B. Stebbins [Mich.]—The Single
Tax Platform—History of the Movement—Speech of Representative
Henry George, Jr., on "The Road to Freedom"; Questions and Ob-
jections by George W. Norris [Neb.], Swagar Shirley [Ky.], Edward
L. Hamilton [Mich.], Benjamin K. Focht [Pa.], John E. Raker [Cal.],
Philip P. Campbell [Kan.], Rufus Hardy [Tex.], James M. Graham
[Ill.]

IN the decade following the introduction of the Homestead Act, and preceding the Civil War, the question of private property in land was seriously pon-
dered in America, although not to the same extent as
it was in Great Britain, owing to its obscuration here by
the absorbing issue of private property in man (chattel
slavery).

Herbert Spencer, the English philosopher, in chapter IX of his "Social Statics" (1850), demonstrated with
Euclidean clearness and cogency the common right of
all men to the use of the earth. This work made a profound impression on a number of progressive thinkers
in America, although it was not until the close of the

Civil War that the philosophy of the author, expressed in this and succeeding works, became generally known and appreciated here.

Even in the days of youth (Spencer was thirty years of age when he published "Social Statics," after several years' cogitation on the subject) when, if ever, a man is optimistic, Herbert Spencer had little hope that the restoration of the land to the people would be accomplished, in view of the fact that the institution of private property in land, by law and custom, had permeated every fiber of the social system. Therefore it was little wonder that in advancing years he repudiated chapter ix of his early work, claiming that, in view of the vested private interest in land, the appropriation of rent by the public would be unethical unless the landowners were compensated. On this point Henry George replied to him in his "A Perplexed Philosopher" (1892).

In the same year which saw the publication of "Social Statics" (1850), Patrick Edward Dove, a Scots philosopher, published "A Theory of Human Progression," in which he came independently to the same philosophic conclusion reached by Spencer, but, in opposition to the despair of the English philosopher, he proclaimed that the restoration of the land to the people would be the next great step in democratic government. He further declared that when the land was taken there would be no compensation to the owners, since this would be no advance in civilization, the people becoming slaves to the debt incurred (literally "bond" slaves) instead of to the land. His conclusions were drawn from the compensated emancipation of the slaves in the British West Indies. By what right, he asked, do you tax the English white laborer to pay the Jamaica man-owner for foregoing an unnatural and unjust privilege in the labor of a black man? When the land question is settled, said he, it will be upon no such inequitable basis.

Dove's book was little read in this country, only the Abolitionists, to whom it was highly recommended by Senator Charles Sumner, being interested in it, and that chiefly because of its position on slavery—Dove's highly optimistic, but yet true, prophecy, that this barbaric institution was doomed to perish within a very few years, being most encouraging to the little band of advanced thinkers who were fighting against forces apparently indomitable.

Neither Spencer nor Dove presented a practical program for the restoration of the land to the people. This remained for political thinkers in America—at that period the most prolific of all countries in invention, which is the adoption and utilization of existing forces and instrumentalities for the accomplishment of new

ends in every field of human activity, political and social, as well as industrial. These thinkers, being inheritors of the mental slant of the Revolutionary patriots who had revolted from an empire and founded a republic on the basic democratic idea of the control of the taxing power by the people, naturally turned at once to taxation as the instrument for maintaining that republic by abolishing abuses which had been permitted to remain in the Government at its foundation, either because it was thought that the abuse would die out of itself (as in the case of slavery), or because the abuse had not made itself felt at the time (as in the case of land monopoly).

Now the Constitution, by forbidding the Federal Government to interfere with the domestic institutions of the States, and by recognizing slavery in compelling the return of fugitive slaves, and in counting five slaves as three freemen in apportioning the basis of representation in the popular house of Congress, compelled a *political* solution for the first great abuse, the private ownership of man (chattel slavery), which had to be abolished before the promise of the Declaration of Independence could be fulfilled and this country become a land where all men had equal rights to "life, liberty, and the pursuit of happiness." No economic solution was possible, although economic arguments were presented by anti-slavery men to induce the slave States *voluntarily* to abolish the institution which gave them their evil distinction.

But the second great abuse, private ownership of land, or industrial slavery, as the thinkers regarded it, had been left a purely *economic* question, and so the instrumentality of taxation could here come freely into play.

Indeed, the use of this instrumentality was invited by the Constitution itself, which expressly gave the Federal Government the power to tax the value of land in the States in ratio to population. Furthermore, the opinion of the Supreme Court, delivered by Chief Justice John Marshall, that "the power to tax involves the power to destroy,"[1] permitted the use of this grant to

[1] The case in which Chief Justice Marshall said that "the power to tax involves the power to destroy," was McCulloch *vs.* Maryland, reported in 4 Wheaton, 316, in the year 1819.

The question before the Court was the validity of a statute of Maryland requiring the notes of the branch of the United States Bank established in that State to be issued upon stamped paper, subject to a stamp tax levied by the State. There was at issue not only the constitutional power of Congress to establish the bank, and the bank to establish its branches, but, also, the power of the State to tax such branches. After holding that Congress had the constitutional power to establish the bank, and the bank the right to establish its branches in the State, it was held further that the State, within which the branch was located, could not, without violating the Constitution, tax that branch. The State government had no right to tax any of the constitutional means employed by the government to execute its constitutional powers, and no power by taxation

the practical destruction of private ownership of land, and the practical creation of public ownership thereof. Whatever be the nature of a tax, and however small its rate, it accomplishes this conversion or redistribution of property in some manner and to some degree, and is essentially confiscatory in that the principle of compensation to the loser in cases of changes in taxation is not recognized in our laws as obligatory.

Thus the American philosophers who belonged to the class of Spencer and Dove (although they developed their theories independently of these, and, indeed, of each other) made a great advance on the British philosophers, who never thought of taxation as the means of restoring the land to the people.

The first of these American economic revolutionists was Edwin Burgess.

Edwin Burgess (born in London in 1807, died in Racine, Wis., in 1869) emigrated to the United States in the middle 40s, locating in Racine and engaging in his trade as tailor. Acquiring a modest competence and failing in health, he retired from business shortly before the breaking out of the Civil War, and thereafter devoted himself to advancing his theory of restoring the land to the people through the instrumentality of

or otherwise to retard, impede, burden or in any manner control the operation of the constitutional laws enacted by Congress to carry into effect the powers vested in the national government.

At page 431 the Court says: ''That the power to tax involves the power to destroy; that the power to destroy may defeat and render useless the power to create; that there is a plain repugnance in conferring upon one government the power to control the constitutional measures of another, which other, with respect to those very measures, is declared to be supreme over that which it exerts the control, are propositions not to be denied. . . . If the State may tax one instrument, employed by the Government in the execution of its powers, they may tax every other instrument. They may tax the mail; they may tax the mints; they may tax patent rights; they may tax the paper of a customs house; they may tax judicial process; they may tax all the means employed by the Government to an excess which would defeat all the ends of government. This was not intended by the American people. They did not design to make their government dependent on the States . . . The question is, in truth, a question of supremacy; and if the right of the State to tax the means employed by the General Government be conceded, the declaration that the Constitution, and the laws made in pursuance thereof, shall be the supreme law of the land, is an empty and unmeaning declaration.''

taxation. A series of letters from him on this subject were published in the Racine *Advocate* during 1859-60. They have been republished in 1912 in pamphlet form by Hyland Raymond and William S. Buffham, Racine, Wis. Say his publishers:

We who were young at that time remember him as a man of liberal ideas in both politics and religion, yet most kindly, moderate, and thoughtful in all things, but in the overshadowing presence of the anti-slavery campaign and the impending Civil War these letters of his were passed over as the irrelevent dreams of a crank, and at the time excited but little note or comment.

Yet here was a man who probably never read the writings of any of the great political economists, yet who, out of a heart overflowing with sympathy for his fellowmen, and especially for the masses of his fellow-countrymen and a wonderful keenness of intellect, evolved practically the whole theory of the single tax as set forth and elaborated twenty years later by Henry George.

LETTERS ON TAXATION

By Edwin Burgess

In his first and second letters Mr. Burgess showed the evils which arose from the existing use of the powerful instrument of taxation and the good which would result from confining it to its sole beneficent purpose, the destruction of monopoly.

Being in the county clerk's room of the court house, I saw a large pile of papers headed "Statement of Property," to be filled out and sworn to by every resident owner. "The number and value of horses and cattle, mules, and asses, sheep, hogs, pleasure carriages of every description, watches, moneys and credits, merchant's stock, manufacturer's stock and other articles of personal property," which is everything that one person could sue another for stealing.

Now I could not help thinking somewhat on the cost as well as consequence of such a method of taxing people for the support of government.

1. Taxing people for their personal property—on their oath—is a premium on perjury, because those who lie the most

pay the least taxes, and children born under such influences will be famous for lying—if there is any connection between cause and effect in the condition of parent and offspring.

2. The means of valuing or assessing are very expensive, thus increasing the cost of government as well as the cost of corruption.

3. Taxing personal property prevents production, because the tax being added to the article for sale increases its price in proportion to the means of buying. Hence, less is sold and less is made, and the makers are less employed; and, having consequently less with which to buy, the makers of other things will be less employed also—till the surplus workers will become paupers and suffer much misery in consequence; many will become hopeless and reckless because hopeless. Some will be tempted to commit crime for the temporary alleviation of their misery, which, repeated, soon becomes a habit; thus the tax on personal property, or the product of industry, increases the amount of paupers and criminals, while the cost of keeping paupers and criminals, officers and legislators, increases the amount of tax and the cost of government, of course. If any person puts up a new fence, or makes any visible improvement which employs the unemployed and beautifies the city—he is taxed annually in proportion to the evil he prevents and the good he does.

4. Taxing personal property is inquisitorial, burdensome, and aggressive against our right to labor and enjoy the fruit of our toil unmolested; so long as we injure no one, we should be protected against aggression instead of suffering aggression.

5. Taxing people in proportion to their industry prevents industry, because when an industrious person labors twelve hours per day successfully he must pay twelve times as much taxes because he has made twelve times as much property to be taxed as if he had worked only one hour per day, and besides the limit of his means to pay the tax, whether in a watch, a piano, or a horse, no one likes to be taxed for the idleness of others, and he feels the injustice also, and improvements are thus prevented which would profitably employ the idle.

6. Taxing personal property raises the price of land, and thus promotes its monopoly by the rich, because land being the source of our subsistence, which labor develops or increases, from which, and on which, all must live, and money instead of manhood being the qualification for owning land, it follows that, in proportion as the taxes are on personal property, the land will be exempt, and it will be thus comparatively cheap

or easy for the rich to monopolize; so that if all the taxes were
on the land it would sell for the lowest price and would be
most difficult to monopolize, but, if all the taxes were on
personal property and none on the land, then the land would
sell for the highest price, and labor would sell for the lowest
price because of the excessive competition of the landless and
destitute workers, who, by selling their labor for the smallest
portion of its produce, would keep the land at the highest
possible price; so, when you want land to be low and wages
high, put all the taxes on the land, but, if you prefer labor
to be low and land high, you have only to put all the taxes
on personal property. All articles of productive industry cost
the keeping of the maker and contriver, but the land costs
nothing for either. It is the natural inheritance of all, for all
time, and all should be protected in their possession, and those
who own all the land should certainly pay all the taxes for
keeping them in possession and their neighbors out of it.

7. Taxing personal property promotes the monopoly of
capital (as well as land) because whenever labor can be bought
for a small portion of its produce the larger portion (or the
unpaid labor) is owned by the capitalist in the name of profit,
with which he can starve the landless workers into worse terms
as long as they continue landless in proportion to their numbers
and necessities.

8. Taxing personal property by preventing production and
promoting the monopoly of land and its products makes the
means of living the most precarious, especially for the landless,
because there is less produced in proportion to the wants of
the community, and as the land is high and labor low (from
the taxes on industry and competition of the landless), it is
proportionally beyond the means of the cheaply paid laborer
to purchase the land, or even to rent it; and, when the means
of living are the most precarious, the greatest anxiety is suffered
by the landless, and the continuance of that anxiety causes
nervousness, sleeplessness, misery, and insanity, which is transmitted to the offspring with increased force, and thus is insanity
made hereditary.

9. Taxing personal property promotes intemperance by
making labor so cheap that the labor must toil excessively for
a living, thus causing bodily exhaustion as well as mental
anxiety to the landless workers, and indolence also on the part
of those who live on the labor of others. Those whose bodies
are exhausted by excessive toil, and whose minds are suffering
from mental anxiety, crave stimulants to recruit the body and

make the mind forget its care, while those who live in idleness on others' toil crave stimulants to quicken the circulation which should be sustained by honest, temperate toil, carrying with it the moral satisfaction that for all they enjoy no one suffers. Then, and not till then, will the good be transmitted to the offspring instead of the evil as now.

10. Taxing personal property by making land dear and labor cheap promotes prostitution and disease to a fearful extent. Is not woman more sensitive and weaker physically than man, and when she can get no just reward for her labor, and frequently no right to labor, need we wonder that she sells herself legally or illegally for the means of living? Are not the high price of land and the low price of labor, or the no right of land and consequently no right of labor, the main causes? And thus is woman driven by injustice, poverty, and misery into temptation, and prayed out occasionally in revivals.

> Pray folks out of temptation, while driving them in,
> Is the usual way to atone for the sin;
> To fight the effect, while feeding the cause,
> You will find the foundation of most of our laws.

11. Taxing personal property is the main cause of rent, interest, and usury, for rent of land is but interest on the price, so that when the land is high the rent will be in proportion, and all the wages of the landless are required for their support; they cannot buy land or build houses, or have capital for business, but must pay rent or interest for all. Usury is but interest or rent of money—more than the law allows—which is sustained by the extremes of rich and poor, caused by land monopoly and its causes. Do we really want permanent prosperity and the interest of all to be honest and live on their own labor instead of speculating on the unpaid labor of others? Do we desire purity and truth instead of corruption and perjury to prevail? Then repeal all taxes on industry, and let the monopolists of land, the source of our living and the rightful inheritance of all, pay taxes in proportion to the value of what they monopolize, then poverty, prostitution, and intemperance will soon be among the things that were.

Letters III and IV criticized the Wisconsin tax laws. In Letter IV he used a term which has become the accepted definition of the single tax. It is a pity that Mr. Burgess's definitive phrase, the "*ad valorem* land tax", has not also been adopted in place of the present meaningless title.

Mr. Burgess said:

I would not tax any personal property or product of industry in any form, but the land alone, according to its market value, irrespective of all improvements.

In Letter V Mr. Burgess wrote of merchants shifting their stocks of goods from one State to another to escape taxation; of rich men "swearing off" their personal property assessments. He doubted if one-half the personal property in the country were taxed, the conscientious paying, therefore, not only for themselves but for the unscrupulous.

Returning to the *"ad valorem* land tax" he said:

If all taxes were on the land, would railroad monopolists want to steal the land (the birthright of all) by millions of acres while they deny to the landless and moneyless any land on which to get their "daily bread," while they hire ministers to open their robbery meetings in Congress by prayer? Do they not know well that it is only by keeping the workers landless that they can buy their labor for the smallest portion of its produce, and if all had what land they needed their plundered land would be almost valueless for sale, though its value for production and human sustenance would be undiminished?

If all the taxes were on the land, and none on improvements, then there would be the greatest encouragement for improvements and industry; then farmers and merchants would not turn land speculators, and run all over creation to buy land at ten shillings per acre with the produce of their toil, but make and enjoy the comforts of life with their families at home instead of being a curse to the landless and their families elsewhere; they could then have no fear that their children would suffer for want of land whenever they might need it.

Were all the taxes on the land and the people's land free to the landless, then none would be driven into the wilderness to suffer the changes of climate and want of society, but those who desired could then settle nearer to their kindred and friends and enjoy the blessings of friendship, love, and home with much less cost and inconvenience.

Were all the taxes on the land and the people's land free, then the hitherto landless could soon build their own homes on their own land and raise all they needed to consume or exchange, and no longer need the land, houses, or capital of others; then rent, interest, and even usury would cease for want of poverty to sustain them, for, the curse, land monopoly, being removed, the effect would cease with the cause. Thus would the happiness of mankind be immeasurably increased and misery be proportionately diminished; then would earth be redeemed from the giant sin of land robbery, and the Paradise of the present or future be as far above that of the past as the intelligence of the philosopher is beyond the ignorance of the child.

In Letter VI Mr. Burgess attacked the tariff, even in the mild form of tariff for revenue only, as set forth in the report of Howell Cobb, Secretary of the Treasury, December 6, 1858.

Does not all such taxation go directly to promote the profit of land monopoly and man monopoly (or slavery)? Does it not take the taxes out of the pockets of the toiling consumers, and, by exempting the land from so much taxes, enable the landlord to sell or rent his land for so much more? Do people buy these imported goods in proportion to the land they hold, or in proportion to the slaves they hold? If not, who pay the taxes and make landholding and slaveholding profitable?

He then discussed the relation of land monopoly to slavery.

Land monopoly is really the parent of chattel slavery, for if no persons owned the land of others, or more land than they needed to cultivate by their own labor for their own support, they would not covet their fellow-men as slaves; but, having obtained the land of others by legal or illegal robbery, they crave their fellow-men as slaves to work it for them, and Africa must be robbed, and slaves must be bred, and men and women and children reduced to bondage to maintain in luxury and idleness a land-robbing and man-robbing aristocracy, a nobility forsooth, based on the lasso, the manacles, and the lash; the gag, the fetter, and the thumbscrew; the whipping-post, the chain and ball, the man-stealer, and the bloodhound.

The law might sanction slavery to all eternity if it was

unprofitable and no law worshipers would be patriotic enough
to hold slaves any more than they would carry white men to
Africa for slaves at a loss. Let us, then, remove this cause
or temptation which is the profit by putting all the taxes on
the land, and the effect will assuredly cease.

Letter VII was devoted to the arguments for free
trade. In place of deriving revenue from taxes on consumption he would do so from taxes on monopoly, that
is, land.

To illustrate the relative merits of the tariff and the land
tax, let us suppose, for example, that Racine exempted all
merchants' and manufacturers' goods from taxes, and all grain,
farm produce, etc., and all improvements from taxes, and put
all the taxes on the land, and at the same time Milwaukee
exempted all land from taxes and put all the taxes on the farm
produce and merchants' and manufacturers' goods and improvements, where would the mechanics, merchants, and manufacturers settle? Where would the farmers go to sell their
produce and buy their goods? Would not Racine grow rapidly
while Milwaukee dwindled? And will not this be true of any
city, town, county, State, or nation?
The land tax, unlike the tariff, would require no extra
officers for assessing and collecting revenue for the general
Government, as the expenses would be defrayed by a percentage
on the assessment for State purposes, which would be transmitted to the general Government in the best manner.
Think what a saving that would be over the old feudal
system of barbarian despots! No buying Cuba or any other
country on the plea of the benefits of free trade, but free
trade without buying the country for it; no custom houses
and officers; no revenue service to diminish our liberties, increase
our expenses, and rob us of our right of free trade on the plea
of protection; no commercial treaties abroad for special
monopolies or vexatious litigation on tariff violations at home;
more producers and fewer destroyers; standing armies and
navies being no longer needed while our commercial motto
shall be "Free Trade with All the World."

In Letter VIII Mr. Burgess spoke of the present tax
system as depopulating the country districts and crowd-
ing the cities until these became "cess-pools of pauperism, prostitution, misery, disease, and crime."

But the land tax would abolish land monopoly and make the means of living honestly the most easy and certain for all, and make it unprofitable to keep land idle; then people would settle near each other for convenience, comfort, society, and profit, and farmers would not need to send their children to cities for education. We should save millions weekly in cost of local government, in rents, interest, and usury, besides diminishing pauperism, prostitution, disease, and crime.

Letter IX continued the comparison of the *ad valorem* land tax with the tariff. The former had the advantage not only in defraying all governmental expense, but in increasing, instead of decreasing, the productive power of the country to pay it. With cheaper land there would result cheaper food. Rents would diminish, the saving being distributed among the manufacturer, the laborer, the merchant, and the consumer.

For, with all the taxes on the land, it would not pay to keep it idle, therefore speculation in land would soon cease and be transferred to untaxed manufactures or labor, which would increase the demand and raise the wages of labor and reduce the profits of capital and speculation, and at the same time we should create and sustain the most permanent and profitable home market for produce and manufactures. For, when farmers desire to settle near factories for the benefit of market and exchange, they may be sure the land will never be high nor manufactures either; because the tax is on the land and not on the manufactures, which keeps the landlord's rent and the speculator's profit from the land, and the robber tariff from the manufactures also.

Letter X amplified the former suggestion of the intimate relation between slavery and land monopoly.

By the operation of the *ad valorem* land tax the poor white man in the South as well as in the North will possess and cultivate land now held for speculation. As slave cultivation is always poor and exhausting, slave farms surrounded by free farms and slave States surrounded by free States could not commercially compete with either in their surplus productions, and thus the profit of slaveholding would be diminished or destroyed.

Were all the taxes on the land, it would not pay to keep it idle; the result would be cultivation to make it pay, which would cause an abundance of produce for which manufactures would be made to exchange. And as the land would be free or cheap, the wages of labor would rise, because, whenever manufacturing paid less than farming, many more would farm the land, and thus equalize the wages of labor between farming and manufacturing.

With cheap free land, with the aid of machinery, we could easily produce a super-abundance of all that is best for mankind, and have an abundance of leisure for the cultivation of our physical, mental, and moral faculties, and thus produce that physical, mental, and moral elevation which slavery, either wages slavery or chattel, must inevitably dwarf instead of develop.

Letter XI was in rebuttal to a reply to Mr. Burgess's letters which had been made in the Racine *Advocate* by one who signed himself "S. S."

"S. S." thinks it wrong that the farmers, who, he says, "make the least cost of government," should pay in proportion to the land which they own. I think if the farmers do make the least cost of government it is because they enjoy their right of land and are less exposed to the destitution, privation, and temptations of the landless, and this is one of the reasons why I put all taxes on the land. With the high price of land caused by the labor tax, the landless and moneyless have no choice but to labor for others if they can get the work, or beg, steal, or starve. So that it is not the honest and thrifty, but the lazy and greedy farmers and land monopolists who own vast quantities of land and cultivate but little, who make paupers, drunkards, and criminals of the landless which "S. S." charges on the citizens, and would fain make the citizens support all the drunkards, paupers, and criminals whom the land monopolies have made. Why, he might as well buy up and monopolize the breasts of the mother and then blame the babe for crying for its food, for the land is to mankind what the breast is to the babe—the source of subsistence.

believe that no one has a moral right to land because he has bought it and paid for it any more than the slaveholder has a moral right to the man, woman, or child he has bought and paid for, because no one can have a moral right to sell the land which belongs equally to all, or to sell the man,

X—5

woman, and child whose persons, liberty, and labor belong to themselves.

Mr. Burgess showed that the *ad valorem* land tax was a "single" tax, in that it was paid only once, while all other kinds of taxes were liable to be laid again and again on the same property in its varying aspects.

"S. S." says the whole system of balances and averages would be changed, and this to the detriment and pecuniary ruin of the present and future farmers. Now, the farmers, as well as mechanics, could change their occupation if they found manufacturing more profitable, and much more easily than at present, because the land for the factory would cost probably nothing, and there would be no inquisitorial, pauperizing "labor tax" on manufactures to prevent them. So also it would be easier to commence farming because the land would cost less, and every implement and machine needed for cultivation would cost less also, and there would be no tax on the stock of the farmer or manufacturer, or on the improvements of either, so that the changes in values would be good for farming and manufacturing, and no "ruin" could result to present or future farmers or manufacturers from the land tax, but permanent prosperity to both.

"S. S." says: "If the great burden of the land tax causes one to sell out, the same cause will prevent others buying." I contend that the taxes will be much less and consequently less burdensome, because, the land being priceless, any persons, or, at least, many, could till the lands for themselves, whom we now keep as paupers and criminals. This would diminish the cost of government (or taxes), which will be less burdensome in proportion to the cheapness of land, and only the land kept idle or badly cultivated would be obliged to be sold because it would not pay the tax. And none can rightly keep land idle and make others suffer for their indolence, else, if one man could buy all the land he might keep all of it idle except enough to support himself and starve every one else to death.

"S. S." says: "At the low price of produce resulting from an increase of producers and a decrease of consumers, the farmer cannot sustain himself and pay his increased and increasing tax." This is the old fallacy of supposing that cheap land would compel people to farm while manufacturing paid better.

"S. S." says: "But, supposing the prices remain relatively the same, what better is a man off by paying a large tax to a government than paying the same amount in rent to a landlord?" I reply: Not only would the taxes be diminished by all the cost of the revenue service, but by that of every pauper and criminal who ceased to be landless because of the free or cheap land, also by that of every pauper and criminal who found labor in manufacturing for the increased supply of the produce of the land, while the very rent to which "S. S." refers would be saved also by any houses that were placed on the free or cheap land by their owners, and all interest and usury would cease also, as all could easily own their own homes and make all the capital they needed. Then bankers, brokers, and usurers would soon die out from the universal prosperity of mankind.

"S. S." complains that the land tax would change the actual and relative value of land. The actual value is its productive power which it would not change except by encouraging its use and making its idleness unprofitable. Its relative or money value might be changed by the Homestead bill which "S. S." might charge with destroying the hard-earned property of millions of monopolies by giving their birthright to millions of mankind. Let us remember that when we trade in the rights of others in buying risk, and not at the cost of the innocent or the wronged.

"S. S." says: "No man can have any more right to the soil another has bought than to the food that another has raised from it, or to the clothing or other products that he has earned by its cultivation." "S. S." still fails to distinguish between the land, which naturally and morally belongs to all, and the produce of the land, which naturally belongs to the producer. Suppose one man or many could buy all the land, who has the right to sell it? Would the buyers have the right to starve all the rest of mankind and entail the land to their children with the eternal power of starving all other children? I think not, and therefore think the right of land is as inalienable as our existence, and that everyone who buys the land of others ought to lose it, just as the slaveholder who buys a man, woman, or child ought to lose what he paid for his covetous villainy.

It is interesting to note in this last opinion the unyielding opposition to "compensation" which distinguished Patrick Edward Dove and Henry George.

HENRY GEORGE

From twelve to twenty years after Mr. Burgess wrote his "Letters on Taxation," Henry George, a compositor and journalist of San Francisco, developed the same theory and program. The vast fortunes acquired in California through the sudden and great increase of values in land and in properties, such as railroads, dependent on franchises in land, and the increase, at the same time, in poverty, not merely relative but absolute, as shown in constantly diminishing wages, had called his attention to the land question as the fundamental problem of government.

He published his views on the subjects in 1871 in a pamphlet entitled "Our Land and Land Policy." The basic principle was that private appropriation of the value of land is a monopoly.

The germinal idea of this book George developed into a treatise which he published in 1879. This was "Progress and Poverty."

In this, his greatest work, Mr. George attacked the "wages fund theory" of John Stuart Mill, which, though Mill had abandoned it in the last years of his life, was generally accepted, forming, indeed, the basis of the trades union movement and the doctrine of protection. According to this theory wages are paid out of capital. George held that wages are directly labor's own creation, and therefore that there is no essential conflict between labor and capital, but that both should coöperate in destroying the common enemy, monopoly, which in all its forms rests upon absorption of public revenues by private persons through special privileges granted them by the State and protected by law.

"Progress and Poverty" became recognized within a few years after publication as an epoch-making work in economic and social science. It elicited many replies from persons of greater or less eminence and ability, among which may be mentioned "The Prophet of San Francisco" [1884], by George J. D. Campbell, the eighth Duke of Argyle, and "Property and Progress" [1884] by

Henry George

W. H. Mallock, a leading English writer on social and economic matters.

In 1881 Mr. George wrote a book specially applying his philosophy to the burning issue of the day in British politics, which he called at first "The Irish Land Question," and, later, simply "The Land Question," since its principles were applicable to the solution of the problem in all countries. He visited Great Britain several times in the early eighties in the interest of his doctrines, promoting a "Land Restoration League," which steadily grew in influence in the Liberal party, until in 1909 David Lloyd George, Secretary of the Exchequer, embodied the land value tax in the national budget.

In 1886 George became the Labor candidate for mayor of New York against Abram S. Hewitt, Democrat, and Theodore Roosevelt, Republican. Mr. Hewitt was elected, George running a close second. Believing that there had been an agreement between the Democrats and Republican managers, whereby sufficient Republican votes were counted for Mr. Hewitt toward the close of the poll to secure Mr. Hewitt's election, Mr. George devoted from that time forward much of his energies to secure ballot reform. For this, in connection with the propaganda of the single tax, he visited Australia, where the secret ballot was used. To the exertions of himself and his followers is largely due the general adoption of this system throughout the United States.

In 1886 Mr. George wrote a work called "Protection and Free Trade," in which he made special application of his philosophy to the tariff.

In 1892, when the discussion on the McKinley bill had made the tariff the leading political question of the hour, Tom L. Johnson [O.], who was the leading Single-Taxer in Congress, and who knew the self-sacrificing devotion of Mr. George to his cause, secured his consent that the entire contents of the book be incorporated in speeches to be delivered in Congress by Mr. Johnson and others, and, being spread upon the *Record,* to be "franked" in the form of reprints as public documents by these Congressmen to persons in every part of the country. There were 1,062,000 copies so circulated. Naturally the sales of the regular edition of the book were greatly impaired, to the author's financial loss. In the political campaign of 1912 a million more of these copies were sent out under franks of Representative Henry George, Jr. [N. Y.], and other Congressmen friendly to free trade and the single tax.

The Congressmen who joined with Mr. Johnson in 1892 in incorporating the book in their speeches were William J. Stone [Ky.], Joseph E. Washington [Tenn.], George W. Fithian [Ill.], Thomas Bowman [Ia.], and Jerry Simpson [Kan.].

Mr. Johnson introduced his quotation with the following speech (March 31, 1892):

FREE TRADE AND THE SINGLE TAX

TOM L. JOHNSON, M. C.

I am for free trade, not merely as a matter of wise policy, but as a matter of natural right. I hold that the right freely to trade with whomever one pleases and on whatever terms he pleases is one of the most important of those natural rights asserted by our Declaration of Independence, and that to deny this to the American citizen is to that extent to enslave and rob him. To the open enunciation of this clear principle I hope to see the Democratic party come. When it does it will be invincible.

I hope to see this Congress, before we adjourn, pass a bill putting lumber, coal, and iron ore on the free list, and, to show that as a manufacturer I am ready to take just what I propose, I am willing to put steel rails also on the free list.

MICHAEL D. HARTER [O.].—And agricultural implements?

MR. JOHNSON.—Yes, and agricultural implements. My colleague, who is one of the largest of agricultural implement makers, has, too, the spirit of true free trade, and stands ready, and more than ready, to vote for the abolition of every duty that applies to what he makes.

I was very much interested, a few days ago, at the explanation of the gentleman from Iowa [Walt H. Butler] of what he meant by free trade.[1] Let me say frankly that I am not that kind of a free trader. As a Democrat I am here simply to enter my protest against that part of the tariff that is protective, for that is as far as party divisions yet go, both Democrats and Republicans agreeing that we shall continue to raise the revenue by a tariff. But in my humble opinion in this matter, both are wrong.

Speaking for myself, and speaking too for a large and rapidly increasing body of men within the Democratic party, I wish to say that what I mean by free trade is not a tariff for revenue only, but nothing less than free trade itself; the abolition of all custom houses and the same freedom to trade with all the world that we now have between our States.

Though the Democratic party has not yet got so far, I hope some day to see it advocating that principle. The discussion now going on must broaden till it brings up the whole question of taxation, and it is in this that the real solution of the labor question is to be sought.

We talk of taxing things—as taxing sugar, or taxing iron, or taxing wool. But inanimate things cannot pay taxes. At last taxes are levied on men. Discussions of taxation are in reality discussions of how burdens shall be levied, not on merchandise, but on men. Already the discussion of the tariff question is bringing out this fact, and as it goes on we constantly hear expressions that show that it is working in the minds of the people.

In discussing the question of taxation what we are really discussing is how men shall be taxed for the support of the Government. A poll tax taxes men by the head. An income tax taxes men in accordance with their incomes—or aims at doing so. A property tax taxes men in accordance with their property. A tax on land values taxes men according to the value of the land they hold, irrespective of the improvements on it. So a tariff tax taxes men in accordance with their consumption. And I protest that it is therefore a most unjust mode of taxation.

It is in some respects even worse than a poll tax, for that would not tax the married man more than the bachelor, the man who rears children more than the man who supports only himself. It is really a system that taxes men according to their necessities, and therefore much worse by comparison than our State taxes on property. It is fairer to tax men on what they have than on what they consume, and therefore the

[1] Mr. Butler had defined free trade as a tariff for revenue only.

general property tax of our States is very much better than the tariff taxes, even when imposed for revenue only, and without the sheer robbery of some to enrich others that is involved in protective taxes. Even an income tax, which is open to so many objections, which makes a nation of liars, and opens so many avenues to fraud, and is a miserable tax, is still a great deal better than a duty on sugar.

But if we abolish the tariff how can we get our revenue? Mr. Chairman, it would have been better for the country if that question, How can we get revenue? had been oftener asked in this House. The question for years heretofore has been, How can we spend our revenue? And if there were nothing else to damn the system of raising revenue by custom house taxation, the manner in which this imposing of taxes for the sake of taxation—this pouring of taxes into the treasury for the sake of giving monopolists opportunity to levy additional taxes on the people—has demoralized our Government and debauched our politics is enough to do so.

So long as you have a system of taxation dictated by private interests that wish to use it to make the people pay them more for what they have to sell, and where similar interests band together to prevent every repeal or reduction, no number of watchdogs will be able to prevent the millions poured into the treasury by the robbery of the poor from slipping out again in extravagance and corruption. If the people want economy, if they want purity, if they want an end to the spectacle that we will see again this year of the money scraped from their hard earnings being used to influence their votes, they must insist on some system of taxation that will not foster private interests.

How shall we raise our national revenue? There is no way in which we could raise it that would be more unjust than our present system of raising it by tariff taxes that fall upon consumption, and most heavily on those articles of necessity and common luxury that are used by all. Any system of taxing men according to their means is better and fairer than the system of taxing according to what they use. For, since the poor must use far more of their incomes to live than do the rich, these taxes fall with heaviest weight on those who are least able to bear taxation and inevitably tend to make the rich richer and the poor poorer. They are taxes, not upon surplus earnings, but upon life, upon comfort, upon decency, upon the accumulation of the little capital that enables a man to get a start, upon marrying and having children.

Is it not certain that we can find some better way than this; is it not time that we should at least make up our mind that tariff taxes must go?

Do not be afraid of the intelligence of the people. The American mechanic and the American farmer, the great mass of our people who find year after year of hard toil and close saving go by without leaving them a whit ahead, and who feel that in spite of all our wonderful advances in production it is getting no easier to live, are fast coming to the conclusion that there is something radically wrong with our system of taxation. Of the superstition of protection, of the notion that the capitalists who spend so much money and so much effort to put on and keep on tariff taxes do so simply out of their benevolent regard for the farmer and the laborer, there is really nothing left but the shell. And the moment the Democratic party have the courage of Democratic principle, and, stopping their paltering with six-penny measures of tariff reform, will boldly raise the banner of opposition to all protection, they will break that shell.

The Knights of Labor lodges, the Farmers' Alliance, the thoughtful men in all occupations, have been and are still doing a great deal of thinking about this matter of taxation. They are fast making up their minds that they want a system of taxation that will not bear on the millionaire like a feather and on the day laborer like a millstone; that will not fetter labor; that will not hamper industry; that will not fine enterprise; that will not muzzle the ox that grindeth out the corn and let the dog in the manger go free to monopolize and waste; a system that will not require a horde of officials; that will not provoke extravagance and engender corruption, but will take from each man for the use of the community the fair and just return of the special pecuniary benefits that he receives from the community.

That system is the single tax. All over the country it is steadily and swiftly making its way in the popular mind—nay, all over the English-speaking world. It won in the last New Zealand Parliament, and is already in large measure in force in that country. It carried the city of London by a tremendous majority in the municipal elections a few weeks ago. It is on the verge of practical politics here. It may be too soon yet to ask this House to consider it, but we shall move toward it as we move toward free trade. And I am a free trader because I believe free trade leads to the single tax. [Loud applause.]

I desire to have printed with my remarks the following,

being an extract from Henry George's book, "Protection or Free Trade." This book, written by a man who views the matter from the standpoint of the interests of the great laboring masses, and who is acknowledged through the civilized world as the foremost of political economists, is the clearest, most thorough exposition of the whole subject ever yet made.

One of the quotations from Mr. George's book, which presented his philosophy, was as follows:

Restoration of the Land to the People

Henry George

To make either the abolition of protection or any other reform beneficial to the working class we must abolish the inequality of legal rights to land, and restore to all their natural and equal rights in the common heritage.

How can this be done?

Consider for a moment precisely what it is that needs to be done, for it is here that confusion sometimes arises. To secure to each of the people of a country his equal right to the land of that country does not mean to secure to each an equal piece of land. Save in an extremely primitive society, where population was sparse, the division of labor had made little progress, and family groups lived and worked in common, a division of land into anything like equal pieces would indeed be impracticable. In a state of society such as exists in civilized countries to-day, it would be extremely difficult, if not altogether impossible, to make an equal division of land.

Nor would one such division suffice. With the first division the difficulty would only begin. Where population is increasing and its centers are constantly changing; where different vocations make different uses of lands and require different qualities and amounts of it; where improvements and discoveries and inventions are constantly bringing out new uses, and changing relative values, a division that should be equal to-day would soon become very unequal, and to maintain equality a redivision every year would be necessary.

But to make a redivision every year, or to treat land as a common, where no one could claim the exclusive use of any particular piece, would only be practicable where men lived in movable tents and made no permanent improvements, and would effectually prevent any advance beyond such a state.

No one would sow a crop or build a house, or open a mine, or plant an orchard, or cut a drain, so long as anyone else could come in and turn him out of the land in which or on which such improvements must be fixed. Thus it is absolutely necessary to the proper use and improvement of land that society should secure to the user and improver safe possession.

This point is constantly raised by those who resent any questioning of our present treatment of land. They seek to befog the issue by persistently treating every proposition to secure equal rights to land as though it were a proposition to secure an equal division of land, and attempt to defend private property in land by setting forth the necessity of securing safe possession to the improver.

But the two things are essentially different.

In the first place equal rights to land could not be secured by the equal division of land, and in the second place it is not necessary to make land the private property of individuals in order to secure to improvers that safe possession of their improvements that is needed to induce men to make improvements. On the contrary, private property in land, as we may see in any country where it exists, enables mere dogs-in-the-manger to levy blackmail upon improvers. It enables the mere owner of land to compel the improver to pay him for the privilege of making improvements, and in many cases it enables him to confiscate the improvements.

Here are two simple principles, both of which are self-evident:

1. That all men have equal rights to the use and enjoyment of the elements provided by nature.

2. That each man has an exclusive right to the use and enjoyment of what is produced by his own labor.

There is no conflict between these principles. On the con-ary, they are correlative. To fully secure the individual right of property in the produce of labor we must treat the elements of nature as common property. If anyone could claim the sunlight as his property and could compel me to pay him for the agency of the sun in the growth of crops I had planted, it would necessarily lessen my right of property in the produce of my labor. And conversely, where everyone is secured the full right of property in the produce of his labor, no one can have any right of property in what is not the produce of labor.

No matter how complex the industrial organization, nor how highly developed the civilization, there is no real difficulty in carrying out these principles. All we have to do is to

treat the land as the joint property of the whole people, just as a railway is treated as the joint property of many shareholders, or as a ship is treated as the joint property of several owners.

In other words, we can leave land now being used in the secure possession of those using it, and leave land now unused to be taken possession of by those who wish to make use of it, on condition that those who thus hold land shall pay to the community a fair rent for the exclusive privilege they enjoy— that is to say, a rent based on the value of the privilege the individual receives from the community in being accorded the exclusive use of this much of the common property, and which should have no reference to any improvement he had made in or on it, or to any property due to the use of his labor and capital. In this way all would be placed upon an equality in regard to the use and enjoyment of those natural elements which are clearly the common heritage, and that value which attaches to land, not because of what the individual user does, but because of the growth of the community, would accrue to the community, and could be used for purposes of common benefit. As Herbert Spencer has said of it:

"Such a doctrine is consistent with the highest state of civilization; may be carried out without involving a community of goods, and need cause no very serious revolution in existing arrangements. The change required would be simply a change of landlords. Separate ownership would merge into the joint stock ownership of the public. Instead of being in the possession of individuals, the country would be held by the great corporate body—society. . . . A state of things so ordered would be in perfect harmony with the moral law. Under it all men would be equally landlords, all men would be alike free to become tenants. Clearly, therefore, on such a system the earth might be inclosed, occupied, and cultivated, in entire subordination to the law of equal freedom."

That this simple change would, as Mr. Spencer says, involve no serious revolution in existing arrangements is in many cases not perceived by those who think of it for the first time. It is sometimes said that while this principle is manifestly just, and while it would be easy to apply it to a new country just being settled, it would be exceedingly difficult to apply it to an already settled country where land had already been divided as private property, since, in such a country, to take possession of the land as common property and let it out to individuals would involve a sudden revolution of the greatest magnitude.

This objection, however, is founded upon the mistaken idea that it is necessary to do everything at once. But it often happens that a precipice we could not hope to climb, and that we might well despair of making a ladder long enough and strong enough to scale, may be surmounted by a gentle road. And there is in this case a gentle road open to us, which will lead us so far that the rest will be but an easy step. To make land virtually the common property of the whole people, and to appropriate ground rent for public use, there is a much simpler and easier way than that of formally assuming the ownership of land and proceeding to rent it out in lots—a way that involves no shock, that will conform to present customs, and that, instead of requiring a great increase of governmental machinery, will permit of a great simplification of governmental machinery.

In every well-developed community large sums are needed for common purposes, and the sums thus needed increase with social growth, not merely in amount, but proportionately, since social progress tends steadily to devolve on the community as a whole functions which in a ruder stage are discharged by individuals. Now, while people are not used to paying rent to government, they are used to paying taxes to government. Some of these taxes are levied upon personal or movable property, some upon occupations or businesses or persons (as in the case of income taxes, which are in reality taxes on persons according to income); some upon the transportation or exchange of commodities, in which last category fall the taxes imposed by tariffs; and some, in the United States at least, on real estate—that is to say, on the value of land and of the improvements upon it taken together.

That part of the tax on real estate which is assessed on the value of land irrespective of improvements is, in its nature, not a tax, but a rent—a taking for the common use of the community of a part of the income that properly belongs to the community by reason of the equal right of all to the use of land.

Now it is evident that, in order to take for the use of the community the whole income arising from land, just as effectually as it could be taken by formally appropriating and letting out the land, it is only necessary to abolish, one after another, all other taxes now levied, and to increase the tax on land values till it reaches, as near as may be, the full annual value of the land.

Whenever this point of theoretical perfection is reached,

the selling value of land will entirely disappear, and the charge made to the individual by the community for the use of the common property will become in form what it is in fact—a rent. But, until that point is reached, this rent may be collected by the simple increase of a tax already levied in all our States, assessed (as direct taxes are now assessed) upon the selling

value of land irrespective of improvements—a value that can be ascertained more easily and more accurately than any other value.

For a full exposition of the effects of this change in the method of raising public revenues, I must refer the reader to the works in which I have treated this branch of the subject at greater length than is here possible. Briefly, they would be threefold.

In the first place, all taxes that now fall upon the exertion of labor or use of capital would be abolished. No one would be taxed for building a house or improving a farm or opening a mine, for bringing things in from foreign countries, or for adding in any way to the stock of things that satisfy human wants and constitute national wealth. Everyone would be free to make and save wealth; to buy, sell, give, or exchange, without let or hindrance, any article of human production the use of which did not involve any public injury.

All those taxes which increase prices as things pass from hand to hand, falling finally upon the consumer, would disappear. Buildings or other fixed improvements would be as secure as now, and could be bought and sold, as now, subject to the tax or ground rent due to the community for the ground on which they stood. Houses and the ground they stand on, or other improvements and the land they are made on, would also be rented as now. But the amount the tenant would have to pay would be less than now, since the taxes now levied on buildings

or improvements fall ultimately (save in decaying communities) on the user, and the tenant would therefore get the benefit of their abolition. And in this reduced rent the tenant would pay all those taxes that he now has to pay in addition to his rent—any remainder of what he paid on account of the ground going, not to increase the wealth of a landlord, but to add to a fund in which the tenant himself would be an equal sharer.

In the second place, a large and constantly increasing fund would be provided for common uses without any tax on the earnings of labor or on the returns of capital—a fund which in well-settled countries would not only suffice for all of what are now considered necessary expenses of government, but would leave a large surplus to be devoted to purposes of general benefit.

In the third place, and most important of all, the monopoly of land would be abolished, and land would be thrown open and kept open to the use of labor, since it would be unprofitable for anyone to hold land without putting it to its full use, and both the temptation and the power to speculate in natural opportunities would be gone.

The speculative value of land would be destroyed as soon as it was known that, no matter whether land was used or not, the tax would increase as fast as the value increased, and no one would want to hold land that he did not use. With the disappearance of the capitalized or selling value of land, the premium which must now be paid as purchase money by those who wish to use land would disappear, differences in the value of land being measured by what would have to be paid for it to the community, nominally in taxes but really in rent. So long as any unused land remained, those who wished to use it could obtain it, not only without the payment of any purchase price, but without the payment of any tax or rent.

Nothing would be required for the use of land till less advantageous land came into use, and possession thus gave an advance over and above the return to the labor and capital expended upon it, and, no matter how much the growth of population and the progress of society increased the value of land, this increase would go to the whole community, swelling that general fund in which the poorest would be an equal sharer with the richest.

Thus the great cause of the present unequal distribution of wealth would be destroyed, and that one-sided competition would cease which now deprives men who possess nothing but power to labor of the benefits of advancing civilization, and forces wages to a minimum, no matter what the increase of wealth. Labor, free to the natural elements of production, would no longer be incapable of employing itself, and competition, acting as fully and freely between employers as between employed, would carry wages up to what is truly their natural rate—the full value of the produce of labor—and keep them there.

On April 6 Charles E. Belknap [Mich.] introduced in a speech on the free wool bill a reply to Henry George by Giles B. Stebbins, of Detroit.

In this book were "rounded up" other replies to George by more eminent persons than the collector, and it is for these that the work is chiefly valuable. The following are extracts:

PROGRESS FROM POVERTY

GILES B. STEBBINS

Henry George has written a book, the title of which outlines its theory. Progress and poverty implies that wealth and want walk side by side, and that as the one thrives and grows fair the hideousness of the other grows more gaunt and grim— as the few go up the many are pushed lower down. If he is right, civilization is a failure, inventive genius and progress in mechanism must crush millions that a few may be "clad in purple and fine linen and fare sumptuously every day," and man's mastery over nature's forces by which wealth is won (which indeed is wealth) is a curse. The savage in his hut with his club and dugout, his helplessness against wind and tide, his alternate gorging and starving, his vacant thoughtlessness and brutish contest, has a better life than the modern workingman, whose poor existence, as Mr. George seems to think, tends downward with our progress in wealth and invention.

But he is not right. The highest civilization of each age is the flood tide of the thought and life of its time, and the last is the best, for the world runs in upward grooves. The last half century has been marked by an immense increase of the precious metals, by a wealth of varied mechanism and inventive skill, a boldness and power in engineering, a mastery of man over nature never before known. This has vastly increased our power of productiveness, making the stroke of a great engine forge and weld more than a hundred hammers, or the click of curious machinery do the work of a hundred hands. It has increased the world's commerce and added vastly to the wealth of all civilized lands. It has tended to change the old methods of production and to put workmen into great shops and mills to make or to guide costly machines.

Capital moves in masses, and its coworker, labor, moves in masses also. The old way was one or two men working in their own little shop; the new way is a hundred or a thousand men working for a great corporation. The old method of transportation was the stagecoach and the freight wagon carrying a dozen passengers or a ton or two of freight; the new mode is the railway train of two hundred passengers or 200 tons of freight—more done and greater capital combined for the larger result.

The change has been so great and so sudden that we have not rightly adjusted the new order of things. Capital, grown greatly, feels its power and presses hard on labor, which has also grown stronger and able to push back against capital. The intelligent and humane among employers and employed are recognizing their common interest and aiming for unity and harmony; the domineering and ignorant are nursing the blind pride of power and the equally blind spirit of vengeful hate. How shall justice be done? Is to-day better or worse than yesterday? As wealth grows and productive power increases does labor gain or lose? These and other like questions are asked and answered in ways wise or otherwise by Henry George and others.

In his "Protection or Free Trade," page 284, the robbers, assailing and plundering labor, are described as follows:

"Labor may be likened to a man who, as he carries home his earnings, is waylaid by a series of robbers. One demands this much, and another that much, but last of them all stands one who demands all that is left, save just enough to enable the victim to maintain his life and come forth next day to work. So long as this last robber remains, what will it benefit such a man to drive off any or all of the other robbers?

"Such is the situation of labor to-day throughout the civilized world. And the robber that takes all that is left is private property in land."

While repudiating all lawless violence or crime as remedies for social wrongs, the writer of this gloomy view of the condition of labor helps to feed the fire wherein the anarchist forges his bombs for the fatal dynamite. If it be true, none need mar-

X—6

vel at the desperate sullenness of that forger; but it is not true. Even in England, where the "robber" protection is driven off, but where free trade and low wages bear rule, the deposits in savings banks, largely the savings of laborers, increased $350,-000,000 in thirty-four years, up to 1880.

Still less is it true in this country. From 1860 to 1881 the savings bank deposits of nine States, all except California in the manufacturing Eastern section, increased $628,000,000, and reached a total of $787,000,000—the protection robber system having full sway all this time, and land being higher and wealth of capitalists greater than in other sections where the accumulated savings were far less.

Millions of dollars are invested in homes, owned and earned by working people in those States, and their value must be added to the savings bank deposits.

George Basil Dixwell, of Boston, wrote an admirable criticism of "Progress and Poverty," courteous yet searching. From it is this extract:

"Mr. George describes eloquently the century's increase in wealth-producing power, and thinks that if a Franklin or a Priestley had seen it in a vision he would have expected the very poorest to be lifted above the possibility of want.

"But Franklin and Priestley were far from rhapsodists. They were cool and wary thinkers and observers. They saw about them much vice, crime, ignorance, and brutality that were the cause of poverty, instead of being caused by poverty, as Mr. George assumes. They saw much poverty which need not then exist had the sufferers been as free from vice and ignorance as they might have been under the then conditions of society; they saw, indeed, much vice, crime, ignorance, and brutality which even then had not the apology of poverty; moreover, they would have foreseen a vast increase of cities where temptations are more numerous and restraints less powerful, where there is much wealth to be preyed upon and comparatively great opportunity of escaping detection, where charity rushes out eager to relieve the deserving and often carelessly giving to the undeserving the funds which should have been better bestowed, where there are a thousandfold more opportunities for self-indulgence than in the village where everyone knows and is known to all and each man and woman is a wholesome restraint upon the rest.

"Franklin and Priestley, then, would hardly have expected as much as our author supposes, possibly not as much as has actually been accomplished. If they could have foreseen the condition of society to-day and compared it, class for class, with what existed in their times, they probably would have gone down to their graves with bright hopes for the future. They would have seen cities grow as healthy as the village was in their days, and they would have seen a great and general advance in the real wages of all classes of those willing and able to work. Wages, fees, salaries, emoluments of every kind, have risen every ten years from 1840 to 1880—at each period more to divide and every portion of the community obtaining a larger dividend.

"The problem, then, for the solution of which Mr. George wrote his eloquent book, seems not to exist. It appears that wages do not tend to a minimum, but that, on the contrary, they are continually and steadily increasing. If we examine them at considerable intervals and under similar circumstances, it would appear that 'where population is the densest, wealth the greatest, and the machinery of production and exchange most highly developed' we do not find 'the deepest poverty, the sharpest struggle for existence, and the most enforced idleness.' His proposition is universal, and is demolished the moment we compare Ireland with England, Portugal with France, or the farmer of fifty years ago with the farmer now, or the domestic servant or 'longshoreman of those days with the same class to-day.''

Mr. George sees in private ownership of land the great scourge which crushes and curses labor. Material progress, inventive genius, wealth, protective tariffs, and dense population are attendant evils, grinding to dust the poor workingman.

His sole remedy and panacea is: "To abolish all taxation save on land values," on the theory that no man has any right to own land. "To satisfy the law of justice," he says, would be "at one stroke to declare all land public property," but he would not suddenly shock our present arrangement to that extent, and he proposes a gradual appropriation of rent through taxation.

Land taxes would increase as taxes on the personal property of the rich were abolished. How would this operate in practice? Suppose the present tax on a farm of a hundred acres to be $50 a year, and that this scheme should raise it to $100, would that help the owner of the farm or enable him to pay higher wages to his workmen?

Suppose a cottage hired by a workingman now pays a tax on house and lot of $40, and the lot should pay $60 under this new plan, the owner would add the extra $20 to his rent, and the workingman, his tenant, would have to pay it. How would this added price of rent raise wages, or give remunerative employ, or do any of the fine things promised? This land tax would be as grinding a rack rent as ever Irish peasants, or Scotch crofters, or poor Hindoo ryots starved under or revolted against. Nor would it abolish rent, the evils of which are so constantly emphasized. Could a man afford to build houses on land which he did not own and not charge rent to tenants who occupied them? Plainly, he could not, and therefore landlords and tenants would still exist.

Mr. George gives warning of a growing tendency to hold land in larger quantities in this country. No doubt purchases of great tracts are more frequent than formerly, yet our census shows that the average size of farms decreases instead of increasing. That average was 199 acres in 1860, 153 acres in 1870, and 134 acres in 1880.

The real evils that come from land monopoly are not to be ignored. With our broad domain and our freedom from the English usages and laws of primogeniture and entail, they are but little felt, yet their possible coming has been partly guarded against, and may well be guarded against anew and with more strength.

Our homestead and preëmption laws have greatly helped many industrious men to buy Government lands at low prices, and have secured to worthy settlers the first right to enter upon the full possession of farms they have opened. They have done much good in keeping the land divided into farms of moderate size.

Purchases of great tracts of Government land by syndicates of capitalists should be checked, and such purchases by foreign nonresidents even prohibited. We want the farmer on his own soil, not a great landlord and tenant system like that which is so grave an injury to Ireland and Great Britain. But to correct the abuses of a good thing is a far different matter from abolishing the good which is abused and putting a bad thing in its place. We want the fixed and settled feeling, the home and family unity and security, the sense of free citizenship and responsibility, the motive and stimulus to industry, the wise conservatism, the independent dignity which the ownership of our three million farms increases so much in the thought and life of their occupants.

To the millions of home owners in towns and cities come the same benefits—great and noble elements needed in our free civilization. Land ownership by the state, such as Henry George advocates, would be a bane and not a blessing.

We quote from the *Christian Union,* a journal especially fair and friendly to the labor movement, the words of Mr. George, as follows:

"By the time the people of any such country as England or the United States are sufficiently aroused to the injustice and disadvantages of individual ownership of land to induce them to attempt its nationalization, they will be sufficiently aroused to nationalize it in a much more direct and easy way than by purchase. They will not trouble themselves about compensating the proprietors of land."

That journal is compelled to pronounce this utterance "immoral," as well it may.

George says:

"God made the land; it is His bounty to the human race. Where does any man, or set of men, get the right to parcel out and sell this heritage of our Heavenly Father to all his children alike?"

God made iron and gold. What right has any man to sell these bounties to the human race? He made "the cattle on a thousand hills." What right has a farmer to sell an ox? Land and iron and cattle were created for us to use and improve. They will not support any human being who sits idly with folded hands. It is our task to mold and shape and make more productive. He who forges and fashions the iron owns the bar, as the fruit of his toil and skill. He has changed it from the useless ore to the useful bar. Wild land is as useless as iron ore. Make this earth a wilderness and the scanty fruit would not keep a quarter of the human race alive. Labor and skill have transfigured the wilderness with fruitful farms and gardens. Has the man who has done this, or have the generations of men who have wrought this beneficent result, no right to the soil they have improved? If not there can be no right to iron or gold or cattle—common property must rule, no man can own anything.

Henry C. Carey tells us the farm lands of New York and Pennsylvania were valued at $950,000,000 in 1860; and that, were they all put back in their wild state and their present estimated value given to a company of capitalists who should drain and clear and improve them up to their present condition, the money would not pay for a quarter of the great cost. The same showing could be made in regard to costly city lots even. To take these lands, which Mr. George holds is right, would be to rob men of the fruits of their toil.

Is it true that wages are relatively high where land is low, or low where land is high? Exactly the reverse is true. Let us first look at manufacturing wages as given in the United States census for 1880.

In Massachusetts and Rhode Island land is high, but in the first State the average yearly wages per head are $364; in the second, $340. In Michigan land is lower in price, and the wages average $326. Iowa, with land still lower, gives an average of $309; and North Carolina, with land least valuable, had an average of only $152 in its few manufactures.

These averages include both city and country. If we look at cities, where land and rent are highest and where, in accord with the "Progress and Poverty" theory, wages should be relatively lowest, we find by a report on labor from the State Department at Washington in 1878 that the average weekly wage in seventeen trades—bricklayers, blacksmiths, shoemakers, etc.— was $12.70 in New York and $11.50 in Chicago. In the latter city it was said that the daily pay of the thousands of meat packers engaged in the late strikes was over $2.50. Relative to cost of living city wages in these leading trades are quite as good as those in the country, and both refute the assertion that wages are low where land is high.

How is it with the millions employed in agriculture? There wages, too, will be found highest where land is most valuable. The value of farm land increases in the vicinity of large mills and factories.

In the Eastern States, with land worth $40 per acre, the average farm wages were $26.61; Western States, with land about $30 and fewer manufactures, $23.63; Southern States, land $8.27 per acre and fewest manufactures, the lowest average was found, $15.30.

We are told that "wages are relatively the lowest where capital is most abundant," and that "wages constantly tend to a minimum which will give but a bare living." But we have shown wages twice as high in Massachusetts manufactories, where capital is larger, as in North Carolina, where there is less capital, and that, in our whole country, wages have increased and savings-bank deposits grown larger in the past twenty years.

There has been meanwhile a gradual decrease of the hours of work, sometimes by law and sometimes by change of custom —a fact noteworthy and important as showing the growth of a spirit of fraternity as well as the power and influence of labor.

All this shows progress from poverty. Want and weakness, pride and greed are painfully seen, but the increase of poverty is not wrought into the very heart and structure of our free civilization. The people's step is up, not down. Let us all join to clear the way, that the upward march may be peacefully triumphant.

Henry George died on October 29, 1897, in the midst of a campaign for the mayoralty of New York, in which he was candidate of an independent party called "The Democracy of Thomas Jefferson." His opponents were Benjamin F. Tracy [Republican], Seth Low [Citizens' Union], and Robert A. Van Wyck [Democrat]. Mr. Van Wyck was elected. Mr. Low's and Mr.

George's candidacies were in opposition to the two political machines, Republican and Democratic, and not to each other. Mr. George tersely summed up his position in a platform utterance as follows: "Mr. Low is a Republican reformer: he would help the people. I am a Democratic reformer: I would help the people to help themselves."[1]

During this campaign the present editor, who was secretary of his campaign committee, called Mr. George's attention to the "Letters on Taxation" by Edwin Burgess, showing him a manuscript copy of the letters which was the property of Joseph F. Darling, of New York City, who subsequently did much to secure the publication of the letters in England and Australia. Mr. George had not heard of Mr. Burgess, and was greatly delighted to learn that the single tax theory had been developed before his time and in a form so strikingly like his own, as this corroborated his claim that it was a fundamental philosophy. He asked to see the manuscript after the campaign was over. Two days later Mr. George died of apoplexy brought on by the labors of the campaign.

After Mr. George's death his son, Henry, published a work which his father was about completing when he entered the campaign. The book was broader than its title—"The Science of Political Economy"—being a treatise upon the author's entire philosophy, which he styled in the work as "The Philosophy of the Natural Order." The son also wrote a biography of the father, which was published in 1900.

The first national conference of single taxers, held in New York City on September 3, 1890, adopted the following platform, which, with minor alterations to suit the changing phases of politics, has been reaffirmed at the succeeding national conferences up to that held at Boston November 29–December 1, 1912.

Henry George drafted this platform.

[1] Another utterance of Mr. George showed his political kinship to Thomas Jefferson, the great opponent of paternalism; this was: "It is not a function of government to save a fool from the consequences of his folly."

The Single Tax Platform

We assert as our fundamental principle the self-evident truth enunciated in the Declaration of American Independence, that all men are created equal, and are endowed by their Creator with certain inalienable rights.

We hold that all men are equally entitled to the use and enjoyment of what God has created and of what is gained by the general growth and improvement of the community of which they are a part. Therefore, no one should be permitted to hold natural opportunities without a fair return to all for any special privilege thus accorded to him, and that value which the growth and improvement of the community attach to land should be taken for the use of the community.

We hold that each man is entitled to all that his labor produces. Therefore no tax should be levied on the products of labor.

To carry out these principles we are in favor of raising all public revenues for national, State, county, and municipal purposes, by a single tax upon land values, irrespective of improvements, and of the abolition of all forms of direct and indirect taxation.

Since in all our States we now levy some tax on the value of land, the single tax can be instituted by the simple and easy way of abolishing, one after another, all other taxes now levied, and commensurately increasing the tax on land values, until we draw upon that one source for all expenses of government, the revenue being divided between local governments, State governments, and the general Government, as the revenue from direct taxes is now divided between the local and State governments; or a direct assessment being made by the general Government upon the States and paid by them from revenues collected in this manner.

The single tax we propose is not a tax on land, and therefore would not fall on the use of land and become a tax on labor.

It is a tax, not on land, but on the value of land. Thus it would not fall on all land, but only on valuable land, and on that not in proportion to the use made of it, but in proportion to its value—the premium which the user of land must pay to the owner, either in purchase money or rent, for permission to use valuable land. It would thus be a tax not on the use or improvement of land, but on the ownership of land, taking

what would otherwise go to the owner as owner, and not as
user.

In assessments under the single tax all values created by individual use or improvement would be excluded, and the only
value taken into consideration would be the value attaching to
the bare land by reason of neighborhood, etc., to be determined
by impartial periodical assessments. Thus the farmer would
have no more taxes to pay than the speculator who held a similar piece of land idle, and the man who on a city lot erected

a valuable building would be taxed no more than the man who
held a similar lot vacant.

The single tax, in short, would call upon men to contribute
to the public revenues, not in proportion to what they produce
or accumulate, but in proportion to the value of the natural
opportunities they hold. It would compel them to pay just as
much for holding land idle as for putting it to its fullest use.

The single tax therefore would—

1. Take the weight of taxation off of the agricultural districts where land has little or no value irrespective of improvements, and put it on towns and cities where bare land rises to a
value of millions of dollars per acre.

2. Dispense with a multiplicity of taxes and a horde of tax
gatherers, simplify government, and greatly reduce its cost.

3. Do away with the fraud, corruption, and gross inequality inseparable from our present methods of taxation, which
allow the rich to escape while they grind the poor. Land cannot

be hid or carried off, and its value can be ascertained with greater ease and certainty than any other.

4. Give us with all the world as perfect freedom of trade as now exists between the States of our Union, thus enabling our people to share, through free exchanges, in all the advantages which nature has given to other countries, or which the peculiar skill of other peoples has enabled them to attain. It would destroy the trusts, monopolies, and corruptions which are the outgrowths of the tariff. It would do away with the fines and penalties now levied on anyone who improves a farm, erects a house, builds a machine, or in any way adds to the general stock of wealth. It would leave everyone free to apply labor or expend capital in production or exchange without fine or restriction, and would leave to each the full product of his exertion.

5. It would, on the other hand, by taking for public use that value which attaches to land by reason of the growth and improvement of the community, make the holding of land unprofitable to the mere owner, and profitable only to the user. It would thus make it impossible for speculators and monopolists to hold natural opportunities unused or only half used, and would throw open to labor the illimitable field of employment which the earth offers to man. It would thus solve the labor problem, do away with involuntary poverty, raise wages in all occupations to the full earnings of labor, make overproduction impossible until all human wants are satisfied, render labor-saving inventions a blessing to all, and cause such an enormous production and such an equitable distribution of wealth as would give to all comfort, leisure, and participation in the advantages of an advancing civilization.

With respect to monopolies other than the monopoly of land, we hold that where free competition becomes impossible, as in telegraphs, railroads, water and gas supplies, etc., such business becomes a proper social function, which should be controlled and managed by and for the whole people concerned, through their proper government, local, State, or national, as may be.

Beginning in the early nineties the Single-Taxers adopted the policy of securing their reform in separate States. Now the constitutions of the original thirteen States had a common provision which was, in essence, that all property should be taxed equally on the basis of its money value, and this provision was incorporated in the constitutions of the States subsequently admitted into the Union. Until it was stricken out it was impossible to apply the single tax to a district within the State, and hence the advocates of the principle agitated for home rule in taxation, which would permit any municipality or county to abolish the tax on any form or forms of property that it chose. With home rule adopted they felt confident that they could persuade the majority of the citizens of at least one district to abolish all taxes on labor products, such as personal property and improvements on land. They were even more confident that, after such abolition, the community would prosper at the expense of its neighbors which continued the old system of taxation, drawing from them manufacturers and laborers, and so inducing them, in self-defence as well as emulation, to follow its example.

Thus far this policy has proved unsuccessful, except in inducing increasing minorities in each State to advocate the single tax. In 1912 a referendum on the subject was held in Oregon and Missouri, and the single tax was defeated by considerable majorities. The new constitution of Ohio, adopted in 1912, specifically excepted change in the principle of taxation from those matters to which the referendum could apply—which would seem to indicate a fear on the part of the present majority opposed to single tax principles that it might shortly become a minority.

On June 10, 1911, Henry George, Jr. [N. Y.], made a speech in the House on a bill to reduce the duties on wool and woolen manufactures, which developed into an exposition of single tax philosophy.

The Road to Freedom

Henry George, Jr., M. C.

Mr. George compared the Democratic assault upon the tariff by reducing the duties schedule by schedule to the Roman attack upon the Macedonian phalanx under Pyrrhus.

When the Roman soldier met the phalanx he had a new military problem on his hands: a gigantic oblong of spears bristled before him like a vast porcupine. How was he to get within arm's reach of the body of the Greek soldier, for do this he must to use his weapon—the short sword. Then was Roman genius called upon to invent a weapon that should destroy the phalanx. It was the pilum, a short spear that could be hurled with great force and accuracy fifty feet or more. Each Roman soldier marked out an individual behind the wall of spears. Watching for an exposed part, he hurled the pilum. If a spearman fell, he made confusion and a breach in the line of spears. That was the Roman chance. The legionaries ran in between the points and with their swords had the spearmen, helpless in heavy armor, at their mercy. One such breach made, there was a wedge-like rush from the Roman ranks and the whole phalanx was destroyed. Thus was Pyrrhus vanquished. The Roman with his broadsword and his *pilum* became the world's master.

Mr. Chairman, the tariff beneficiaries have been the economic and political phalanx for long years in the United States. They have formed one great compact united body. Realizing that they must stand together or be destroyed in detail, they have acted as a mass, their shields spread, their spears advanced; from time to time moving forward to new ground of vantage; making at all times a common bristling defence against all general attack.

And so it has been until this Congress. In this special session the method of attack on the tariff phalanx has changed. The *pilum* has now come into use in this Democratic House. This wool bill which we are now debating; the Canadian reciprocity bill and the free-list bill which we have passed; the other schedule bills that may hereafter pass are our Roman lances which we hurl at weak points in the tariff ranks. We break down the spears here, we break down the spears there, we make a breach and widen it with a rush, and then the cry in the tariff ranks is each for himself. Small and insignificant as these bills may appear, they carry destruction. Hurled by the Democratic side in this Congress, the tariff army line will at points be pierced and breached, and the monopoly phalanx, which, so long as it could stand intact, was invincible, will end in utter rout and destruction. [Applause on the Democratic side.]

Therefore, Mr. Chairman, I have great joy in voting for this wool bill. I do not regard it as much of a bill, but since it unites the Democratic side in battle order it will do. I would have liked the bill to declare for free trade in wool and woolens. [Applause.] But, thank you, I shall take what I can get. [Applause.]

I believe that the gentleman from Georgia [William G. Brantley] is perfectly right in stating that any tariff at all involves protection. I am against any protection whatever, and therefore I am altogether against a tariff. [Applause.] I am against a tariff for revenue, for I regard it as one of the worst ways for raising revenue.

But, Mr. Chairman, suppose that we reach a revenue basis; suppose we cut out much of the tariff, how are we to supplement the revenue? Shall we go to an income tax? Some thirty States have approved of a change in the Constitution that will enable us to do that, and, some half dozen more States approving it, Congress will have authority to pass such an act. If I should be a member of this House at that time, I should take great pleasure in voting for it. [Applause.] It has one merit over a tariff tax; it is direct. You can see it; you know just exactly what you are paying. Who in the world knows what he is paying under a tariff tax?

A MEMBER.—Or who gets it?

MR. GEORGE.—Ay, or who gets it? For, as has been said of old, the tariff is a device for getting the most feathers with the least squawking. [Laughter and applause.]

But, while an income tax is better than a tariff tax, I am opposed to it. Why tax incomes? Men toil away their days in trying to get incomes. Why should they not keep them to spend as they please? Why should the Government tax any part into the public treasury? To support the Government, it is said. But to get support in that way is all a mistake. The British have had a high income tax, but they are now lowering it. The whole trend of taxation is away from that idea. The march of enlightenment opposes a tax of any kind upon production. It opposes personal property taxes. It opposes taxation upon the improvements on land—upon dwellings, stores, factories; upon the buildings of the farmer, his fences, ditches, drains—opposes the taxation of anything and everything that comes from human toil.

To him that produceth should go the fruits thereof. This is getting to be the current of thought. Consequently I believe that just so surely as this country shall establish an income tax that surely will the mass of those who pay it become active in quest of some substitute tax. They will be far more active against an income tax than they may now be against a tariff tax, because an income tax is direct in its incidence. It can be seen plainly by the man who pays it. Therefore income-tax payers will rebel against this tax upon their industry. They will look for a tax that will raise revenue, but not tax thrift.

What tax will do that? A tax on land values will do it; do it absolutely. It will fall on privilege, and not any part of it on toil.

This brings us to a consideration of the single-tax philosophy. I am a single taxer. I do not believe in taxes upon any kind of industry, or upon anything that comes from industry. I believe the whole burden of taxation—Federal, State, and municipal—should fall upon monopoly. I believe it should fall upon the mother of all monopolies; upon the earth; upon that value which comes to any piece of land not by reason of the toil of its owner—for all improvements should be exempted— but from the development of the community; from social growth and social improvement.

That part of New York City known as Manhattan Borough, Manhattan Island, comprises land officially valued at more than three thousand million dollars. The island was bought from the Indians by Dutch traders in the seventeenth century for $24 worth of calico and glass beads. Yet now that same piece of land stands on the tax books at three thousand millions. That is the official value of the ground alone. It does not include the value of buildings or other improvements of any kind. Who made the increase in value from $24 to three thousand million dollars—who but all the people? The coming of population did part; the birth of babies did part; the laying out of streets, the making of great public improvements, the general toil, the building this island into a great center of production, of manufacturing and trade made parts. Social growth and social improvement brought the value to that piece of land. Why should it not be taken into the public treasury for social uses? Why not abolish all other taxes and take by taxation this publicly made value for the uses of government—municipal, State, and Federal?

Now, such action is not so far away. Bills are in the State legislature to abolish the personal-property tax and to reduce taxation on improvements on land. This would involve a corresponding increase in the tax now falling on the ground value.

To tax land values, ground values, alone is not a mere dream. It is not the utterance of a man so far in the advance of practical affairs as just to be listened to for a brief hour and then be dismissed. My colleagues, it is a principle that is now and here. It is claiming the grave attention, shaping the legislation, of the advanced nations of the earth. It is in the Orient; it is in the Occident; it is in the Antipodes; it is among the progressive people to the north of us with whom we are seeking closer ties; it has made a momentous, convulsive drive forward in Great Britain.

GEORGE W. NORRIS [Neb.].—In fixing the value of the land for the purpose of taxation, you would not take into consideration any improvements?

MR. GEORGE.—As though it had no improvement on it; what it would sell for in the open market. That market price is the sum of advantages in the situation; if there be public streets or other public improvements, for instance; if there be improvements on adjoining lots—all such considerations enter into value.

MR. NORRIS.—So that you would not consider the improvement of the land you are fixing, but you would consider the other improvements on other land that had a tendency to put a value into that land which you were taxing?

MR. GEORGE.—Yes; but you would not have to bother about that. You simply determine the selling value of the land.

Up north of us, in Vancouver, British Columbia, they have applied what is called the "single tax." So far as local revenues are concerned, it is a single tax; but it is not the single tax I am advocating, since it is very small in amount—not sufficient to check the great land "boom" now in progress there in consequence of the exemption of buildings and all other improvements from taxation.

The city began some years ago by exempting 25 per cent. of the value of improvements from taxation. That worked so well that 50 per cent. were exempted. Then they exempted 75 per cent.; and for two years, I think it is, they have entirely removed improvements from the tax rolls. The course of personal-property exemption was similar. No personalty tax now exists there. The sole source of revenue in that advancing city is the land value, ground value; the value called "economic rent" by the political economists.

As a result, Vancouver has increased in improvements faster than any city in the world. I was informed by Mayor Taylor during a visit there that the increase in Vancouver's improvements during the last year was 87 per cent. There being no tax on buildings or other things a man might put on his land, industry and thrift are encouraged.

Indeed, there is so much benefit from this policy that land values are rising. There is very active speculation in land. The advantage from the exemption of improvement is likely to be absorbed by land speculation. Against this the people of Vancouver will be compelled to defend themselves by increasing the tax rate on land values.

But, this aside, the idea of exempting improvements from taxation is spreading all through western Canada. Wherever tried, it is working most prosperously. And nowhere, in Canada, Australia, or anywhere else, is there the least disposition to go back to the old taxes. The people in Washington and Oregon, as you can find if you go out to those States, are looking with amazed eyes at Canada and her exemption of industry from any taxation. Attracted by that, many are going up over the border. Many more will most assuredly go unless those Western States shall adopt a similar policy of exempting improvements from taxation.

Some say the farmers would object to this single tax. But have we not seen in the newspapers how the Canadian farmers from the West went to the Dominion Parliament and asked for the adoption of the reciprocity treaty with us? They offered to make up any loss of revenue by submitting to a tax upon land values. They believed that they would get benefits from even that small measure of free trade with the United States, and were willing to pay for such benefit by accepting a tax upon ground values—on the ground values alone, of course, less all improvement value. Certainly, this is an answer to any who say that the farmers of this country would never bear such taxation. For, let me repeat, this tax is upon land values exclusively. When you come to consider the values in a farm you find that they are largely betterments—improvements the farmer's labor has wrought. Exempting them, the value that remains to be taxed is very much shrunk up. Moreover, speculative value in the land would lessen. Indeed, speculative value would disappear with heavy taxation of land values.

Why should we in this country not go to land values for all our revenues? We get part there; why not all? Abolish the tariff and other taxes on production and increase our present taxation on land values. If the older countries find it good, if the newer parts of the world, Australia and Canada, find it good, why should not this country find it good?

Is there in any part of the world a greater, more damaging, more damning kind of land monopoly than in this country? Can you find in any part of the world landlords so great, so mighty? Where will you find, among the peerage of Europe, dukes or earls or counts or viscounts so powerful from their landed possessions as are simple citizens of our country?

A steel trust has vast possessions. Those possessions form the very core of its monopoly. An oil trust has great landed

"Ye build! ye build! but ye enter not in,
Like the tribes whom the desert devoured in
their sin;
From the land of promise ye fade and die,
Ere its verdure gleams forth on your wearied eye."

"They toil not; neither do they spin,
Yet Solomon, in all his glory, was not
arrayed like one of these."

THE WORKER AND THE WORKED
From "The National Single Taxer"

possessions—vast possessions, of which it choses to use only a small part, shutting all the rest off from use by anybody. You will find the roots of most of the trusts in land monopoly. Why not apply the single tax? All the revenue raised in this country—Federal, State, local—amounts in round numbers to $2,000,000,000 a year. The ground-rent roll of the country probably approximates four thousand millions, so that there is an ample source of revenue for all needs.

Land monopolies such as find example only, if there be any comparison whatever, in the imperial days of Rome exist here. The great Warwick, the king maker, could go to Parliament with 600 liveried men. But a simple citizen, a Carnegie, or any one of a large number that any of us might name, could, if he chose, have not 600 but 6,000—we might say, in some instances, 60,000—retainers, should he choose to go abroad in such a style.

X—7

Whence comes all this? Primarily from ownership of the soil. That is the very essence of these monopoly fortunes. Given a condition where the few own the soil that all others there must use for their subsistence, the few are the masters of the many.

SWAGAR SHERLEY [Ky.].—The gentleman has alluded to Mr. Carnegie. Does he think he is accurate in giving the impression that Mr. Carnegie's fortune came as the result of the ownership of land?

MR. GEORGE.—Yes, I do; mainly.

In his most recent book, "Problems of To-day," Mr. Carnegie himself describes in exact terms and with precise instances the greatest factor in the production of the great combinations and great individual fortunes. He says it lies in the monopoly of land.

It was by holding a monopoly of the Connellsville coal fields, the best coking coal in the world, and subsequently by possession of practically all the best or most available iron and steel ore in the country that the United States Steel Corporation received material advantage over all competitors—which were sufficient, at any rate, to force a gentleman's agreement with competitors in America, while the tariff shut off competition from abroad.

MR. SHERLEY.—I would like to have the gentleman define just what he means by "land."

MR. GEORGE.—By "land" I do not mean mills, I do not mean railroad tracks, I do not mean anything made by labor. By "land" I mean the superficies of the earth. By "land" I mean the thing on which we stand, from which we came, to which we return.

MR. SHERLEY.—The gentleman says he means that which, if I may paraphrase his language, is the gift of nature and not the result of man's handiwork. Does he consider iron ore when it comes out of the land to be land within the meaning of his definition?

MR. GEORGE.—No; I do not.

MR. SHERLEY.—Then, to the extent that the general ownership of iron ore produced the fortune, it does not relate to land?

MR. GEORGE.—I call land that which nature offers to man before man has put his hand to it.

MR. SHERLEY.—In that sense there is practically nothing; there is no value at all until he puts his hand to it.

MR. GEORGE.—I can have a vacant lot here in Washington, and it may lie just as it was at the time the Indians occupied

it. I can sell it for a price. Yet not a stick or a stone has been touched upon it.

MR. SHERLEY.—Yes; it has a potential value.

MR. GEORGE.—It has an actual value, for value proceeds not only from labor, but also from a power to exact labor.

Now, Mr. Chairman, observe the Coal Trust. I do not believe that any amount of regulation, any amount of examination into financial accounts, any amount of acts here in Congress for the reorganization, if you please, of the Coal Trust will do any lasting good. You pass regulations and set up regulators, and then you have got to have somebody regulate the regulators. [Laughter.] The only way to hit a combination like the Coal Trust is to hit the monopoly principle underlying it.

Take the Anthracite Coal Trust in Pennsylvania. It possesses practically all of the hard-coal land of that State. Nature has put into eastern Pennsylvania a great deposit of hard coal. It has been the business of the anthracite railroad companies, beginning with the Reading Railroad years ago, to get possession of these deposits by purchase, by long lease, and by contract for the carriage of the coal. These railroads acting together have in these ways got control of the hard coal of all eastern Pennsylvania. The purpose has not been to mine coal. It has been, rather, *not* to mine coal. Their purpose has been to limit the output and to force up the price of coal—to work only part of their land, a small part, and to let the remainder lie idle, as though it did not exist, and to keep others from the use of it. Why could they do that? There was no tax upon it, no penalty on their doing it. The law does not discourage it; nor does even public opinion. People do not realize that it could and should be stopped; that it could be absolutely destroyed by the simple process of taxation. The law of Pennsylvania requires a tax on the market value of that land. The actual practice is not to assess at the market value, which would be as valuable mineral land. The practice is to assess it as inferior agricultural land. Then, the tax upon that preposterously low valuation is very small, so that these great coal barons go practically without taxation upon their holdings.

But if we were to make an absolute market value and put that upon the tax books, and then increase the tax upon that valuation, you would see whether the Anthracite Trust could hold its lands idle or keep the price of its coal high. Its purpose then would not be to make a scarcity in output in order to put up prices and keep down the wages of labor by limiting

opportunities for employment. A heavy tax upon the real market value of these lands would compel their use. Their use would mean more demand for labor. The price of labor would go up in the hard-coal regions. Because of the larger output of coal, the price of coal would go down. Consumers in the United States would get cheaper coal. Laborers in the coal regions would have higher wages, shorter hours, and God knows their little boys would not have to work in the breakers or their little girls go into the silk mills to help get the family subsistence. [Applause.]

EDWARD L. HAMILTON [Mich.].—The method of taxation which the gentleman is expounding so very ably would result in what is known as expropriation eventually, would it not, of the coal lands? That is to say, the title of the coal lands would pass to the State, would it not?

MR. GEORGE.—No, sir.

MR. HAMILTON.—You think that the corporations would be able to continue to pay the tax and to sell the coal?

MR. GEORGE.—Yes; the whole policy would be to use land, not to hold it out of use. Instead of high prices and small sales of the mined coal, there would be large sales at low prices.

BENJAMIN K. FOCHT [Pa.].—I will ask the gentleman two questions. The assertion was made by the gentleman from New York that under some changed conditions the boys would not be allowed to work in the breakers of Pennsylvania. Is the gentleman not aware of the statute there that prohibits boys from working in the breakers?

Second, with reference to the labor problem, does not the gentleman know that in the mining section there is a perfectly satisfactory agreement between the United Mine Workers of America and the producers of coal?

MR. GEORGE.—The law, not only in Pennsylvania, but in California, in New York, and in the South and all over the United States, forbids children under a certain age from working at all, but their parents, driven by poverty, have to lie about their children's ages. [Applause on the Democratic side.]

The gentleman asks me if I am not aware that there is a satisfactory relation between the United Mine Workers and the mine owners of Pennsylvania. I know that it is satisfactory in a state of war. I do not deny that. I am not talking about that. I am talking about a condition where men do not have to join labor organizations in order to get even a small measure of social justice. [Applause.] I stand for unions. I am the son of a trade unionist. I went to the printer's trade myself. If

I were working at a trade, I should certainly be an active trade unionist; but I do not consider that a natural condition. It is an unnatural condition. It is a condition where men who have nothing but their labor to sell must band themselves together into an organization, offensive and defensive, to make the best terms of sale they can in respect to price, to time, and the like. [Applause.] I do not regard that as natural. I regard it as unnatural. That is the kind of arrangement that has to be made by men in a state of industrial warfare. I am talking of men in a state of freedom, where every man can look every other man in the eye as a free man.

Mr. Sherley.—Now, if the gentleman will permit, assuming the correctness of his statement, that a tax of this kind would result in the lowering of the price of coal because of the necessity to mine and sell it, does the gentleman also think that such a tax would help conservation of the natural resources?

Mr. George.—Mr. Chairman, I do not care anything about this conservation of natural resources if I am permitted to apply the single tax. What do the conservationists want to do—keep the public lands out of the hands of monopolists and speculators? Well, if you hit land monopoly with taxation, no man will want to own land simply for monopoly's sake. Monopoly's profit would be gone. This single tax would tax land monopoly to death in the United States. Any value attaching to land would be taken into the public treasury and used by all. Therefore there would be no advantage in getting hold of farming land or mineral land or timber land or urban or suburban land unless to use it.

Mr. Sherley.—Does the gentleman consider that there is any difference in principle as to the view that the Government should assume toward private property that consists of land and private property that consists of things other than land; and, if so, what is the basis for it?

Mr. George.—Yes; a very great difference; for who made this world? God Almighty. And for whom did he make it? For all men, without any distinction whatsoever; and, if anything in man's laws belies that everlasting truth, it must in the end go down. But as to other things—this building, a newspaper, a book, glass, iron things that we see here about us, or any similar things outside—they have come from man's exertion. Their title springs originally from labor. I see a vast difference, for instance, in property in the ocean and in property in the fish taken by labor out of the ocean.

Mr. Sherley.—Very well, but can the gentleman state any

condition of land ownership that does not have a value as the result of man's labor?

MR. GEORGE.—Does the gentleman mean the owner's labor only.

MR. SHERLEY.—Oh, we are not discusisng the labor of the owner. We are discussing man's labor. The gentleman undertakes to make the distinction between those things that are the gift of God and those things that are the result of man's labor. Now, it is a perfectly proper distinction if it exists, but, if it is applied artificially to things, then the whole fabric based upon it must fall.

MR. GEORGE.—I said that that value should be taken into the public treasury which was the consequence of social growth, meaning increase of population; and of social improvement, meaning the laying out of streets, the putting in of grades and bridges, the erection of public buildings, the watering, sewering, lighting, heating, the providing of transportation for the city, and matters of that sort. This value comes from the exertion of the community and the increase in numbers of the community. It is a public value, and should be so considered and be publicly taken.

MR. SHERLEY.—If the gentleman will permit me, I am not quarreling with that statement, that so far as an unearned increment is concerned it belongs more to the community than to the individual who is the fortunate possessor of it; but the proposition the gentleman announced in answer to my question was that he differentiated between private land ownership and private ownership of other property, and when I asked him why he said because he considered land to be the gift of God and private property to be the act of man's labor. When I asked him to further evolve that he brings me back to the proposition of unearned increment.

Now, the whole meat of the gentleman's position, as it was of his father's book—one of the most interesting and epoch-making books ever written—was that very question. It is the crux of the whole proposition, whether land, as he uses the word "land," represents something that belongs to the community at large any more than the other property.

MR. GEORGE.—Yes; the land was made by God, and the value that attaches to it may be quite apart from the owner's labor. The owner may do nothing. Any value that attaches to that particular piece of land is a public value. To illustrate: Here you have in the center of Washington a lot, a vacant piece of property. It has nothing whatever upon it. It

has never been improved in any way. Yet it has a selling value and will increase in price. Who made that value? Surely not the labor of the man owning the land. He did not turn a hand. He might have gone into the mountains as did Rip Van Winkle and slept for twenty years, and, returning, found a value in his land that he had nothing to do with making. Why should not such value be taken as a public value? I certainly separate it from any value that might be put upon that land in the way of a house or a machine. Such value perfectly clearly is a private value and belongs to labor.

Mr. Chairman, this land-value tax meets, as no other kind of a tax does, the four canons of taxation. First of all, as laid down by Adam Smith, the father of political economy, in his "Wealth of Nations," it is the most equal kind of a tax.

Mr. Hamilton.—Just a moment. A little while ago the gentleman stated that by the operation of the method of taxation which he is advocating monopoly would be destroyed, a monopoly of coal holdings, for illustration. I want to know where the title of the property would go when the monopoly is destroyed by this method of taxation.

Mr. George.—The title of the land would stay where it is. We do not propose to change titles. You kill monopoly's powers by taxing the value of land. You force the land into use. The power of monopoly is the power to hold land out of use.

Mr. Hamilton.—But could not the monopoly, having to pay the increased tax, charge the increased tax upon the consumer?

Mr. George.—I invite the gentleman to consider the political economists. This is one thing in political economy that is not in dispute.

Mr. Hamilton.—Might he not undertake to do that, as he does it now in coal properties?

Mr. George.—No, sir. When you put a tax on production, you limit production. Men will not produce unless they can get compensation for the tax. They add the tax to the price of the product, and thereby they get recompensed for the tax. But not so when you tax land values. By putting a tax on land values you do not lessen the amount of land. You cannot lessen it by one grain. It is just the same in amount. But you will increase the available quantity. You will force land into use that has been kept out of use by speculation. This will put down the price of land, instead of putting it up.

Mr. Hamilton.—Precisely. Now, if I understand the gentleman, this coal monopoly which he is discussing is a monopoly which controls coal lands and is lying dormant so far as the actual mining of a part of its lands is concerned. It is proposed, then, to tax it so as to compel it to dig all of its coal as rapidly as possible and put it upon the market, so as to be able to pay the increased tax, and that, failing to do this, the monopoly must die. But the gentleman denies the monopoly would actually die so far as the actual mining of coal is concerned. Am I right that it would have to be more active and mine more coal?

MR. GEORGE.—If the trust shall itself use the land it is now holding shut up, then it practically becomes broken as a trust, because the feature of monopoly has gone, the essential part of which is to withhold from use the natural resources and thereby make a higher price for the product from such parts as are used.

MR. HAMILTON.—Suppose the gentleman's theory, then, is correct, and the public refuses to pay the increased price of coal which the corporation has been obliged to impose in order to pay the increased tax, and then the monopoly is unable to pay the tax, does not the monopoly then lose its coal property, and does it not, then, go to the State?

MR. GEORGE.—No, sir. If the land contains valuable coal, and the trust will not pay the tax, then somebody will take the land who will. Valuable land does not run around without an owner. Somebody will use it. If the Coal Trust will not use that land, somebody else will, subject to the tax.

MR. HAMILTON.—The grantee himself takes it at the same rate as the original owner, does he?

MR. GEORGE.—If the owner does not want to use the land and yet, because the tax is too heavy he cannot afford to hold it idle, he will sell it for whatever he can get, subject to the tax by the State. I am not proposing to change titles. I am not a Socialist. I do not propose to put the land into the hands of the Government. I do not propose government management of land. I propose the plain application of the Thomas Jefferson principle of the least possible government. I propose to tax out speculators and monopolists and to throw land open to private initiative.

JOHN E. RAKER [Cal.]—Suppose the taxes were so high the man could not pay them; is it your idea, then, that this land should eventually go back to the State and then as the people wanted it the State would sell it back to some one who desired to put it into actual use?

MR. GEORGE.—No, sir. If a land owner did not pay the tax, he would get sold out for taxes. Whoever bought would buy subject to taxation. Somebody will buy it if it has any value at all. The application of a single tax should not be a hundred per cent. application. It should fall short just enough to leave enough value in the land untaxed to make a basis for sales. This basis for sales will become the market basis for valuation and taxation. Now, if a man, we will say, who is a speculator, a monopolist, or who is "land poor" cannot or will not pay the tax imposed, he will have his land sold for taxes.

The land will go into the hands of a new man. That man will have to pay the tax. If the value of the land should fall, then the tax would correspondingly diminish. If the value should disappear, then there would be nothing to tax, and the owner would hold his land subject to no tax whatever.

The hope of speculation gone, it is probable that there would be an abundance of free land open to whoever might wish to use it. Instead of having to go away out to the remote fastnesses of our mountains to find free land, we could then find free land accessible to our city populations, and, some part of the people going out upon it, city congestion would be relieved.

Mr. Raker.—In California all the public sales under taxation are to the State. There are no private sales in the first instance.

Mr. George.—The gentleman is asking me how the single tax would apply under the Torrens system. This Torrens system is an introduction from Australia. By it the government—in this instance California—at a transfer guarantees the title. That is to say, in the tranfer of land, the title must go through the hands of the government, which thereby guarantees the title. The application of the single tax would not change this. The present small tax on land values does not affect it. Why should a large tax? All I am proposing with respect to land is to increase the amount of the tax—now existing—now imposed on the ground, or what is at times called the "site" value of land.

Philip P. Campbell [Kan.].—The gentleman from New York would break up the coal monopoly by taxing the land it owns in its mining enterprise. Suppose, instead of owning the land, it took a lease upon the land of other people, or of several other people, what effect would taxing the land have upon the monopoly in that instance?

Mr. George.—It would fall upon the owner; and in the leasing of land the man who took the land would take it subject to the taxation condition.

Mr. Campbell.—But there are several owners in this instance, and the mining corporation simply owns the personal property, which is not taxed at all.

Mr. George.—The mining corporation, like any individual, should not be taxed on its personal property; as to the land, it should pay on its market, its real selling, value. Idle land it would sell off; get rid of. It could not afford to pay taxes on valuable idle land.

Rufus Hardy [Tex.].—We understand there is a vast carrying occupation in this country. All our coast-line vessels are engaged in transportation. Our railroads, likewise, are engaged in transportation. Now, I would like to know what solution there is in the gentleman's theory as to a monopoly of transportation, particularly on the ocean? What shipping line has to-day such a monopoly?

Mr. George.—In the first place, the railroads have the most valuable kind of land. The terminals have a very great value. Besides, most railroads, especially the Western railroads, have very valuable lands: Ore beds, oil deposits, timber tracts, water rights, agricultural lands, lands in and about cities. The taxation of land values would fall upon that. But, as to railroads, I would go further, and this is beyond this taxation question. I would treat them as public highways. I think there is no getting away from that. The railroads must be taken into public hands as public highways, along with telegraphs and telephones and every function of a public highway. We must have them in our civilization. Yet it is impossible to have permanent competition in respect to them. Some individuals, getting the privilege to the exclusion of others to engage in the transportation business, will thereby get a serious advantage over others in the community. It therefore becomes a function of the State to perform.

Mr. Hardy.—Mr. Chairman, I do not think the gentleman answered my question as to monopoly and water transportation. For instance, across the water the shipping company does not own the wharf, but the Government has made vast improvements in order to have a port. Now, there is a company organized that monopolizes the transportation from New York to Liverpool. Its property is all on the water. How would the gentleman's land tax affect that?

Mr. George.—It would not affect it directly, assuming that the company itself owned no land; for instance, no wharf or warehouse privilege. But there would be a very material indirect effect. Removing taxation from steamships and steamship building would tend to beget competition. Opening idle lands of every kind to production would increase demand for such shipping competition, and then, beyond this, changing railroads from private administration to public administration would be the greatest stimulus to competition; for now the railroads feed traffic to particular ocean carriers which they control.

JAMES M. GRAHAM [Ill.].—Would you tax the coal which would not be mined for many years to come so heavily that those who have possessed themselves of hundreds of thousands of acres of it could not hold it?

MR. GEORGE.—I should if the assessment were based on the market price. I should discover what such lands would sell for. That is easily obtainable.

MR. RAKER.—For instance, a man owned a good deal of coal land. You would tax it to the extent that he had to use it to make a profit out of it, and if he did not do that the land would be sold.

MR. GEORGE.—I would not pay any attention to whether he used it or not. I would tax it on its value. It is the owner's business to pay the tax and keep the land out of use or to use it. My belief is that a man who pays a heavy tax upon idle land would very rapidly discover that too much of a burden. He would use the land or get rid of it.

MR. RAKER.—How would you make the application to timber land?

MR. GEORGE.—I would put timber land on the tax roll for the price that it would sell for. If it has good trees on it it would sell for such and such a price; if poor trees, a less price. Do not men every day buy and sell timber lands? Take that price and tax the land on that.

MR. RAKER.—The owner can use but little of it as he goes along.

MR. GEORGE.—It does not matter whether he can use little or much. If he wants to monopolize it, he must pay the price. The price is the market price. Tax that.

Mr. George closed his speech by showing how the single tax fulfilled the four canons of taxation.

It is the most equal tax. It falls upon men according to the natural bounties they have in their possession. The man who has little pays little. The man who has much pays much, so that it is the most equal kind of a tax.

Then it is certain. It is not intermittent and wavering. It falls regularly, so that all dependent matters can be arranged accordingly.

In the next place, it is direct. It cannot be shifted. It stays where it falls. There can be no addition of this tax to the value of the land. The land owners are getting as much as they can get now. They are not waiting for taxation to put up the price of their land. On the contrary, any proposal to put a tax on values immediately causes a discouragement on the part of some owners who have idle lands, and the tendency is for the price of land to go down. This tax can be seen. It is not the kind of a tax that falls and no man knoweth how much or where. There lies the land and there lies the value and there falls the tax.

And then it is the most economical tax in its incidence. It lays no burden beyond the revenue received from it. It is cheap in the collection. This tax is not like a tariff tax. That falls upon things coming into the country. To the extent of the tax and the volume of the things so imported is the revenue that goes into the public treasury. But the tax on imports enables an increase in the price of similar commodities made in this country. There is not a cent of revenue from this home production. In the case of the tax on land values, the more the tax the less the speculation, and, therefore, the lower the price of land. So that in application it is the most economical of all taxes.

But, Mr. Chairman, I do not stop with the canons of taxation; for that, after all is said, is a fiscal question. This land tax means far more than that. It means the opening to the use of labor and capital the vast quantities of land now shut off by speculation.

There is no real scarcity of land anywhere. There is no scarcity even in the city of New York with its great population. Great areas are vacant on the outskirts, and you can go along Broadway and Fifth Avenue, the greatest and proudest thoroughfares on the whole hemisphere, and find vacant lots, and one and two-story shacks and shanties where there ought to be imperial buildings.

Why is this? Because the penalty of holding land out of use is so slight that men can pay the small tax and yet, owing to social growth and social improvement, and the consequent increase in value, realize handsome profits by the speculation. Some men acquire fortunes in a short time by simply getting hold of a piece of land, sitting down, and letting society do the rest.

This is so in every State; it is so in every village, town, and hamlet of our country. It is so throughout the agricultural regions; it is so throughout the mineral and timber regions. Apply this tax and you tax out the speculators, you tax in the users, you produce a new order in the United States.

We, of all the peoples of the world, ought to be the most advanced. We ought to be the greatest people, because we have the greatest possible opportunities. But what are we doing to rise to these opportunities? We have instituted a condition by which a few own the country. A few here, a few there, practically control villages, towns, cities, counties, and almost whole States. We have the greatest landlords that have ever been seen. Should we meet this condition, should we apply taxation to land values so as to break down land monopoly and throw open the soil of our country to our fast-growing population, a prosperity will come such as will dumfound mankind and give to America the glory of carrying civilization to a point higher than ever reached in the destinies of the race. [Applause.]

CHAPTER III

CONSERVATION OF NATURAL RESOURCES

Theodore Roosevelt on ''The Conservation of Natural Resources''—Speech of Gov. John F. Shafroth [Col.] in Favor of ''State vs. National Conservation''—Speech of Sen. George E. Chamberlain [Ore.] in Favor of National Conservation, but against Abuses of Its Administration: Remarks by Reed Smoot [Utah], James P. Clarke [Ark.], Duncan U. Fletcher [Fla.], Knute Nelson [Minn.].

B EGINNING with the specific idea of the preservation of forests on the public domain, a subject which was referred to in the annual messages of the Presidents from Johnson to Taft, the idea of the conservation of all natural resources grew in the mind of our statesmen. In President Roosevelt it found its foremost champion. For a summary of his activities in the cause see the speech of Senator Chamberlain later in the chapter.

Mr. Roosevelt's ideas on the subject are summed up in his speech of August 6, 1912, before the national Progressive convention in Chicago.

THE CONSERVATION OF NATURAL RESOURCES

PRESIDENT ROOSEVELT

There can be no greater issue than that of conservation in this country. Just as we must conserve our men, women, and children, so we must conserve the resources of the land on which they live. We must conserve the soil so that our children shall have a land that is more and not less fertile than that our fathers dwelt in.

We must conserve the forests, not by disuse, but by use, making them more valuable at the same time that we use them. We must conserve the mines. Moreover, we must insure so far

110

as possible the use of certain types of great natural resources
for the benefit of the people as a whole. The public should not
alienate its fee in the water power which will be of incalculable
consequence as a source of power in the immediate future.

A PRACTICAL FORESTER

From "A Cartoon History of Roosevelt's Career"

The nation and the States within their several spheres
should by immediate legislation keep the fee of the water power,
leasing its use only for a reasonable length of time on terms
that will secure the interests of the public.

Just as the nation has gone into the work of irrigation in
the West, so it should go into the work of helping reclaim the

swamp lands of the South. We should undertake the complete
development and control of the Mississippi as a national work,
just as we have undertaken the work of building the Panama
Canal. We can use the plant, and we can use the human experience, left free by the completion of the Panama Canal in
so developing the Mississippi as to make it a mighty highroad
of commerce and a source of fructification and not of death to
the rich and fertile lands lying along its lower length.

In the West, the forests, the grazing lands, the reserves of
every kind should be so handled as to be in the interests of the
actual settler, the actual homemaker. He should be encouraged to use them at once, but in such a way as to preserve and
not exhaust them. We do not intend that our natural resources
shall be exploited by the few against the interests of the many,
nor do we intend to turn them over to any man who will waste-
fully use them by destruction and leave to those who come after
us a heritage damaged by just so much.

The man in whose interests we are working is the small
farmer and settler, the man who works with his own hands,
who is working not only for himself, but for his children, and
who wishes to leave to them the fruits of his labor.

His permanent welfare is the prime factor for consideration
in developing the policy of conservation, for our aim is to preserve our natural resources for the public as a whole, for the
average man and the average woman who make up the body
of the American people.

Alaska should be developed at once, but in the interest of
the actual settler. In Alaska the Government has an opportunity of starting in what is almost a fresh field to work out
various problems by actual experience.

The Government should at once construct, own, and operate
the railways in Alaska.

The Government should keep the fee of all the coal fields
and allow them to be operated by lessees, with the condition in
the lease that nonuse shall operate as a forfeit. Telegraph lines
should be operated as the railways are. Moreover, it would be
well in Alaska to try a system of land taxation which will, so
far as possible, remove all the burdens from those who actually
use the land, whether for building or for agricultural purposes,
and will operate against any man who holds the land for speculation or derives an income from it based, not on his own exertions, but on the increase in value due to activities not his own.
There is very real need that this nation shall seriously prepare
itself for the task of remedying social injustice and meeting

social problems by well-considered governmental effort; and the best preparation for such wise action is to test by actual experiment under favorable conditions the devices which we have reason to believe will work well, but which it is difficult to apply in old settled communities without preliminary experiment.

A "Conservation Congress" of those interested in the subject was held at St. Paul, Minn., in September, 1910, at which considerable opposition developed to the plan of conservation by the nation rather than by the States which are immediately concerned.

This opposition grew until it formed the leading feature of the Trans-Mississippi Commercial Congress, held at Kansas City, Mo., on November 15, 1911.

Governor John F. Shafroth [Col.] spoke as follows:

STATE VS. NATIONAL CONSERVATION

GOVERNOR SHAFROTH

There has been a strong sentiment in the East in favor of conservation of the natural resources of the public domain. All rational people are in favor of such conservation, if by that term is meant prevention of waste. But the sentiment has gone further, and has assumed the meaning of making enormous forest reserves, and taxing the natural resources of the public domain by means of leases of grazing, oil, phosphate, asphaltum, coal, and mineral lands for the benefit of the Federal treasury, and of making water-power plants pay a royalty to the national Government for each horsepower generated by falling water. The recent Conservation Congress adopted resolutions indorsing such a policy.

Fifteen million acres of land in Colorado have been set aside as forest reserves and 9,425,239 acres of coal land have been withdrawn from entry until reclassified, and on reclassification there have been placed such enormous values upon the same (in some instances as high as $400 per acre), that it practically operates as an absolute withdrawal of all the coal lands from entry. This is an enormous area and is equal to that of Massachusetts, Connecticut, New Hampshire, and Rhode Island combined.

Most of these forest reserves are on the mountains, situate more than 7,500 feet above sea level, where nature has decreed

X—8

that large timber cannot grow, and many millions of acres are above timber line, where no timber whatever can grow.

It has been estimated that of the forest reserves in Colorado 30 per cent. contain good merchantable timber, 30 per cent. scrub timber, and 40 per cent. no timber at all. Thus 70 per cent. of the forest reserves in Colorado have no connection whatever with forestry. It is ridiculous to contend that these reserves can be reforested in Colorado, because, according to a report of the Agricultural Department, it takes in my State 200 years to grow a pine tree 19 6-10 inches in diameter at an altitude of 7,500 feet above sea level.

This is not a partisan question, as President Cleveland set aside 25,686,320 acres of forest reserves in the West, and President Taft, in his message to Congress of December 6, 1910, declared that these are not questions pertaining to partisan politics. Nine-tenths of the Senators and Representatives of these Rocky Mountain States, irrespective of political affiliations, are opposed to this policy. The total area of the forest reserves established by the Presidents up to this time amounts to 192,931,197 acres.

Congress, time and again in its acts, has referred to all of that property acquired by the national Government as the "public domain," and, in all references to the same, has never intimated that such lands should be retained in perpetuity by the Government. Until recently it has been held, as its name implies, in trust by the Federal Government for the benefit of those citizens of all the States who will settle upon, develop, and improve the same. Not even residence in the State is required in order to locate a gold, silver, or mineral mine, a claim under the coal, timber, or stone acts. Certain improvements and payments only are necessary, and the work can be done by hired men. The right to so locate claims constitutes the interest which every citizen of the United States has in the public domain. It is truly a domain for the public.

It has never been the policy of the United States to make money out of its lands. The sums charged are presumed to amount to very little more than sufficient to cover the expenses of properly regulating the disposition of the same.

It was not until during the last eight or ten years that we have heard people seriously contend that a revenue should be derived for the national treasury from the leasing of these lands.

This Rocky Mountain region was the least inviting to the pioneer. It was Daniel Webster who used this language as to the Western territory which we acquired from New Mexico:

"What do we want of that vast and worthless area, that region of savages and wild beasts, of deserts, of shifting sands and whirling wind, of dust, of cactus and prairie dogs? To what use could we ever hope to put those great deserts and those endless mountain ranges, impenetrable and covered to their very base with eternal snow? What can we ever do with the Western coast, a coast of 3,000 miles, rockbound, cheerless, and uninviting?"

The Government recognized that it was the explorers, settlers, and developers who made the value of everything in a wild and uninhabited country; that if the lands were not exploited and improved they would remain as worthless as they had been for 6,000 years.

Under this general policy of rewarding the pioneer citizens of the United States in the development of the natural resources of the public domain, thousands of people crossed the trackless desert for California, and there discovered the richest gold fields ever known in the history of the world. These gold mines were upon the public domain. There was no law providing for the location of mines. The miner locating gold fields in California could have been considered by the Government a trespasser and liable to refund to the Government the value of all the gold extracted; but, under the policy of the Government as to the settlement of lands in Ohio, Indiana, Illinois, and Missouri, no one ever suggested that the miner was not entitled to the fruits of his discovery; and the miners themselves proceeded to frame rules and regulations as to the manner of locating and developing the mines. These rules and regulations afterward were enacted into laws by Congress, not for profit to the national Government, but for the production of the greatest wealth to the nation and benefit to the citizens thereof.

Under that policy there has been a development of the Western country unparalleled in the history of the world. Three billions of dollars in the precious metals, produced at a cost of perhaps that amount of money, but, turned into the channels of trade, have contributed largely toward making this country the most prosperous nation on earth. It is the increase of basic money that has always given a quickening impulse to business and commerce. An enormous development has been produced in all the other industries of that region.

When the Rocky Mountain territories applied for admission to the Union, no power existed in the President or any other officer to permanently withdraw lands from entry or location either for agricultural, mining, timber, stone, or coal purposes. The laws providing for disposition of the lands had been fixed for years, and no officer was vested with power to change those laws. The fact that all the laws provided for the settlement, location, development, and improvement of all the public domain and did not provide for the Government retaining any part thereof, excepting for military purposes and purely governmental uses, shows conclusively that the policy was intended to be fixed in favor of the disposition of the lands as against the perpetual ownership of the same by the Government.

The enabling act of each State, as did similar acts of all the States of the Mississippi Valley, provided that the property held by the nation until disposed of should be exempt from taxation. There had been no effort upon the part of the Government to hold in perpetuity lands in the Mississippi Valley, and the people of the Rocky Mountain region had a right to presume that the same policy would be pursued as to the new territory. Yea, more, this fixed policy would be pursued as to which the national Government had placed upon all enabling acts, inducing settlement and development, and thereby had made it an implied agreement with the Western States admitted thereafter into the Union that lands should not be held in perpetuity by the Government.

Now it is proposed, by bills introduced in Congress and advocated by the followers of Mr. Pinchot, to change this policy, to impose royalties upon powers generated by falling water and to lease the oil and phosphate lands and the coal and metalliferous mines upon a rental basis payable to the treasury of the United States. No other States have had their national resources taxed by the national Government, and we deem it is unfair that the people of the States which had all the products of their natural resources for themselves should now require, through their Senators and Representatives, these less-favored States in the West to not only undertake the development of the natural resources of these States, but to pay into the Federal treasury a tax upon the very development thereof.

What does the leasing of the natural resources of the mountain States mean? It means perpetual ownership residing in the national Government, and that means exemption from taxation forever.

Perpetual exemption from taxation of vast territory in a State is almost destructive of the development of that State. It is an injustice which it seems to me every fair-minded person must recognize. The State must maintain government for State, county, and school purposes over all the lands within its borders, whether reserved or not

In the West the taxes upon land for a period of thirty years, including reasonable interest upon each yearly payment, amount to the value of the land. Therefore, when the lands privately owned must pay all of the taxes for State, county, and school purposes it is equivalent to them paying every thirty years, in addition to their just taxes, an amount equal to the value of the public lands. Thus the people of these States must pay for these public lands every thirty years, and yet never own a foot of the same. Is that right; is it just; is it the way a parent would treat a child? Is it a compliance with the enabling acts, which provide that each State is "admitted into the Union upon an equal footing with the original States in all respects whatsoever"?

The national Government was formed for national affairs and the State governments for local control. It was a dual form of government, a partnership in which the people of each were interested in and a part of the other; both were necessary, and both must be supported by taxes. It would not have been right for the States alone to have the power of taxation, nor that the nation alone should possess that power, because, by this dual form of government, there were imposed upon each certain duties, the performance of which required revenues. Now, would it have been right for the States to cripple the national Government in the raising of revenue, or for the national Government to hamper the States in their exercise of such an indispensable power? The power of taxation is the most important of all governmental prerogatives. It is the very foundation upon which the administration of law is builded, and without it the superstructure must fall. It is the very law of its being.

In the constitutional distribution of the powers of taxation the Federal Government has obtained great advantage; its revenues have been so enormous that it has been difficult to devise ways of spending the amounts thus collected. It was Senator Aldrich who stated not long ago that he could curtail the expenses of the Government to the extent of $300,000,000 per annum without detriment to the public service. The States, being principally limited to taxation upon real and personal property, have always had scant amounts with which to maintain their administrations. Every State in the Union is now limited in its work by reason of the small revenue derived from direct taxation.

Here the governor enumerated the many expenses of State governments.

This new policy would not only deprive the States of the means of raising the necessary revenues to establish and maintain good government, but in addition to that injustice the advocates thereof propose to make revenue for the Federal treasury by taxing the natural resources of the West. By so doing they propose to make the Mountain States pay an undue proportion of the burdens of the national Government.

It has been estimated by the Geological Survey at Washington that there are contained within the boundaries of the State of Colorado 371,000,000,000 tons of coal. More than three-fourths of this coal is upon the public domain. If a rental of 10 cents a ton is to be imposed upon that natural resource of the State of Colorado it will mean ultimately that the citizens of our State must contribute $27,000,000,000 to the Federal treasury. This tax is advocated on the ground that it will prevent waste. According to this geological report, Colorado alone has sufficient coal to supply the world, at the present rate of consumption (of about one and a quarter billion tons per annum), for 300 years.

It has been estimated by the authorities at Washington that from 1,000,000 to 2,117,000 horsepower can be generated from falling water in the State of Colorado. If the Government is to charge $1 per horsepower as a rental for a temporary right of way for transmission lines, and conducting that water on Government land until it attains a height sufficient to generate power, it will mean, when this power is fully developed, a rental to the national Government from the inhabitants of Colorado of from $1,000,000 to $2,117,000 a year. It must be remembered that every horsepower generated by falling water saves the burning on the average of twenty-one tons of coal each year.

Is it equal or fair treatment to our commonwealth for the Government to impose any tax whatever upon our natural resources, which it has never imposed upon the older and richer States of the Union? It must be remembered that the act of Parliament of Great Britain, imposing duties upon goods shipped to the thirteen colonies, against which our forefathers rebelled, provided that the revenues derived therefrom should be expended in America for its protction and defence.

All taxes upon production must ultimately be paid by the consumer. Yea more, such policy means that the people will have to pay additional prices for such products far in excess of the royalties which will be obtained by the national Government. It will put our people at a disadvantage in the struggle for industrial supremacy.

The excuse for imposing a tax and terms upon the water-power plants of our States is that Congress will prevent monopoly, whereas the State governments will not; that they at Washington are better able to administer local affairs than the people of the States in which the lands and the resources are situate.

It has been my good fortune to represent my State in Congress for nine years, and I and all other members of Congress know that it is more difficult to pass through the United States Senate and House of Representatives an act which will prevent monopoly than it is to get through the general assemblies of the various States the same character of legislation.

When we realize that the National Government has given away in 43 different railroad grants lands aggregating 155,504,-994 acres, it comes with poor grace from the Federal offices to say that they can conserve and administer the lands better than the people of the States wherein the lands are situate. These railroad grants comprise an area equal to that of Maine, New Hampshire, Vermont, Massachusetts, Connecticut, Rhode Island, New York, New Jersey, Pennsylvania, Delaware, West Virginia, and Ohio combined. If the Western States had donated to railroads one-tenth of such grants, such action would have been looked upon as the most horrible example of waste and extravagance, if not corruption, that had ever occurred in the history of the world.

The Supreme Court of the United States has determined time and again that the waters belong to the States and not to the National Government. Congress has only jurisdiction over navigable streams, and it cannot interfere with the use of the waters of a State. In accordance with that belief, laws in every arid State in the Union have been enacted providing for the use of water for irrigation and for power purposes. The Supreme Court of the United States has sanctioned such laws and has held that they have always been in existence as laws of necessity.

The man who first applies the water to beneficial uses, either for irrigation or the generation of power, is entitled to priority of right to the flow of that water. We have a system of administering these waters. Water commissioners exist in 70 water districts of the State of Colorado. The water commissioners possess the power of turning water into ditches, according to their priority of right, and, when there is a scarcity of water, of shutting down the headgates of the ditches in the inverse order of their priority of appropriation.

The national officials now recognize the ownership of the water in the States, but in order to get some jurisdiction over the same they claim that inasmuch as the Government owns the lands lying along our streams they will not grant a permit or right of way to a power company to conduct the water along that land and by a steep descent send it back to the stream, thereby generating power, unless the owner of such power plant agrees to pay a royalty on the water which he uses and until he makes certain other terms which they may prescribe. This is simply doing indirectly what the Government cannot do directly. It is annulling that inherent power of sovereignty in the States called eminent domain, by which rights of way can be condemned for great public enterprises. It was Secretary of the Interior James R. Garfield who two days before he retired from office revoked 40 permits for power plants to transmit their electricity across public lands. In several instances the electric plants had cost hundreds of thousands of dollars and were being operated. He no doubt thought he was doing right, but we thought he was doing a most egregious wrong to our States.

The people living in these public land States are more interested in the development of their water powers than Congress or the officials at Washington. It is they who ultimately must pay the penalty if monopoly obtains possession of their water plants, and consequently they are sure to be more careful with respect to these water powers than the National Government.

The fact that water power plants can be operated every five or six miles of a mountain stream, and that in the Rocky Mountain States there can be generated by falling water 33,000,000 horsepower, makes it almost impossible to create a monopoly, even if there were no laws to prevent the same. But it is absurd, under the present State laws, to talk about a monopoly of the water powers.

The owners of these water power plants are simply public carriers, to transmit the power generated to be used for commercial purposes. They are expressly declared by statute in my State to be common carriers. They are identically in the same position as railroads. That the rates of railroads, or rates of power companies, can be made reasonable by the States has been settled too many times to need citation of authorities. It is absurd to say that the legislatures of the States will not curb and prevent excessive prices for the transmission of electrical power. If they should fail to do so, it is the right of the people in my State to initiate statutes which will compel reasonable rates. These laws constitute the guaranty that no monopoly in charges for electricity could possibly become permanent in the State of Colorado.

The policy of the nation holding in perpetuity great forest reserves, and coal, gas, oil, phosphate, and mineral lands, and rights of way for water power plants, and controlling the same, is an interference with local affairs which, according to our theory of government, should belong to the States.

It was the late Justice John M. Harlan, of the Supreme Court of the United States, who said:

"A National Government for national affairs and State governments for State affairs is the foundation rock upon which our institutions rest. Any serious departure from that principle would bring disaster upon the American system of free government."

The permanent administration of public lands in a State, sovereign as to all functions except those which were delegated to the National Government, is an interference with local affairs never before attempted in the history of this country. Such administration by a bureau at Washington, with its thousands of guards imported from other States patrolling these gigantic areas, can never be satisfactory to the people of the States in which such lands are situate. The bureau will always be controlled by officers who are not in sympathy with the people of such States. Carpetbag government of such local affairs is bound to follow, with its antagonism to everything that interferes with the National Government's control and use of these reserves, which control and use we think are so destructive of the development of our States.

The Federal bureau cannot want settlement of lands or location of mining claims upon these forest reserves, and its rules are and will be continuously harassing to those who desire to settle upon or locate mineral claims upon the same. I have no doubt the officers and employees of the Forestry Bureau are honest, but, representing the National Government, which has a policy antagonistic to the public land States, they naturally will favor its side, especially when they earnestly believe in that policy.

When timber reserves were first established it was the advocates of this forestry policy who contended that it was impossible to maintain forest reserves and yet permit the ownership of private property within the reservations; that the right of access to private lands through forest reserves for the owners of horses, cattle, sheep, and other live stock would interfere with the Government's use of the same.

It was not until Congress, seeing the serious interference with the development of the Western States, enacted a law opening such forest reserves to homestead and mineral entry that the advocates of this forestry policy yielded upon that point. It is asserted in Congress that during the years 1907 and 1908 the number of homesteads allowed on reserves was only 1,563, while the number of reservations for rangers' lodges, with adjacent land, during that same period was 3,227.

While it was well known that Congress was going to forbid the creation of any more forest reserves in Colorado, Wyoming, Idaho, Montana, Washington, and Oregon without its consent, the Senate, having passed the measure on February 25, 1907, and the House, on March 3, 1907, having concurred in the same, it was the advocates of this forestry policy who circumvented the effect of that law by inducing a President, on March 1 and 2, 1907, before he signed the bill, to establish by proclamation forest reserves to the extent of over 30,000,000 acres.

The Forestry Bureau knew full well the antagonism of the people of the Western States to these large reserves, and yet, while that bill guarding the interests of the West was about to become a law, forest reserves, mapped out and described by this Federal bureau, were established at its' request.

Every time these foresters see a tract of land which has been cleared of timber they repeat the poem, "Woodman, spare that tree," and expostulate over the great waste of that natural resource. They do not seem to realize that every stick of timber so cut was used in the mines, in the erection of houses, and in other improvements necessary to man, and that the use has been most beneficial in the development of our country.

The timber cut upon the public domain in my State is infinitesimal compared to the losses by fire. It is not profitable to cut timber except near streams, where the logs can be floated to market, or where a railroad exists, which is usually along the streams. The lands cleared of timber are mere threads through these gigantic reservations. The people of the Western States have endeavored in every way possible to prevent forest fires, but the most destructive fire we ever had occurred since the Forestry Bureau had full control of the reservations. Those catastrophes will happen, and it is not the fault of either the State or the forestry officials.

The discouragement to the prospector of mineral lands, by means of the rules adopted by the Forestry Bureau, has been so great in my State that there are now practically no prospectors left. And yet we know that the hills of our State have hardly been scratched in prospecting for the minerals therein contained. It is impossible for these reserves to be managed to the best interest of our people by a bureau administered two to three thousand miles away.

The employees of the forest reservations of the West consist of 243 forest rangers, 1,050 assistant forest rangers, 558 forest guards, 2 game wardens, and 6 hunters and trappers. I have no doubt that three-fourths of those employees are not citizens of the commonwealth in which they do their work. I have heard it stated that the former chief of the Forestry Department said that when these reserves were scientifically managed it would require 100,000 employees. It must be remembered that in the Declaration of Independence our forefathers arraigned King George III in these words: "He has erected a multitude of new offices, and sent thither swarms of officers, to harass our people and eat out their substance." The people of the South have felt the effect of carpetbag government in a reign of misrule and corruption unequaled in the history of the world. It was that experience which brought the American people to a realization that home rule is to the best interest of a State.

Why impose upon the Western States a rule which interferes with what they think are the rights belonging to the States:

First. Which will make the people of those States, by taxation upon their own land for government over all the lands, pay for these reserves every 30 years without owning any of the same?

Second. Which, in addition to the burdens imposed upon those States for the support of the National Government, will compel them to pay millions of dollars into the Federal Treasury as taxes upon their natural resources, which no other States have been required to do? And

Third. Which must foist upon those States landlordism and a bureaucratic control of these great reserves, which policy in the administration of government has always proven a failure?

Heed the advice of the great justice of the Supreme Court— let our Government be "a National Government for national affairs and State governments for State affairs," and then there will follow a development of the resources of the Rocky Mountain region which will be the marvel and wonder of the world.

On May 16, 1912, George E. Chamberlain [Ore.]
spoke in the Senate in connection with an appropriation
bill for the Agricultural Department in defence of the
conservation of natural resources by the nation, but
against abuses that had grown up under it.

NATIONAL CONSERVATION AND ITS ABUSES

SENATOR CHAMBERLAIN

This should not be considered as a political question or as
a partisan question. Both the great political parties of this
country are committed to the question of the conservation
of our natural resources. I will read the plank of the Democratic party adopted at Denver in its last national convention
on this subject, as well as the plank adopted by the Republican
party in its national convention at Chicago.

REPUBLICAN PLATFORM, 1908—CONSERVATION OF FORESTS

We indorse the movement inaugurated by the Administration for the
conservation of the natural resources. We approve of measures to prevent
the waste of timber. We commend the work now going on for the reclamation of arid lands, and reaffirm the Republican policy of the free distribution of the available areas of the public domain to the landless settler.
No obligation of the future is more insistent and none will result in
greater blessings to posterity. In the line of this splendid undertaking is
the future duty equally imperative to enter upon a systematic improvement
upon a large and comprehensive plan just to all persons of the country of
the waterways, harbors, and Great Lakes, whose natural adaptability to
the increasing traffic of the land is one of the greatest gifts of benign
Providence.

DEMOCRATIC PLATFORM, 1908—NATURAL RESOURCES

We repeat the demand for internal development and for the conservation of our natural resources contained in previous platforms, the enforcement of which Mr. Roosevelt has vainly sought from a reluctant party;
and to that end we insist upon the preservation, protection, and replace-
ment of needed forests, the preservation of the public domain of home
seekers, the protection of the national resources in timber, coal, iron, and
oil against monopolistic control, the development of our waterways for
navigation, and every other useful purpose, including the irrigation of arid
lands, the reclamation of swamp lands, the clarification of streams, the
development of water power and the preservation of electric power generated by this natural force, from the control of monopoly; and to such
end we urge the exercise of all powers—national, State, and municipal—
both separately and in coöperation.

We insist upon a policy of administration of our forest reserves which
shall relieve it of the abuses which have arisen thereunder, and which shall,
as far as practicable, conform to the police regulations of the several

States wherein the reserves are located, which shall enable homesteaders as of right to occupy and acquire title to all portions thereof which are especially adapted to agriculture, and which shall furnish a system of timber sales available as well to the private citizen as to the large manufacturer and consumer.

I take the position, Mr. President, that the forest service has been criticized, and very severely criticized, for a condition of things for which it is not at all to blame. I am willing to admit that in the administration of the land laws of the United States not only are the subordinate officers sometimes too arbitrary, but this criticism applies as well to the heads of the land and many other departments. Technical and arbitrary rulings not infrequently make it impossible for a man to perfect his title to public lands, where he is making an honest endeavor to acquire a home.

I am also willing to agree with the Senator from Idaho [William E. Borah] when he repudiates the suggestion that every man who attempts to secure a home in the West is a thief, and I only differ from him in this respect, that I do not think that that charge is generally made. Whenever and wherever it is made it is usually by persons who do not understand the situation in the West.

An investigation will disclose that where individuals have been guilty of fraudulently acquiring lands under either the homestead or preëmption acts, and in a great many cases under the timber and stone act, they have been the homeless hirelings and agents of timber syndicates or others in the East who have been interested in acquiring a part of the public domain for speculative purposes.

Now, Mr. President, I make the broad statement that the Forestry Bureau and the Agricultural Department are not responsible in the first instance for the wrongs which have grown up under the forest reserve system. Congress itself is and has been responsible, and it is responsible now, wherever these evils exist, for it has it in its power to correct them, and it ought to correct them. As a matter of fact, there has not been a single piece of constructive or corrective legislation suggested except on the floor of the Senate in the heat of discussion, and that has not had the consideration it ought to have had when it affects so great a national question.

The act authorizing the President by proclamation to create forest reserves was passed March 3, 1891. The creation of these reserves was recognized as almost a necessity at that time, and the President proceeded, in pursuance of the power vested in

him, to create these reserves in order to protect the great
wealth of timber and mineral resources against monopolization
by those who wanted to acquire them for speculative purposes.

In the creation of these reserves it became necessary, Mr.
President, to include lands that were owned by entrymen under
the several Federal statutes, railroad and wagon road grants,
and others who had acquired holdings before the reserve was
created. Now, let us note the evolution and development of a
great national wrong under an act that was beneficent in its
purposes.

Occasionally there would be a homestead near the top of a
mountain or on a mountainside or in an isolated valley at the
time of an executive proclamation creating a reserve. These
holdings were, of course, not extinguished by the creation of
the reserves, but where there was one private holder or one
entryman under the land laws there were hundreds of thousands of acres that belonged to railroad and wagon road grant
companies and others who, through mesne conveyances, had
acquired title from them.

Then began to be heard a plea in behalf of the poor entryman, who had a home in the center of a reserve without possibility of having any neighbors or churches or schools; that he
ought to be protected, and allowed to surrender his little holding
in the reserve, which could never be otherwise than isolated;
and that he should be permitted to select in lieu thereof other
lands outside of the reserve, where he would have the benefit
of neighbors, schools, and churches. That was a plausible plea
for the entryman, and nobody on earth could object to allowing
that entryman to release his land to the Government of the
United States and to select in lieu thereof an equal area in
some other part of the public domain. The same plea is being
made for the poor settler now as a reason for abandoning
the forest reserve policy. It looks ominous, Mr. President. The
unwritten history of that plea is that it originated, not by
the fireside of the poor entryman, but in the office of a great
railroad company in the Middle West; it was gotten up, not
for the benefit of the small holder, but for the purpose of
enabling the big grant corporations, railroads, and others, and
their successors in interest to release their holdings within the
forest reserves, and to take up in lieu thereof other vacant
Government lands in other sections of the country, which were
far more valuable for all purposes than were the lands within
the reserves. This was the origin of the indemnity selection
or lieu land law. It was conceived in iniquity and resulted

in robbing the people of untold millions in land and money. On June 4, 1897, Congress passed what was known as the indemnity selection law, ostensibly in the interest of the entryman who had his home within the forest reserve, allowing him and incidentally all others who had holdings within the reserves to release their holdings to the Government and to take up lands elsewhere in lieu of the lands which they might surrender to the Government.

Bear in mind that this law, ostensibly in the interest of the settler, was not confined to him. It would have been harmless with such a limitation. But it applied to the grant companies of all kinds and their successors in interest and millions of acres of land in these reserves, consisting of lava beds, denuded forests, and rugged peaks, were released under the act of 1897 to the United States, and lands valuable for agricultural purposes, for timber, for minerals, for coal, and for oil, surveyed and unsurveyed, were taken up in every State in the Union where there were vacant lands by these companies that hastened to surrender their holdings within the reserve and to take advantage of a law which it was pretended was in the interest of the settler.

REED SMOOT [Utah].—Mr. President, I know in some of the States, after the law was passed and was in operation perhaps for four years or more, there was a move made by men to enter lands and to make selections in forest reserves under State selections that were not agricultural in character, and the selections were made with no other view than to have them turned back to the Government, and in lieu of them to select lands outside.

JAMES P. CLARKE [Ark.].—I think it would tend to a clearer understanding of just how this abuse came about to repeat a brief statement made by the late Senator from Montana, Mr. Carter. He said that in the construction of the act of 1897 the Secretary of the Interior made a ruling that was obviously correct, that it never was the intention of Congress that the railroads holding arid lands under their early grants should be permitted to surrender them wholesale and to take certificates that would enable them to file on better lands elsewhere in the United States. That ruling was accepted by the railroads for a number of years. Subsequently, Mr. Hitchcock, of Missouri, came to be Secretary of the Interior, and, without any sort of foundation for his action, he reversed that ruling and permitted the surrender of the railroad grants and the selection of lands elsewhere. Arkansas fell a victim to the

extent of 270,000 acres of land to that ruling made by Mr.
Secretary Hitchcock.

SENATOR CHAMBERLAIN.—This thing had become so notorious
and so infamous in every Western State that a demand went up
everywhere that this old indemnity selection law should be
abolished and repealed. What happened? On the 3d of March,
1905—I want the Senate to notice the wording of this repealing
clause—there was passed and approved "An act prohibiting the
selection of timber lands in lieu of lands in forest reserves,"
which is as follows:

> *Be it enacted, etc.*, That the acts of June 4, 1897, June 6, 1900, and
> March 3, 1901, are hereby repealed so far as they provide for the relin-
> quishment, selection, and patenting of lands in lieu of tracts covered by
> an unperfected *bona fide* claim or patent within a forest reserve.

If they had stopped there the act would have repealed the
indemnity selection acts and would have stopped the looting
of the public domain, but it goes on:

> But the validity of contracts entered into by the Secretary of the
> Interior prior to the passage of this act shall not be impaired: *Provided*,
> That selections heretofore made in lieu of lands relinquished to the United
> States may be perfected and patents issued therefor the same as though
> this act had not been passed, and if for any reason not the fault of the
> party making the same any pending selection is held invalid another selec-
> tion for like quality of land may be made in lieu thereof.

Here was a qualified repeal of the indemnity selection acts
that were on the statute books at that time, but it excepted
from the effect of the repeal contracts which had been made
by the Secretary of the Interior in the face of all sorts of
protests, whereby the railroad and lumber companies and
others surrendered to the Government of the United States lands
which, in many instances, were absolutely denuded of timber,
and got the right to select other lands out of the public domain
in lieu thereof. The repealing clause did not name these companies. It would not have been policy to have named them
in the repealing clause, because it would have aroused a protest in and out of Congress against legislation which had for
its purpose the protection of the Santa Fe Railroad Co. and
others instead of the protection of the citizens of the country.

DUNCAN U. FLETCHER [Fla.].—I think, under the circumstances, it would be a little bit enlightening at least to know
who was Secretary of the Interior at that time, and whether

these protests were brought to the attention of the President at that time as well as to the attention of the Secretary of the Interior.

SENATOR CHAMBERLAIN.—The old Latin maxim, *de mortuis nil nisi bonum*,[1] appeals to me in this case. I want to observe it as far as it is possible consistent with the truth. It was Mr. E. A. Hitchcock who in his lifetime seems to have assumed that every man who undertook to acquire title to public land was a thief, and yet he was a party to the scheme to give away over a million acres of land by contracts he could have refused to make. Commissioner Hermann had called attention to these very dangers and he was removed from office at the instance of Mr. Hitchcock, as many believe, because he did not stand for these things, but for the interest of the people of this country in reference to these indemnity selections.

Mr. President, there are numerous other indemnity selection acts that I am not going to take up the time of the Senate in discussing. I have discussed them thus far for the purpose of showing conditions as they existed at the time this conservation movement had its origin. Lands in nearly all the States of the Union had been and were being taken up and placed under monopolistic control.

Mr. Gifford Pinchot, former forester, has been denounced here as a despoiler by one of the distinguished Senators who has discussed this subject. Mr. President, I say to you that, instead of criticising him as a despoiler, the American people ought to erect a monument in his honor and engrave his name upon it as the man who originated the idea of placing these resources of the Government—timber, coal, iron, and oil—beyond the reach of monopolistic control, and saving them, not only for the generous use of our own generation, but for generations yet unborn, because to him more largely than to any other individual in this country it is due that the people of America were first aroused to the fact that our public lands and the things under them, including the water powers and everything else, were being taken up and monopolized by selfish interests. He aroused an interest and created a public sentiment that has made Congress do something to protect these natural resources. Therefore, even if I do agree with some of the criticisms which have been indulged in against the administration of the forest reserves, and with others that have been indulged in against other governmental bureaus, I must state that, in its larger view, Mr. Pinchot and those who have succeeded him have done

[1] "Say nothing but good of the dead."

X—9

a work that entitles them to the everlasting gratitude of the people.

Mr. President, we can see, in view of the looting of the public domain by these big corporations, why the idea of the conservation of natural resources had such an impetus given to it from the start. Really, it sprung into importance only four years ago, in 1908, when the governors of the several States met here in Washington for the purpose of discussing the whole subject.

The growth of the conservation movement has been slow, but, involving, as it does, a great moral question, it will never be retired from political or economic discussion until it has been rightly solved, and the party or the individual who opposes it must eventually be crushed by an outraged public opinion. So well is this recognized that you can not find anyone in public life upon whom responsibility rests in this important matter who will not claim that he is in favor of the conservation of our natural resources, and some there are who, while professing to believe in the doctrine, are nevertheless willing, on one pretext or another, to oppose any measure looking to the advancement of the cause.

It may not be inappropriate to call attention briefly to the evolution of the movement. As early as 1903 President Roosevelt appointed the Public Lands Commission. The first partial report of this commission was presented to Congress in a message by the President March 7, 1904, and the last was presented in the same way February 13, 1905. These reports deal at length with the antiquated land laws, and the abuses which have grown up under them, the sale of timber on the public lands, grazing thereon, and other kindred subjects. They contained many valuable suggestions, such as the repeal of the timber and stone act and the commutation clause of the homestead act. Attention was called to the frauds which had been and were being perpetrated under these laws, and if the recommendations of the commission had been followed by Congress a long stride would have been taken toward saving the public domain for the homesteader instead of allowing it to pass into the hands of speculators.

In 1907, the President created the Inland Waterways Commission and charged it with the consideration of "the relations of the streams to the use of all the permanent natural resources, and their conservation for the making and maintenance of prosperous homes."

Acting upon the suggestion of the Inland Waterways Commission, the President called a conference of governors [1] of all the States and Territories, which was held at the White House in May, 1908. For the first time in history the executives of the sovereign States met with the Executive of the United States, and the occasion for that gathering was the consideration of the important problem of conservation. Acting upon the recommendation of the governors, all of whom recognized the importance of the great question they were called upon to consider, the President, on the 8th of June, 1908, appointed the National Conservation Commission, which thereafter proceeded to take the first inventory of the natural resources made by any nation in the world. The results of that inventory are recorded in the report of the National Conservation Commission, which the President transmitted to Congress with a special message in January, 1909.

Not only did Congress not then see fit to enact any legislation therein recommended, but unfortunately declined to print the report in sufficient numbers for its adequate distribution among the people. More disastrous than this, however, was the congressional enactment forbidding this or other executive commissions from pursuing their important work in the service of the people. This action, plainly designed to wipe out the National Conservation Commission, accomplished its purpose. It put an end to the activities of that commission, removing the only national organization which was dealing with the conservation question as a whole. Thus was presented the strange spectacle of a nation-wide movement, inaugurated by the governors of the States, the presidents of great organizations of our national industries, and other distinguished citizens, and heartily indorsed by the people of the country, by legislative enactment denied not only an appropriation, but even permission to continue its work.

That the conservation work is going on to-day is due to the approval of the people, crystallized into an organization formed by patriotic men and supported by individual citizens, whose desire it is that the conservation movement, to which such uniformly popular approval has been given, shall not fail, but shall go on until the principles for which it stands have been carried into practical effect. I refer to the National Conservation Association, the patriotic service of which to the nation cannot be too strongly emphasized.

[1] This assembly (which has been held every year since 1908) is popularly known as "The House of Governors," the name given it by the originator of the idea, William George Jordan, of New York City.

Mr. President, if we should abandon the present policy it would not be three months until every acre of timber in this country would be taken up by agents and hirelings of those whose interest it is to get them under monopolistic control. This is not guesswork. I call your attention to the very able argument of my friend, the Senator from Minnesota [Knute Nelson], published in the annals of the American Academy of Political and Social Science a year or two ago.

The mode in which these lumbermen have carried on their operations has been in the main, and in outline, this: They have in person or through agents and employees secured, by divers means, a large number of men and women in various parts of the country—people who knew nothing about such lands and who had no thought of acquiring the same—to apply to purchase and enter such lands, supplying them with money to travel from remote interior towns to examine and select the land and make the necessary application to purchase at the district land office, and supplying them with money to pay for the land, and then, after the purchase and entry were completed, procure a conveyance of the land to themselves for a moderate bonus.

I remember how, a few years ago, a large number of lady school teachers in a Western city—the headquarters of some big lumbermen—were induced to "take up" timber and stone claims in Oregon, Washington, and California, more than 1,500 miles from where the teachers lived. Most of these lands afterwards passed into the hands of these lumbermen.

Instead of denouncing and criticising the Forestry Bureau officials and undertaking to defeat a proper appropriation, as has been attempted in the Senate, I think the American people ought to take their hats off to the men who have inaugurated this movement; they ought to take their hats off to Mr. Graves, the present Forester, who is here devoting the best energies of his life to the protection of the great interests of the public; they ought to take their hats off to the young men in all the States of the West who are risking their lives and doing all in their power to protect the public domain, not only for the interest of those living, but for the interest of those who are coming after us.

Mr. President, differing from the Administration in politics, as I do, I am yet willing to stand here and give them my support in every way possible, to defend them against unjust charges, to assist them to do their duty in the future as they have done it in the past; and I predict that the time is not far distant when the American people, with one accord, will extend to these men their appreciation of the efforts which they have made to protect the national resources of this country from the looting of monopolistic interests.

CHAPTER IV

INTERNAL IMPROVEMENTS

[POST-ROADS AND CANALS]

Debate in the House on Federal Control over Post-roads: In Favor, Theodore Sedgwick [Mass.]; Opposed, John Vining [Del.], Thomas Fitzsimons [Pa.]; Opposition Wins—Surveys of Post-roads at Government Expense: In Favor, Abraham Baldwin [Ga.]—President Jefferson on Federal Aid to Education and Public Improvements—Speech of Sen. James A. Bayard, Sr., in Favor of Federal Investment in the Chesapeake Canal—President Madison's Message to Congress (December, 1815) Referring to Internal Improvements—John C. Calhoun [S. C.] Introduces in the House a Bill to Apply Profits of the National Bank to This Purpose—Debate on the Bill: In Favor (in Whole or Part), Mr. Calhoun, Timothy Pickering [Mass.], Erastus Root [N. Y.], Henry Clay [Ky.]; Opposed, Thomas B. Robertson [La.]—Bill Is Vetoed by the President—His Constitutional Objections—Debate in the House on Federal Administration of the Cumberland Road: In Favor, Tomlinson Fort [Ga.], Oliver H. Smith [Ind.]; Opposed, James Buchanan [Pa.], Philip P. Barbour [Va.]; Opposition Wins—President Jackson Vetoes Maysville [Ky.] Turnpike Bill on the Ground That Federal Operation of Public Works Is Unconstitutional—Speech on This Principle by Senator John Tyler [Va.]: "The First Entanglement of Government by Capital."

DURING the organization of the Government the question of the constitutional power of the Executive arose in connection with a bill to establish post-roads, in which discretion was given the Postmaster-General in choosing mail routes, in permitting mail stages to carry passengers, in granting the franking privilege, etc.

In the debate on the measure, which took place in the House at various times between December 6, 1791, and February 3, 1792, Theodore Sedgwick [Mass.] argued that Congress could *delegate* the constitutional requirement that it "establish post-offices and post-

133

roads," as it had done in borrowing money, which function also was given it by the Constitution, it being the office of Congress to determine the *principle* on which the business was to be done, and then delegate the *execution* of the work.

JOHN VINING [Del.] argued that the assignment of the execution was explicit in the Constitution. He also doubted the expediency and safety of the amendment. The function assigned by it would be to a good President a burden, to a bad one a dangerous power of establishing offices and roads in those places only where his political interests would be promoted, and removing others of long standing in order to harass those persons whom he might suppose inimical to his ambitions.

The motion to delegate was negatived. Power, however, was given the Postmaster-General to form contracts for extending mail routes under certain restrictions.

In regard to the carriage of passengers by the mail it was argued by Thomas Fitzsimons [Pa.] that the clause of the Constitution which empowers the Federal Government to establish post-offices and post-roads cannot be understood to extend farther than the conveyance of intelligence, which is the proper subject of the post-office establishment: it gives no power to send men and baggage by post.

If, by the construction of that clause of the Constitution which authorizes Congress to make all laws necessary for carrying into execution the several powers vested in them, they may proceed farther, and so regulate the post-roads as to prevent passengers from traveling on them; they may say what weights shall be carried on those roads, and at what seasons of the year; they may remove everything that stands in the way; they may level buildings to the ground, under the pretence of making more convenient roads; they may abolish tolls and turnpikes; they may, where an established ferry has been kept for a hundred years past in the most convenient place for crossing a river, give the post-rider authority to set up a new one beside it, and ruin the old establishment; they may say that the person who carries the mail shall participate in every privilege that is now exclusively enjoyed by any man or body of men, and allege, as a reason for these encroachments, that they are only necessary encouragements to carry the mail of the United States; in short, the ingenuity of man cannot devise any new proposition so strange and inconsistent as not to be reducible within the pale of the Constitution by such a mode of construction. If this were once admitted the Constitution would be a useless and dead letter, and it would be to no purpose that the States in convention assembled had framed that instrument to guide the steps of Congress. As well might they at once have said, "There shall be a Congress who shall have full power and authority to make all laws which to their wisdom will seem meet and proper."

The motion was voted down.

Four years later (on February 11, 1796) the temper of Congress had so changed that a resolution was carried ordering a survey, *at the expense of the Government,* of a system of post-roads. In support of this resolution Abraham Baldwin [Ga.] said:

In many parts of the country there were no improved roads, nothing better than the original Indian track. Bridges and other improvements are always made with reluctance while roads remain in this State, because it is known, as the country increases in population and wealth, better and shorter roads will be made. All expense of this sort, indeed, is lost. It was properly the *business of the general Government to undertake the improvement of the roads,* for the different States are incompetent to the business, their different designs clashing with each other. It is enough for them to make good roads to the different seaports; the crossroads should be left to the government of the whole. The expense, he thought, would not be very great. Let a surveyor point out the shortest and best track, and the money will soon be raised. There was nothing in this country, he said, of which we ought to be more ashamed than our public roads.

This was the first step taken by the Government in making Federal internal improvements. The common-sense argument for doing so, which was presented by Representative Baldwin (who, though from Georgia, was born and bred a Connecticut Yankee), grew more cogent with the years, and now is unquestioned.

"THE MAN WOT PAYS NO POSTAGE"

[Hit at "Graft" in the Post-Office Department]

From the collection of the New York Historical Society

JEFFERSON ON FEDERAL AID TO EDUCATION AND INTERNAL IMPROVEMENTS

In his annual message to Congress in December, 1806, President Jefferson advocated the retention of the tariff, especially on luxuries, and the expenditure of the revenue remaining after the operating cost of government had been defrayed upon public education and internal improvements.

Patriotism would certainly prefer its [the tariff system's] continuance and application to the great purposes of the public education, roads, rivers, canals, and such other objects of public improvement as it may be thought proper to add to the constitutional enumeration of Federal powers. By these operations new channels of communication will be opened between the States; the lines of separation will disappear; their interests will be identified, and their union cemented by new and indissoluble ties. Education is here placed among the articles of public care, not that it would be proposed to take its ordinary branches out of the hands of private enterprise, which manages so much better all the concerns to which it is equal, but a public institution can alone supply those sciences which, though rarely called for, are yet necessary to complete the circle, all the parts of which contribute to the improvement of the country, and some of them to its preservation.

I suppose an amendment to the Constitution, by consent of the States, necessary, because the objects now recommended are not among those enumerated in the Constitution, and to which it permits the public moneys to be applied.

The present consideration of a national establishment for education particularly is rendered proper by this circumstance; also that, if Congress, approving the proposition, shall yet think it more eligible to found it on a donation of lands, they have it now in their power to endow it with those which will be among the earliest to produce the necessary income. This foundation would have the advantage of being independent in war, which may suspend other improvements, by requiring for its own purposes the resources destined for them.

The principle of Federal aid to education was put into practice during the Civil War, when land grants to the States were made for the purpose of establishing agricultural and mechanical colleges. Out of these have since been developed our great State universities.

Federal Investment in the Chesapeake Canal

The question of applying public revenue to internal improvements came up in the Senate on February 13, 1807, in the form of a resolution to invest a portion of the receipts from the sale of public lands in shares of the Chesapeake Canal. On this subject James A. Bayard, Sr. [Del.], said:

It is admitted that the Constitution does not expressly give the power to cut canals, but we possess, and are in the daily exercise of, the power to provide for the protection and safety of commerce, and the defence of the nation. It has never been contended that no power exists which has not been expressly delegated.

There is no express power given to erect a fort or magazine, though it is recognized in the delegation of exclusive legislative powers in certain cases. The power to erect lighthouses and piers, to survey and take the soundings on the coast, or to erect public buildings, is neither expressly given nor recognized in the Constitution, but it is embraced by a liberal and just interpretation of the clause in the Constitution which legitimates all laws necessary and proper for carrying into execution the powers expressly delegated. On a like principle the Bank of the United States was incorporated. Having a power to provide for the safety of commerce and the defence of the nation, we may fairly infer a power to cut a canal—a measure unquestionably proper with a view to either subject.

In his message to Congress on December 5, 1815, President Madison advised an amendment to the Constitution permitting the Federal Government to establish a system of national roads and canals.

"No objects," he said, "within the circle of political economy so richly repay the expense bestowed on them; there are none, the utility of which is more universally ascertained and acknowledged; none that do more honor to the government whose wise and enlarged patriotism duly appreciates them. Nor is there any country which presents a field where nature invites more the art of man to complete her own work for his accommodation and benefit. These considerations are strengthened, moreover, by the political effect of these facilities for intercommunication in bringing and binding more closely together the various parts of our extended confederacy. While the States, individually, with a laudable enterprise and emulation, avail themselves of their local advantages, by new roads, by navigable canals, and by improving the streams susceptible of navigation, the general Government is the more urged to similar undertakings, requiring a national jurisdiction and national means, by the prospect of thus systematically completing so inestimable a work. And it is a happy reflection that any defect of constitutional authority which may be encountered can be supplied in a mode which the Constitution itself has providently pointed out.''

Owing to the great need of building up the finances of the country, the subject was postponed until the next session of Congress.

On December 16, 1816, John C. Calhoun [S. C.] moved in the House of Representatives that a committee be appointed to consider the expediency of applying the profits of the National Bank to internal improvements.

After some opposition the committee was appointed, and he was made its chairman. On December 23 he reported a bill to this effect. The bill came up for discussion on February 4, 1817, and was debated until February 8, when it was passed by a vote of 86 to 84. The Senate passed it on February 27 by a vote of 22 to 16. The bill then went to the President, who vetoed it on March 3. His veto was sustained in the House, the vote being 60 to 56 in favor of the bill, which thus lacked the two-thirds vote requisite to overrule the veto.

In the debate in the House, John C. Calhoun [S. C.] and Henry Clay [Ky.] were the chief speakers in favor of the bill. Thomas B. Robertson [La.] objected decisively to it. Timothy Pickering [Mass.] objected to the constitutional argument of Calhoun in favor of the measure, but presented one of his own in its place. Erastus Root [N. Y.] objected to Federal roads as interfering with State affairs, but advocated Federal canals.

INTERNAL IMPROVEMENTS

HOUSE OF REPRESENTATIVES, FEBRUARY 4-8, 1817

MR. CALHOUN observed that it seemed to be the fate of some measures to be praised, but not adopted. Such, he feared, would be the fate of that on which they were now deliberating. From the indisposition manifested by the House to go into committee on the bill, there was not much prospect of its success, yet it seemed to him, when he reflected how favorable was the present moment, and how confessedly important a good system of roads and canals was to our country, he might reasonably be very sanguine of success. At peace with all the world, abounding in pecuniary means, and, what was of most importance, and at what he rejoiced as most favorable to the country, party and sectional feelings immerged in a liberal and enlightened regard to the general concerns of the nation—such, said he, are the favorable circumstances under which we are now deliberating. Thus situated, to what can we direct our resources and attention more important than internal improvements? What can add more to the wealth, the strength, and the political prosperity of our country? The manner in which facility and cheapness of intercourse added to the wealth of a nation had been so often and ably discussed by writers on political economy that he presumed the House to be perfectly acquainted with the subject. It was sufficient to observe that every branch of national industry—agricultural, manufacturing, and commercial—was greatly stimulated and rendered by it more productive. The result is, said he, that it tends to diffuse universal opulence. It gives to the interior the advantages possessed by the parts most eligibly situated for trade. It makes the country price, whether in the sale of the raw product or in the purchase of the articles for consumption, approximate to that of the commercial towns. In fact, if we look into the nature of wealth we will find that nothing can be more favorable to its growth than good roads and canals. Let it not be said that internal improvements may be wholly left to the enterprise of the States and of individuals. He knew, he said, that much might justly be expected to be done by them, but in a country so new and so extensive as ours there is room enough, said he, for all the general and State governments and individuals in which to exert their resources. But many of the improvements contemplated, said Mr. Calhoun, are on too great a scale for the resources of the States or individuals, and many of such a nature that the rival jealousy of the States, if left alone, might prevent. They required the resources and the general superintendence of this Government to effect and complete them.

But, said Mr. Calhoun, there are higher and more powerful considerations why Congress ought to take charge of this subject. In many respects no country of equal population and wealth possesses equal materials of power with ours. The people, in muscular power, in hardy and enterprising habits, and in a lofty and gallant courage, are surpassed by none. In one respect, and, in my opinion, in one only, are we materially weak. We occupy a surface prodigiously great in proportion to our numbers. The common strength is brought to bear with great difficulty on the point that may be menaced by an enemy. It is our duty, then, as far as in the nature of things it can be effected, to counteract this weakness. Good roads and canals judiciously laid out are the proper remedy. In the recent war, how much did we suffer for the want of them? Besides the tardiness and the consequential ineffacy of our military movements, to what an increased expense was the country put for the article of transportation alone! In the event of another war the saving in this particular would go far toward indemnifying us for the expense of constructing the means of transportation.

It is not, however, in this respect only that roads and canals add to the strength of the country. Our power of raising revenue, in war particularly, depends, said he, mainly on them. In peace our revenue depends principally on the imposts; in war this source, in a great measure, fails, and internal taxes, to a great amount, become necessary. Unless the means of commercial intercourse are rendered much more perfect than they now are, we shall never be able in war to raise the necessary supplies. If taxes were collected in kind; if, for instance, the farmer and mechanic paid in their surplus produce, then the difficulty would not exist, as in no country on earth is there so great a surplus in proportion to its population as in ours. But such a system of taxes is impossible. They must be paid in money, and, by the Constitution, must be laid uniformly. What, then, is the effect? The taxes are raised in every part of this extensive country uniformly, but the expenditure must, in its nature, be principally confined to the scene of military operations. This drains the circulating medium from one part and accumulates it in another, and perhaps a very distant, one. The result, said he, is obvious. Unless it can return through the operation of trade, the parts from which the constant drain takes place must ultimately be impoverished. Commercial intercourse is the true remedy to this weakness, and the means by which that is to be effected are roads, canals, and the coasting trade. On these, combined with domestic manufactures, does the moneyed capacity of this country, in war, depend. Without them, not only will we be unable to raise the necessary supplies, but the currency of the country must necessarily fall into the greatest disorder—such as we lately experienced.

But on this subject of national power, what, said Mr. Calhoun, can be more important than a perfect unity in every part, in feelings and sentiments? And what can tend more powerfully to produce it than overcoming the effects of distance?

No country enjoying freedom ever occupied anything like as great an extent of country as this Republic. One hundred years ago the most profound philosophers did not believe it to be even possible. They did not suppose it possible that a pure republic could exist on as great a scale even as the Island of Great Britain. What then was considered as chimerical, said Mr. Calhoun, we now have the felicity to enjoy, and, what is most remarkable, such is the happy mold of our Government, so well are the State and general powers blended that much of our political happiness draws its origin from the extent of our Republic. It has exempted us from most of the causes which distracted the small republics of antiquity. Let it not, however, be forgotten; let it, said he, be forever kept in mind that it exposes us to the greatest of all calamities, next to the loss of liberty, and even to that in its consequence—*disunion.* We are great and rapidly—he was about to say fearfully—growing. This, said he, is our pride and danger—our weakness and our strength. Whatever impedes the intercourse of the extremes with this, the center of the Republic, weakens the Union. The more enlarged the sphere of commercial circulation, the more extended that of social intercourse, the more strongly are we bound together, the more inseparable are our destinies. Those who understand the human heart best know how powerfully distance tends to break the sympathies of our nature. Nothing, not even dissimilarity of language, tends more to estrange man from man. Let us then, said Mr. Calhoun, bind the Republic together with a perfect system of roads and canals. Let us conquer space. It is thus the most distant parts of the

Republic will be brought within a few days' travel of the center; it is thus that a citizen of the West will read the news of Boston still moist from the press. The mail and the press, said he, are the nerves of the body politic. By them the slightest impression made on the most remote parts is communicated to the whole system, and the more perfect the means of transportation the more rapid and true the vibration. To aid us in this great work, to maintain the integrity of this Republic, we inhabit a country presenting the most admirable advantages. Belted around as it is by lakes and oceans, intersected in every direction by bays and rivers, the hand of industry and art is tempted to improvement. So situated, said he, blessed with a form of government at once combining liberty and strength, we may reasonably raise our eyes to a most splendid future if we only act in a manner worthy of our advantages. If, however, neglecting them, we permit a low, sordid, selfish, and sectional spirit to take possession of this House, this happy scene will vanish. We will divide, and in its consequences will follow misery and despotism.

Such, then, being the obvious advantages of internal improvements, why, said Mr. Calhoun, should the House hesitate to commence the system? He understood there were, with some members, constitutional objections. The power of Congress is objected to because the public moneys can only be appropriated to effect the particular powers enumerated in the Constitution. He was no advocate for refined arguments on the Constitution. The instrument was not intended as a thesis for the logician to exercise his ingenuity on. It ought to be construed with plain, good sense, and what can be more express than the Constitution on this very point? The first power delegated to Congress is comprised in these words: "To lay and collect taxes, duties, imposts, and excises; to pay the debts and provide for the common defence and general welfare of the United States, but all duties, imposts, and excises shall be uniform throughout the United States." First—the power is given to lay taxes; next, the objects are enumerated to which the money accruing from the exercise of this power may be applied; to pay the debts, provide for the common defence, and promote the general welfare, and, last, the rule for laying the taxes is prescribed—that all duties, imposts, and excises shall be uniform.

If the framers of the Constitution intended to limit the use of the money to the powers afterwards enumerated and defined, nothing could be easier than to have expressed it plainly.

He knew it was the opinion of some that the words "to pay the debts and provide for the common defence and general welfare," which he had just cited, were not intended to be referred to the power of laying taxes, contained in the first part of the section, but that they are to be understood as distinct and independent powers, granted in general terms, and are gratified by a more detailed enumeration of powers in the subsequent part of the Constitution. If such were in fact the meaning, surely nothing can be conceived more bungling and awkward than the manner in which the framers have communicated their intention. If it were their intention to make a summary of the powers of Congress in general terms, which were afterwards to be particularly defined and enumerated, they should have told us so plainly and distinctly, and, if the words "to pay the debts and provide for the common defence and general welfare" were intended for this summary, they should have headed the list of our powers, and it should have been stated that, to effect these general objects, the following specific powers were granted. The whole section seemed to him to be about taxes. It plainly commenced and ended with it, and nothing could be more strained than to suppose the intermediate words "to pay the debts and provide for the common defence and general welfare" were to be taken as independent and distinct powers. Forced, however, as such a construction was, he might admit it and urge that the words do constitute a part of the enumerated powers. The Constitution, said he, gives to Congress the power to establish post-offices and post-roads. He knew the interpretation which was usually given to these words confined our power to that of designating only the post-roads, but it seemed to him that the word "establish" comprehended something more. But suppose the Constitution to be silent, said Mr. Calhoun, why should we be confined in the application of money to the enumerated powers? There is nothing in the reason of the thing, that he could perceive, why it should be so restricted, and the habitual and uniform practice of the Government coincided with his opinion. Our laws are full of instances of money appropriated without any reference to the enumerated powers. If we are restricted in the use of our money to the enumerated powers, on what principle, said he, can the purchase of Louisiana be justified? To pass over many other instances, the identical power which is now the subject of discussion has, in several instances, been exercised. To look no further back, at the last session a considerable sum was granted to complete the Cumberland road[1] in reply to this uniform course of legislation, Mr. Calhoun expected it would be said that our Constitution was founded on positive and written principles, and not on precedents. He did not deny the position, but he introduced these instances to prove the uniform sense of Congress, and the country (for they had not been objected to), as to our powers; and surely, said he, they furnish better evidence of the true interpretation of the Constitution than the most refined and subtle arguments.

Let it not be urged that the construction for which he contended gave a dangerous extent to the powers of Congress. In this point of view he conceived it to be more safe than the opposite. By giving a reasonable extent to the money power it exempted us from the necessity of giving a strained and forced construction to the other enumerated powers. For instance, he said, if the public money could be applied to the purchase of Louisiana, as he contended, then there was no constitutional difficulty in that purchase, but, if it could not, then were we compelled either to deny that we had the power to purchase, or to strain some of the enumerated powers to prove our right. It had, for instance, been said that we had the right to purchase under the power to admit new States— a construction, he would venture to say, far more forced than the one for which he contended.

MR. PICKERING said he did not admit the latitude of construction given by the gentleman from South Carolina [Mr. Calhoun], who introduced the bill, to the terms of the Constitution which he had quoted. Congress had power "to lay and collect taxes, duties, imposts, and excises"—for what purpose? in order "to pay the debts and provide for the common defence and general welfare of the United States." Hence, the gentleman inferred, that as public roads and canals would promote the general welfare, therefore Congress had power to make roads and canals. If this interpretation of the Constitution be correct, then the subsequent enumeration of powers to be exercised by Congress was superfluous; for the terms "to provide for the general welfare" would embrace the following enumerated powers and every other imaginable power, the exercise of which would promote the "general welfare." The object for which the Constitution was ordained is explicitly declared to be "to promote the general welfare," and the like

[1] The so-called "National Road," running from Cumberland, Maryland, to Wheeling, Virginia, and afterwards extended through Ohio and Indiana to Springfield, Illinois. It formed a great highway of emigration.

words at the head of the specified powers appeared to Mr. Pickering as intended to mark the line within which the powers expressed or fairly implied should be exercised: they must all have for their object the "general welfare." Then follows the enumeration of the powers granted to Congress, all of which are manifestly calculated "to promote the general welfare." From the specific powers granted to Congress "to establish post-offices and post-roads" the gentleman from South Carolina had inferred that Congress had power to make roads on which the post-riders might travel. This construction Mr. Pickering believed to be altogether erroneous. He remembered that the supposition that Congress might, under that clause, exercise the power of making roads in any State, and where they pleased, was offered as a serious objection to the adoption of the Constitution in the convention of Pennsylvania, of which Mr. Pickering (then living in that State) was a member. And his recollection was probably the more perfect because he answered the objections observing that the power "to establish post-offices and post-roads" could intend no more than the power to direct where post-offices should be kept, and on what roads the mails should be carried; and this answer appeared then to be entirely satisfactory.

But while the gentleman from South Carolina was speaking it had occurred to Mr. Pickering that, if Congress had the power to make roads and canals, it must necessarily be an implied one, and under the express power "to regulate commerce with foreign nations and among the several States, and with the Indian tribes." To give facility and safety to foreign commerce, and to that between the several States, in what is called the coasting trade, Congress had caused lighthouses and beacons to be erected, piers in rivers to be constructed, and the coast to be surveyed to ascertain and mark dangerous shoals. But commerce (which consisted in the exchange of commodities) was carried on by land as well as by water, and if Congress, under the clause for regulating commerce, could rightfully do what, from the formation of the Government, they had been doing, and without a single objection—erecting lighthouses, beacons, and piers to give facility and safety to commerce by water, why should they not exercise the like power to facilitate, secure, and render less expensive, by means of roads and canals, the commerce *by land?* This, as it had occurred, Mr. Pickering suggested for consideration.

Mr. Root said if the national resources were to be directed to the internal improvement of the country, let them be applied to objects the least interfering with State policy, with State rights and sovereignty, and the best calculated to promote the general welfare and to aid in the regulation of commerce. It would hardly be pretended, he said, that the constitutional authority to establish post-offices confers the power to lay out and work roads in despite of State regulations. The construction of roads is a municipal regulation, generally much more limited in its operation than the confines of a State. Except in some great leading roads the convenience of counties and towns and even of neighborhoods is and ought to be chiefly consulted. Roads, said Mr. Root, even great leading ones, are used more by the inhabitants of their vicinity than by travelers from a distance. Not so with canals. They may connect distant States, unite in commercial connections remote parts of the nation, and chain them together in bands not to be severed by ambition or faction. The distant boatman, the distant merchant, make use of the canal, and by that means enhance the value of the farmer's produce, and reduce the price of merchandise necessary for his comfort. The inhabitants of its immediate vicinity derive no material advantages from it which are not shared in nearly an equal degree by their more remote neighbors, unless, as sometimes may happen, a village or town shall spring up in consequence. Canals are therefore, said he, more properly an object of national regard. Let your surplus treasure, Mr. Chairman, for it would seem that you have much of it, and I shall not urge the more rapid reduction of the public debt, nor the repeal of any of the taxes at this time; let your surplus treasure, destined by this bill, not to be wasted, I hope, but to the achievement of great schemes of national grandeur, be directed exclusively to the construction of canals. Gentlemen, said Mr. Root, may suppose that I have my eye directed to the contemplated great canal to connect the waters of the upper lakes with those of the Hudson River. I have, sir; I candidly confess I have. If we are to go on in this way, if we are to expend the national resources on objects of this kind, said he, without waiting to examine our constitutional powers, I wish to see a great national work accomplished; to see the waters of the Lakes connected with the Hudson and the Mississippi, Michigan with the Wisconsin and the Illinois, and Erie with the Wabash and Ohio. The intercourse between the Eastern and Western States might then form a ligature and a cement which no Hartford convention could ever dissolve.

MR. CLAY [Speaker] observed that he had long thought that there were no two subjects which would engage the attention of the national legislature more worthy of its deliberate consideration than those of internal improvements and domestic manufactures. He conceived the first and only step necessary to be taken at the present session was to set apart and make an inviolable pledge of the fund.

Mr. Clay said that as to the constitutional point which had been made by Mr. Pickering he had not a doubt on his mind, but it was not necessary, in his judgment, to embarrass the passage of the bill with the argument of that point at this time. It was a sufficient answer to say that the power was not now to be exercised. It was proposed merely to designate the fund, and, from time to time, as the proceeds of it came in, to invest them in the funded debt of the United States. It would thus be accumulating, and Congress could, at some future day, examine into the constitutionality of the question, and, if it had the power, it would exercise it; if it had not, the Constitution, there could be very little doubt, would be so amended as to confer it. It was quite obvious, however, that Congress might so direct the application of the fund as not to interfere with the jurisdiction of the several States and thus avoid the difficulty which had been started. It might distribute it among those objects of private enterprise which called for national patronage in the form of subscriptions to the capital stock of incorporated companies, such as that of the Delaware and Chesapeake Canal, and other similar institutions. Perhaps that might be the best way to employ the fund, but he repeated that this was not the time to go into that inquiry.

In reply to those who thought that internal improvements had better be left to the several States, he would ask, he would put it to the candor of every one, if there were not various objects in which many States were interested, and which, requiring therefore joint coöperation, would, if not taken up by the general Government, be neglected, either for the want of resources, or from the difficulty of regulating their respective contributions? Such was the case with the improvement of the navigation of the Ohio at the rapids; the canal, from the Hudson to the Lakes; the great turnpike road parallel with the coast, from Maine to Louisiana. These, and similar objects, were stamped with a national character, and they required the wisdom and the resources of the nation to accomplish them. No particular State felt an individual interest sufficient to execute improvements of such magnitude. They must be patronized, efficaciously patronized, by the general Government or they never would be accomplished.

My friend from Louisiana [Mr. Robertson] says his State wants no roads. Does she want no levees? But Mr. Clay conceived that no State was more interested in the making of good roads. The most vulnerable to a foreign enemy of all the points of our country, Louisiana is, at the same time, the most dependent upon the other parts of the Union for the means of her defence. Is she not, therefore, deeply interested in multiplying the channels by which those means may be transported to her? If two great roads, the one following the valley of the Ohio and that of the Mississippi, and the other the maritime coast, shall terminate at New Orleans, will not the security of Louisiana be greatly increased?

President Madison presented the following reasons for vetoing the bill:

I am constrained by the insuperable difficulty I feel in reconciling the bill with the Constitution of the United States to return it with that objection to the House of Representatives in which it originated.

The legislative powers vested in Congress are specified and enumerated in the eighth section of the first article of the Constitution, and it does not appear that the power proposed to be exercised by the bill is among the enumerated powers, or that it falls by any just interpretation within the power to make laws necessary and proper for carrying into execution those or other powers vested by the Constitution in the Government of the United States.

To refer the power in question to the clause "to provide for the common defence and general welfare" would be contrary to the established and consistent rules of interpretation as rendering the special and careful enumeration of powers, which follows the clause, nugatory and improper. Such a view of the Constitution would have the effect of giving to Congress a general power of legislation instead of the defined and limited one hitherto understood to belong to them; the terms, "common defence and general welfare," embracing every object and act within the purview of a legislative trust. It would have the effect of subjecting both the Constitution and laws of the several States, in all cases not specifically exempted, to be superseded by laws of Congress, it being expressly declared "that the Constitution of the United States, and laws made in pursuance thereof, shall be the supreme law of the land, and the judges of every State shall be bound thereby, anything in the Constitution or laws of any State to the contrary notwithstanding.'' Such a view of the Constitution finally would have the effect of excluding the judicial authority of the United States from its participation in guarding the boundary between the legislative powers of the general and state governments; inasmuch as questions relating to the general welfare being questions of policy and expediency are unsusceptible of judicial cognizance and decision.

A restriction of the power ''to provide for the common defence and general welfare'' to cases which are to be provided for by the expenditure of money would still leave within the legislative power of Congress all the great and most important measures of government, money being the ordinary and necessary means of carrying them into execution.

If a general power to construct roads and canals and to improve the navigation of water courses, with the train of powers incident thereto, be not possessed by Congress, the assent of the States in the mode provided in the bill cannot confer the power. The only cases in which the consent and cession of particular States can extend the power of Congress are those specified and provided for in the Constitution.

As has already been noted (see Volume V, chapter II), almost every debate in Congress during the nullification agitation developed into a discussion of Federal vs. State rights.

This was the case with a bill for the repair of the national road from Cumberland, Md., to Ohio and westward, which came before the House of Representatives on January 19, 1829. The question involved the institution and administration of toll gates by the Federal Government, in order to acquire revenue for the repairs. The bill was passed by the House, but returned to it from the Senate with the provision for toll gates stricken out as unconstitutional. On March 2, 1829, the House agreed to the amendment of the Senate by a vote of 80 to 52.

In the debate on the bill in the House, the chief speakers in favor of the toll-gate clause were Tomlinson Fort [Ga.] and Oliver H. Smith [Ind.]. Those opposed to the clause were James Buchanan [Pa.] and Philip P. Barbour [Va.].

The Cumberland Road

HOUSE OF REPRESENTATIVES, JANUARY 19-MARCH 2, 1829

MR. BUCHANAN.—It is not a question whether we shall keep the road in repair by annual appropriations, nor whether we shall extend other millions in constructing other Cumberland roads; these would be comparatively unimportant, but it is a question, upon the determination of which, in my humble judgment, depends the continued existence of the Federal Constitution, in anything like its native purity. Let it once be established that the Federal Government can enter the dominion of the States, interfere with their domestic concerns, erect toll-gates over all the military, commercial, and post-roads within their territories, and define and punish by laws of Congress, in the courts of the United States, offences committed upon these roads, and the barriers which were erected by our ancestors with so much care between Federal and State power are entirely prostrated. This single act would in itself be a longer stride toward consolidation than the Federal Government has ever made, and it would be a precedent for establishing a construction for the Federal Constitution so vague and so indefinite that it might be made to mean anything or nothing.

It is not my purpose, upon the present occasion, again to agitate the questions which have so often been discussed in this House as to the powers of Congress in regard to internal improvements. For my own part, I cheerfully accord to the Federal Government the power of subscribing stock in companies incorporated by the States for the purpose of making roads and canals, and I entertain no doubt whatever but that we can, under the Constitution, appropriate the money of our constituents directly to the construction of internal improvements *with the consent of the States* through which they may pass.

Before I enter upon the subject it will be necessary to present a short historical sketch of the Cumberland road. It owes its origin to a compact between the State of Ohio and the United States. In 1802 Congress proposed to the convention which formed the constitution of Ohio that they would grant to that State one section of land in each township for the use of schools; that they would also grant to it several tracts of land on which there were salt springs, and that five per cent. of the net proceeds of the future sales of public lands within its territory should be applied to the purpose of making public roads, "leading from the navigable waters emptying into the Atlantic to the Ohio, to the said State, and through the same." The act, however, distinctly declares that such roads shall be laid out under the authority of Congress, "with the consent of the several States through which the road shall pass." These terms were offered by Congress to the State of Ohio, provided she would exempt, by an irrevocable ordinance, all the land which should be sold by the United States within her territory from every species of taxation for the space of five years after the day of sale. This proposition of Congress was accepted by the State of Ohio, and it thus became a compact, the terms of which could not be changed without the consent of both the contracting parties.

In March, 1806, Congress passed "An act to regulate the laying out and making of a road from Cumberland, in the State of Maryland, to the State of Ohio." Under the provisions of this act, before the President could proceed to cut a single tree upon the route of the road, it was made necessary to obtain the consent of the States through which it passed. The Federal Government asked Maryland, Pennsylvania, and Virginia for permission to make it, and each of them granted this privilege in the same manner that they would have done to a private individual or to a corporation created by their own laws.

Congress at that day asserted no other right than a mere power to appropriate the money of their constituents to the construction of this road after the consent of these States should be obtained. The idea of a sovereign power in this Government to make the road and to exercise jurisdiction over it for the purpose of keeping it in repair does not, then, appear to have ever entered the imagination of the warmest advocate for Federal power. The federalism of that day would have shrunk with horror from such a specter. This road has cost the United States more than thirteen thousand five hundred dollars per mile. This extravagant expenditure shows conclusively that it is much more politic for us to enlist individual interests in the cause of internal improvements by subscribing stock than to become ourselves sole proprietors. Any government, unless under extraordinary circumstances, will pay the third more for constructing a road or canal than would be expended by individuals in accomplishing the same object.

What, then, does this precedent establish? Simply that the United States may appropriate money for the construction of a road through the territories of a State with its consent, and I do not entertain the least doubt but that we possess this power.

What does the present bill propose? To change the character which the United States has hitherto sustained in relation to this road from that of a simple proprietor to a sovereign. We will not ask the States to erect toll-gates for us. We are determined to exercise that power ourselves. The Federal Government first introduced itself into the States as a friend by permission; it now wishes to hold possession as a sovereign by power.

The right to demand toll and to stop and punish passengers for refusing to pay it is emphatically a sovereign right and has ever been so considered among civilized nations. The power to erect toll gates necessarily implies, first: The stoppage of the passenger until he shall pay the toll. Second. His trial and punishment, if he should, either by force or by fraud, evade, or attempt to evade, its payment. Third. A discretionary power as to the amount of toll. Fourth. The trial and punishment of persons who may wilfully injure the road, or violate the police established upon it. These powers are necessarily implied. Without the exercise of them you could not proceed with safety to collect the toll for a single day. Other powers will soon be exercised. If you compel passengers to pay toll, the power of protecting them while traveling along your road is almost a necessary incident. The sovereign who receives the toll ought naturally to possess the power of protecting him who pays it. To vest the power of demanding toll in one sovereign and the protection of the traveler's person in another would be almost an absurdity. The Federal Government would probably, ere long, exercise the power of trying and punishing murders and robberies, and all other offences committed upon the road. To what jurisdiction would the trial and punishment of these offences necessarily belong? To the courts of the United States, and to them alone.

Can any man lay his hand upon his heart and say that in his conscience he believes the Federal Constitution ever intended to bestow such powers on Congress? The great divisions of power, distinctly marked in that instrument, are external and internal. The first are conferred upon the general Government—the last, with but few exceptions, and those distinctly defined, remain in possession of the States. It never—never was intended that the vast and mighty machinery of this Government should be introduced into the domestic, the local, the interior concerns of the States, or that it should spend its power in collecting toll at a turnpike gate.

MR. BARBOUR.—All the powers of government may be considered as emanations from its sovereignty, but what I now speak of is that complete and perfect jurisdiction which necessarily includes, as a part of its definition, the right in, and power over, the domain or territory. Whensoever and wheresoever this jurisdiction is exercised directly over the soil, as the subject of its action, it must be exclusive, because, as the jurisdiction of a government embraces the whole right in and power over the soil, whenever it exercises it directly on that subject, the jurisdiction of any other government must necessarily be absolutely and totally contradictory and repugnant if brought to act upon the same subject. Thus, to illustrate: When the general Government shall have turnpiked a particular road, and established toll gates, if a State were to attempt to regulate or to claim the same road, the two powers could not exist together—the action of the first government directly upon the right of soil having exhausted the whole subject, and expended the whole power over it. Accordingly, with a view to prevent this necessary collision of jurisdiction in the clause relating to the seat of government, etc., the jurisdiction or legislation is, *totidem verbis,* declared to be exclusive, and in the other to dispose of and make all needful rules as to the public land, it must be exclusive, from the necessity of the case, because no other power can exercise jurisdiction, inasmuch as that implies the ownership in the domain, which is in the general Government alone. No one can doubt but that the erection of toll gates and demanding toll is an exercise of jurisdiction which can be founded only on a right to, and power over, the soil. If so, and the principle be true, that the jurisdiction in the Federal Government, in its direct action upon the soil, must, where it exists at all, be exclusive, then it results that the States have not, in this respect, concurrent power—that is, that they cannot turnpike any road which is declared to be a post-road—thus giving to the general Government exclusive jurisdiction over one hundred and fourteen thousand miles of post-road, which we now have, without the assent of the States, though the Constitution requires that assent before it can be divested of its jurisdiction, in the small surface which is the seat of government, and the other inconsiderable places which it enumerates. Again, sir. See to what lengths this principle would carry us. If Congress have a right to turnpike roads, then they have a right to adopt the accustomed means of doing it, but one of the most usual means is the incorporation of companies, and thus we might have every road in the Union in the hands of incorporated companies, demanding tolls of the people, which Congress must make high enough to yield them a dividend upon their stock. This is not all: we are told that the right to create implies the right to preserve. Upon this principle Congress might, with a view to preservation, prohibit any citizen from passing it, unless his wheels were of a given width, and, indeed, in this very bill, it is provided that those whose wheels exceed six inches in width shall be exempt from toll.

But, sir, I affirm the proposition, and I call upon gentlemen to refute it if they can, that, with the exception of the cases provided for in the Constitution, of a seat of government, the sites of forts, magazines, etc., it is not competent for the general Government to exercise jurisdiction, or to acquire by purchase, jurisdiction and property in and over one square foot of territory in one of the States. Let me not be misunderstood; I speak not here of our public lands lying within any of the States; our power over them results from a substantive and distinct provision of the Constitution. But my proposition applies to those States, in all the soil of which the State governments have the right both of soil and jurisdiction, such, for example, as the State of Massachusetts.

Mr. Fort opposed the State Rights theory at length with the usual arguments for Federal power over the States. His last point was as follows:

Do the States enjoy a paramount and exclusive jurisdiction over the soil they cover? So long as this Government exists, its enactments are nothing, unless of force in the States. They are worse than nothing, if subject to be repeated, directly or indirectly, by the individual States. And how, let me ask, can this Government carry on its indispensable operations without exercising sovereignty over the soil? True, this sovereignty, although paramount for its purpose, is not exclusive, even for forts, arsenals, etc., unless by the consent of the States in which they lie, so abundantly guarded are the rights of the States. But for all the necessary purposes of its institution this Government, by the declaration of the people themselves, the uniform decision of its courts, and the legislative enactments of every administration, from its commencement, is declared to have a paramount jurisdiction over the whole Union. The powers of this Government are co-equal with its duties. It must establish post-roads, regulate internal commerce, defend us against our enemies, have fortifications, march its armies, and occupy so much space as these operations require. Suppose a State were to refuse her consent to each and every one of these operations, by what right would this Government enter her territory for either purpose if the State sovereignty over the soil is exclusive?

I have used freely the term sovereignty. I am apprised that it is at the risk of being misunderstood or misrepresented. I disclaim all definitions of this term which signify a power unknown to the Constitution. I have used it because it is so liberally and exclusively applied to the States by those in opposition to my views. I grant that each government is equally entitled to the term, but must again repeat that the people of this country acknowledge no sovereignty inconsistent with that liberty which they have again and again declared is dearer than life, the one who surrenders it being unworthy to live. I think I have shown that the United States is a Government of the people, and that its powers are all sovereign and paramount, though in many instances not exclusive. That if it can make a road it must do so as a sovereign power, and, if so, a power to tax for the use is a necessary and proper incident.

Mr. SMITH.—Was it not remarkable that those old sages and heroes [who formed the Constitution] who had fought the good fight in times that tried men's souls should not have been alarmed at the idea of letting the people become more closely united? Was there no voice then to raise the cry of State rights—of bleeding State rights? Yes, there were in those days such men as these; they represented, in glowing colors, the same—yes, the very same—doctrines that are now contended for on this floor. They contended that the States had much better continue under the Articles of Confederation than for the people to adopt a Federal Constitution with such tremendous powers as to authorize Congress "to provide for the common defence and the general welfare," but all to no purpose. It was believed that the people were capable of self-government; that they would be more likely to act together for the public good than to destroy each other without inducement. It was believed that a government, to do good and to "promote the general welfare," must have the power to act. The convention said so; the people said so, and the unparalleled prosperity of the United States, under the exercise of this power, enters a *caveat* against the confederation doctrines of the gentleman from Virginia [Mr. Barbour].

The question of the Government operation of public works, particularly those connected with transportation, came prominently before the country for the first time in the case of the Maysville [Ky.] Turnpike bill. This passed Congress in May, 1830. President Jackson vetoed it, basing his action on the lack of authorization in the Constitution for the *operation* (although not the *construction*) of public works, and suggested, as his predecessors had done when the subject of Federal internal improvements had come before them, amending the Constitution to justify such measures. When the bill was before the Senate, John Tyler [Va.] spoke as follows in opposition to it:

THE FIRST ENTANGLEMENT OF GOVERNMENT BY CAPITAL

SPEECH OF SENATOR TYLER AGAINST OPERATION OF PUBLIC WORKS

It has become customary of late years to ridicule the Virginia doctrines, as they are called. That State which has stood by this Union through good and through evil report is sneered at and reviled. So was it in former times. Under the first Adams she was declared rebellious and factious, and it was said that her Republicans should be trampled into dust and ashes. She nevertheless, with Kentucky, raised her voice against the infractions of the Constitution. She does the same now. And what were the infractions against which she then protested in comparison with those against which she now protests? Bad enough they were, it is true. But the art of construing the Constitution, and the efforts to make it a nose of wax, were then but barely commenced. The sedition law was passed, and thereby the principle of force was resorted to. Now, sir, a more insidious and a more dangerous principle is brought into action. Money is now relied upon; cupidity—avarice, are the infernal agents now invoked. These are the fatal sisters who weave the web of our destiny, and if we do not destroy that web before we come to be more fully entangled, if we permit first an arm and then a leg to be tied up, there will be left to us no means of escape. Let us now begin the effort, and, by drawing back this Government to its legitimate orbit, save our institutions from destruction. My untiring efforts shall not be wanting in so holy a cause. But if we surrender ourselves into the hands of ingenius politicians, those aspirants for high office who seek evermore to enlist in their support the strongest passions of human nature, with a view to their individual aggrandizement, the ark of the covenant will be destroyed and the temple rent in twain. Let us expel the money changers from that temple, and introduce the only true worship. In this way only, I am fully satisfied, can we preserve the Union of these States and secure their unceasing happiness.

CHAPTER V

National Aid to Railroads

[The Pacific Railroad]

Sen. Daniel Webster [Mass.] on Sympathetic Aid by the Government to Transportation Enterprises (The Baltimore and Ohio Railroad)—William M. Gwin [Cal.] Introduces Bill in Senate for the Government to Build a Railroad from the Mississippi River to the Pacific Ocean: It Is Opposed by Robert F. Stockton [N. J.]; Bill Is Committed—Debate on the Committee's Bill: In Favor, Thomas J. Rusk [Tex.], John B. Weller [Cal.], John Davis [Mass.], Stephen A. Douglas [Ill.], Henry S. Geyer [Pa.], Joseph R. Underwood [Ky.], George E. Badger [N. C.]; Opposed, James A. Bayard, Jr. [Del.], James Cooper [Pa.], William C. Dawson [Ga.], Andrew P. Butler [S. C.], James M. Mason [Va.], Isaac Toucey [Conn.]—Subsequent History of Pacific Railroads.

THE question of Federal aid to and partnership in private transportation enterprises came before the Senate on May 22, 1830, in the proposition that the Government subscribe to the stock of the Baltimore and Ohio Railroad Company. Daniel Webster [Mass.] advanced the suggestion

"That the funds of the general Government in works of internal improvement ought to be a circulating fund, to be applied as circumstances might demand, for the purpose of encouraging and promoting those works in different sections of the country, and when the works have been effected the stock should be sold out and again applied to the encouragement of similar works."

The bill was laid on the table by a vote of 21 to 19.

A system of granting public lands to the States for the encouragement of railroad construction was begun in 1850. On September 20 an act was passed for the benefit of the Illinois Central and the Mobile and Ohio railroads, donating over two and a half million acres to the States through which the roads were to run.

159

The rapid growth of the Pacific States after the discovery of gold in California caused a great national demand to arise for railroad connection between these and the Eastern States. Owing to the great cost of construction it was universally recognized that if the project were to succeed there would have to be a combination of private enterprise and public capital.

The chief subject of discussion in Congress during the session beginning December 6, 1852, and ending March 3, 1853, was the construction of a railroad from the Mississippi River to the Pacific Ocean. On December 22 William M. Gwin [Cal.] introduced in the Senate a bill authorizing the grant of the public lands to the States through which the railroad was to pass to be used for this purpose, the Government building the road through the Territories.

THE PACIFIC RAILROAD AND TELEGRAPH

SENATE, DECEMBER 22-FEBRUARY 22, 1853

Robert F. Stockton [N. J.] opposed the consideration of the bill at the time, saying:

I am opposed to this whole scheme of a great national road. I go against it from the beginning to the end, from first to last; therefore it cannot be expected that I will yield any of the common and usual forms of legislation to facilitate its progress. I have no idea that such a bill as the one contemplated can pass the Congress of the United States at the present day. Sir, those who are endeavoring to extend the powers of this Government with the expectation and hope of making a splendid and magnificent empire of ours may well approve of this scheme, but I think the day has not yet arrived when the Congress of the United States will lend itself to such a project or proceed to make a railroad from the Atlantic to the Pacific. I am for a simple and frugal government, and against the proposed bill, and intend from the very start to oppose it.

On January 27 Thomas J. Rusk [Tex.] moved that the entire subject be referred to a special committee with instructions to report a bill. This was done, and he was made chairman of the committee.

On February 2 the Select Committee reported its bill to the Senate. This empowered the President to select the route of the railroad after surveys had been made; gave a right of way 300 feet in width for the road, and a telegraph line; appropriated for the construction of the road alternate sections of public lands six miles on either side, and not over $20,000,000 to supply any deficiency in the funds resulting from the sale of the lands; authorized the President to give out contracts to the lowest and best bidders; reserved to the Government preference in the use of the road; limited the period of construction to ten years; secured to the Government the right to purchase the road thirty years after its completion at ten per cent. advance on the cost of construction with the right of Congress to regulate tolls, etc., before this time; gave to Congress the power to "authorize individuals, companies, or States to form a connection between said railroads and any other railroad or railroads under their control"; and created "The Pacific Railroad and Telegraph Company" out of the contractors and their associates.

Upon this bill James A. Bayard, Jr. [Del.], spoke as follows:

When I look at this bill as it stands, it is, in my opinion, a project to create a corporation with a power which, if you ever do create it, will be fourfold the power of that corporation [the United States Bank] against which the Democratic party of the United States were at war for a series of years.

I do not mean to desert my Democratic principles on any ground of expediency, or on any of the magnificent ideas entertained by the honorable Senator from Maine [Hannibal Hamlin] as to the benefits of this road to the commerce of this country. There is a question with me, independent of the benefit to be conferred: whether it is within the constitutional power of this Government to create such a corporation as this bill proposes to create. And, further, beyond the question of constitutional power, there is a question whether the corruption that would result from the irresponsible power vested in such a corporation would not be greater than all the benefits to commerce which could flow from such a road.

This question is pressed at the close of the second or short

X—11

session of this Congress, when the people of this country, by their late vote, have decreed a change of the political power which controls the Executive Department. Under such circumstances, it looks as if there was something like a fear on the part of the honorable Senator from California that the incoming President of the United States [Franklin Pierce], judging by his previous opinions, might never be brought to sanction a bill to make such a road as this; and that, perhaps, is the reason why it is pressed upon us at this time without any preliminary surveys at all.

SENATOR RUSK.—Mr. President, it is very easy to talk of the powerful corporations. It is very easy to talk about a violation of the Constitution of the United States, and the enormous expenditure of money involved in this proposition, and the unlimited powers we are about to confer upon a corporation; but there is some difficulty in drawing that from the bill which has been reported to the Senate by the Select Committee. The honorable Senator from Delaware has chosen to characterize this bill as involving an unlimited amount of expenditure, and says we do not know the cost to which it will lead. Sir, the President cannot go beyond its limits. He is to contract "on the terms and conditions" prescribed in the bill. Who supposes that, with an appropriation of $20,000,000, the President will go beyond it?

Then, with regard to the "tremendous corporation" spoken of by the Senator from Delaware. Why, the only question with regard to corporations raised in any bill is the power of Congress to create a corporation in the Territories; for it goes on to declare, in more places than one, that it is to have no force or effect in any of the States of the Union until it is assented to by the legislature of such State. So much for the tremendous powers that have alarmed the Senator!

If gentlemen say there is a violation of the Constitution, let them point it out. Let them take up the bill, and point out where it conflicts with the Constitution. Let them prove that you cannot carry a mail to California. Let them prove that it is not your duty to protect that defenceless frontier. Let them take up the Constitution and prove that you cannot adopt the means necessary to defend all your possessions; and then prove that it is not your duty to do it. Let them select from the bill, and not from the workings of imagination, its objectionable features. Let us have no more of this raw-head and bloody-bones business of allusions to the United States Bank, and talk about Democracy. Why, sir, the chief apostle of Democracy,

General Jackson, said that he would vote money out of the treasury, or that he would sanction the voting of money out of the treasury, for internal improvements of a general and national character. Then, to keep within the pale of Democracy, let gentlemen take up and prove that the Pacific Railroad, without which you cannot defend California in case an attack should be made upon her, is a matter of local, and not of general, importance, then I will submit.

SENATOR BAYARD.—Let me ask, will not the President be bound to contract for the whole road, at whatever price may be proposed by the lowest and best bidders? There is no limitation as to the price for which a contract is to be made; and, if the contractors should make a contract for a very large amount of money, they know perfectly well that they could fall back on this Government, and say, "Here is the contract—we have half made the road, and your appropriations have failed, and now you are bound by your public faith, in addition to the benefits arising to the community from the construction of the road, to comply with the contract, although it may cost $300,-000,000 or $500,000,000."

Mr. President, this bill should not pass until we have accurate surveys made and know the cost of the road.

On February 3 John B. Weller [Cal.] replied to the opponents of the bill:

My friend from Delaware [Mr. Bayard] has discovered that there is an immense corporation covered up somewhere in the bill of the Senator from Texas.

If that Senator can show me that the effect of this bill is to incorporate a dangerous company, with the immense power which he claims can be exercised in controlling a work of this sort, I am against it. But what is this corporation? The President of the United States is authorized to make a contract with some private individual or individuals for the construction of this road. This is all. As well might it be claimed that, in all contracts which are made between the executive department of the Government and individuals, corporations are constituted. If my friend from Texas has been overreached, or if he is attempting to overreach me by forcing a bank of the United States upon this country, under the pretext of constructing a railroad, I desire that my able friend from Delaware shall give me the necessary information that I may convict that Senator, and then he shall be read out of the Democratic party.

The Senator from Indiana [Jesse D. Bright], who also says here is an incorporation which is going to eat out the liberties of the country, contended that this work was not within the constitutional powers of the Government. I desire to know whether there is no power in Congress to construct a military road? Is there no power in Congress to establish a post route? Is there not an obligation resting upon this great and powerful Government to protect the people who stand upon its frontier? Sir, the man who stands upon the remotest portion of the Republic is as much entitled to the protection of this Government as he who stands in its center. If you desire the confidence and support of the people, you must take care to protect them.

I had supposed that it was long since settled that Congress had a constitutional power to appropriate the public money for works of internal improvement of a national character. The Cumberland or National road, which was designed to connect the East with what was then the far West, was first sanctioned by Mr. Jefferson. It was approved by all our Democratic Presidents down to Mr. Polk. Yet, sir, a new light has sprung up here in the State of Indiana, discovering that there is no constitutional power to do that which all those apostles of Democracy have sanctioned. I am inclined to think that they were right and the Senator wrong.

SENATOR BAYARD.—By the bill the contractors are made a body politic and corporate, a great corporation, extending throughout the whole line of the road, and created for the express purpose of constructing the road. Then the last section refers to the existence of a company for the purpose of working this road. It secures the rights of that company, but provides that, at the lapse of thirty years, the Government may purchase the road from them, paying them their capital, with ten per cent. interest.

Now, if, after looking at all these sections, anyone can say that this bill does not create a corporation, that it does not contemplate the construction of this road by means of a great corporation, which is only to a very limited extent to be within the control of the Congress of the United States, I confess that I cannot understand the meaning of language and the objects of the bill.

Senator James Cooper [Pa.] added his arguments to those of Senator Bayard.

The honorable Senator from Texas told us yesterday that the bill prescribed the cost, and that the $20,000,000, for which bonds are to be issued, and the expense of keeping engineers upon the road, to inform the President of its progress, was all the cost the United States would be called upon to incur. Sir, I doubt it very much. If the route should be found to be practicable by the company undertaking its construction, when the $20,000,000 have been expended by the Government, and after $50,000,000 or $100,000,000 have perhaps been expended by private individuals, would not the Government be besought by this huge corporation—for a corporation it is to all intents and purposes? And do you believe that Congress would resist an application backed by the influence of such a company, with such interests at stake? You, sir, have seen enough—I, sir, have seen enough in the short period I have been here—to know that any great, influential corporation or company can bring means to operate upon Congress to induce it to overstep the boundaries of prudence in making appropriations; and such would be the case here. But suppose they should go on and complete it by the aid that the Government is to lend in money or lands, and it should be found out afterward to be unprofitable. Gentlemen may say there is no danger of that; but I am not at all sure that there is no danger of that kind.

I do not care how many individuals may be employed in the construction of this road—how many companies may be engaged in it—their interests will be similar; they will have the same object in view; there will be a combination from one end of it to the other; all the interests embarked in it will be combined; and when combined do you suppose that Congress could resist the influence which would be brought to bear?

A money influence of hundreds of millions would be vested in such a company, and who can suppose that Congress would be able to resist an application that it should take such a work out of their hands, if it should be found unprofitable?

Who ever before heard of such an enterprise—spanning a continent of three thousand miles in width, over territory larger than the whole territory of Great Britain and Ireland? Who can foretell—who can judge, with any degree of accuracy, the amount of power which such a corporation as this would possess? The honorable Senator from California has said that this bill, as it now stands, created no corporation. If it does not do that, what does it?

SENATOR WELLER.—I confess that when I made the remarks which I did make this morning I was not aware of the last section contained in that bill; but, after having heard it read by the Senator from Delaware, I do regard it as an act of incorporation, and that, under the power which is thus conferred upon the company, they can, if they choose, exercise almost unlimited control. This I regard as a dangerous power, which ought not to be conferred even by implication.

SENATOR RUSK.—We have drawn up this bill for the purpose of restricting this company to the strict performance of the contract for the construction of the road. If gentlemen are not satisfied with this language, let them draw up the most restrictive clause possible, and I will agree to it, because it has been the object of the Select Committee to endeavor to control these men, and to keep them under the supervision of Congress.

On February 4 John Davis [Mass.] came to the aid of Senator Rusk.

The objection made to the bill is that it proposes to invest this company, who may undertake the work, with corporate powers. This seems to have excited very great alarm in the minds of some Senators. This corporation seems to be, in their judgment, a Trojan horse, filled with armed men; and we who come here to support this bill to be voluntarily prostrating the walls of the citadel to let the monster in, that those concealed in it may prey upon the confiding and unsuspicious. But, Mr. President, I think a little calmer view of this subject will greatly modify their idea of the magnitude of this evil. The proposition in this bill is to confer upon this company the corporate powers which are daily conferred on those who undertake to construct railroads. If there be a State in this Union that has not had the rashness, the temerity, to create just such corporations, I do not know which State it is. It is, certainly, a fact that just such corporations exist in nearly all, if not all, the States of the Union created by the legislative authority of those States.

The danger resulting from a corporation seems to spring entirely from the character of its paternity. If it be within a State, its claws are cut, its teeth are drawn; if it be a work of the United States, it becomes a savage monster, full of evil and full of defilement. The only question here is whether this work shall be done by a corporation, or done by the direct act of the Government, if it is done at all.

Why, sir, if we are to go to either of the two modes, that by means of a corporation, or that of the Government itself, for

the construction of a railroad, the former is infinitely preferable
to the latter, because we all know from our experience and observation, and we might know by reasoning *a priori,* that, if
the Government undertakes, by its own immediate exercise of
power, to carry on such a work under its own direction and
superintendence, abuses will creep in, and that it will become
a political engine necessarily. That is precisely the objection
made to a corporation, and yet how infinitely greater are the
abuses under the management of a government itself than those
which arise under the management of any corporation whatever.

What is it feared this monster corporation will do? I should
be very greatly obliged to gentlemen if they will point out the
probable abuses which will grow out of the power proposed to
be vested in it. We hear gentlemen saying, substantially, that
a corporation of that sort will come here and control Congress
itself—having a power greater and higher than the legislature
of the nation. I should like to have gentlemen point out the
process by which that is to be done; I should like to see the
means exposed by which such results are to be produced. I
should be gratified to see both the sources of the power and the
corruption, if they are to exist necessarily in a body of that
sort; and, if there be not a way of avoiding the evils predicted,
it will be some consolation to have that which seems so manifest
pointed out, that we may be admonished by it, and inquire
whether a purer and better course cannot be adopted—one more
free from the objections raised here, and one which shall be
carried forward more to the satisfaction of the country.

William C. Dawson [Ga.] made a number of pertinent inquiries relative to the relations of the general
and State governments in respect to what is now called
"interstate commerce."

Gentlemen have spoken about the corporation to be created
under this act. I will not, in this stage of proceedings, raise
the question as to the power of Congress to grant corporations
within the limits of the States, but I would make this suggestion: After this corporation shall be formed for the construction of a road three thousand miles in extent, those portions of
the road within the limits of the States will be, of course, within
the jurisdiction of the respective States. The corporation will
have received its power from the general Government. Will

not the general Government, therefore, have the right to regulate that corporation, either to extend the grant of powers to
it, or limit it? If we yield to Congress the power to grant an
act of incorporation to a company within the limits of the
States, do we not yield the whole question as to the power to the
Federal Government? Although it is provided that this corporation shall not be within the limits of the States, except by
their consent, yet the question arises, Can Congress exercise an
unconstitutional power, even with the assent of one of the
States? Can we take upon ourselves to exercise a power which
we admit by this bill does not belong to us, merely because a
State says it may be exercised within her limits? This road
may pass through the State of Texas. Who is to obtain the
right of way there? Is it the Government of the United States?
The provision of the bill is that the right of way shall be granted
for the construction of this road through the public lands.
There is not an acre of the public lands belonging to the United
States within the limits of Texas. You will then have to acquire
from that State the right of way. How is it to be procured?
Have we made any arrangement for that?

SENATOR RUSK.—Texas has already granted the right of
way.

SENATOR DAWSON.—To whom has she granted it?

SENATOR RUSK.—To anybody who will make the road.

SENATOR DAWSON.—Has she granted the right of way to
anybody who may be under the control of the United States?
Has she granted the right of way to any corporation which
may be created by the Government of the United States to run
the road through her limits?

SENATOR RUSK.—She has given the right of way for the construction of a road through that State to the Pacific Ocean to
anybody who chooses to construct it.

SENATOR DAWSON.—If that be true, and I have no doubt it
is, she never contemplated that she was going to yield the jurisdiction over that road to any other government than her own.

SENATOR RUSK.—Nor will she do so under this bill, unless
she expressly consents to it after its passage.

SENATOR DAWSON.—Then let her do so. Will Texas give up
all her power to control that matter, and give jurisdiction to the
Government of the United States if we pass this bill?

SENATOR RUSK.—Try her.

SENATOR DAWSON.—But, sir, I care nothing about that question. The corporation which is to be created by the bill now
under consideration is a tremendous one, as we all know; but

the dangers growing out of it I shall not now depict. If we grant them the act of incorporation, and it is carried into execution, who, I ask, will become the corporators, and upon what terms? The contractors, whoever they may be, are to be the corporators, together "with their associates and successors"; and the word "associates" I suppose is intended to mean such persons as these contractors may permit to associate with them. Who holds the stock that this company is to put before the country? Who authorizes the issue of the stock? Does the Government of the United States authorize it? Suppose these parties do issue stock, what are they to pay for it? The railroad is not to be built by the contractors' own money; and the Government is to grant fifty millions or thirty-five millions, or, according to some gentlemen, only fifteen millions of acres of land. Besides that, it is to issue five per cent. bonds to the amount of $20,000,000. That will cause a large portion of this road to be executed. To whose benefit will this inure? To the men who perform the labor. They get the pay for constructing the road; and, after the road shall be constructed, what are you to do? You are to pay them for constructing the road, and to give it to them. That is what you are to do. Is there a Senator here who denies it?

SENATOR RUSK.—Yes, sir.

SENATOR DAWSON.—Do we not, according to this bill, give the road to them?

SENATOR RUSK.—We do not pay them for taking it.

SENATOR DAWSON.—Why, the bill allows them to hold it for thirty years, and then they can dispose of it to the Government of the United States at an advance of ten per cent., after deducting the $20,000,000 in five per cent. bonds and the value of the lands. The Government then would only have to pay the additional sum the road may cost beyond that. How much will the road cost? That is a question in regard to which we should have information before we undertake the work. How are we to ascertain this? Men in private life, when their own interests are involved, when their own judgment and honor are involved in a transaction, when they propose such a work as this, first want to know its probable cost. I think that should be so in this case. Private individuals would not go into such a proposition without first understanding what they were about to do.

Suppose any one of the contractors should fail to execute his contract, or that any one of them could not procure means sufficient to connect different links of the road together, when the contracts shall be divided, as they no doubt will be, into hundreds of sections. I suppose he would forfeit it, according to the bill, and then you would redispose of it to some other person. Can you take the money which you have already paid to the first contractor to complete the road? Will he not have the money, although he may have done scarcely anything, and will you not have to pay the same amount over again before you can connect together the various links? But this feature may be no objection, because the bill may be amended in this respect. This bill certainly requires amendment in many respects. If the Government of the United States is to enter upon the construction of this road, from one end of it to the other, and if the twenty millions of bonds, and the public bonds proposed to be granted, should be found not to be sufficient for the purpose, would they be able to proceed? Would not the contractors call upon us, from time to time, to make additional appropriations for the purpose of carrying on this great and magnificent enterprise, and should we be able to resist the appeal?

Private capital is not going to connect itself with this road, and why? Because every man who has an eye to his own interests must see that a railroad three thousand miles in length through a wilderness country, stretching to a population not over three hundred thousand or four hundred thousand, never can sustain itself by the ordinary profits on freights and passengers. No gentleman upon this floor can pretend to pledge his opinion that this is to be a money-making road? Hence it is that, if there is to be a total failure in the way of profits arising from the road, the Government of the United States should say at once and boldly: "We will build the road out of our lands and money entirely, and not seek in this indirect way to pledge ourselves to a large amount, in order that the people may not see the extent of the appropriation, and be mistaken in regard to the consequences." If it be true that this road will not pay, it is certainly true that no intelligent man will invest his money in it; and the contractors will take their contracts according to the limits of your capacity to pay under this bill. The road, therefore, will be carried to such an extent as the appropriations which you may make will carry it, and not an inch farther. Do gentlemen suppose that by passing this bill they will induce individuals to take stock in this road? If they do, I think they are mistaken. But by passing the bill, you pledge yourselves that if the road shall be built by your means, by your money, and by your lands, you will give it to the company after thirty years; and suppose they should say they would not take it, because it would not pay the expenses?

That would be an end of the matter. So I conclude that in my judgment—and I say it reluctantly—the friends of this measure cannot suppose that it is to be a money-making road.

I would rather vote for a bill appropriating hundreds of millions of dollars to build this road than to vote for this bill under the idea that we are merely extending a little aid to those companies which may make it.

But, Mr. President, has the period arrived when nobody is alarmed as to the extent of the public debt? Has nobody any fear that we shall have to increase the tariff in order to support the Government? Examine the matter in any of its bearings, it is certainly an extraordinary proposition. I have looked at it with a great deal of care. I have endeavored to comprehend it; and there is not a Senator upon this floor who would feel greater pleasure, and who, as an American, would feel prouder than I should to see a railroad extending from the Atlantic to the Pacific; and whenever the period comes when I can act understandingly, and keep myself within what I believe to be the pale of the Constitution, I will be found one of those as willing to do everything to promote the interests and greatness of this country as any gentleman here.

Stephen A. Douglas [Ill.] defended the bill.

I apprehend that gentlemen travel beyond the terms of the bill, and make arguments which are negatived by its provisions. They argue in defiance of it, when they pretend to show that the Government of the United States is about to go into an unknown expenditure, and to create a boundless public debt. One great merit of this bill is that it fixes precisely and exactly the liability of the Government; and it not only does that, but it contains such guards that by no possibility, under its terms, can there be a loss to the United States. By no possibility can the contractors get one dollar of public money, until they have expended on the road five times that amount, and given us a priority of lien on that fivefold amount as security for our advance. We do not part with our security even when the road is completed. I think, therefore, that an examination of the provisions of the bill will put an end entirely to any apprehensions upon that score.

The Senator from Georgia says he would like to see this road made, provided it can be done consistently with the Constitution. I did not understand distinctly from him that it violated the Constitution.

SENATOR DAWSON.—I said I would do all I could to bring it within the pale of the Constitution.

SENATOR DOUGLAS.—But if it is already within the pale of the Constitution, of course the limitation amounts to nothing; and if it is not within the pale of the Constitution I would like to see the objection to its constitutionality pointed out; and I will tell the Senator that, when it shall be pointed out, I will undertake either to answer the argument, or I will write an amendment to avoid the force of the objection.

The Senator from Georgia says no man dreams that the road is going to pay a fair dividend after it is made. I presume he was speaking in his usual beautiful, rhetorical manner, without pinning himself down to what he would expect us to regard as seriously the facts of the case. There are men who think that this road will pay when it is made. There are men who think they have some data by which they can arrive at that conclusion. I have seen, within the last four years, a road started within my own State through a country where hardly one-tenth of the land was under cultivation, and where the same predictions were made that it would never pay, and yet that road, although only half done, now yields twenty-seven per cent. upon its cost.

I undertake to predict to the honorable Senator from Georgia that, although the country through which this road is to be constructed is now a wilderness, before it is finished the line of the road and the country for a wide extent on either side will be more densely populated than the State of which he is the able representative on this floor. I undertake to say to the Senator that I am willing to put myself on the record as predicting that, when you get this road half done, the local travel along the finished portion of it will be beyond the capacity of a single track to perform. Each one hundred miles that you penetrate the wilderness, you shorten the distance for hauling supplies, and a greater number of teams will be required to concentrate upon it, and population will be swelling in upon each side to raise provisions to sell to the men engaged in the work.

One of the best markets that can be opened to the agriculturists anywhere will be along the line of this road, to supply your five thousand workmen who will be employed in its construction. Storekeepers and shopkeepers will be needed to supply them with goods and other materials. You will find mechanic shops growing up all along the road to make and repair tools and implements for the workmen. You will find the whole country turning from a wilderness into one of the most densely populated and highly cultivated portions of America. Such will be the natural result of the construction of this road. That being the case, I do not see the force of the gentleman's argument that this work is to be constructed through a vast wilderness.

I am free to say to you, sir, that I believe it is the first and the highest duty of this nation to see that this road is made. I believe that the integrity of the Union itself depends upon its construction.

Then, how are we to do it? Some say with land; some say with money. This bill says by a combination of both. Then come in gentlemen who say, "It is all right; we are for the road; but let us have a survey first." Sir, we have been at that for three years, and when we bring up a bill for a road it is said we must have a survey. When we get up bills providing for a survey, it is said we must have the road immediately. And thus alternately one proposition or the other has received the go-by. The proposition now made to have a survey is simply a postponement of the building of the road, and is to result in doing nothing. I do not mean to say that gentlemen mean that; but I say that will be the result.

The Senator from Georgia says that no individual, no nation, no State, ever undertook a work of this magnitude without a survey. They never did, either with or without a survey; for never has a road of this magnitude been proposed, much less executed, anywhere. Works of less magnitude have been devised and executed without surveys. You objected to me, two or three years ago, because I was asking a grant of land, without a survey, for a railroad from Chicago to Mobile. You made the grant, although there had been no survey on a portion of the line for four hundred miles. But I have now the pleasure of telling you that the road is under contract. It is more than half done, and it will be finished in two years, although you gave us ten years within which to do it. The Senator from Georgia then told us that we were squandering the public lands for the purpose of encouraging railroads in a State. I told him, in reply, that the Government had had lands in the market for forty-two years, at $1.25 an acre, which were upon the line of the proposed road, and they could not be sold because of the absence of timber, and their distance from market; but that, if you would give us alternate sections, we would make the remaining half worth more than the whole was originally, and enable you to sell them at $2.50 an acre. He shook his head, and doubted my argument. He said it was very good in theory, but the result would not turn out as I predicted, and that, if he thought it would, he would vote for the bill. I have now the pleasure of informing him that the alternate sections reserved to the Government have, some of them, been brought into market at public auction, and more of them have been sold within the last few months, since they have been brought into market, at $2.50 an acre, than were sold for years previously at $1.25. That demonstrates that all apprehensions upon the subject of a grant of lands for roads through a wilderness country where settlements have never penetrated vanish as the dew before the rising sun when there is an inducement for opening these lands and a means of communication by a railroad to be constructed.

Well-informed men in regard to the geography and topography of that country know that a railroad route from the Mississippi to the Pacific is practicable. Sir, instead of having difficulty in selecting an engineer that can find a practicable route, I think the engineer will immortalize himself who can find a route in our own territory which is not practicable. These mountains are full of passes—practicable passes. Gentlemen talk about the great deserts that lie there, impassable and uninhabitable. There are such tracts which are not very large, but I undertake to say that there is no continuous line which is not susceptible of a higher degree of cultivation and a greater yield of product than the line from here to New Orleans, or the line from here to Portland, in Maine.

When people start from their old homes and go to the Western wilds, they are apt to find fault with everything they see which they do not find exactly as it was in the country which they left. They grumble at everything that is not exactly agreeable to them. If they get sick, they charge it upon the new country; if any misfortune happens to them they charge that upon it. Hence you find the first explorers of every country always underrate its value. Who does not remember that, shortly after the close of the last war, President Monroe sent commissioners into the Territory of Michigan for the purpose of selecting lands upon which to locate military bounty land warrants? Those intelligent commissioners, after spending one year in Michigan and traveling all over it, reported officially to the War Department that there was no land in that Territory susceptible of cultivation. [Laughter.]

ANDREW P. BUTLER [S. C.]—Julius Cæsar reported the same thing of England.

SENATOR UNDERWOOD.—My country was called "Barrens."

SENATOR DOUGLAS.—My friend from Kentucky has reminded me that the country where he lives was once called the "Barrens." That brings to my mind a thing which used to puzzle me very much when I first emigrated to the State of Illinois. .I found that the State was divided into prairie country and barrens. The barrens consisted of portions of land on the borders of the prairies that had grown up to shrub oaks; but after a while the people cultivated the barrens and raised better wheat on them than on the prairies.

I could not find out, at that time, how it was that the best land in the State was called barrens. The people told me they did not know how it was, but that the Kentuckians, who were some of the first settlers, came over there and named it barrens, and it was said that it was a sort of Kentucky notion that the best lands in any country must be called barrens. [Laughter.] The first settlers who came from Virginia found a part of Kentucky so destitute of timber and of water that they thought it ought certainly to be called barrens. They passed round it, and settled every other nook and corner in the State, and even ascended the mountains, and fixed themselves in their deep gorges, in preference to entering these barren wastes. In later years other people went and settled upon these lands, and it was found that these spots called barrens were among the very best lands in the Mississippi valley or on the broad continent of America.

I remember that my intelligent friend from Connecticut [Mr. Smith], when we had the subject of annexing California before us, made a speech, in which he described utter desolation as pervading every valley, and every stream, and every mountain top in the whole Territory. But we find out now, sir, that the only trouble in regard to California is that it is so productive that it is actually asserted that when a man plants a ten-acre patch of potatoes, he has got to rent an adjoining tract to pile them up on. [Laughter.] And until I saw some Californians, who returned from that country, I could not comprehend the story that I heard from a gentleman who was in Texas several years ago. He said that while traveling through that country he entered the camp of a distinguished general who was in command of the Texan army, and there he found a fellow sitting on one end of a sweet potato while he was roasting the other in the fire. [Laughter.]

Sir, I am under the impression that the vast regions of desert in the slopes on either side of the mountains west of the Mississippi will disappear before investigation and settlement, in the way that other deserts have.

On February 5 Andrew P. Butler [S. C.] opposed the bill.

Mr. President, we are engaged in the consideration of a bill of unusual importance, and it seems to be assumed, as I understand, that it is to be carried through this body and through the other House by the momentum of its own magnitude.

The reason given by the friends of this bill, why we should not have such lights before us as are usually consulted in such cases, is because this is a measure whose magnificence puts at defiance everything that has preceded it, either in the Congress of the United States, or in any other deliberative body of the world. A measure, the success of which must therefore depend more upon the chances of blind fortune than upon the counsels of wisdom or lights of experience.

Since I have been referred to as one that may have constitutional objections to this measure, I will present, by way of illustration, a proposition involving principles the same as those of this bill which many of the gentlemen now advocating it have condemned as opposed to party creed, upon the ground that it was subject to the same objections which I might well urge to it now. Suppose the proposition, once made, to construct a Federal road from Buffalo to this city, and hence on to New Orleans, were now to be revived. Gentlemen would then take party alarm, and cry out that this savors of a general system of *internal improvement,* and violates the cardinal doctrines of the Democratic creed. In principle, the cases supposed cannot be distinguished from the measure under consideration, for this bill proposes to make a railroad to run through two or more of the States west of the Mississippi by the direct appropriation of money from the Federal treasury. The difference, then, between these systems of internal improvement is simply the fact that part of the Pacific road runs over territory, and that a desert belonging to all the United States—a distinction that cannot avail gentlemen unless they are prepared to give up conviction or party professions to the force of interest and the temptations of sectional aggrandizement; to this complexion it must come at last. They cannot even lay the flattering unction to their souls, which seems to have sustained Mr. Jefferson, in his disregard of the Constitution, by the purchase of Louisiana, upon the broad doctrine of *State necessity.* Such a doctrine might afford a place of refuge for a virtuous and wise magistrate, acting under the duress of necessity, while it might become a dangerous hiding-place for selfish expediency or criminal ambition. Gentlemen do not pretend to plead this necessity: indeed, they cannot, for a communication with California can be now had, within thirty days, by the ocean and Panama route. And when a railroad shall be completed, at some one of the many points in contemplation across the isthmus, it is very doubtful whether this one will have any advantages over it. In a commercial point of view, it is a common opinion that there will be none. These natural facilities of communication seem to have been pointed out by the finger of God, while this road to be indicated, without reconnoissance or survey, will be the work of guessing man.

Now, Mr. President, let gentlemen look at it. Is not this a measure of internal improvements, to be constructed by the direction and the means of the Federal Government?—not by the direction of the Federal Government, in its full meaning, but one of its departments—the executive. It is but an illustration of many of the lessons of history that doctrine and principle melt and crumble under the temptations of interest. Creeds and party platforms are but as barriers of sand against the tide of power and the force of local combinations.

Mr. President, we are standing on the threshold of an eventful future. We are about to embark upon a system that will swallow up all others, and will increase the tendency of this Government, once a free confederacy of Republican States, to become a consolidated empire. We are departing from old landmarks and entering upon a boundless wilderness of unknown powers, without chart and without compass. We are committing our destinies to the discretion of irresponsible legislation, instead of allowing it to be controlled and protected by the obligations and the guaranties of a written and once-respected Constitution.

Mr. President, I have lived too long and seen too much of the predeterminations upon subjects of this kind to enter here upon discussions that are regarded as the stale notions of our ancestors under the tide of what is called *progressive democracy.* Yes, sir, I have seen enough to convince me that the machinery of this Government, in its actual operation, is stronger than the Constitution. The law of progress has superseded the law of the Constitution. I was reminded by a friend, no longer ago than last night, of the futility of resisting what is called the progressive tendency of the age. The question was asked me:

X—12

Will you continue to think with your ancestors? I will give the same reply to you that I gave to him: I am willing to obey the law of progress, for we would not fulfill the great designs of Providence if we were to oppose it. But to conform to that law, as I would have it observed, it must be regulated by wisdom, freedom, and justice; otherwise it becomes rash, slavish, and aggressive—running into the doctrine that "might makes right." Under the influence of this law, as I have heard it so often interpreted upon this floor, conservative restraint and guidance are looked upon as stupid impediments, restraining the wisdom and suppressing the genius of Young America.

In looking at all nature, I find there are salutary vetoes upon the unrestrained energies and impulses of progress. No nation, or great people, ever attained security and greatness by a disregard of these wise lessons, and a disregard of them, even in our own history, characterized as it is by such wonderful developments, would be like Apollo giving up to Phaëton the reins of the horses of the Sun. It is a law to be conducted very much as the concerns of society are, under the impulsive energy of youth and the restraining wisdom of age.

Shall we trust this law of progress to the judgment, I would rather say the decision, of an unrestrained majority, having no other control than the wisdom of its discretion and the policy of progression? Those who are for trusting alone to the impulsive energy of progress may sow the seeds of the storm and reap the whirlwind. I have not more caution than other men, but surely I may be permitted, at least, to appeal to *conservative principles* and the *spirit* of the *Constitution* to save us from the dangers of acceleration and the consequences of transgression.

And now, so far from my suffering the Constitution of the United States to restrain this great law of progress, I say that it ought to have been consulted, and its expansibility ought to have been developed, in order to embrace everything that would accommodate it to this law of progress. Sir, the Constitution within itself contains the very element of self-existence—the provision of amendment. Have you amended it? Have you not practically disregarded that provision which allowed the Constitution to expand with the progress of events? Let this be answered; there stands the Constitution a dead letter, in many respects, I will not say in all. You have not expanded it by the wise interposition of the legislature, allowed by the instrument itself, to amend it according to the exigencies of the change of human affairs. But what have you done? I intend to speak boldly, and freely, and fearlessly before the Senate upon that subject. If I had the eloquence of Cicero, I might pay a decent tribute to the memory of the Constitution; but I could not restore it no more than he could restore the life and virtue of the Roman Senate, over which he wept in such strains of eloquence as have survived Rome itself, and given immortality to the memory of the violated institutions of the commonwealth as it existed in the days of its primitive purity and simplicity, and before they were tarnished by Augustan casuistry or imperial pollution. The Constitution has not been amended and expanded to accommodate itself to the progress of events. But what has been resorted to to supply that wise provision? Construction—a construction like India rubber that accommodates itself to the interests of those who choose to avail themselves of the Constitution whenever an advantage is to be gained by any measure. And *compromises* where there is no provision of the Constitution. I say, deceptive and dangerous *compromises,* to be violated whenever there is a temptation to do so; and platforms, deceptive, fallacious platforms, to whip parties into harness and to keep them there, and scarcely for any other purpose. These are the miserable expedients that have been resorted to to supply the place of amendments to the Constitution. If I am to be reproached because I appeal to the spirit of that sacred instrument, allow me to say that I have been doing more to preserve this Union and the integrity of the institutions of this Confederacy than those who blindly obey the aggressive spirit of progress. Progress, left entirely to legislative discretion, is a law without limit or certain direction, and must vary according to the fluctuation of the times and the temptations of men. It is as easy to obey it as to float with the current, but would be as unwise as to follow that current without knowing over what cataracts it may fall. It would be like committing the vessel to the wind, without rudder or compass. To make it safe in a political point of view, it "must have a right direction, and be kept within constitutional limits."

The last resort which an intelligent people should make is to revolution for the vindication of their rights, and the greatest danger of such a resort will be a disregard of the organic law of existence. When it shall be ascertained that this Confederacy, in the name of its Union, shall have survived the Constitution of its existence, it deserves to perish.

On February 18 Senator Cooper again spoke against the bill.

Sir, our friends on the other side of the chamber used to be terrified by a monster which had its den in my own good State—the bank of the United States—and they supposed that with its capital of $35,000,000 it had it in its power to break down and trample under foot the liberties of the country. Sir, are the powers that are conferred here of a character which would be likely to permit of an unwholesome exercise, such as in the case of a bank? In my judgment they permit of greater abuse. I have seen, in a neighboring State, the influence of these railroad corporations. There are two or three railroads, not, perhaps, more than four hundred or five hundred miles in extent, and yet they control, politically, socially, and morally, the whole population of that State. They make and they unmake at pleasure. And let a railroad of this kind be built across the continent; let the company have at its command the transportation of the commodities of the whole eastern world, as you are told it will—supposing that fuel and everything else can be found in sufficient abundance to make the communication between the East and the West in this way practicable and easy—and what kind of powers will it possess? Unexampled in the history of the world. I repeat, I cannot particularize in what way it might affect the public interests; how it might eventually be used to the danger of the public liberties. There are things in the future which wisdom cannot foresee. It is not necessary that I should particularize, that I should, in short, do that which is impossible to be done; but it is enough to repeat that possessing such powers as it will possess, and such vast pecuniary resources, it will use them as other corporations have used theirs, and it will abuse them as other corporations have abused them. There is nothing more certain than this.

I agree in many of the suggestions which have been made as) the value of this great enterprise of the Pacific Railroad. I think it will be one of the most magnificent that human genius and human skill have carried out and perfected. But this is nothing to the purpose. It can only be thus magnificent, it can only add to the character and the grandeur of this country by being what it ought to be—as perfect as possible. I therefore, in view of the character of the country, desire that this enterprise shall be undertaken upon such principles as will insure as much perfection as possible. I desire that we shall not disgrace American genius by hurrying forward into a great enterprise of this kind, and making it a miserable patchwork thing, when it ought to be one grand and magnificent whole, honorable to the skill and genius of the country, as it will be beneficent to the world.

Senator Cooper was followed by Henry S. Geyer [Mo.] who spoke in favor of the bill.

The Senator from Pennsylvania supposes that, although Congress can be trusted in the location of the road, and in the bargain which it will make for the construction of it, when it is made, influences may be brought to bear upon them hereafter by which a much larger and unlimited expenditure may be made. If the Senator had looked at the bill carefully he would have seen that that contingency was not likely to arise, because the bonds are to be issued as the road is built by sections; and, if there is a failure to construct any section of fifty miles, there is a forfeiture of all the work that has been done, and not another dollar or another acre of land will go into the hands of the company.

SENATOR COOPER.—The Senator misconstrues my argument. My argument is that, although the amount of twenty millions was fixed in the bill, and the number of acres, though not fixed, is ascertainable by calculation, yet, if it became necessary, this company would have it in its power, by its pressure upon Congress, to obtain as much more as was necessary. It does not matter at all whether Congress is subject to such influences or not; it does not affect my argument at all. I may have been wrong, but, if I was right in supposing that Congress was subject to such influences, my argument was good.

SENATOR GEYER.—The argument is one in favor of a dissolution of this Union, or at least of the incompetency of Congress. If a great and beneficent measure cannot be compassed, because we cannot trust Congress, we had better cease to legislate. Sir, I do not believe that any influences can be brought to bear upon a future Congress which cannot be brought to bear upon this. There are influences adverse to this measure. There are the roads across the isthmus. There is the influence of the Atlantic cities, which want the ocean transportation, and which would be somewhat reluctant to erect a rival road. Why, even now we are so very solicitous to get a means of transportation across Tehuantepec that there is a threat of war. We are to seize it *per fas et nefas*,[1] to get a line of transportation between the Atlantic seaports and the Pacific. We would prefer to go to war, and hazard all the expenditure of blood and

[1] "Right or wrong."

money to which it would lead, and the calamities which it would bring upon us, than to give it up.

Another objection to the bill is that the work is to be committed to individuals, who, in consequence of its magnitude, will have a fearful power. Sir, when we look at the thirteenth section of the bill—which is all that it contains about a corporation—we shall see that its powers are very limited; more so than those of any railroad corporation in the State of Pennsylvania. To contend that these powers may be abused is to contend that no corporation should ever be created; nay, sir, that no trust shall be confided to any individual, for it is liable to be abused. But in this country we have no reason to apprehend any great abuse of power. If the corporation should exceed its powers, we have a judicial tribunal that will rebuke it. Its powers may be tested by the same law and by the same tribunal that our rights of property are inquired into.

But the alarm is in the name "corporation." The honorable Senator from South Carolina [Mr. Butler] intimated that within the States it was clearly unconstitutional, though with their consent, and of doubtful constitutionality, to say the least of it, within the Territories. I will not enter at large into the argument of the power of Congress to incorporate a body of men employed by them to do a work under an acknowledged power under the Constitution; but I would ask the honorable Senator what is a territorial government but a municipal corporation? You have two bills now on your table, one to incorporate the inhabitants of the Territory of Washington, so called, and the other of Nebraska—municipal corporations with general legislative powers—an "abdication," in the language of the Senator from Ohio, of the power of Congress to legislate. Sir, if it be an "abdication" to intrust any person with the execution of work for which it is in the power of Congress to provide, the Constitution has been broken at almost every session of Congress from the time it was first signed down to the present day.

Senator James M. Mason [Va.] followed with a speech against the bill.

This is not a new subject. Those with whom I have always acted in public life have denied the power of Congress to appropriate either money or land for the purpose of internal improvement. They have denied to Congress the power by any agency, either directly or indirectly, to construct works of internal im-

provement; but this bill, by one fell swoop, declares, as an order of the Congress of the United States, that it shall be done;
and that, if it cannot be done by ordinary legislation, it shall
be done by the fiat of executive will. What is the discretion
given to the Executive? The Executive is to determine, upon
the whole Mississippi border, and upon the whole Pacific border—on the east and on the west—where this road is to begin,
and where it is to end. You will see at once the immense discretion vested in the Executive, and the inordinate power that
it gives him when it invests him with that discretion. Why, he
may control the legislation of a whole district of country, of
whole tiers of States, by his will, in fixing where this road is to
begin and where it is to end. But that is nothing in the world
to gentlemen. The destinies of this country are well confided
to an Executive, who is not responsible to the Constitution, provided they can get the road. Could such a power as this be
given to the Executive, unless there was an interest behind it
greater than the control of constitutional obligation—that interest with which gentlemen are so much impressed here—the
indispensable importance of having this road? But that is not
the only power. He is to fix the termini, and, in the vague language of the bill, he is to fix all the important intermediate
points. He is to control the immense interests that will be involved in and affected by this work, between the North and the
South, by his fiat alone. The representatives of the people in
the other branch of Congress and of the States in this branch
are not to be consulted in this matter. Everything that pertains
to legislation and the expenditure of the public money, or to
the regulation and adjustment of the vast and great interests of
the different portions of the Confederacy, I had thought were by
the Constitution vested in Congress; but the bill takes them from
Congress, great and extensive as they are, and leaves them to the
discretion of a single man. Why, we all know—gentlemen here
admit—the conflict that will arise whenever it is determined
what route this road shall take; whether it shall go to the north
or to the south. They know the immense influence it will exercise in building up the section of country where it goes, and in
injuring that where it does not go. Yet, gentlemen say, so in-
dispensably necessary is it to have the road that they will take
all the power from the representatives of the people and vest
it in executive discretion alone.

Mr. President, there is but one term, in my judgment, which
will characterize a measure of this kind. It is a *rape* of the
Constitution. The Constitution has vested these powers in the

legislature. The bill wrests them from the legislature, and confides them to an irresponsible Executive; for he is not responsible under the Constitution for the exercise of this discretion.

What is the next power? The Executive is to make the contracts—these immense contracts which are to involve an expense, as all admit, of at least $100,000,000. The Executive is to make these contracts and to dispose of them at his discretion. Congress has no part nor lot in making them. The people of the United States create one agency, through their representatives, by which the public money is to be expended; but it is given by this bill, almost by rapine, to an irresponsible Executive. And the bill instigates the President to dispense, as far as practicable, with preliminary surveys. The language of the bill is that he shall act under it "at an early day." And that emphatic language is repeated in a subsequent part of the bill, instigating him to go immediately to work, to determine where the road is to go, and at an early day commence its construction. Is this the language of solidity of judgment? Is it language which becomes the representatives of the States of this Confederacy when they are ordering an expenditure of some $100,000,000 of the public money? It is to be done at an early day—almost with indecent haste.

Sir, there is another clause in that bill, one that struck me with extraordinary force. It is proposed to pass through the Territories of the United States by the potentiality of a law of Congress, and it is proposed to pass through the States by the assent of the States. That is to say that, if the States assent to be invaded by this Federal power, then the Federal power is to construct the work within their limits. Now, I submit it to the honorable Senator from Texas, and I submit it to every Senator upon this floor, where do you find anywhere in the Constitution the power in a State to enlarge or curtail or qualify to any extent the power of the Federal Government. Is this to be added to the platform which was spoken of by the honorable Senator from South Carolina [Mr. Butler] as presenting a fundamental law more potent than the Constitution itself; that where the Constitution is silent any State can increase its power or enlarge it by its single assent? Sir, the language of the Constitution is this—and I beg to call the attention of Senators to it—that the laws made pursuant to the Constitution are supreme within the limits of the States, and when the Federal power goes into a State, armed with a law of Congress, it goes there with supreme power, and the State legislation bows before it. But by the terms of this bill the law of Congress goes

within the limits of a State, and asks that State to give its sanction to it. If this be the law of the Constitution, then it is in
the power of any State whatever to enlarge and amplify, or to
restrain and control it at its own pleasure. And yet the honorable Senator who reported this bill from the Special Committee I apprehend found himself under the necessity of so
construing the Constitution, in order to give his bill any value.

Again, sir: the bill creates a corporation, and a corporation to act where? To act through the whole Confederacy and
based upon the public treasury—not such a corporation as the
Bank of the United States, and, by the way, that never could be
chartered by Congress until, as was most eloquently said by a
Senator from Kentucky, now no longer living, they resorted to
almost every clause in the Constitution to find authority for it,
and he called it a vagrant power. Here is a corporation proposed to be created for the purpose of a Federal agency, based
upon the Federal treasury. And what is the corporation, and
who are the corporators? They are the body of the contractors
for the work. The President, then, is to control this corporation, for he selects the contractors. The President is to designate who these corporators are to be, and it is by his fiat, in
the exercise of the patronage given to him, that this corporation
is to be called into being. The bill offers these extraordinary
features. You are to bring a body of contractors to make this
railroad from the Pacific to the Mississippi, and you are to pay
them from the public treasury, partly in land and partly in
money. You pay them a full equivalent for the work they are
to do, and then, when you have done that, you create them into
a corporation and present them with the work, and they are to
draw the whole emoluments from it. Sir, this extraordinary
machinery it is found necessary to invoke in order to enable the
Federal Government to exercise a power not granted, and
through an agency unknown to the Constitution.

There is another provision in this bill, on which, in this connection, I should like to comment. The provision is this, one
that the Senator from Illinois [Mr. Douglas] said, a few days
ago, furnished ample security to the Government: that, if the
contractor fails to comply with his contract, his work shall be
forfeited. Forfeited! And who ever heard of a forfeiture enforced which was caused by a failure of that kind? Why, sir,
between man and man, equals in society, the courts of justice
are open, for the purpose of relieving a party from such forfeiture. It is done every day. Forfeitures are odious in law, even
between man and man, and what would be a forfeiture between

a citizen and the Government? It would not be enforced; and, if it were enforced, what becomes of the property? Where do you find a clause in the Constitution making this Government the residuary legatee of a bankrupt contractor, to take his effects and administer them for the benefit of Government? But by the provisions of this bill it is declared that, if he do not comply with his contract, Government may take not only the work he has done, but his effects, being the residuary legatee of the bankrupt contractor. Sir, it will never be done. If the contractor fails to comply with his contract, and remains there ready to go on, he will be reinstated, especially if he is a pet of the Executive or has political influence.

I should like to know—for it has been a part of my professional duty to be engaged in the construction of laws—what is the meaning of the bill when it says, in the thirteenth section, the corporators are to be "the contractors, their associates and successors." Who are the associates? I can understand who the contractors are. Thomas Wilson proposes to contract to build a certain portion of road for a given sum; or Thomas Wilson and John Thompson, with others, propose to contract. They are associated together, but they are the contractors. But who are to be the associates of the contractors?

THOMAS G. PRATT [Md.].—Those who take stock.

SENATOR MASON.—What is the stock for? Stock in what? Railroad stock, I presume, in the "Pacific Railroad and Telegraph Company," inviting subscriptions by an association with the contractors making them a part of the corporators, and entitling them to part of the profits. I should like to see the machinery by which that could be done. I should like to see how these certificates of stock will read; I should like to see them presented to the President for his approbation, to be conferred upon his pet class of contractors. I should like to see the privileges and immunities and advantages that the Executive patronage may deal out to these contractors, or their associates, or successors. Who are the "successors"? The bill says, "the contractors, their associates, and successors." I suppose they are the assignees of the stockholders.

Well, if we are to have a joint stock company, in which the United States Government is to hold barren stock, and the contractors and associates the profitable or productive stock, if that is the character of it, if the Government of the United States goes in with millions of dollars, in money and lands, to be used at the discretion of the President, and any number of contractors and associates come in with an unlimited amount of stock, and the Government stock is to be barren, and the contractors' stock is to be productive, let it be so understood by the country.

Mr. President, there was a day in this Republic when we were accustomed to scan carefully and closely executive power. The fathers of the Republic transmitted it to us as a legacy that we should scan all power, and more especially the power of the Executive. But what does this bill do? It not only gives him the power, but it gives it to him alone. This immense body of corporators, with $100,000,000 of barren stock on the part of the Government, and an unlimited issue of their own, are to be handed over to the President as the source of its authority and the dispenser of its influence and patronage.

There is another provision in this bill, which authorizes the President to employ such military officers and troops as he may deem necessary. It puts the army of the United States at the disposal of this immense corporation.

How much of the army is to be required for this purpose nobody can tell; but if the distance be, as is said, from two thousand to three thousand miles from the Mississippi to the Pacific, and through a large portion of which you are to meet predatory and hostile bands of Indians—if you allow five soldiers to every ten miles, you have a large army employed at once. The military of the United States will not be equal to the duty unless the army be increased for the purpose of protecting this body of corporators.

Mr. President, who doubts how this bill will be construed if it becomes a law? Who doubts how it will be carried into effect? Who can now resist, in far smaller matters, the tremendous collateral pressure of capital that is every day at the doors of the Senate? Capital is a power so potent that we are told monarchs reel before it upon their thrones. We are told every day that the strongest monarchs of Europe are powerless before the Rothschilds and the Barings, and it is true. How do we stand in this country? We have no Rothschilds or Barings, but we have men who aspire to be such: men who wield capital potentially, who, it may be, without actual bribery and corruption, bring a thousand influences to operate, which are not known until they are felt. Yes, sir, pass this bill into a law, and you will begin the work, utterly ignorant whether you will ever be able to finish it; and that is to be the character of the legislation of an American Senate at this early day of our Republic!

Mr. President, if this bill becomes a law there will be no

longer parties in this country except the party in power and the party in opposition. The whole character of the Government will be changed, never to be reclaimed; and it will have been done by gold, and, worse than all, by gold out of the public treasury. The Constitution will be gone. There will be no appeal to that, and the Government will be one of unlimited power.

Sir, this bill, with its appropriation of a hundred millions, will make a breach in the Constitution through which everything will pass. It will be perfectly idle, after such a power, to talk about the tenets of party. After that, the only parties will be the party in power and the party in opposition, and the party in power will have no restraint or control but the will of a majority. I would recall to the Senate the vaticinations of one of our greatest men and most gifted statesmen—a statesman to whom at his death the honorable Senator from Texas paid a beautiful tribute of feeling and sensibility. I refer to the illustrious Calhoun. When the order was given by the President of the United States to march an army to the frontier of Mexico, Mr. Calhoun said to his friends, "It dropped a curtain between me and futurity; I cannot see beyond that." It was, in his view, the first aggressive march taken by an American army; and said that prophetic man, "It dropped a curtain between me and the future." "I told my friends," said he, "that here closed the first book of the history of this Republic; the second book is unwritten and unread." Mr. President, if that man were here now, he would find the curtain lifted. He would see something written which is to go into the next book of American history; and it is written on the pages of this bill. It is a measure forced upon the country. Honorable Senators may say that it is forced upon the country because we have these Pacific possessions, and cannot get to them without it.

Sir, I shall deeply deplore the passage of this bill. I make no factious opposition to it, and I have made none. Sir, the State of Virginia will be as deeply interested in access to the Pacific as any other of the Atlantic States. She is very deeply interested; but the State of Virginia, I trust, never will take it at the expense of the Constitution which she has bound herself to support. This bill cannot stand with the Constitution. You must take one or the other; and, if you take the bill, you make a breach in the Constitution through which everything can pass. I move that the bill be referred to the Committee on Roads and Canals.

Isaac Toucey [Conn.] on February 19 spoke against the bill.

What, I ask, will be the condition of this Western country fifty years hence with a dense population, with a line of States across the continent, with this colossal corporation, with its immense commercial business, vast beyond any present conception? Sir, I tell you that the States which will exist in the vicinity of this road, which will embrace the line of the road, will make war upon it. They will not consent to have this colossal corporation overriding them in the hands of the money power of this country, transporting for their own profit the great commerce that will find its way through that channel to and from the different continents of the world. The States will make war upon this corporation. It will be a war whether the corporation can exist. It will be a war whether you can exercise the power that you have reserved in this bill of regulating merchandise and passengers in crossing this road. It will be a war whether this act of Congress can override the sovereignty of those States. It will be a war with this Government; aye, sir, with its own government, whether the men now upon the stage of action, by assenting to the exercise of a jurisdiction of this kind, can debar the generation that will then be conducting the affairs of the country from exerting the usual legislative powers of their government for the management of their own internal affairs.

Joseph R. Underwood [Ky.] followed with a speech in favor of the bill.

If you cannot create a corporation, you have undertaken to protect them in foreign countries, when created by others. You did that in the treaty with New Granada. You did the same thing by the Clayton-Bulwer treaty. I want the people of the United States to consider these *democratic* ideas advanced here. Government, according to the Democratic creed, has no power to establish a corporation by which we may execute a great national object and fulfill our constitutional powers and duties. But, if other nations will form one by which we can derive benefit, we can go into treaty guaranties to defend that corporation, on foreign ground, in the execution of its work. The interest which we have in, and the benefits which we derive from, the action of foreign corporations may be such that we can pledge the whole force of the country, the army and the navy, to defend these corporations and protect them against all dangers; but we cannot find the power to do for ourselves, at home and upon our own territory, the same things which we can go to war to protect foreign corporations in doing for us abroad! I ask the people if we can pledge the whole force of the country and go to war in order to protect a foreign corporation in which we may have an incidental advantage, in order to secure a right of way and a free passage across the Isthmus of Darien, may we not make a corporation and build a road for ourselves in our own country? If, under the Constitution, we may rightfully go to war and fight, to protect the railroad from Chagres to Panama, or a ship canal from Lake Nicaragua to the Pacific Ocean, so that we may travel these routes in going to California and Oregon, why may we not, under the same Constitution, shorten our line of travel thousands of miles by building a railroad all the way within our own country? If you can do the one, by virtue of the post office, commercial and military powers of the Constitution, why will not these powers enable you to do the other also? I cannot perceive a reason for the difference, and, if I had the power of the people, I would cast overboard all politicians who pretend that there is a difference.

Mr. President, I want the country to understand another thing which I see here whenever gentlemen from the seaboard get up to offer an argument or make a speech on subjects of this kind. Sir, in 1789, when our Constitution went into operation, we had a little settlement—it deserves no other name than that when compared with things as they exist at this time—a little strip of settlements along the salt water, and the Contitution at that time seems to have been puffed up by a sort of salt-water impregnation. It has certainly brought forth a spawn of all kind of improvements for the seaboard and little or nothing for the interior. One of the salt-water constructions of the Constitution is that the interior States of the Union—although the Constitution expressly gives to Congress the right to regulate commerce between the several States, and of course through the several States—are to be entirely dependent upon the seaboard States for a channel of commercial communication through their borders. They assume the sole right of making railroads, and of taxing travel and transportation, just as they please and as much as they please. They can neglect to keep common highways in repair, in order to force the citizens of other States to use and pay tolls upon artificial works. They may refuse to grant facilities in constructing direct lines of railroad or canal between important commercial points in order to force the citizens of other States to travel circuitous routes to promote local interests and the sectional schemes of particular States. This has already been done by Pennsylvania, if I am correctly informed, in refusing the Baltimore and Ohio Railroad a direct route across her territory to Wheeling. Sir, if the doctrine be conceded that this Government can, under no circumstances, make a road or canal in or through a State, then may the seaboard States prescribe what terms they please to the people of the interior States as to the manner in which they shall reach the ocean, that common highway of all nations. They may block up all dirt roads and turnpikes, and compel all travelers and merchants to seek transportation for themselves and property on such railroads or canals and under such tolls as shall be prescribed by a local and sectional policy. Sir, I protest against any such doctrine. It is no answer to tell me that the States will never do these things. That is not the question. If they should do so, have I any remedy? If they cut me off from the ocean, have I a right to appeal to Congress to give me a right of way and a commercial road, so that I may enjoy the privilege of getting to the ocean?

SENATOR BUTLER.—Do I understand the Senator from Kentucky to lay down the broad principle that if Kentucky, or if a corporation created by Congress, should design having a road, by way of regulating commerce, it could be done as against the consent of the State of Tennessee, Georgia, or South Carolina, through those States?

SENATOR UNDERWOOD.—I shall lay down this proposition: that if Tennessee shall undertake to say that the people of Kentucky shall not, with their wagons and produce, pass through her territory to get to Georgia, Alabama, or Mississippi, then the people of Kentucky have a right to appeal to Congress to open a way for them, and to guarantee a safe passage through it, so that they may freely trade with the people of the South.

SENATOR BUTLER.—That is not the proposition. But have you a right to go through by a road to be created by Congress?

SENATOR UNDERWOOD.—If the object cannot be accomplished in any other way, I have.

SENATOR BUTLER.—I wanted to make the proposition pretty broad.

SENATOR UNDERWOOD.—Just as broad as you choose to have it. I maintain, if the State of Tennessee should declare to the people whom I represent, "You shall not go to Georgia, to Alabama, or even to South Carolina, through my territory; you may go around by the way of Virginia and North Carolina, if you please, or you may cross the Father of Waters and go around by Arkansas and Mississippi, but you shall not pass through Tennessee," and undertake to enforce the declaration, that I have a remedy for the evil in the legislation of the Congress of the United States, and in the judiciary of the United States, to abrogate and annul all State laws which obstruct free intercommunication and commerce between the several States. Sir, there is no danger that Tennessee will ever deny Kentuckians the right to pass through her borders as freely as her own citizens; but, if she should be so unmindful of good neighborship, and attempt to do it, I believe her legislation, to accomplish such an object, would be void, as an infraction of the Constitution of the United States, upon two grounds: first, it would be directly in conflict with that provision of the Federal Constitution which declares that "the citizens of each State shall be entitled to all privileges and immunities of citizens in the several States"; second, it would conflict with the rights of intercommunication and commerce among the several States, which can alone be regulated by Congress, and which are clearly guaranteed to the people of every State by the Federal Constitution. The power to regulate "commerce among the several States" is part of the same clause which grants to Congress power "to regulate commerce with foreign nations." The powers are identical, and a State can no more interfere with the internal trade and intercourse among the several States than it can interfere with the same thing with foreign nations. We have, from the origin of the Government, improved and preserved harbors for the benefit of foreign commerce. We have passed law after law, under Democratic administrations as well as Whig, to improve the Mississippi and other rivers for the benefit of internal commerce. Now, if we can improve upon nature, and make rivers and harbors for commercial purposes better than they were, will not the same reasons justify us in building a road? Sir, we have the power, and we ought to exercise it whenever any State shall undertake to cripple and regulate the travel and commerce of another State upon local motives and sectional considerations.

Sir, if that power is not already in the Constitution it ought to be there. I think it is there. If it is not there what is the consequence? You allow the seaboard States of the Union to regulate the business of the interior States at their pleasure; you allow a seaboard State to cut off an interior State from access to the ocean, except upon terms which that seaboard State may prescribe. If this Government is nothing but a confederation—though I deny that—but if it is nothing but a confederation, and each State can make its own transit laws, just as it pleases, governing persons and property in passing through its territory, imposing onerous taxes in the shape of railroad tolls, and setting slaves free, as has recently been done, my word for it, such a confederation will not last. Sir, the people of my State will never consent that the State of Louisiana shall block up the mouth of the Mississippi and prevent their access to the ocean, or allow Louisiana to tax their commerce and navigation upon that stream. That is a good illustration. Will the gentleman from South Carolina [Mr. Butler], when he comes to make his speech, say that Louisiana has a right to block up the mouth of the Mississippi, and prevent Kentuckians from going down to the gulf and thence across the ocean to any country of the world? The Senator from Virginia [Mr. Mason], though I think he carried his doctrine a little too far, contended for a right of way across the Isthmus of Tehuantepec upon legal principles. If we may insist upon a right of way over foreign territory, much more may we insist upon a similar right across a State of this Union. If Tennessee will not give or allow that right to the people of Kentucky, how are we to get it?

SENATOR BUTLER.—Tennessee will allow you to use her roads as she uses them, but will not build one because you want it built.

SENATOR UNDERWOOD.—Suppose she will not. I have no right to ask her to build a road for my use. But suppose she makes a law against my using the roads she builds for herself, or imposes such conditions on me that I cannot comply, and consequently cannot use her roads, then what is my remedy? I cannot go to war with her, because the Constitution ties my hands in that respect. What remedy have I? There is none on earth, unless it is found in the powers of the Federal Constitution. Sir, I want the people to think about these things. Some gentlemen, when they come to construe the Constitution of the United States, construe it as if all the means for executing the powers of Government, except those known in 1787, are illegitimate, and cannot be resorted to. I think that if Wise, the aëronaut, should ever teach us to navigate the atmosphere successfully, we may use balloons, and just as many of them as we please. And I also think, when it comes to that, no State, under the ideas of "State Rights," and "State sovereignty," and the old common-law notion of owning from the center *"usque ad cœlum,"* [1] could rightfully prevent the passage of the

[1] "Clear to the sky."

X—13

balloons of Congress over her territory. I believe that Congress may make roads over and through the territories of the States whenever they are "necessary and proper" auxiliaries in executing constitutional powers. I believe that Congress may properly execute the powers of the Constitution by using the most appropriate means furnished by the inventions of the age in which we live, and that it is both "necessary and proper" to avail ourselves of all means to accomplish constitutional ends which science and *"progress"* have made since the Government commenced its operations.

If Congress shall erect its own lines of telegraph, and allow the President to appoint sworn officers to transmit his orders (and that might be necessary to prevent publicity), what reason can be assigned against doing it, unless it be that such a thing was not known at the origin of the Government in 1789, or even as late as the enlightened age of the Virginia resolutions of '98? I insist that Morse's telegraph may be adopted as legitimate and constitutional means by which the President may transmit his orders. I do not know that this argument has been presented before to the country, and I want the people to see it. Here is a clear power given the commander-in-chief to issue orders to the military and naval forces of the country. These orders must be sent by some means. Science has discovered a new mode of communicating intelligence. Can we use it? And, if so, can a State prevent our using it, and arrest the erection of the posts and wires in her territory, any more than she could prevent our courier from passing under whip and spur through her borders? Like the gentleman from Michigan [Mr. Cass], I hold that the powers of Congress do not at all depend upon the consent of the States.

This bill, in my judgment, presents no question of constitutional power. We, the present Congress, have found power in the Constitution, by adopting the Wheeling bridge as a post road, to save it from abatement as a nuisance, under the decision of the Supreme Court. If we have power to prevent pulling a bridge down, we can build it. If we can protect a bridge, or build a bridge over a river within a State, under our post office powers, we can make a road and preserve it. This body, in the Wheeling bridge case, has settled the constitutionality of this bill. But, if it must be argued over and over again, then I say that speed and facility of concentrating supplies and soldiers is military strength and power. To defend our possessions on the Pacific, the railroad would be invaluable. You know that a navy of your enemy is sailing around Cape

Horn. Let us have a national telegraph, and orders can be given with the rapidity of thought; troops can be concentrated as circumstances require, your country defended. But start your courier—give him relays of the fleetest race horses, keep him mounted on the back of Henry or Eclipse, Boston or Fashion, and let him distance the wild Comanche on the open plains, and beat the antelope in the mountains; and yet, sir, before he can deliver an order or a warning, your Pacific possessions may be invaded, your army captured in detail, your ships sunk, and your commerce ruined.

Why, sir, destruction of life by thousands, and loss of property by millions in value, may be saved, and the Union preserved from dismemberment, by the proposed railroad and telegraph; and yet we are told gravely, at this day, that there is no constitutional power to construct them. In other words, we are gravely told that the organic functions of the Government are so imbecile that it lacks the capacity of self-preservation. If this be true, its rickety existence will soon perish, and but few mourners will weep at the grave. Let the people look into these things, and hold to accountability, as I shall do when I retire from this body, all those who virtually deny to this Government the necessary powers of self-defence, saying, if the States will not or cannot build railroads and telegraphs where they are wanted for national purposes, then we are to go without them. Sir, we might just as well call upon the States to build for us our steamships, manufacture our cannon, or furnish any other means of national defence.

WILLIAM H. SEWARD [N. Y.].—It is a hundred and fifty miles from New York to Albany.

SENATOR UNDERWOOD.—The Senator from New York says the distance is one hundred and fifty miles; will he tell me how many lighthouses there are in that distance?

SENATOR SEWARD.—There are five. [Laughter.]

SENATOR UNDERWOOD.—I saw a great many more, according to my recollection.

SENATOR SEWARD.—They are double reflectors. [Laughter.]

SENATOR UNDERWOOD.—The gentleman says they are *double reflectors,* and, if so, I should suppose a fewer number might answer the purpose of inducing us to *reflect twice* upon what I am about to state. I saw some other things as I passed up the river. I saw buoys to point out the channel. I saw these internal improvements made by Congress, with national funds, in the State, without the consent of the State, and without ever having asked its consent. That is the idea which I wish to bring to your mind. When and how did the idea originate that Congress might erect lighthouses and plant buoys without the consent of a State? It originated with the birth of the general Government, and it has been put in practice from that day to this. The idea sprang from the Constitution, correctly interpreted by its makers and the founders of the Government. The idea suited and promoted *salt-water* regions and *salt-water* interests. Then we had no interior. At length the fertile and great interior had opened her dense forests, and her agriculture sought means to reach foreign markets with her rich products. The great interior then wanted internal improvements of the same kind to benefit her commerce. But, when she applied to the general Government for them, she was met by a new generation of politicians—not statesmen—with the objection: "There is no constitutional power to gratify your wishes." To protect and aid commerce is the foundation on which the doctrine and practice originally stood. Now, I appeal to the common sense of mankind and ask, if our ancestors had constitutional power sixty years ago to aid commerce, by building lighthouses and planting buoys along the seaboard, may not their posterity aid commerce by building a railroad from the seaboard into the interior, without violating the Constitution?

Senator John B. Weller [Cal.], seeing the opposition to the corporation authorized in the bill, moved on February 21 to amend the measure by striking out this provision. This motion, however, had the disastrous effect of alienating some of its strongest supporters, such as Rusk and Underwood, and so doomed the bill to defeat. On this point Senator Weller spoke on February 22.

The bill came into the Senate lame, halting, impotent, and scarcely half made up. Notwithstanding the paternal care that was exercised over it by my friend from Texas, it came in here impotent for all practical purposes, impotent to carry out the objects he had in view—most potent so far as it violated principles heretofore considered sacred. He will therefore allow me to say this much in answer to the remarks of my friend from Texas, in derision of the amendment which I had the honor to propose to this bill. I was glad that he did see wisdom in that amendment. I am sorry, however, that he is now laboring to defeat the bill. But, sir, the Senator from Kentucky, who has taken his seat, thinks the mortal wound was inflicted when the corporation was stricken out.

SENATOR UNDERWOOD.—I do.

SENATOR WELLER.—Sir, that Senator belongs to a class of politicians who believe that nothing good can be accomplished except through the medium of a corporation. He would have a corporation to transact the most ordinary business of life!

SENATOR UNDERWOOD.—No, sir.

SENATOR WELLER.—If he desires the construction of a railroad, or that any labor shall be performed, or any public improvement made, he thinks it can be accomplished in no other way so well as through the aid of a corporation. I differ from him in regard to that point, and I therefore moved the other day to strike from this bill the section which incorporated these contractors into a great corporation, an overshadowing one, which, in my judgment, would, under the patronage of the general Government, have exercised a more disastrous influence than that which was exercised by the late Bank of the United States. With such a provision in it, I could not sustain the bill. The Senate, by a vote of nearly two-thirds, concurred with me in that opinion, and upon my motion this unconstitutional and dangerous provision was stricken from the bill. By that decisive vote, the favored corporation put in here by my friend from Texas, who claims to represent Democratic principles, was stricken out. That was an improvement; and I then began to think that there might be virtue enough in the bill to effect the object which so many of us had near to our hearts —the completion of a road to the Pacific. This amendment gave offence to the fathers of the bill, and hints were then thrown out that it was ruined. Wedded to the scheme which they reported, they could not be expected to look with a favorable eye upon any change which might be made. That corporation, as proposed by the committee, could have exercised all the privileges of bankers, and flooded the country with irredeemable paper money. The destruction of this feature of the bill alarmed the committee, and they began to show symptoms of abandonment.

Now, is the bill dead? My friend from Texas, who "is an honorable man," says that it is. An attempt was made to bury it this morning. Some of those who have claimed to be the especial friends of the bill joined in the effort. They failed. Now, I ask my friend from Texas to stand by me and sustain this bill, and I pledge what little reputation I may have in this country that there are plenty of contractors who would be glad to take contracts under it, not only for the construction of the road in his State, if that should be selected as the most desirable route, but for its construction from the Mississippi valley to the Pacific Ocean.

I know, and I admit, that the Senator from Texas has labored more assiduously than any Senator on this floor in the preparation of this bill; I know that all his energies—and great they are—have been devoted to accomplish this great national work; and that section of the Union from which I come owes him a deep debt of gratitude for the friendly interest he has exhibited in it. But I was sorry that, at the very moment when his power and influence were particularly required, at a time when the adoption of a simple amendment was calculated to give life and vigor to the bill by avoiding a constitutional difficulty, he abandoned it, and declared that it was dead, and that it remained for the Senate but to inter it. If he withholds his support, it can scarcely be expected that the bill will pass. If gentlemen have made up their minds to defeat it, they certainly can do so. On their heads the responsibility must rest.

SENATOR RUSK.—The honorable Senator from California says the bill came in lame, halting, deformed, and unfinished, until his master hand got hold of it, and then it became perfect. I am sorry to differ from my honorable friend in this particular; but I cannot vote for the bill as it now stands. I do not believe it will build the road. I am sure that in its present "perfected" form it will split up the road into three different pieces, and perhaps four; and I cannot vote for such a disjointed bill.

There have been appeals on both sides of the chamber to the country about the subject. Sir, I am not talking to the country. I have not been working for applause. I have been working for this railroad bill. I have no disposition to put the honor of killing Cock Robin upon anybody. Those who did it may divide the honor among them.

When I first reported the bill, the clause in relation to a corporation was the "rawhead and bloody bones" that troubled the conscience of some of my Democratic friends. I did not care six snaps of my finger for the corporation, and in fact I rather agreed to put it in, because I saw that it would draw the enemy's fire; that it would bring forward a great deal of patriotic thunder in opposition to that feature of the bill. Well, sir, in that I was right. We went on; thundering licks were struck; the artillery roared, and the small arms crashed against the terrible corporation; and I should have voted to strike it out myself, but I thought that if I did so some of these gentlemen would think they had frightened me off the track [laughter], and so I voted in a very small minority to keep it in, not, however, that I cared a sixpence about it.

After the corporation was stricken out, the first constitutional scruples that I heard of were brought forward against appropriating any money in the States. The idea started, and it rolled on with the fury of a hurricane, and out went that provision of the bill by a majority of two votes. The honorable Senator from California thinks that it made the bill a perfect instrument; made it an instrument by which the road could be built. There is a difference of opinion between us on this point. If I thought so, I should vote for it. It would be tolerably hard work for me to do it even then; but I would trust to Providence. As the bill now is, however, the road is divided up, and we have no means of controlling the ends of it. It is to be given by the States to railroad companies, who are to do as they please. We have no means of saying that passengers and freights shall pay only so much; the power has gone out of our hands, and we shall have no control over the subject in the States, because the very ground on which the amendment goes is that you have no constitutional power to control the road in the States.

Under such circumstances, believing that we have no further use for the bill, and, as the Senator from California does not appreciate my courtesy in keeping the bill up, I now announce to him distinctly that I want a favorable opportunity of putting my name on the record against the bill in its present shape, and that may go to the country also. Cock Robin is killed! As to who killed him I do not care six straws. He is dead. I expected to get a road, but I know that, under the provisions of the bill as it now stands, I cannot get one, and I do not care about the credit or discredit of it. I shall have the proud satisfaction of reflecting that I have performed my duty faithfully upon this important subject, and with that I must be content.

GEORGE BADGER [N. C.].—Mr. President, I am a very earnest and decided advocate for the establishment of this road, and in that I present no exception to the Senate generally. Everybody is in favor of the road.

SENATOR MASON.—No!

SENATOR BADGER.—The Senator from Virginia is not in favor of it?

SENATOR MASON.—Decidedly not.

SENATOR BADGER.—I am glad to hear there is one man not

in favor of it. Now I am sure that I am right since the Senator is against me in the main project. [Laughter.] I was about saying that everybody in the Senate was in favor of the road, but there were so many conflicting opinions as to the mode in which, conveniently, constitutionally, and consistently with the principles of the Democratic party it could be accomplished that it seemed as if the general wish for a railroad was an abstraction, and the general difficulties in the way of its construction, a reality, which made the abstraction of no value.

Well, sir, I have been in favor of any measure that is a practical one, that would accomplish the object which is of so great importance to the country. But I find that there are insuperable obstacles in what are called the principles of the Democratic party. I never hear of them without alarm, for I have generally observed that they are brought forward and operated precisely to the extent, and precisely for the purpose, of preventing the accomplishment of some great good to the country.

Now, Mr. President, it has been said over and over again that this bill is dead. Gentlemen on all sides agree as to that except the Senator from California [Mr. Weller] who has a manifest State interest in keeping it alive and who I think mistakes certain galvanic motions in the dead body for the evidence of life and conjures up for it future exertion and usefulness.

It is agreed on all hands that, whether by what has been done or not, it is the general sentiment in the Senate, and the deleterious effect of the administration of Democratic principles upon the measure, that it is dead, and the only inquiry on all sides has been how it should be decently and respectably disposed of by an honest burial.

Now, instead of moving that this bill lie on the table as a test question, having very great respect for the bill as it was originally reported, and the greatest respect and kindness for my honorable friend from Texas, who reported it, and who has pressed it with so much anxiety, I think the best course we can adopt with this distinguished member of the once practical measures, but now abstractions and humbugs of the age, would be to treat it exactly as we treat a member of Congress when he is dead. And, by way of taking final leave of it and testifying our respect for its memory, I move that the Senate do now adjourn [laughter] with the understanding that that makes an end of the Atlantic and Pacific railroad at least for this session.

The motion to adjourn was passed by a yea-and-nay vote, Senator Douglas desiring to put the members on record.

COMPLETION OF THE PACIFIC RAILROADS

By 1855 the Government had ascertained by surveys the passes practicable for railroads through the Rocky Mountains.

In 1860 all parties declared either in platform or in statements of their candidates in favor of constructing a Pacific Railroad by the Government. The outbreak of the Civil War caused the Lincoln Administration to urge the completion of the road in order to bind the Pacific States more closely to the Union, even though this involved the expenditure of funds sorely needed for the prosecution of the war. Owing to the great Republican majority in Congress an act to this effect was pushed through that body on July 1, 1862, with only a feeble opposition from the few State Rights Democrats who remained in the House and Senate. This act was in favor of the Central Pacific, Kansas Pacific, and Union Pacific railroads. Vast tracts of land were granted directly to these corporations instead of to the States for the benefit of the roads. This method has been invariably followed since that time. The largest grants to single corporations have been 47,000,000 acres to the Northern Pacific Railroad, and 42,000,000 acres to the Atlantic and Pacific Railroad. The amount of bonds issued to the various Pacific railroads, interest payable by the United States, was $64,623,512.

The Union Pacific Railroad was completed on May 10, 1869.

CHAPTER VI

NATIONAL ABOLITION OF STATE RAILROAD MONOPOLIES

[THE CAMDEN AND AMBOY RAILROAD]

Bill in Senate to Prevent Discrimination by State Governments between Railroads—Debate on the Bill: In Favor, Zachariah Chandler [Mich.], Charles Sumner [Mass.]; Opposed, Reverdy Johnson [Md.], John P. Hale [N. H.]; Bill Is Not Brought to Vote.

D URING the Civil War the Government was compelled by military necessity to seize and operate certain railroads. In addition to this executive action the House passed a bill in 1864 authorizing every railroad company in the United States to carry freight, mails, passengers, troops, and Government supplies on their way from one State to another, and to receive compensation therefor from the national treasury. This gave the Government precedence of private individuals or corporations whenever it so desired.

The bill, while general in its application, was designed especially to abolish the monopoly of the Camden and Amboy Railroad in New Jersey, which, in 1832, by a State charter, had received the exclusive right of transit through the State in consideration of a bonus of the stock of the railroad. The charter, with its grant of monopoly, was afterwards extended until 1869, upon the agreement of the railroad to charge passengers no more than three cents per mile for transportation.

The bill was brought up in the Senate on January 16, 1865.

STATE MONOPOLIES IN TRANSPORTATION

SENATE, JANUARY 16-MARCH 3, 1865

Zachariah Chandler [Mich.] supported the bill. He said:

If the State of New Jersey has a right to levy a small tribute upon either passengers or freight passing through that State, she has a right to levy a large tribute, and if she has a right to levy a large tribute she has a right to prohibit their passing absolutely if she, in the exercise of her sovereignty, sees fit thus to prohibit it. No man would claim that the State of New Jersey possessed that right; probably she would not attempt to exercise it, but it is a well-known fact that she has exercised the right of levying a tribute for years, and this monopoly has been grinding upon the people of the United States, grinding upon every man who has had occasion to pass from the great capital of the nation [Washington] to the actual capital of the nation [New York].

Senator Chandler showed that the State government had recognized in the charter of the railroad the right of Congress to control commerce through the State by providing that the bonus of stock paid by the railroad to the State government in consideration of the exclusive privilege granted it should revert to the railroad if Congress should recognize another road through the State.

Reverdy Johnson [Md.] opposed the bill on constitutional grounds. Every State has exclusive jurisdiction over its internal commerce. Congress can exercise jurisdiction only with the assent of the State. It has been the unvarying practice of the United States Government to procure this assent in establishing navy yards, mints, etc.

There was at one time a doubt as to the true meaning of the clause to be found in the eighth section of the first article which gives to Congress the right "to establish post-offices and post-roads." The question turned upon the meaning of the word "established," as there used. Some few contended that it gave to Congress the right to make roads as well as to say what roads already made by the States they would use for the transportation of their mails, but the received opinion after a while, which was adopted and has been uniformly acted upon, and since recognized as the correct opinion by the judiciary in every instance in which any analogous question has been before the Supreme Court of the United States and the circuit courts of the United States, has been that the meaning of the clause giving to Congress the right to establish post-roads meant only that they had the power to designate roads already existing.

Senator Johnson entered into the history of transportation in New Jersey.

The State of New Jersey in the infancy of the railroad system, as far back as the year 1830, when we had no experience which would enable a man or a government or a company to decide whether it would be a profitable business to engage in enterprises of this description—authorized the construction of a railroad under a charter granted to the Camden and Amboy Railroad Company. At the same time they authorized a company to make a canal called the Delaware and Raritan canal. The latter, perhaps, was under all the circumstances supposed to be a more perilous enterprise than the former, for a canal of this length had never been constructed through a State like New Jersey, not then with the population that now teems upon her fields; and its termini (the cities of Philadelphia and New York) did not then as now number a population of millions, but were comparatively in their infancy. It was exceedingly doubtful whether either of these enterprises would prove to be lucrative on the part of the corporators. What did New Jersey say? What was she obliged to say? What was her object in saying it? She wanted a railroad between Philadelphia and New York; she wanted canal transportation between those two termini; it was not only important to her, and it was not only important to Pennsylvania and New York; it was important to the United States. Every man who came from the West, traveling north to the East, and every man who came from the opposite quarter traveling west, and every man who had any merchandise to send of any description from west to east or east to west was interested in having a mode of transportation for himself and merchandise through New Jersey. New Jersey, then, actuated by that enlightened and patriotic policy which I think has illustrated her career, determined that she would, if she could, have made through her limits a railroad and a canal which would operate so beneficially, not only for herself, but for the rest of the country. But how to do it was the question.

This enterprise required an expenditure of millions; she could not make the expenditure without very heavy and onerous taxation. Who would make it? Individuals. How could they be induced to do it? By giving them a charter that promised to make the railroad and the canal, when they should be constructed, profitable. How was that to be accomplished? There were two ways to accomplish it: the first was to authorize them to levy any amount by way of toll that they might think proper; the other was to guard them against all competition. It was better, in her judgment, and, as I think, she decided rightly, that she should hold out the latter motive to the individuals who might be willing to construct this railroad and this canal, because to tax by a heavy imposition of toll would be not only to injure those of her own citizens who might want to travel on these improvements, but would also be to injure us and the other citizens of the United States who might want to travel and to transport their merchandise upon them.

Now, Mr. President, a word or two will show, as I think, that New Jersey had a right to do both. New Jersey was under no obligation to make a road or a canal. There is nothing in the Constitution of the United States which compels New Jersey to spend a dollar for the benefit of other States, to spend a dollar in the construction of roads or canals in her own State. What she does for the benefit of her own citizens she is authorized to do, and may be compelled to do, not by the United States, but by the influence of her own population. They elect her legislature and, if they, the people of New Jersey, are willing to have roads constructed, they, the people, will instruct the members of their legislature to construct any particular road or canal that they want, but the United States have no right to interfere. If New Jersey was not under any obligation to the United States, or any citizen whatever living in any other State, to construct a road or canal in 1830, when these two improvements were authorized, and she determined upon constructing a road and canal, had she not a right to say upon what terms she would authorize them to be constructed? Who can doubt that? She had the power to make either of these improvements, and nobody had a right to enforce as against her the execution of that power. It was a power confided to her own sole discretion, and, being in the full and unlimited possession of the power, she had a right to exert it just in the manner she thought proper; and if she, in her judgment, believed that she could make this road by means of this charter, and by force of all the provisions contained in the charter, including that provision which secures the company as against competition, who has a right to complain of it? Can the corporators complain after they have got the charter? I suppose that question answers itself. And, if they cannot complain, who else can complain?

My friend from Michigan is a citizen of the United States, but also a citizen of Michigan. He wants to come to Washington. He gets to the eastern limit of New Jersey and insists upon the right to come through. When he gets there, there is no road to bring him through. What is he to do? File a bill in equity against the State of New Jersey to compel the specific performance of some duty which she owes to the United States, to compel New Jersey to make a road over which my friend from Michigan can travel to Washington or from Washington home? Certainly not. When he gets there, and there is no road, does he stand in a stronger relation to the government of New Jersey than every Jersey man stands in relation to that government? And, if no Jersey man could complain that New Jersey had not provided for a road through her limits, it would follow necessarily that my friend could not complain that she was without such a road and that he had to foot it the best way he could. How was it before the system of railroads was adopted? How were the turnpike roads made? Not by any act of Congress; not by any power supposed to be derived to the States by any act of Congress, but by virtue of a power antecedently existing in the States, not surrendered by the Constitution of the United States to the Government of the United States, and therefore remaining just as effective and operative as it would have been if the Constitution of the United States never had been adopted. Does anybody doubt that upon those turnpikes, such as were made in all the States of the Union before the railroad system was adopted, no man had a right to travel without paying toll? That question also, I presume, is too clear for debate.

Then, if you cannot travel upon a railroad or a turnpike without conforming to that provision to be found in the charter under which turnpikes or railroads are made that authorizes the companies to charge toll, either for the transportation of passengers or the transportation of merchandise, what right have you to complain—I mean legal right, constitutional right? You may think it unkind in New Jersey, a want of comity, the absence of an enlightened policy, that she will have her system of railroads such as it is now, but what right have you to complain that you are placed in the position of all the citizens of the State of New Jersey, and all the other citizens of the country at large?

Why, Mr. President, if you do not pass this bill, cannot

these companies surrender their charters to New Jersey to-morrow, and then can she not close the road permanently, and permanently close the canal? I suppose nobody doubts that, and if New Jersey could do both, or either, it is only because over the construction of a road or a canal the jurisdiction of a State is not concurrent with any jurisdiction possessed by the United States, but is exclusive of all power on the part of the United States.

There have been some doubts as to the extent of the provision of the Constitution of the United States which prohibits the States from passing only laws impairing the obligations of contracts. In the beginning of the Government it was supposed that it did not apply to anything assuming the form of a contract to which a State was a party, and therefore no legislation constituting a company, or making a grant of land, and entering into stipulations with the grantee on the part of the State, was by some supposed to be embraced by the prohibition against the States impairing the obligation of contracts. But in the case of the State of New Jersey *vs.* Wilson, reported in 7 Cranch, and recognized ever since by all subsequent cases, the Supreme Court decided that the contract made in that case was protected. What was that? It was a very strong case, and about which a good deal might have been said at the time, and a good deal was said. There were differences of opinion—not on the bench, for the court was unanimous, but at the bar—whether that contract, if it could be called a contract, was binding at all upon the State, on the ground that it was a contract which the State had no right to enter into. The State of New Jersey took possession of certain lands belonging to Indians within her limits, and agreed to purchase for them other lands, and agreed that the other lands which she was to purchase should not be subject to the taxing power of the State. The Indians sold those lands, and they came into the hands of the parties who were in possession of them, and who were parties to the case which I have just mentioned, and the question before the Supreme Court of the United States, on appeal from the courts of New Jersey, was whether it was competent for the State to surrender at all the taxing power; whether it was not simply void legislation, not because of any clause of the Constitution of the United States, but because of the nature of the power itself. It was imagined to be a power so necessary to State existence that a State could not deprive herself of it. The Supreme Court, however, decided that in that case the agreement was a contract, and therefore protected by the constitutional inhibition upon the States interfering with contracts.

Now, Mr. President, if I am right so far, what does this bill do? It says, no matter what are the limitations to be found in any railroad charter, no matter what they are prohibited from doing, whether carrying all freight, all passengers, or any particular freight, or any particular class of passengers, they are to have that privilege by virtue of this act. Is not that altering the franchise—the contract with the State?

The act has even a greater power than authorizing the road to be made. It is denying to the State the right to make roads of this description as she thinks they ought to be made, because to admit that she has a right to impose limitations as between herself and the holders of the franchise, and to hold at the same time that it is within the power of Congress to free the holders of the franchise from the obligation of the franchise, is to tell New Jersey (to apply it to New Jersey): ''Your authority to make railroads is to be exercised in subordination to our authority to extend the privileges and to do away with the conditions without which you never would have authorized the roads to have been made at all.''

Under this bill they are authorized to receive, for the transportation over their road of what by it they are authorized to transport, compensation. What compensation? How is it to be regulated? What limitation is there upon it? The charter has no limitation, because (according to the assumption I have made, that this is to apply to a road which is not authorized to carry passengers and freight through) the charter does not authorize them to charge at all for carrying passengers and freight through. Then, if there is no authority in the charter to carry passengers and freight from one terminus to the other, there is no limitation in the charter upon the right to carry such passengers or freight, and, as you are about to authorize them to carry passengers and freight, and to receive compensation therefor, without limiting the compensation which they are to receive, you are about to give them the authority to charge just what they please.

It may be said that New Jersey has no right to say that a citizen from Michigan or from Massachusetts shall not come through her territory. It will be sufficient to argue that question when New Jersey says it. She has not said any such thing. She has not said that unless you go upon the Delaware and Raritan canal or upon the Camden and Amboy road you cannot go through her territory. Go upon the other road;

if she has turnpikes, resort to the turnpikes; if she has no turnpikes, travel what are called the country roads; if she has no country roads, walk through. New Jersey is bound, with a view almost to her own existence, certainly to the promotion of her own prosperity, to furnish the means by which travel into or through her territory from the other States may be made, but she is under no obligation to say that she will spend her money to give you a favorite mode of transportation except upon her own terms. She is under no obligation to make these roads at all.

If there was no obligation upon her to make this railroad, and nobody else but herself could make it or authorize it to be made, then she had a right to say upon what terms she would make it, and he who undertakes to make it, or does make it, under a charter which subjects him to certain conditions, does not act honestly, certainly does not act legally, unless he complies with the condition. If he abuses the power, transcends the authority conferred upon him by the franchise, the franchise will be taken from him; the road is no longer his, and vests in the sovereign.

But here you propose to step in and say to New Jersey, who alone could have made the road, to whose exclusive jurisdiction the subject itself is confided, because not delegated by the Constitution, "It is true you had a right to make the road; you have made it; it has been made under your authority; you never would have authorized it to be made except upon the conditions included within that authority, but Congress now says to you your limitations are wholly inoperative as against us; it is our right not to assist anything that you have done, not to complete your road, not to appropriate money for the purpose if money should be wanted, but to step in and annul the very conditions without which you never would have authorized the construction of the road."

I warn Senators that there is involved in this measure a principle which is destructive of the sovereignty of their own States. If you pass this measure, and it can stand judicial examination—I am sure it will not, at least I think so—you submit the authority of the States now supposed to be exclusive to the unlimited power of Congress.

Congress may do with any of your needs just what Congress may think fit to do, and in a controversy between any one State and all the other States in which the Representatives from the other States may be brought to believe that the interest of their particular constituencies will be promoted by

X—14

disregarding the limitations in the franchises under which the roads in the particular States have been made, they will be done away with, and then see how we shall stand with our people. We are sent here to take care, among others, of the rights of our States. Our oath to support the Constitution of the United States is not merely to execute all the powers which it confers, but to abstain from exerting any powers which it does not confer.

On February 14 Charles Sumner [Mass.] spoke in favor of the bill.

Mr. President, the question before us concerns the public convenience to a remarkable degree. But it concerns also the unity of this Republic. Look at it in its simplest form, and you will confess its importance. Look at it in its political aspect, and you will recognize how vital it is to the integrity of the Union itself. On one side we encounter a formidable railroad. Usurpation with all the pretensions of State rights, hardly less flagrant or pernicious than those which have ripened in bloody rebellion. On the other side are the simple and legitimate claims of the Union under the Constitution of the United States.

New Jersey lies on the great line of travel between the two capitals of the country, political and commercial. It cannot be avoided except by a circuitous journey. On this single line commerce, passengers, mails, troops—all must move. In the chain of communication by which capital is bound to capital— nay, more, by which the Union itself is bound together, there is no single link of equal importance. Strike it out, and where are you? Your capitals will be separated and the Union itself will be loosened.

New Jersey, in the exercise of pretended State rights, has undertaken to invest the Camden and Amboy Railroad Company with unprecedented prerogatives. These are the words of the legislature: "It shall not be lawful, at any time during the said railroad charter, to construct any other railroads in this State without the consent of the said companies, which shall be intended or used for the transportation of passengers or merchandise *between the cities of New York and Philadelphia*, or to compete in business with the railroad authorized by the act to which this supplement is relative." (New Jersey Session Laws for 1854, page 387.) Here, in barefaced terms, is the grant of a monopoly in all railroad transportation, whether of commerce, passengers, mails, or troops, between *New York,* a city *outside* of New Jersey, and *Philadelphia,* another city *outside* of New Jersey. Or, looking at this grant of monopoly again, we shall find that, *while it leaves the local transportation of New Jersey untouched,* it undertakes to regulate and appropriate the transportation between two great cities outside of New Jersey, constituting, from geographical position, the gates through which the whole mighty movement, north and south, must pass.

If this monopoly is offensive on its face, it becomes still more offensive when we consider the motive in which it had its origin. By the confession of its supporters, it was granted in order to raise a revenue for the State out of men and business not of the State.

Here the speaker quoted statements of original officers of the road.

But the character of this usurpation becomes still more apparent in the conduct adopted toward another railroad in New Jersey. It appears that a succession of railroads has been constructed, under charters of this State, from Raritan bay, opposite New York, to Camden, opposite Philadelphia, constituting a continuous line, suitable for transportation, across New Jersey and between the two great cities of New York and Philadelphia. This continuous line is known as the Raritan and Delaware Bay Railroad. On the breaking out of the rebellion, when Washington was menaced by a wicked enemy, and the patriots of the land were aroused to sudden efforts, the Quartermaster-General of the United States directed the transportation of troops, horses, baggage, and munitions of war from New York to Philadelphia over this line. The other railroad, claiming a monopoly, filed a bill in equity, praying that the Raritan and Delaware Bay Railroad "be decreed to desist and refrain" from such transportation, and also praying "that an *account* may be taken to ascertain the amount of damages." The counsel of the monopoly openly insisted that, by this transportation, the State was "robbed of her ten cents a passenger," and then cried out, "I say it is no defence whatever if they have succeeded in obtaining an order of the Secretary of War, *when we call upon them to give us the money they made by it;* and that is one of our calls. They have no right to get an order to deprive the State of New Jersey of the right of transit duty, *which is her adopted policy."* Such was the argument of Mr. Stockton, counsel for the monopoly, November 12, 1863. The *transit duty* is vindicated as the *adopted policy* of New Jersey. Surely, in the face of such pretensions, it was time that something should be done by Congress.

Such, sir, are the pretensions of New Jersey to interfere with commerce, passengers, mails, and troops *from other States,* on their way, it may be, to the national capital, even with necessary succors at a moment of national peril. Such pretensions, persistently maintained and vindicated, constitute a usurpation not only hostile to the public interests, but menacing to the Union itself. Here is no question of local taxation, or local immunities, under State laws, but an open assumption by a State to tax the commerce of the United States on its way from State to State.

From the nature of the case, and according to every rule of reason, there ought to be a remedy for such a grievance. No usurping monopoly ought to be allowed to establish itself in any State across the national highway, and, like a baron of the middle ages perched in his rocky fastness, levy tolls and tribute from all the wayfarers of business, pleasure, or duty. The nuisance should be abated. The usurpation should be overthrown. And happily the powers are ample under the Constitution of the United States.

Following unquestionable principles and authentic precedents, the committee have proposed a remedy which I now proceed to discuss.

The bill under consideration was originally introduced by me into the Senate. It was afterward adopted and passed by the other House as a substitute for a kindred bill which was pending there.

The entire and unimpeachable constitutionality of the present measure is apparent in certain familiar precepts of the Constitution, which were brought to view in the title and preamble of the bill as introduced by me, but which have been omitted in the bill now before us. The title of the bill as introduced by me was "to facilitate commercial, postal, and military communication among the several States." This title opens the whole constitutional question. This was followed by a preamble, as follows:

"Whereas the Constitution of the United States confers upon Congress, in express terms, the power to regulate commerce among the several States, to establish post-roads, and to raise and support armies: Therefore, *Be it enacted.*"

In these few words three sources of power are clearly indicated, either of which is ample, but the three together constitute an overrunning fountain.

First. There is the power "to regulate commerce among the several States." Look at the Constitution and you will find these identical words. From the great sensitiveness of States this power has been always exercised by Congress with peculiar caution, but it still lives to be employed by an enfranchised government.

In asserting this power I follow not only the text of the Constitution, but also the authoritative decisions of the Supreme Court of the United States. Perhaps there is no question in our constitutional history which has been more clearly illustrated by our greatest authority, Chief Justice Marshall. In the well-known case where the State of New York had undertaken to grant an exclusive right to navigate the waters of New York by vessels propelled by steam, the illustrious Chief Justice, speaking for the court, declared the restriction to be illegal, because it interfered with commerce between the States precisely as is now done by New Jersey. In his opinion commerce was something more than traffic or the transportation of property. It was also "the commercial intercourse between nations and parts of nations in all its branches," and it embraced by necessary inference *all interstate communications* and the whole subject of intercourse between the people of the several States. It was declared that the power of Congress over the subject was not limited by State lines, but that it was coextensive with commerce itself according to the enlarged signification of the term. Here are the words of Chief Justice Marshall:

"But in regulating commerce with foreign nations, the power of Congress does not stop at the jurisdictional lines of the several States. It would be a very useless power if it could not pass these lines. The commerce of the United States with foreign nations is that of the whole United States. Every district has a right to participate in it. The deep streams which penetrate our country in every direction pass through the interior of almost every State in the Union, and furnish the means for exercising this right. *If Congress has the power to regulate it, that power must be exercised wherever the subject exists.* If it exists within the States, if a foreign voyage may commence or terminate at a port within a State, then the power of Congress may be exercised within a State."— Gibbons *vs.* Ogden, 9 Wheaton, 196.

This important decision of the Supreme Court was before railroads. It grew out of an attempt to appropriate certain navigable thoroughfares of the Union. But it is equally applicable to these other thoroughfares of the Union where the railroad is the substitute for water. It is according to the genius of jurisprudence that a rule once established governs all cases which come within the original reason on which it was founded. Therefore I conclude confidently that the power of Congress over internal commerce by railroad is identical with that over internal commerce by water. But this decision does not stand alone.

Mr. Justice Story, who was a member of the Supreme Court at this time, in a later decision thus explains the extent of this power:

"It does not stop at the mere boundary line of a State; nor is it confined to acts done on the water, or in the necessary course of the navigation thereof. *It extends to such acts done on land as interfere with,* obstruct, or prevent *the free exercise of the power to regulate commerce* with foreign nations and *among the States.*" United States *vs.* Coombs, 12 Peters, 78.

From various cases illustrating this power I call attention to that known as the Passenger case, where the Supreme Court declared that the statutes of New York and Massachusetts imposing taxes upon alien passengers arriving at the ports of those States was in derogation of the Constitution. On this occasion Mr. Justice McLean said:

"Shall passengers, admitted by act of Congress without a tax be taxed by a State? The supposition of such a power in a State is utterly inconsistent with a commercial power either paramount or exclusive in Congress."

Mr. Justice Grier said with great point:

"To what purpose commit to Congress the power of regulating our intercourse with foreign nations and among the States, *if these regulations may be changed at the discretion of each State?*" . . . "It is, therefore, not left to the discretion of each State of the Union either to refuse a right of passage to persons or property or to exact a duty on permission to exercise it."—7 Howard, 464.

But this is the very thing that is now done by New Jersey, which "exacts a duty" from passengers across the State.

I call attention also to the case of the Wheeling bridge, where Congress, under peculiar circumstances, exercised this identical power. In this case the State of Pennsylvania claimed the power to limit and control the transit across the Ohio River to the State of Ohio, and this power was affirmed by the Supreme Court so long as Congress refrained from legislation on the subject. But under the pressure of a public demand, and in the exercise of the very powers which are now invoked, Congress has declared the Wheeling bridge to be a lawful structure, anything in any State law to the contrary notwithstanding. The Supreme Court, after the passage of this act, denied a motion to punish the owners of the bridge for a contempt in rebuilding it, and affirmed that the act declaring the Wheeling bridge a lawful structure was within the legitimate exercise by Congress of its constitutional power to regulate commerce. (13 Howard, 528.)

Such are the precedents of courts and of statutes showing how completely this power belongs to Congress in the regulation of internal commerce. It would be superfluous to dwell on them. There they stand like so many granite columns, fit supports of that internal commerce which in itself is a chief support of the Union.

Secondly. There is also the power "to establish post-roads," which is equally explicit. Here, too, the words are plain, and they have received an authoritative exposition. It is with reference to these words that Mr. Justice Story remarks that "constitutions of government do not turn upon ingenious subtleties, but are adapted to the business and exigencies of human society, and the powers given are understood, in a large sense, in order to secure the public interests. Common sense becomes the guide and prevents men from dealing with mere logical abstractions." (Story, "Commentaries on Constitution," Vol. 2, sec. 1134.) The same learned authority, in considering these words of the Constitution, seems to have anticipated the very question now under consideration. Here is a passage which may fitly close the argument on this head:

"Let a case be taken *when State policy*"—

As, for instance, in New Jersey at this time—

"or State hostility shall lead the legislature to close up or discontinue a road, the nearest and the best between two great States, rivals, perhaps, for the trade and intercourse of a third State; shall it be said that Congress has no right to make or repair a road for keeping open for the mail the best means of communication between those States? May the National Government be compelled to take the most inconvenient and indirect routes for the mail? *In other words, have the States the power to say how, and upon what roads, the mails shall and shall not travel?.* If so, then, in relation to post roads, the States, and not the Union, are supreme."—Story, "Commentaries on the Constitution," Vol. 2, sec. 1144.

Thirdly. Then comes the power "to raise and support armies," an unquestionable power lodged in Congress. But this grant carries with it, of course, all incidental powers necessary to the execution of the principal power. It would be absurd to suppose that Congress could raise an army, but could not authorize the agencies required for its transportation from place to place. Congress has not been guilty of any such absurdity. Already it has by formal act proceeded "to authorize the President of the United States in certain cases to take possession of railroads and telegraphs, and for other purposes." (12 Statutes at Large, p. 334.) By this act the President is empowered "to take possession of any or all the railroad lines in the United States, their rolling stock, their offices, shops, buildings, and all their appendages and appurtenances," and it is declared that any such railroad "shall be considered as a post-road and a part of the military establishment of the United States." Here is the exercise of a broader power than any which is now proposed. The less must be contained in the greater.

Such is the argument in brief for the constitutionality of the present bill, whether it be regarded as a general measure applicable to all the railroads of the country, or only applicable to the railroads of New Jersey. The case is so plain and absolutely unassailable that I should leave it on this simple exhibition if the Senator from Maryland [Mr. Johnson], who always brings to these questions the authority of professional reputation, had not most zealously argued the other way. According to him, the bill is unconstitutional. Let me say, however, that the conclusion of the learned Senator is only slightly sustained by the reasons which he assigns. Indeed his whole elaborate argument, if brought to the touchstone, will be found inconclusive and unsatisfactory.

The Senator opened with the proposition that the internal commerce of a State is within the exclusive jurisdiction of the State, and from this he argued that the present bill is unconstitutional. But the Senator will allow me to say that his proposition is not sufficiently broad for his conclusion. The present bill does not touch the internal commerce of a State, except so far as this may be a link in the chain of "commerce among States," which is committed by the Constitution to the jurisdiction of Congress. Mark this distinction, I pray you, for it is essential to a right understanding of the case.

From this inapplicable proposition the Senator passed to another equally inapplicable. He asserted that the jurisdiction of a State over all territory within its limits was exclusive, so that the United States cannot obtain jurisdiction over any portion thereof, except by assent of the State, and from this again he argued the unconstitutionality of the present bill. But this very illustration seems to have been anticipated by Mr. Justice Story in his learned commentaries, where he shows conclusively, first, that it is inapplicable, and, secondly, that so far as it is applicable, it is favorable to the power. Here are his words:

"The clause respecting cessions of territory for the seat of Government, and for forts, arsenals, dock yards, &c., has nothing to do with the point. *But, if it had, it is favorable to the power.*" . . .

"But surely it will not be pretended that Congress could not erect a fort or magazine in a place within a State unless the State should cede the territory. The only effect would be that the jurisdiction in such a case would not be exclusive. Suppose a State should prohibit a sale of any of the lands within its boundaries by its own citizens, for any public purposes indispensable for the Union, either military or civil, would not Congress possess a constitutional right to demand and appropriate land within the State for such purposes, making a just compensation? *Exclusive jurisdiction over a road is one thing; the right to make it is quite another.* A turnpike company may be authorized to make a road, and yet may have no jurisdiction, or at least no exclusive jurisdiction, over it."—2 Story on Constitution, Sec. 1146.

Had the distinguished commentator anticipated the argument of the Senator from Maryland, he could not have answered it more completely.

Passing from these constitutional generalities the Senator came at once to an assumption, which, if it were sustained, would limit essentially the power of Congress with regard to post-roads. According to him the words of the Constitution authorizing Congress "to establish post-roads," mean only that it shall designate roads already existing, and in support of this assumption he relied upon the message of Mr. Monroe in 1822, on the Cumberland road. The learned Senator adds that this is "the received opinion uniformly acted upon and since recognized as the correct opinion by the judiciary." Of course his testimony on this point is important, but it is overruled at once by the authority I have already cited, which says that "the power to establish post-offices and post-roads has never been understood to include no more than the power to *point out* and *designate* post-offices and post-roads." (Story's "Commentaries," Vol. 2, sec. 1136.) In the face of Mr. Justice Story's dissent, expressed in his authoritative commentaries, it is impossible to say that it is "the received opinion," as has been as-

serted by the Senator. But the learned commentator insists that
"the Constitution itself uniformly uses the word *establish* in the
general sense and never in this peculiar and narrow sense,"
and after enumerating various places where it occurs, says, "it
is plain that to construe the word in any of these cases as
equivalent to *designate* or *point out* would be absolutely absurd.
The clear import of the word is to create and form and fix in
a settled manner." "To establish post-offices and post-roads
is to frame and pass laws, to erect, make, form, regulate, and
preserve them. Whatever is necessary, whatever is appropriate
to this purpose, is within the power." (*Ibid.*, sec. 1131.) I
might quote other words from the same authority, but this is
enough to vindicate the power which the Senator has denied.

But here it is my duty to remind the Senate that the argument of the Senator from Maryland on this head is not only
false in its assumption, but that the assumption, even if correct,
is entirely inapplicable on the present occasion. The bill now
before the Senate does not undertake to create, but simply to
designate or *point out*, certain roads. Therefore it does not
fall under the objection which the Senator has adduced. Even
by his own admission it is constitutional.

But the Senator, not content with an erroneous assumption
concerning post-roads, which, even if correct, is entirely inapplicable, made another assumption concerning another clause
of the Constitution which was equally erroneous and inapplicable. The Senator argued that the railroad charters in New
Jersey were grants in the nature of a contract, and that they
were protected by "the constitutional inhibition upon States
interfering with contracts," and here he referred to several
decisions of the Supreme Court of the United States. I do not
trouble you with the decisions. It will be enough if I call
attention to the precise text of the Constitution, which is: "*No
State* shall pass any law impairing the obligation of contracts."

Look at these words, and it appears, in the first place, that
this prohibition is addressed to the States and not to Congress,
whose powers are not touched by it. Look still further at
the railroad charters, and even admit that they were grants in
the nature of a contract, but you cannot deny that the contract
must be interpreted with reference to the Constitution of the
United States. Learned judges have held that the law of the
place where a contract is made not only regulates and governs
it, *but constitutes a part of the contract itself.* (Sturgis *vs.*
Crowninshield, 4 Wheat. 122.) But if the law constitutes a part
of the contract, still more must the Constitution. Apply this

principle and the case is clear. Every railroad charter has been framed subject to the exercise of the acknowledged powers of Congress, all of which are implied in the grant as essential conditions, not less than if they were set forth expressly. The Supreme Court has decided that "all contracts are made subject to the right of *eminent domain,* so that they cannot be considered as violated by the exercise of this right." (The West River Bridge *vs.* Dix, 6 Howard, 507.) But the powers of Congress, invoked on the present occasion to regulate commerce among the several States, to establish post-roads, and to raise and equip armies, are in the nature of an *eminent domain,* to which all local charters are subject. Therefore, I repeat again, nothing is proposed "impairing the obligation of a contract," even if that well-known prohibition were applicable to Congress.

From these details of criticism the Senator jumped to a broader proposition. He asserted that the pending measure was destructive of the sovereignty of the States, and he even went so far as to say that it was the same as if you said that all State legislation is null and void. These, sir, were his exact words. How the Senator, even in any ardor of advocacy, could have ventured on this assumption it is difficult to comprehend. Here is a measure, which, as I have already demonstrated, is founded on three different texts of the Constitution, which is upheld by three unassailable supports, and which is in essential harmony with the Union itself, and yet we are told that it is destructive of the sovereignty of the States. Such an assumption seems uttered in the very wildness of unhesitating advocacy. If it is anything but a phrase, it must be condemned, not only as without foundation, but as hostile to the best interests of the country.

Sir, the pending measure is in no respect destructive of the sovereignty of the States, nor does it in any sense say that all State legislation is null and void. On the contrary, it simply asserts a plain and unquestionable power under the Constitution of the United States. If in any way it seems to touch what is invoked as State sovereignty, or to set aside any State legislation, it is only in pursuance of the Constitution. It is simply because the Constitution, and the laws made in pursuance thereof, are *the supreme law of the land.*

But the assumptions of the Senator bring me back to the vital principle with which I began. After exhibiting the public convenience involved in the present question, I said that it concerned still more the unity of the Republic. It is in short that identical question, which has so often entered this Chamber, and which is now convulsing this land with bloody war. It is the question of the Union itself. In his ardor for that vampire monopoly, which, brooding over New Jersey, sucks the life-blood of the whole country, the Senator from Maryland sets up most dangerous pretensions in the name of State rights. Sir, the Senator flings into one scale the pretensions of State rights. Into the other scale I fling the Union itself.

Sir, the Senator from Maryland is a practiced lawyer, and he cannot have forgotten that Nathan Dane, whose name is an authority in our courts, tells us plainly that the terms "sovereign States," "State sovereignty," "State rights," and "rights of States" are not constitutional expressions. Others of equal weight in the early history of the country have said the same thing. Mr. Madison, in the convention which framed the Constitution, said, "Some contend that States are *sovereign*, when, in fact, they are only political societies. The States never possessed the essential right of sovereignty. These were always vested in Congress." Elbridge Gerry, of Massachusetts, in the same convention, said: "It appears to me that the States never were independent. They had only corporate rights." General Pinckney, of South Carolina, said: "I hold it for a fundamental point that an individual independence of the States is utterly irreconcilable with the idea of an aggregate sovereignty." ("Madison Papers," page 631.) Both Patrick Henry and George Mason, in the Virginia convention, opposed the Constitution on the very ground that it superseded State rights. But perhaps the true intention of the authors of the Constitution may be best found in the letter of General Washington, as President of the Convention, transmitting it to Congress. Here are his words:

"It is obviously impracticable *in the Federal Government of these States to secure all rights of independent sovereignty to each,* and yet provide for the safety of all. Individuals entering into society must give up a share of liberty to preserve the rest." . . . "In all our deliberations we kept steadily in view that which appears to us the greatest interest of every true American—THE CONSOLIDATION OF OUR UNION—in which are involved our prosperity, safety, perhaps our national existence.
"GEORGE WASHINGTON."

I content myself on this head when I find myself with the support of this great name.

By the adoption of the Constitution the people of the United States constituted themselves *a nation*, one and indivisible, with all the unity and power of a nation. They were no longer a confederation, subject to the disturbing pretensions, prejudices, and whims of its component parts, but they became a body-politic, where every part was subordinate to the Constitution, as every part of the natural body is subordinate to the principle of life. The sovereignty then and there established was the sovereignty of the United States, where the States were only "parts of one stupendous whole." The powers then and there conferred upon the nation were supreme. And it is those very powers which I now invoke, in the name of the Union, and to the end that pretensions in the name of State rights may be overthrown.

I have already presented a picture of these intolerable pretensions. But they must be examined more minutely. They may be seen, *first*, in their character as a monopoly, and, *secondly*, in their character as a usurpation under the Constitution of the United States. I need not say that in each they are equally indefensible.

If you go back to the earliest days of English history, you will find that monopolies have from the beginning been odious, as contrary to the ancient and fundamental laws of the realm. A writer, who is often quoted in the courts, says: "Monopolies by common law are void as being against the freedom of trade and discouraging labor and industry, and putting it in the power of particular persons to set what prices they please on a commodity." (Hawkins's "Pleas of Crown," Vol. 1.) But, without claiming that the present monopoly is void at common law, it is enough to show its inconsistency with the Constitution. And here I borrow Mr. Webster's language in his famous argument against the monopoly of steam navigation granted by the State of New York, as follows:

"Now I think it very reasonable to say that *the Constitution never intended to leave with the States the power of granting monopolies* either of trade or of navigation; and, therefore, that, as to this, the commercial power is exclusively in Congress."

Then again he says:

"I insist that the nature of the case and of the power did imperatively require that such important authority as that of granting monopolies of trade and navigation *should not be considered as still retained by the States.*"

And then again he adduces an authority which ought to be conclusive on the present occasion. It is that of New Jersey at an earlier day:

"The New Jersey resolutions [on forming the Constitution of the United States] complain that the regulation of trade was within the power of the several States within their separate jurisdiction, to such a degree as to involve many difficulties and embarrassments; and they express an earnest opinion that *the sole and exclusive power of regulating trade ought to be with Congress.*"

And yet, in the face of these principles we have a gigantic monopoly organized by New Jersey, composed of several confederate corporations, whose capital massed together is said to amount to more than $27,537,977—a capital not much inferior to that of the United States Bank, which once seemed to hold "divided empire" with the National Government itself. And this transcendent monopoly, thus vast in resources, undertakes to levy a toll on the commerce, the passengers, the mails, and the troops of the Union in their transit between two great cities, both of which are outside of New Jersey. In its attitude and in its pretension the grasping monopoly is not unlike Apollyon in "Pilgrim's Progress."

New Jersey is the Valley of Humiliation through which all travelers north and south must pass, and the monopoly, like Apollyon, claims them all as "subjects," saying, "for all that country is mine, and I am the prince and god of it."

The enormity of this usurpation may be seen in its natural consequences. New Jersey claims the right to levy a tax for State revenue on passengers and freight in transit across her territory from State to State; in other words, to levy a tax on "commerce among the several States." *Of course, the right to tax is the right to prohibit.* The same power which can exact "ten cents from every passenger," according to the cry of the Camden and Amboy Railroad, by the voice of its counsel, may exact ten dollars or any other sum, and thus effectively close this great avenue of communication.

But if New Jersey can play successfully this game of taxation, and compel tribute from the domestic commerce of the Union as it traverses her territory on the way from State to State, then may every other State do likewise. Then if the Union should continue to exist, it would be only as a name. The national unity would be destroyed.

A profitable usurpation, like that of New Jersey, would be a tempting example to other States. Let this usurpation be sanctioned by Congress, and you hand over the domestic commerce of the Union to a succession of local imposts. Each State will be a tax gatherer at the expense of the Union. If there be any single fruit of our national unity, if there be any single element of the Union, if there be any single triumph of the Constitution which may be placed above all others, it is the freedom of commerce among the States, under which that *free trade* which is the aspiration of philosophers is assured to all citizens of the Union, as they circulate through our whole broad country, without hindrance from any State. But this vital principle is now in jeopardy.

Do not forget that it is the tax imposed on commerce between New York and Philadelphia, two cities outside of the State of New Jersey, which I denounce. I have denounced it as hostile to the Union. I denounce it also as hostile to the spirit of the age, which is everywhere overturning the barriers of commerce. The robber castles, which once compelled the payment of toll on the Rhine, were long ago dismantled, and exist now only as monuments of picturesque beauty. Kindred pretensions in other places have been overthrown or trampled out. The duties levied by Denmark on all vessels passing through the Sound and the Belts; the duties levied by Hanover on the goods of all nations at Stade on the Elbe; the tolls exacted on the Danube in its protracted course; the tolls exacted by Holland on the busy waters of the Scheldt, and all transit imposts within the great Zoll-Verein of Germany, have all been abolished, and in this work of enfranchisement the Government of the United States led the way, insisting, in the words of President Pierce, in his annual message, "on the right of *free transit* into and from the Baltic." But the right of free transit across the States of the Union is now assailed. Strange that you should reach so far to secure *free transit* in the Baltic and should hesitate in its defence here at home!

Thank God! within the bounds of the Union, under the national Constitution, commerce is free. As the *open sea* is the highway of nations, so is this Union the highway of the States, with all their commerce, and no State can claim any exclusive property therein. The Union is a *mare librum* beyond the power of any State, and not a *mare clausum,* subject to as many tyrannies as there are States. And yet the State of New Jersey now asserts the power of closing a highway of the Union.

Such a pretension, so irrational and destructive, cannot be dealt with tenderly. Like the serpent, it must be bruised on the head. Nor can there be any delay. Every moment of life yielded to such a usurpation is like the concession once in an evil hour yielded to nullification, which was kindred in origin and character. The present pretension of New Jersey belongs to the same school with that abhorred and blood-bespattered pretension of South Carolina.

There is a common bond among the sciences, among the virtues, among the vices, and so, also, among the monopolies. The monopoly which was founded on the hideous pretension of property in man obtained a responsive sympathy in that other monopoly which was founded on the greed of unjust taxation, and both were naturally upheld in the name of State rights. Both must be overthrown in the name of the Union. South Carolina must cease to be a slave State, and so must New Jersey. All hail to the genius of universal emancipation! All hail to the Union, triumphant over the rebellion, triumphant also over a usurpation which menaces the unity of the Republic!

JOHN P. HALE [N. H.].—The Senator from Massachusetts represents the Union and commerce and peace, and all the kindred arts as enlisted on one side, and monopoly on the other, and not content with the profundity of his own suggestions he goes to that old English classic, the "Pilgrim's Progress" to illustrate the Heavenly City and the City of Destruction. Which he would represent as the City of Destruction and which the Heavenly City I do not know, but I suppose, from their names, Philadelphia would represent the Heavenly City and New York must represent the other. [Laughter.]

Mr. President, like the Senator from Massachusetts, I could draw a picture, not so eloquent, but as truthful, representing the various interests that are contending here, and if I were to do so I might represent a railroad, a bad speculation, paying no dividends, nor even the interest on its bonds; its stock being worth nothing, I might represent such a railroad, by the magic influence of this act, short and simple as it is, raised to be one of the best stocks in the market. That, I think, would be as near the practical effect that would be brought about (not to say designed) by this bill as any which have been pictured by the Senator from Massachusetts. This would be the immediate and the tangible effect: the Raritan and Delaware Bay road, if that is the name of the corporation, would suddenly find themselves, from being below a fancy stock, raised to a considerable advance in the market, and, as one of the newspapers which advocate this bill says that there are at least twenty men in the Senate that make speeches for money, the wicked world outside perhaps would stop to inquire which side paid the most money.

Mr. President, let me say that I want to put down this rebellion; I want this Union to succeed, I trust, with an ardor and a sincerity of conviction not second even to that which animates the Senator from Massachusetts, but when the war is over, as I believe it will be, when the rebellion is put down, as I have no doubt it will be, I want there to be something left of the Constitution for which we profess to be contending. I do not want to strike giant blows at the rebellion which, when they put that down, shall annihilate the Constitution and all State rights, so that everything shall be consolidated into one despotism. I undertake to say that the right of controlling the railroads within their own limits is one, notwithstanding everything that has been said about it and a great many decisions that have been had, that has been always maintained, preserved, and protected by the legislatures and by the courts of the several States, and by none more so than by the State of Massachusetts. If you pass this bill you strike a blow at the cherished policy of Massachusetts to-day as it exists upon her statute books and is enforced by her judiciary.

Massachusetts has not been alone in this policy. It is essential to every State that it should have the power to exercise this right. There is the great State of New York, what has been her action? She incorporated by a series of acts what is now known as the New York Central Railroad, leading from Albany to Buffalo, a distance of between three and four hundred miles. That road was prohibited from carrying certain articles of merchandise, I think wheat, one of the great necessaries of life—almost as necessary to life as paper [laughter], except upon condition that a certain toll was paid upon the wheat, and I think it was a toll equal to the amount of the whole freight received, to the Erie canal. That was the law of New York for a long time. It was a question of policy for the State of New York whether that prohibition should be continued or not, but I believe, in all the discussions that took place between the advocates of the prohibition and those who were for its repeal, it was never suggested that it was a thing with which Congress had any right to meddle, with which Congress could interfere, in regard to which Congress had any right to exercise any power, but left it for the State of New York to settle for herself, and to settle exclusively as a question affecting her own State policy.

Mr. President, it may well be asked, if this be a power residing in the general Government, why in the whole history of the States and the Union has it not been invoked before? During the whole history of this Camden and Amboy monopoly, why has not the power of Congress been invoked until this time?

X—15

Why was it not invoked in the State of Massachusetts? Why has it not been invoked in New York? Why was it not invoked somewhere else? Why, until the Raritan and Delaware Bay Railroad Company found that they had sunk thousands and hundreds of thousands in their road, and it was a losing concern, that they could not pay dividends on their stock or interest on their bonds, did not those patriotic gentlemen, governed by these public interests, these high motives, these great considerations relating to the Union, enlist the eloquence of my learned friend from Massachusetts to come in here with grandiloquent pæans in praise of the Union, and to excite public sentiments and public opinion in favor of the Union——

SENATOR SUMNER.—How have they "enlisted" me?

SENATOR HALE.—Why, Mr. President, in a hundred ways. They enlisted him by articles in the New York *Tribune* [laughter]; they enlisted him by various articles scattered all over the country; they enlisted him by all the ways and means by which men that have a selfish and a private object to effect appeal to great objects, high considerations, and moral sentiments, and thus operate upon the judgment and the sympathies of the generous, the impulsive, and the unreflecting. [Laughter.]

Despite the strenuous efforts of its advocates the bill was not brought to a vote. Senator Chandler was on his feet asking for the yeas and nays on the bill in the closing hour of the session when the Vice-President [Hannibal Hamlin] entered with the Vice-President-elect [Andrew Johnson] and all business was suspended to hear the inaugural address of the latter.

CHAPTER VII

GOVERNMENT RAILROADS

John Sherman [O.] Introduces in the Senate Bill to Charter Government Railroads from the Capital to Various Points—Debate: In Favor, Sen. Sherman; Opposed, William P. Whyte [Md.], James R. Doolittle [Wis.]; Bill Is Postponed—William H. Kelsey [N. Y.] Introduces Bill in the House of Representatives Authorizing the Construction of a Railroad between New York City and Washington, D. C., to be under Government Control—Debate: In Favor, Burton C. Cook [Ill.], Charles O'Neill [Pa.], Dennis McCarthy [N. Y.], Austin Blair [Mich.]; Opposed, Charles E. Phelps [Md.], William D. Kelley [Pa.]; Passed by House and Not Acted upon by Senate.

ON January 6, 1869, John Sherman [O.] introduced in the Senate a bill "to promote commerce among the States and to cheapen the transportation of the mails and military and naval stores," particularly by chartering three railroad companies respectively from Washington to New York, Pittsburgh, and Cincinnati.

GOVERNMENT RAILROADS

SENATE, JANUARY 6-23, 1869

Senator Sherman, in supporting his bill, discussed the public inconvenience resulting from the monopoly over interstate commerce exercised by railroads not under the control of Congress, instancing in particular the Baltimore and Ohio Railroad. Passengers on this were made to suffer unnecessary inconvenience.

The Baltimore and Ohio Railroad will not connect with the only road from Baltimore to the North. It will not transfer baggage or sell tickets over or to that route. The time tables are arranged to create delay in Baltimore; a rough omnibus or carriage ride across the city one mile, with a scramble for baggage at either end of the transit, are unreasonable, inconvenient, and expensive, but they must be endured. The tracks of the two roads actually meet and connect, but the transfer is not made at the point of connection, and there can be no reason for this except the hostility of rival companies—the desire to force the Western travel over the main line of the Baltimore and Ohio Railroad, and the fact that passengers are utterly helpless to correct the evil. Tens of thousands of passengers have passed through this experience; many ladies and sick persons have suffered severely. In cold and heat, by day and by night, this antiquated system of transfer goes on. It is estimated that the delay and expense of this transit through Baltimore have already exceeded the cost of a new line from Baltimore to Washington. If this inconvenience could fall upon the citizens of Maryland, it would not have been endured, for they could correct it, but all the passengers compelled to undergo this transit are traveling beyond the limits of Maryland, and thus have no remedy unless Congress can give them one. It has been complained of here and everywhere, but the only reply is that it is not the policy of the Baltimore and Ohio Railroad to make this connection. Recently, it is said, efforts have been made to reconcile the petty rivalries and jealousies of these roads, but it is not done, and will not be done until competition compels them to regard the convenience and comfort of their passengers.

The Government as well as the general public had a right to complain.

A President of the United States [Lincoln], to the lasting disgrace of the nation, was compelled, by an organized plot of assassination, to steal through Baltimore at night in disguise. Soldiers duly summoned to the defence of the capital were murdered in the streets of Baltimore. For weeks the railroads in and near Baltimore were in the possession of an armed force in hostility to the United States, and the rolling stock and property of the only railroad to Washington were in the use of the public enemy. At the same time their use was denied to the Government of the United States. Recently an armed mob in the streets of Baltimore took possession of a train of cars and insulted passengers for political opinions. None of these outrages could have occurred if there were free competing railroad lines through and around Baltimore.

Full charges for freight were exacted from the United States without abatement during the war, while all other roads lowered their rates to the Government, and on United States troops the charge was one dollar to one dollar and ten cents.

At the very time the United States was defending Maryland from invasion by the rebels she charged the United States a tax of thirty cents on each soldier who traveled over this road to her protection. The amount thus collected from the United States far exceeded the entire cost of building and running a new road to Baltimore.

It is thus apparent that the railroad transit to Washington is neither direct, convenient, nor cheap, and that from the nature of the existing monopoly no remedy can be expected from the State of Maryland. That State commands every avenue of approach to Washington. It ceded to the United States this District as a national capital. This fact at common law implies a reasonable right of way over her remaining territory to the ceded territory. This is not granted. She obstructs free communication between the capital and the great body of the people. The inevitable tendency of this policy is to unsettle the continuance of the capital at this place. It is now far from the center of population, but its fine location on the Potomac, central between the North and South, the historical associations connecting it with General Washington, and the great expenditure incurred for public buildings will secure the permanence of this location if direct, convenient, and cheap communication may be had to it from all parts of the country. One chief reason urged for this location was its easy access to the West by the old route of the Potomac and Monongahela and Ohio Rivers. This is the great national route to the West—the route of the Indian trails—of the pioneers of Ohio and Kentucky, of Washington as a surveyor and soldier, and apparent on the map as the nearest and easiest connection between the waters of the Atlantic and the waters of the upper Mississippi basin.

When the Baltimore and Ohio Railroad was built the interests of Baltimore and the legislature of Maryland diverted this route from its natural course along the Potomac to Harper's Ferry eastward over a difficult country to Baltimore, while westward from Cumberland the local interests of Philadelphia and Pennsylvania prevented its construction to Pittsburg and forced it over dangerous and difficult mountains to Wheeling. The same adverse local interests have been strong enough thus far to prevent this national route from being occupied. And thus the chief reason for locating the capital of the nation here has been counteracted, so that now this city is more difficult of access from the West than any city on the seaboard. If this anomaly is continued it will be impossible to resist the removal of the capital to a more central location, free from the danger of foreign and domestic violence, and where the policy of the neighboring States invites the freest and fullest competition in modes and routes of transit of persons and property.

The only remedy for all these complaints is free competition in the building and running of railroads to and from Washington. Where this is allowed no legislative restraints or regulations are required. Railroads are vast agencies of commerce vitally necessary to modern civilization, and it is as wrong by law to limit the number of them as to limit by law the number of steamboats, cotton mills, or blacksmith shops.

Free competition in railroads is necessary in another view. The tendency of the age is to the combination of railroads— the union of connecting and competing lines with a view to prevent the reduction of fares. This process has, within a few years, by leases, by divisions of profits, and by running arrangements, united in a single interest, under a common control, over one thousand miles of railroad, reaching through many States. The only way to avoid injury from this combination of capital is to invite new competing lines. The liberty to build these is the only check upon monopolies. But for this, existing railroads would form combinations precisely as they would be formed by merchants and manufacturers if the freedom of new competition did not compel them to gain their business and profit by the cheapness of their commodities and the excellence of their productions, rather than by special privileges.

A greater danger presents itself than mere combinations to regulate freight. It is the combination of great corporations to control Congress. A very marked example of this is presented by the effort of great corporations to oppose this bill. I will ask the secretary to read a circular letter recently published, signed by eight railroad presidents.

The secretary read as follows:

PHILADELPHIA, *December* 26, 1868.

SIR: Two bills are now pending before the Senate of the United States, each of which incorporates several companies, and authorizes them to build railroads, seven in all, radiating from Washington and extending over seven or eight different States. These bills confer very great powers and impose few restrictions. For example, one of them authorizes the construction of a road to any point on any railroad in Virginia.

It is well understood that this is but an entering wedge to a system of railroad legislation by Congress, intended to extend over every part of the country.

Believing that such congressional legislation will be destructive of existing railroad interests, promote wild and dishonest speculation, and be highly demoralizing in its influence, we call your especial and immediate attention to it.

Many of the corporators named in these bills—some of them officers of existing railroads—have never been consulted. This has given the impression that influential men and companies favor this legislation who in fact are strongly opposed to it.

Under the impression that no such bill can pass, railroad companies generally have not opposed the measure. Prominent Senators, however, say that the danger is great and imminent, and that it calls for immediate and vigorous exertions on the part of existing railroad officers to avert it.

Should this matter appear to you as it does to us, we suggest that you use your influence with your friends in Congress, especially in the Senate, to defeat all such measures.

SENATOR SHERMAN.—I know the gentlemen whose names appear attached to this paper. They are among the ablest railroad managers in the United States. But, sir, if they make combinations of capital to prevent competition they must expect new competitors. They control powerful corporations, but these corporations are subject to law. They have no exclusive powers, and let me say to them, in all kindness, that this effort of theirs is ill-advised, and if persevered in will result in political combinations, both in the States and in Congress, that will override at once their efforts to prevent new railroads, new combinations, and improved facilities.

Experience has shown that free competition is not only beneficial to the public, but is not injurious to the railroads. A new railroad develops its own business; the reduction of prices caused by competition increases the amount of business, and often increases the net earnings of a road. Competition promotes economy in railroad management. It destroys corruption, which is usually an instrument of monopoly. In every aspect, and to every interest, a free competition in railroads is beneficial; it develops local resources, it increases subordinate industries, it cheapens the cost of living, while monopoly in railroads has the opposite tendency, and creates a feeling of dissatisfaction, which, in the end, without regard to legal enactments, will overthrow it.

I have thus far considered the question as a local one, affecting alone the citizens of Washington, or those coming to or going from Washington. There is another view far more important. The right of a State to obstruct commerce and communication between the States by imposing taxes on commerce, or by granting special privileges and monopolies, has often been denied in Congress and by the courts, and presents a question of infinitely greater proportions than the dwarfing of Washington or the cost and inconvenience of persons traveling to Washington. It is the same question which mainly led to the adoption of the Constitution, to the formation of the Zollverein of Germany, and to the formation of the present empires of France and Great Britain. It is the struggle between local restrictions and the liberty of commerce. The effort to harmonize these was attempted by the Constitution of the United States. Local government for local purposes is the primary object of cities, counties, and States; general government for general objects affecting the people of the nation was the object of the national Government.

The precise boundary between these must always be the subject of dispute, and this must especially occur where a specific power is given to both the States and the United States. The power over commerce is of this character: Congress has power "to regulate commerce with foreign nations and among the several States and with the Indian tribes." Here the power of Congress is limited only by the nature of the commerce. The power over local commerce between the citizens of a State is left exclusively to the States, but commerce among the States is to be regulated by Congress. Railroads are the agents both of local commerce and commerce among the several States. This creates the difficulty of defining the limits of the power of Congress and the States. Navigable streams, even if within the limits of a State, have been repeatedly held to be subject to the regulation of Congress. States create railroads for local commerce. May not Congress create railroads for commerce among the States? States prescribe fares and freights for local commerce. May not Congress do the same for commerce among the States? This brings us to the general constitutional question involved in this and all the bills referred to the select committee: does the Constitution confer upon Congress the power by general regulations or by new corporations to control and build railroads?

The general design of the Constitution was to secure to Congress all legislative power affecting the interests of more than one State and essential to the general welfare. Thus questions of peace or war, of armies and navies, of foreign intercourse, of commerce with foreign nations and among the several States, are carefully reserved for the consideration of Congress.

It may sometimes be difficult to draw the line between local commerce within the State and general commerce between the States, but there can be no difficulty in classifying the vast operations of modern railroads, telegraph, and transportation companies, reaching from State to State, as commerce among the States. Commerce between New York and Chicago, traversing several States, cannot be classed as local interstate commerce, nor is it made so by being carried on by different agents of the several States. Though chartered by different States, if they form a connecting line for a single voyage they are agents of a commerce between States, and are subject to the regulation of Congress. If, by the policy of their State or by local interests, they fail to conduct this commerce between States in a convenient, cheap, and expeditious manner, they may be superseded by other agencies created by Congress. The power to regulate includes the power to enforce regulations. The law of a State cannot obstruct or oppose this power. Nor can its agents, under shelter of the authority of the State, impede, retard, or delay commerce among the States.

Internal commerce is the life-blood of a nation, as essential to national existence as an army or navy, more essential than separate departments of the Government or the careful division of political power. As an object of government internal commerce is secondary only to the preservation of life and property. This principle was recognized by the framers of the Constitution. They could not foresee the new modes of transit devised in recent times, but they declared the power of the nation, not only over external, but internal commerce, when between States. When the canoe, the scow, the keel-boat, and the raft were the agents of commerce on navigable rivers they secured the power of Congress over them. When the sailing vessels owned by private merchants and engaged in free competition on the ocean and lakes were the agents of commerce, jurisdiction over them, the power to regulate them, was carefully reserved to Congress. The control over commerce, the duties levied upon commerce, the necessity for uniform commercial regulations, were leading inducements for the formation of the National Government, and these powers were clearly and fully given to the new Government. If the framers of the Constitution could have foreseen the forty thousand miles of railroads and the steamships, telegraphs, express, and transportation companies that now are the agents of commerce, overlapping State lines and extending their operations to the remotest hamlets of the country, they could not have adopted language more clearly conferring upon Congress the power over all these agencies than the language of the Constitution.

Reasoning thus from the nature and character of our Government and the language of the Constitution, I cannot doubt the full power of Congress, not only to regulate the commerce among the States conducted by existing railroads, but when it deems it expedient to build new railroads, either directly by the money of the people or by corporations created by it, and this view is strengthened by the history of the Constitution.

The power of the United States to build works of internal improvement within the States has been settled by a series of precedents stretching through our entire legislative history and sanctioned by every department of the Government. The public records show that the policy in some form or other has been coeval with the existence of the Government, and the rapid progress of the nation is evidence of the wisdom of the policy. Vetoes have sometimes limited the general power for a time, but these are exceptions to the general rule. Rivers and harbors have been improved; canals have been made; turnpikes and railroads have been constructed; private property has been appropriated for public use, and almost every form of commercial improvement has been authorized and constructed by the authority of the general Government.

A long list of these appropriations is contained in Professor Baché's report to Congress some years ago, and in Wheeler's History of Congress. From these it appears that appropriations for internal improvement have been made during every Administration, for a great variety of improvement, and varying in character as commercial agencies advanced from turnpikes to canals, steamboats, and railroads.

The Cumberland road was commenced in the time of Mr. Jefferson. In the Administration of Mr. Monroe the system of internal improvements was revived. The instructive debates in the Senate in 1824 and 1830 exhausted the constitutional argument. Mr. Webster, in his second reply to Mr. Hayne, proved conclusively that Mr. Calhoun, the champion of the most limited authority of Congress, had repeatedly conceded and voted for the unlimited authority of Congress over public improvements, with or without the consent of the States. And, sir, when we reflect upon the march of events, upon the debates and acts of this Senate during the last eight years, it seems idle to pause over the exercise of a power to build a national railroad to the capital of the nation when its necessity is so clearly demanded for the public good, and when it is only resisted by the interest of private corporations demanding a monopoly in the name of State rights.

If Senators desire to follow the constitutional argument further, they will find in the memorial to Congress of the Chicago internal improvement convention of 1848, the authorship of which is attributed to John C. Spencer, of New York, an argument that, to my mind, is conclusive upon every objection made to the power of Congress by the several veto messages of Presidents Polk and Tyler. This argument is on the record of Congress, and deserves a place among the ablest State papers of this century. I can add nothing to it.

A claim is sometimes made that, though the power of Congress to build railroads is settled by legislative precedents, yet Congress cannot condemn land for that purpose without the assent of the State. This claim is certainly untenable. The general power includes all the necessary and proper means to carry it into execution. This cannot be done without appropriating land.

The authority of Congress to build roads, canals, and all forms of internal improvement has been sustained by the Supreme Court whenever questioned before that tribunal. Though the direct question whether Congress may, in disregard of a State law, build a railroad within a State has never been presented, yet the tenor of the decisions of that court has always upheld the power of Congress to adopt its own agencies in the execution of its delegated powers and to disregard any obstructions set up by a State. The United States Bank cases and the Wheeling bridge case sustain all that is attempted by this bill. Whether the bank was an agency proper and necessary for the execution of any of the express powers of Congress was a question of doubt, but no man will question but that a railroad between Washington and New York is an agent of commerce between States, essentially and vitally necessary for the postal, military, and commercial service of the United States, and to hold that no such agent shall exist except it be created by a State, controlled by a State, regulated by a State, made a monopoly by a State, and beyond the power of Congress, is to destroy the essential qualities of a supreme National Government. It is secession intensified, for if a State seceded it lost the benefit of the protection of the general Government, but a State that can grapple and control for her own interests merely all communication over her territory could enjoy all the benefits of union and yet inflict upon her sister States all the injuries of separate governments. The case of

New Jersey is a marked and, fortunately for the country, an isolated example of this policy.[1] Now, therefore, is the proper time to assert the authority of Congress to regulate commerce among the States by authorizing new lines of transit; by encouraging competition, improvement, and enterprise; by making the construction of railroads as free as the construction of merchant vessels and blacksmith shops, and by guarding by general laws the lives and safety of passengers on railroads as well as steamboats. We have already by a general telegraph law greatly increased the competition in that agency of commerce. We have often exercised our power to regulate commercial vessels, both on the sea and on the rivers. The iron track is now the great commercial road of mankind. Over it the commerce of men is now greater than by all kinds of navigable water. The locomotive is either superseding or revolutionizing the canal boat, the sailing vessel, and the steamboat. It is creeping up every valley and overleaping every mountain of our vast country. It is everywhere the agent of commerce and civilization. It has added more to the wealth of our country than all the land and houses and possessions were worth forty years ago. If the railroad and telegraph are not national, then nothing is national. If railroads can be built only by a State, regulated by a State, monopolized by a State; if a State can prevent their construction to promote some local interest or monopoly, then our Government is not national.

The fear of Jonathan Dayton, of New Jersey, expressed in the Constitutional Convention of 1787, has come true. A State, under pretence of State law, taxes other States.

It is one of the great beauties of our Constitution, framed by men of rare wisdom, that though man may invent and magnify; though the habits and agencies of their day are swept away by the inventive genius of their children; though our population has increased twelvefold, and our country extends across the continent, yet that the general principles and powers they have ingrafted in the Constitution, like the teachings of the Bible, meet all changes, all time, all diversities of condition, wealth, and population, and, applied with a liberal and fair construction, regulate agencies and things of which they had no conception, in harmony with their central idea of a local government for local purposes merely, affecting only the people of the State; a national government for general purposes, affecting the people of different States. I believe, sir, that in authorizing the construction of these railroads we exer-

[1] See preceding chapter.

cise no doubtful power, while if our legislation is followed, as I hope it will be, by their speedy construction, we will have contributed not only to the local interests of this District, but to the common good and general welfare of the whole people of the United States.

On January 20 William P. Whyte [Md.] opposed the bill.

I hardly think it can be seriously contended that any power in Congress to build roads is to be found expressed in any of the grants of the Constitution, and, if there is no such power in the creator, surely none can be claimed for the creature. The power, therefore, not being expressed, but in fact denied by the framers of the Constitution, the advocates of this bill claim that it is incident to an expressed power. Such a proposition is not new. As early as the time of Mr. Monroe the same claim was set up. In his veto of the bill to extend the Cumberland road he denied the proposition.

This bill, as its title declares, is to "promote commerce" among the States, and the authority of Congress to pass such a measure is asserted to be incidental to the power "to regulate commerce." Says Mr. Madison:

"A power to be incidental must be exercised for ends which make it a principal or substantive power, independent of the principal power to which it is an incident."

It is not enough that it is regarded by Congress as convenient, or that its exercise would advance the public weal. It must be necessary and proper to the execution of the principal expressed power to which it is an incident, and without which such principal power cannot be carried into effect. "To regulate commerce among the States" gives no warrant to take from a State its right of eminent domain over the soil within its territorial jurisdiction. "To regulate commerce" is not to carry it on. In Gibbons *vs.* Ogden (9 Wheaton, 196), the Supreme Court said "to regulate is to prescribe the rule by which commerce is to be governed." It never meant to make bridges, construct roads, canals, or streets, but it could prescribe the rule by which commerce was to be conducted over them "among the States." The distinction is too clear to need further argument. In the Wheeling bridge case, to which my friend, the Senator from Ohio, casually referred, in which the majority of the court only decided that the power to regulate commerce included the power to determine what shall and what shall not be deemed an obstruction of navigation, Mr. Justice John McLean, in his opinion, dissenting from some of the rulings of the court, said:

"If under the commercial power Congress may make bridges over navigable waters it would be difficult to find any limitation of such a power. Turnpike roads, railroads, and canals might on the same principle be built by Congress. And if this be a constitutional power it cannot be restricted or interfered with by any State regulation.

"So extravagant and absorbing a Federal power as this has rarely, if ever, been claimed by any one. It would in a great degree supersede the State governments by the tremendous authority and patronage it would exercise. But if the power be found in the Constitution no principle is perceived by which it can be practically restricted.

"This dilemma leads us to the conclusion that it is not a constitutional power."

I turn from these authorities and these executive expositions of this power in Congress to find some case, or some dictum even, from those high judicial officers who have thrown light upon the jurisprudence of our country, laying down a doctrine in opposition to this, but I look in vain. Not a single case can be found maintaining the power of Congress to construct a railroad in a State without its concurrence, either expressed or implied. If the Senator from Ohio could have laid his hand upon one he would not have allowed the opportunity to have passed. Without the multiplication of words, for I do not wish to trespass unnecessarily upon the time of the Senate, I affirm that no such power exists in Congress under the Constitution.

But should such power exist in Congress as claimed in this bill I should still protest against its passage upon the ground of its injurious effect upon the country. Every man knows the corrupting influences which surround legislative bodies in the interest of corporations and charter seekers, the former striving for ampler powers and privileges and greater immunities from their common law liabilities, and the latter seeking to obtain charters, to be bought up by rival and existing companies. Once establish Congress as a corporation manufacturer and you will transfer to the rotunda of the Capitol the lobbies of thirty-four States. The third house will outnumber both Houses of Congress put together.

Thousands of miles of railways, intersecting the country at all points, and woven over it like a spider's web, costing millions of money, have been built by private enterprise under State charters and fostered by State legislation. The vast capital so expended has, in a great measure, come from foreign lands, and after lying idle for years is now beginning to yield revenues to the holders of these investments. Let it be understood that after a private company, incorporated by a State, has raised capital from Europe and opened up new territory, and brought to the farmer a market for his grain, and is about to realize the profit of its enterprise, Congress shall intervene and grant charters for parallel roads, without responsibility to the States, and you paralyze the whole railroad energy of this country. No more foreign capital will seek investment in railroad securities here. Under the present system, wherever railroads have been needed, charters for them have always been granted by the States, as far as my experience goes, with a single exception. I concur with the Senator from Ohio in his advocacy of competing lines. Competition in railways, as in everything else, ought to be encouraged. Wherever capital and enterprise are willing to open the country every legislative facility ought to be granted. No monopolies ought to be permitted, whether in railways or copper mines or any other branch of industry. They are odious to republicans, and are calculated to build up the meanest of all aristocracies—the aristocracy of money.

But, Mr. President, I contend that there is no necessity for any such new roads, as proposed by this bill. The State of Maryland has been foremost in the promotion of works of improvement. At the previous session its legislature refused to make any change in the charter of the Baltimore and Potomac Railroad which should prevent a direct connection over its line between Baltimore and Washington.

That she may have erred in some of her legislation I do not pretend to deny, but her good far outweighs her evil. The capitation tax on the Washington branch of the Baltimore and Ohio Railroad is, in my judgment, whether constitutional or not, unfounded in justice or in policy. It exacts as well from her own citizens as from strangers an unnecessary and burdensome toll. It ought to be, and I trust will be, repealed by the legislature at its next session, for I do not think it has now the popular sanction.

Another cause of complaint stated by the Senator who reported this bill is the failure in close connections between the Baltimore and Ohio Railroad and the road running northward to Harrisburg. It is a serious inconvenience, and ought to have a remedy, and if any constitutional mode can be suggested for the benefit of the traveler I shall be most ready to support it. I appeal to Senators, to their candor and to their justice—

Maryland having broken all the bonds of the past, if there were bonds in the past; Maryland having opened wide its doors for capital and for enterprise to build these new roads—whether now the power of Congress shall be extended over that State to destroy all the capital and all the interests created there of which I have spoken, and to build up a monopoly in railroads between this capital and the city of New York and the other points named in the bill?

On January 22 James R. Doolittle [Wis.] opposed the bill in an extended speech of which the conclusion was as follows:

It is upon these grounds, Mr. President, first, that by the Constitution Congress has no power to grant an incorporation for any such purpose; that such power is neither expressly given nor can fairly be implied from the powers which are granted; second, because Congress has no power without the consent of the State legislature to assert the right of eminent domain, and thus far to oust the jurisdiction of the State over its property, its own soil; and, third, because Congress has no power to withdraw valuable and important property interests belonging to the State from State taxation, that I am opposed to the passage of this bill. I believe in the truth of what Justice McLean said, that the exercise by Congress of these tremendous powers will, if once entered upon, revolutionize the Government. If Congress once begin, of necessity all railway corporations will seek to be chartered by national authority. I believe if Congress shall bring to itself here, and under its control, all the railway corporations of the United States, it will in the end subject the control of this Government to an aristocracy of concentrated wealth, not an aristocracy of men, which may have some redeeming qualities, but an aristocracy of mammoth corporations, which, as has been said in strong Anglo-Saxon, have neither "bodies to be kicked nor souls to be damned." In the hands of these great mammoth railway corporations, representing thousands of millions, congresses and presidents will be but playthings.

Mr. President, I have observed the fact—it may be entirely by accident, I hope it is—that under the new *régime* every statue has been removed from the rotunda of the Capitol except that of Alexander Hamilton. Is he to be the presiding genius of the coming future? Having always represented in his life the Federal tendency to bring consolidated power to this Government, he may represent the future just before us, and which is soon to come, and which if you pass this bill has already come. The power of the States over their own railways, their own means of communication, their own institutions, even over their suffrage, is to be subjected to the power of this Government. If this measure shall pass and be acquiesced in by the people every railway corporation will desire its charter under this Government. They will seek a national charter. They will seek national authority for all their acts independent of State control. The time would not be far distant before they would seek to relieve themselves from State taxation in whole or in part. They will be here in immense force, the representatives not only of hundreds of millions, but of thousands of millions of dollars, concentrated and controlled by directors who meet in secret and control all their gigantic operations. When the time comes that all this concentrated power is here, I tell you, Mr. President, and I tell you, my brother Senators, the days of this Republic under the Constitution of the United States as our fathers made it, as our fathers understood it, are already numbered. The plea for a strong government will be set up by these moneyed monopolies, and they will not plead in vain. Capital seeks strong governments. Capital seeks to concentrate itself; and concentrated capital, wherever it exists and in whatever form, has a tendency to concentrated despotism. If we would not see the just powers of the States destroyed, if we would not have them broken down and an imperialism established here at Washington, an imperialism not represented by monarch or potentate or aristocracy of birth, but represented by an aristocracy of concentrated wealth held by railway and banking corporations, we must resist the passage of this bill.

The bill was postponed on January 23 by a vote of 33 yeas to 16 nays.

GOVERNMENT RAILROADS

HOUSE OF REPRESENTATIVES, FEBRUARY 3-12, 1869

On February 3, 1869, a bill proposed by William H. Kelsey [N. Y.] authorizing the construction of a military and postal railway from Washington, D. C., to New

X—16

York City was reported in the House from the Committee on Roads and Canals by Burton C. Cook [Ill.], its chairman.

Mr. Cook announced the cause of the introduction of the bill to be the "holding up" of the Government by the existing railroad (the Baltimore and Ohio joined to the Camden and Amboy) in mail contracts, and assaults committed upon passengers over the line because of political opinions. The bill proposed to incorporate a company of capitalists under control of the Government, especially in relation to transportation of mails and troops, and limitation of fares and freight charges.

The power to charter such a railroad Mr. Cook derived from the constitutional power of Congress to regulate interstate commerce. He cited the case of Cooley vs. The Board of Wardens, 12 Howard, 316, as deciding that the means used to transport merchandise from one State to another are the "instruments of commerce," and the case of Gibbons vs. Ogden, 9 Wheaton, 191, as deciding that "wherever commerce among the States goes the power of the nation goes with it to protect and enforce its rights."

But it is insisted that Congress has no power to authorize the construction of a railroad, even if it has the power of regulating commerce over those already existing and extending from State to State.

I do not see how any distinction can be made between the power to widen and deepen a river so that the commerce of the country can be carried on by an avenue through which it could not pass before and constructing a railroad for the same purpose. The end sought in either case is the same, and the exercise of power is the same. If Congress may deepen Lake St. Clair, it may construct a railroad around it if the interests of commerce would be better served thereby. And it is too late now to question the power of Congress to create avenues of commerce which did not before exist by the improvement of those great rivers which, reaching from State to State, may be made instruments of commerce among the States.

It is argued with great earnestness that Congress has no right to create a corporation in a State. I grant that this is so, except in cases where the creation of such a corporation is a

necessary, or at least a proper, means of carrying into effect
some one of the powers expressly granted to Congress by the
Constitution. If the power to regulate commerce among the
several States be one of these powers, if that commerce must
be to a very great extent carried on over railroads, to deny to
Congress the right, under proper restrictions and limitations,
for the benefit of commerce, to create a corporation for the purpose of making that commerce free from the imposts and heavy
charges imposed either by individual States or by corporations
created by such States would be to construe the Constitution
as if it read thus: ''Congress shall have the power to regulate commerce among the several States, subject, however, to the
control of each individual State at its pleasure.'' This is not
a case of first impression. The precise point was argued by
very eminent counsel and decided by the Supreme Court of the
United States in the case of Osborn *vs*. United States Bank,
9 Wheaton, 860, Chief Justice Marshall delivering the opinion
of the court, and deciding that Congress has the power to create
a corporation in any case where it is a proper instrument to
carry into effect any power vested in the Government of the
United States. Whether the bank was a necessary agency in
carrying out any of the express powers conferred by the Constitution upon Congress may be a matter of argument, but no
one can doubt that a railroad between Washington and New
York is an agency necessary for the postal, military, and commercial service of the United States.

But it is insisted that Congress has not the right to authorize the taking the land of individuals within the several States.
The right of eminent domain existing in the States is qualified
by whatever right the Constitution has vested in the United
States. The question is: Is it necessary or proper, for the proper
regulation of commerce among the several States, that a railroad should be constructed between two or more States? If it
is, Congress has clearly the power to authorize its construction,
and it is believed to be precisely the same exercise of power as
would be the improvement by Congress of the navigation of a
river running through several States. In both instances it
would be the creation of a means of transportation of commerce not before existing, and would require in each case the
appropriation of some soil of the State; and yet the power to
improve the navigation of the rivers extending from one State
to another has long been exercised, and is believed to be unquestionable. The right to authorize the building of bridges across
the navigable waters of the country has been repeatedly exer-

cised by Congress, and the exercise of such right repeatedly sustained by the Supreme Court.

It is urged that Congress can pass no law whereby the title to the soil can be divested from the owner and vested in the corporation, and that the power of the Government, uninterruptedly exercised from the beginning, to erect lighthouses, forts, arsenals, and dockyards is derived, not from their authority to regulate commerce, but from the following clause in the Constitution [Art. I, sec. 8, par. 17].

And, contending that the consent of the State was by this clause required to the erection of lighthouses, dockyards, and other needful buildings, it is argued that this is inconsistent with the idea that Congress possessed the power under other grants of the Constitution. The mistake in this argument is evident in not adverting to the real object of the clause in question, which is not to enable the United States to hold lands in the States, but simply to give Congress exclusive jurisdiction over such places as should be purchased with the consent of the States.

The Supreme Court have decided (3 Wheaton, 388) that Congress may purchase land for a fort or lighthouse and erect such buildings without the consent of the States, but that in such cases the jurisdiction remains with the State, and cannot be acquired by the United States except by a cession.

There is no power given in the Constitution to the United States to erect lighthouses, dockyards, etc., except the power to regulate commerce. That the power to take private property for public use is given to the national Government may be clearly inferred from the last clause of the fifth article of the amendment of the Constitution: "Nor shall private property be taken for public use without just compensation." This is simply a restriction upon the power possessed by the Government of the United States under the Constitution. (Fox. vs. State of Ohio, 5 Howard, 434.)

The power to regulate foreign commerce has been always conceded to give the right to build lighthouses, dockyards, and harbors, to open harbors, to deepen the mouths of rivers, and to create avenues of commerce where they did not before exist. Can anyone draw a distinction between the right to do this and the right to create new avenues of commerce between two or more States?

Can one State without appeal authorize or forbid at its pleasure the passage of the commerce of another State through its limits by railroad communication? Is the authority of every

State over the greater portion of the commerce of the several States superior to that of Congress? By what right can you create a new avenue for foreign commerce if you may not do so for commerce among the several States?

The necessity of the exercise of this power may be seen from the fact that it is in the power of great corporations created by the laws of one State, by the use of controlling capital, to become virtually the owners of connecting lines in other States, and thus to form great trunk lines of communication over which the commerce of the interior States must be carried on, and thus to subject that commerce to such impositions as their own interests may dictate, and thus virtually to "regulate commerce among the several States" by a power wholly unknown to the Constitution, and wholly independent of the people. Nor do I believe that any plan can be devised by which the government of any one State can remedy this evil.

There is another reason, which addressed itself to the committee with some degree of force, why Congress should exercise power to regulate railroads as instruments of commerce. The great lines of railroad west of the Mississippi River, which connect the Atlantic with the Pacific Ocean, are being built mainly by means furnished by the national Government; the money which is used in their construction is taken from the common fund belonging to all the States. It is well settled that every highway and all public improvements made by Congress in a Territory, and which the Federal Government has not a right to establish in a State, passes by necessity to the State government when the change from a territorial to a State organization takes place. Congress cannot by legislation for a Territory obtain a power in the future State which it cannot originally exercise without it. This has been frequently decided. The control, therefore, of the Pacific roads can be continued after States are organized along their lines only by the assertion of a power to charter a railway within their limits after their admission.

Such has been the pressing necessity for the exercise of the power to regulate the connection of these roads where they form lines passing through different States that attempts have been made to exercise this indispensable power by authorizing the consolidation of companies chartered by different States. Three or four States get up a new confederation among themselves, under which they attempt to create a corporation by conjoint legislation. What will ultimately be the effect when exigencies occur which call for a legal solution of the difficulties arising from this legislation cannot be foretold. That great confusion has already ensued no one can doubt. What are the powers of a consolidated railroad company whose several charters contain the most conflicting provisions? How can a mortgage be foreclosed upon a railroad in several States? No American court, State or Federal, has jurisdiction beyond the State in which it sits. We see to-day the disgraceful spectacle presented by the Erie Railroad war. Gentlemen take a boat in the evening and row themselves and their corporation out of the jurisdiction of the courts. If followed, no tribunal can be found in which can be impleaded more than a fraction of the property and persons concerned. These facts show the necessity of the exercise by Congress of the power conferred by the Constitution to regulate commerce among the several States, a commerce not limited either in fact or by constitutional definition to the navigable waters of the country, but for the most part carried on over the great national highways extending in every direction through the length and breadth of the land.

The practical question is, Can Congress regulate the vast and increasing commerce among the States carried on by means of railways, or must that commerce be regulated by monopolies whose power over such commerce is limited only by the amount of capital at their command? It will be seen that the details of this bill have been framed with care to prevent the creation of fictitious capital stock, to prevent heavy charges, to prevent unnecessary delays; and it is confidently believed that the road can and will be built should this bill become a law, and a speedier, cheaper, and better communication be established between this capital and New York.

I conceive that the great difficulty with the railroad corporations now existing in the country is that the capital stock does not represent the cost of the road, but represents precisely the amount which in the judgment of the directors or those having control of the road is necessary to carry on its operations successfully. When Massachusetts sought, by legislation, to prevent the increase of the capital stock of her railroads, and also the declaring of dividends greater than a specified per cent., the result was that the usefulness of the roads was greatly diminished, the roads doing no more work than was sufficient to earn the specified rate of dividend upon the capital stock. The only way, it seems to me, by which these evils can be guarded against in a measure of this kind is by fixing, as is done in this bill, the maximum rate of fare and tariff of freight. In other words, we say to this company, "You may earn all the money you can; but you must impose no greater charge for passengers or freight than we here specify; you must make the trip in a certain number of hours; you must comply with certain regulations as to the time of starting and arriving." If this bill should become a law it will be found that, so far as the traffic over this road is concerned, the commerce will be effectually regulated for the interest of the public.

CHARLES O'NEILL [Pa.].—I wish to inquire whether the object the gentleman seeks would not be better accomplished if he would prepare and present to the House a measure to be enacted by Congress as a general railroad law? I think he has shown most clearly the power of Congress to pass a bill of this kind, but, if his object is to assert that power, why not urge upon the House the passage of a general railroad law which might extend, if capital could be raised for the purpose, a railroad from the Atlantic to the Pacific?

MR. COOK.—In the first place, the Committee on Roads and Canals were under instruction, if in their opinion Congress had power over this subject, to prepare a bill regulating commerce on railroads, not authorizing the building of roads, but regulating commerce over them. Now, I agree that until some members of the House shall be able to give time and study to this subject, to the exclusion of every other, and shall be furnished with the necessary statistics and other information, it will be impossible for us to adopt such a law as will be fully operative and effectual. I believe the importance of the subject demands that we should have a bureau of statistics upon the question; that the statistics should be prepared as other important statistics are prepared, by a commissioner, whose attention should be devoted exclusively to this subject.

Now, as to the inquiry of the gentleman from Pennsylvania [Mr. O'Neill], "Why not report a general railroad law?" the answer is very evident. Our power to charter a railroad grows out of the necessities of commerce. We must in each individual case decide upon our sworn responsibility as legislators that in our opinion it is necessary for the purposes of free commercial intercourse that a road should be built upon a particular route. I submit that such being the nature and extent of our power, we cannot authorize a general system of railroads, which might extend anywhere at the pleasure of those who might choose to build them.

On February 9 Dennis McCarthy [N. Y.] supported the bill. Referring to the monopoly of the Camden and

Amboy Railroad exercised in fixing discriminating charges in favor of inhabitants of New Jersey by agreement with the State and without consent of Congress, he said that this was in opposition to the Constitution, which forbade a State, without the consent of Congress, to lay any duty on tonnage, etc.

It is said that this levy upon passengers and freight is not impost or duty. What is it? Direct taxation upon the people of the United States, a violation of the Constitution and the rights of all the people, except those of New Jersey; a monopoly of the carrying trade, conferred upon a corporation and road by that State, thus preventing that healthy competition which insures to the public safety, speed, comfort, and cheap fare, all of which the advocates of special privileges and powers, yes, technical interpreters of the Constitution, forbid to the people at large. The Constitution says:

"The citizens of each State shall be entitled to all privileges and immunities of citizens in the several States."

Certainly, then, no State has the right or power under the Constitution to lay imposts on the citizens of other States who are compelled to cross her domain. Other States occupy an equally important position for controlling commerce, the public defence, and transmission of mails, and will also claim a royalty if Congress shall refuse to regulate this claimed power where it exists. Our remedy is to create and incorporate companies with power to raise capital, secure the right of way, and build roads from this city to New York, or from such points in States, to and through other States, as the wants of the people demand. Look at the condition of this capital, almost isolated from the people outside, subject to great annoyances and cost of time and money from the want of competition; and yet under a claim of vested rights these incorporations hold the people and country under impost and tax for the benefit and use of their stockholders. The power to provide for the "common defence of the nation" confers the right and the necessity of creating competing lines of railroads, running from center to circumference of our vast country, as a means of national defence and safety in times of peril, thus furnishing cheap and rapid transportation of troops and all the materials and munitions pertaining to the nation's safety and defence. The want of this competition added largely to the delay, suffering, and expense of suppressing the rebellion. The creation of competing lines of railways is of vital importance as an auxiliary means of defence, and demands immediate action. By them we overcome time and distance; we prevent rebellion, or we speedily subdue it; we shall prevent Indian barbarities and allay Indian wars; we bring extremes convenient to each other, encourage social and friendly intercourse, hasten emigration, binding the whole people together in one family—one in agriculture, manufactures, commerce, art, sciences, mechanism, labor, and all the interest of our common country.

This great power of commerce diffuses intelligence, destroys prejudice, advances all interests, almost as generally and as rapidly as the rays of light travel over and benefit the earth. "The power to establish post roads" is another of those powers sufficient for all time. No man will claim that the mails can be lawfully held in abeyance by the legislation or power of any State, much less the power created by it on the old idea of post roads; yet to-day nearly all the post office business of the country in the transportation of mails is only allowed and performed by sufferance, by the railroads refusing to enter into contracts as to time, safety, convenience, or cost. This state of dependence on the part of the Government must not be allowed. This great element in the power of government is for the people, and confers benefits and happiness upon all equally; it is a great power of the diffusion of intelligence, stimulating energy and action, aiding prosperity; and when to it is added the telegraph, equally free and equally cheap, and when the shackles of State and individual obstructions are stricken off then will be settled for all time the question of regulating commerce, bringing it into harmony with the other great powers and duties of the Government.

Charles E. Phelps [Md.] opposed "the extraordinary measure."

It is nothing less than the inauguration of a system, now for the first time in the history of this Government, which looks to nothing short of the ultimate consolidation, under congressional auspices, of the forty-two thousand miles of railway already constructed in every State of this Union, and the ultimate Federal control of the $3,000,000,000 of capital which has already been invested by corporations and States in this vast network of internal improvement. The assumption of power extends to the absolute claim of eminent domain over the soil of every State, the absolute claim to enter upon, seize, and condemn the land of every freeholder in each State deemed necessary for the opening and construction of new lines of communication, and, in addition, the complete control, regulation, and management of every mile of railway in operation and every dollar of capital invested through the agency of one or more mammoth corporations, creatures of the national Congress.

It not only does that, but it goes further. It wrests from every one of the thirty-seven States of this Union all the jurisdiction their courts now exercise over rights and remedies affecting these lines of internal improvement, as they come in contact with the citizens and with the property of the various States. It absorbs to the general Government and brings within the sweep of the Federal courts that enormous mass of jurisdiction, civil and criminal, at law and in equity, over cases involving property, liberty, and even life, which of necessity travels with these great lines of intercommunication wherever they penetrate society.

It does more—a consideration which I should think would compel every man who wishes to keep this Government as honest and as pure as circumstances will permit to oppose any such measure as this. It invites the lobbies of thirty-seven State legislatures to pack their carpet-bags and move at once upon Washington. It concentrates these railroad rings, with their intrigue, their log-rolling, and their corruption funds, at the seat of the Federal Government, and intrenches them in the corridors of this Capitol. It exposes members of Congress, not to danger, for they are pure and innocent, but to the annoyance and importunity of solicitation, and subjects their stern and incorruptible virtue to the schemes and manipulations of a combined horde of speculators unprecedented in congressional experience.

William D. Kelley of Philadelphia characterized the measure as a "job."

It is a provision for the incorporation of a number of unprofitable roads into one and a sacrifice of the interests and rights of all save the stockholders of these roads; and it is to be enacted just when the great want which we have always felt is being supplied.

I grant that the conduct of the Baltimore and Ohio road in refusing to make connections with other roads is a great hardship. I am ready to remedy it by the law proposed in the last

Congress compelling roads running to State lines to connect with roads of other States. But this is not necessary in this case, as the Potomac and Baltimore road is nearly completed and will enfranchise travel from the monopoly hitherto maintained by the Baltimore and Ohio company.

Austin Blair [Mich.] supported the bill.

I am not surprised to see gentlemen on the other side of the House unite to raise the cry of State rights against this bill. They live in the ideas of fifty years ago. We cannot convince them that the world moves. If we tell them that the power to regulate commerce between the States is the power to build trans-State railways; that commerce abandons the lakes and the rivers, and even the ocean itself, and speeds across the continent upon the iron rail, the Democratic party only stares at us. The magnetic telegraph itself can give it only a spasm as it feebly croaks "State rights!" If a great nation demands national highways for the encouragement of its industries and the development of its resources, no matter how great the necessity, it must yield to every State the right to veto the project. And thus local jealousies, private greed, and ignorant stupidity must be allowed to defeat the most necessary and beneficial measures. I insist that the only security for cheap and speedy transportation must be looked for in the power of Congress to open the way for trade and that intercourse which is a part of trade by annulling repressive State laws or by providing national highways over which the people of all the States may pass upon equal terms.

We have been solemnly warned that the passage of this bill will bring down upon Congress the terrible lobby from thirty States. There is no danger from the lobby when there are no subsidies, and the virtue of Congress does not need to sound an alarm before the temptation is offered. If the legislatures of Pennsylvania and Maryland have been able to withstand the terrible lobby while voting special privileges, then I will trust the virtue of Congress while it goes about to destroy those monopolies.

The gentleman from Maryland [Mr. Phelps] evidently fears—and I think we all share in that fear—that the time will speedily come when cars will run past Baltimore by steam. Farewell then, sir, to the charming omnibus line; farewell to the great horse teams which, with the crack of the whip and the sound of a tin horn, take us at the rate of two miles an hour through the metropolis of Maryland with a cheery "Gee-up" and "Gee-ho!" It will be some compensation that we shall no longer see women and children, the aged, the halt, and the blind tumbled out of the cars coming in from the Northwest at all times of night and day and in all weather, and delivered over to the howling gang to whom they are compelled to intrust themselves in passing through the Monumental City.

Mr. Speaker, the spirit of American enterprise refuses longer to be bound by these vexatious restrictions upon the speed and comfort of travel. If the States will not furnish the highways required by the people the country calls upon the national Congress to supply the defect, and we shall not long refuse to respond to the call. Let us pass this bill and put upon record our determination to remove out of the way every obstruction placed across the great avenues of commerce and business, whether by State monopolies or otherwise.

On February 12 the bill was passed by the House— yeas, 99; nays, 54. It was not acted upon by the Senate.

CHAPTER VIII

FORFEITURE OF RAILROAD GRANTS

Joseph N. Dolph [Ore.] Introduces Bill in Senate to Restore to the Government Certain Lands of the Northern Pacific Railroad—Debate: Wilkinson Call [Fla.], Sen. Dolph, Charles H. Van Wyck [Neb.], George F. Edmunds [Vt.], James Z. George [Miss.], John H. Mitchell [Ore.], Henry W. Blair [N. H.]; Bill Is Passed—Barclay Henley [Cal.] Proposes Substitute Bill in the House Making a General Forfeiture by the Company; Bill Is Passed; Senate Non-concurs, and Conference Is Appointed—Preston B. Plumb [Kan.] Introduces in the Senate a Bill to Forfeit All Unearned Railroad Grants—Debate: Sen. Dolph, Henry M. Teller [Col.], James H. Berry [Ark.]; Bill Is Passed—Debate in the House: William S. Holman [Ind.], William J. Stone [Mo.]; Bill Is Passed with Amendments; Senate Non-concurs, and a Conference Is Appointed.

A S time passed the people began to regret the lavish donations which their Representatives in the national legislature had made to the railroads, especially since these corporations were not fulfilling the spirit of the grants, and, indeed, in a number of instances were not complying with even the letter of their contracts with the Government, in that they were entering into land speculation before the title to the grants had been completed by construction of the roads.

The Northern Pacific Railroad was especially condemned for this practice, and a loud popular demand was made for forfeiture of the grants with the conditions of which it had not complied. In order to forestall action in the matter, the corporation very shrewdly inspired a bill for that measure of forfeiture which it would accept, the concession being so framed that its acceptance by the Government would confirm the railroad's title to the remainder of the land.

On April 19, 1886, Joseph N. Dolph [Ore.] introduced in the Senate from the Committee on Public Lands a bill

To restore to the United States certain of the lands granted to the Northern Pacific Railroad Company to aid in the construction of a railroad from Lake Superior to Puget Sound, and to restore the same to settlement.

FORFEITURE OF NORTHERN PACIFIC RAILROAD GRANTS

SENATE, MAY 27-JUNE 15, 1886

On May 27 Wilkinson Call [Fla.] opposed the measure on the ground that it was an attempt to appease the public (justly outraged at the retention of vast land grants by the trans-continental railroads to which they had forfeited title by non-performance of obligations imposed in the grants) by a forfeiture of an insignificant portion of the grants, which might be construed as strengthening the title to the remainder.

The bill, he said, was in effect handing over to the corporation 27,539,840 acres of the public domain, worth $100,000,000.

The whole question is before the Senate whether the demand of the people, and their rightful and just demand, that where a railroad company has failed to comply with the provisions of the law the Congress of the United States shall declare that the law which created the grant and which provided that at a certain period of time the grant should expire, and the land should belong to the public domain and be open to settlement and occupation by the people under the homestead laws, shall be observed, or whether Congress will make a new grant of perhaps a hundred million dollars or more of the public money in the form of a land grant to a few individuals.

Instead of complying with the just demand of the associated laboring men and women of the country to enact some measures by which the burden of their toil and poverty shall be lightened, this bill proposes to lay still heavier burdens on them, and to place beyond their reach 27,000,000 acres of the public domain, which partly belongs to them.

There is no question of the construction of the railroad presented by this bill. There is no question that this great high-

LAND GRANTS TO RAILROADS

way failed to be constructed within the time limited by the
act, and that by emigration and the increase of the population
of the country these lands have become immensely valuable.
All the circumstances which require and justify the original
policy, if there was justification for such a vast donation of an
empire of land for any purpose whatever to a few individuals,
have changed and no longer exist.

The power of Congress to declare forfeited a grant of the public lands,
made to either a corporation or a State, by an act containing a clause
providing that the lands should revert upon failure to build the road
within a specified time, is established beyond all controversy by repeated
decisions of the Supreme Court.

It is specifically so held in United States *vs*. Repentigny (5 Wall., 211)
and Schulenberg *vs*. Harriman (21 Wall., 44).

Following these cases is another which even more unequivocally defines the power of Congress in this regard. In Farnsworth *vs*. Minnesota
and Pacific Railroad Company (92 U. S., 66), the court, considering the
question, said:

"A forfeiture by the State of an interest in lands and connected franchises, granted for the construction of a public work, may be declared for
non-compliance with the conditions annexed to their grant or their possession, when forfeiture is provided by statute, without judicial proceedings to ascertain and determine the failure of the grantee to perform the
conditions."

Mr. President, when you consider the fact that has been developed before the Senate in the reports of its Committees on
Interstate Commerce, that a taxing power upon the people of
this country greater than that exercised by Congress, upon every
man, woman, and child, has imposed a debt of $3,000,000,000
upon this people in the shape of fraudulent and fictitious securities, and that, while we are here pretending to exercise the powers of legislation in this most important of all subjects, the
power of taxation, the power to oppress the labor of the country and take from its hire for public purposes, has been exercised without our knowledge or consent, and a debt greater than
the war debt has been imposed and now rests upon the people
by virtue of the issue of fraudulent securities issued by transportation companies with the power to tax for all locomotion
and transportation to pay the interest on their securities—when
we reflect that this expanse of public land is now proposed to be
appropriated to the same purpose, to float additional securities
with the power of taxation upon the people of this country, the
magnitude of the question involved in this bill may be somewhat appreciated. The passage of this bill in its present shape
will be a menace to all the property interests of the country. It

will be a defiance by the Senate of the people and their just demands. It will be a declaration that the Senate will use the powers of legislation in the interests of corporate power and against the people.

On May 28 Senator Dolph supported his bill. The Canadian Government, he said, had been subsidizing the Canadian Pacific Railroad. The Northern Pacific Railroad Company, on the contrary, had to contend with threats of forfeiture of their land grants, greatly impairing their credit, and yet it was making heroic efforts to complete the road.

Thus it appears to me that we owe something to the stockholders of this company, the people who put their money into this enterprise. It seems to me unjust now as an equitable proposition when hundreds of thousands of dollars are being expended upon this link, this 75 miles in the Cascade Mountains, when it is partly graded, when surveying parties have been seeking to find a practicable route through the mountains ever since the company was incorporated; when a great tunnel is being constructed—it seems to me, I repeat, that it is unjust now to declare that they shall be deprived of that land if the road is not completed when this act shall take effect. If they were not now prosecuting the work with energy, if it could be shown that they were not being diligent in the construction of the Cascade branch, if they were delaying the construction and seeking to hold on to the grant, I would not say a word; but with the diligence that is now being used it appears to me that we ought not to throw an obstacle in the way of the construction.

Something has been said here in regard to the conditions of this grant and the character of it. I do not believe that there is a lawyer in this body and there are few out of it but who know that this grant is a grant *in præsenti*, that it transferred the title upon conditions, that when the conditions are performed, no matter whether within the time limited in the act or afterward, the title becomes perfect and beyond the power of Congress to interfere with it; that as this road was to be constructed in sections of 25 miles, and it was provided that whenever a section was completed the President of the United States should appoint commissioners to examine it and accept it and then patents should issue to it; whenever a 25-mile section was constructed and commissioners were appointed to examine it and it was approved by the President of the United States, no matter whether the patents were issued or not, the title of the company became perfect to the lands so far as the road had been accepted. The grant is in its nature divisible, and under the provisions of the act every section stands upon precisely the same basis as if there had been a separate act for each 25-mile section; and no lawyer under a grant with such conditions, in my judgment, after a thorough examination of the question, would contend that the provision as to the completion of the entire road at all affects the condition as to the sections of the road which had been completed, examined, and accepted in accordance with the terms of the act.

He also pleaded for the settlers who had in good faith bought lands from the company.

The Northern Pacific company issued a circular and advertised that, if people would go on the lands and settle on them and improve them, when they had been earned by the company by construction of its road, they would be graded and settlers should have the first right to purchase at an appraised value or in some cases at $2.60 an acre. Some people went onto these lands under those provisions, and have fenced, cultivated, and improved them, and there are great fields of wheat growing on them to-day. Many of the settlers have exhausted their homestead and preëmption rights, and if Congress should not make any provision for such persons they would be liable to lose their lands and we should have them coming here at another session of Congress for relief; others would jump their claims under the land laws, and we should have a great deal of trouble growing out of the matter.

Charles H. Van Wyck [Neb.] opposed the bill.

This land was given to the Northern Pacific on the ground that their road would benefit the remaining land and that the benefit to the Government from this donation would be the enhancement of its other property by building the road; but they delayed building the road for reasons best known to themselves, so that it was not completed until the land had become valuable. I think there would be no injustice even now in saying to this railroad company, "Half the grant at the completion of your road is worth more than the whole would have been had you completed the road within the lifetime of the grant."

X—17

GEORGE F. EDMUNDS [Vt..].—How much would it have been worth if the road had not been built at all?

SENATOR VAN WYCK.—The American citizen went in advance of the road.

SENATOR EDMUNDS.—And would not that be true in the great and growing State of Nebraska, which through her Senator is now asking Congress to help build railroads there?

Senator Call spoke again on June 2.

When a measure of great public importance is pressed upon the attention of Congress by a large body of public opinion, when it has been presented by the platforms of both the great political parties of the country, when the Democratic party in the last canvass presented distinctly to the country the pledge that all unearned railroad grants should be forfeited, that the policy of granting the lands in homesteads to actual settlers was a necessary one for the well-being of the whole country, that the policy of these large land grants to railroad corporations was a hurtful one in every respect, when the great body of the associated labor of this country has indorsed that view and has spoken in the most emphatic terms recently to the country, it can scarcely be justified that we should fail to take action upon it, and it is certainly true that a failure to act when the question is presented and the passage only of a law which relates to a very small portion, an insignificant portion of this vast domain, thus evading the question raised before us by the public opinion of the country, will be regarded as a denial, as hostile legislation, and, whatever the motives, it will in effect and in fact be a denial of this proposition and of this demand by the public opinion of the country.

It does not matter that this small proportion of this unearned land grant shall be forfeited and that it is right that it should be. The great question upon which the people of this country demand Congress to take action, and upon which in my judgment the very stability of our republican institutions depends, is left untouched; and it is left untouched in the interest of these vast land grants; it is left untouched in the interest of accumulation without consideration of vast properties in the hands of a few individuals; it is left untouched in the interest of that great amount of taxation upon securities issued without consideration and taxing the productive power of the people of the United States without the authority of law, but which is as practical and as effective in oppressing the industries of the country as if imposed by an act of Congress itself. And for one, therefore, I am not in favor of allowing this question to pass without some expression of opinion on the part of the Senate.

In the report of the Committee on Education and Labor, the intelligent representatives of the associations of labor presented the views and the opinions of that large and influential body of our fellow citizens upon that subject. Since that time the subject has continued to grow in importance. I will read a few extracts from the testimony taken before the committee on this subject, the testimony of Mr. William Godwin Moody found on the seven hundred and twentieth page of the first volume of that report:

The amount of the public domain that has been absolutely granted to the railroads is 250,000,000 acres—an area equal to the Austro-Hungarian Empire and the Kingdom of Italy, with Switzerland and the Netherlands thrown in.

The hurt is manifold. One of the most manifest features of it is that it has driven our American people off the farms. Under the conditions of the grants of the homestead lands the amount of land so granted to each American citizen was limited to two quarter-sections at the most; one acquired by homestead right or purchase and the other by tree culture, making altogether 320 acres. Under the grants to the railroads no limitations have been made, and no conditions have been imposed as to the disposal of the lands. The railroads take them purely as speculators, and they enter upon the disposal of them as upon a gigantic speculation. They are filling our country with these great estates; estates that sink to insignificance the *latifundia* of old Rome, which were the cause of her destruction. They are planting upon our soil a social system that is in utter and direct conflict with all our institutions, and it is growing with a rapidity that is almost beyond belief. That system is driving from the soil those who should there find their homes with full occupation, abundance, and happiness. Hundreds of thousands, aye, millions, of our people are driven off the land into the towns and cities, where they are hived up in hovels and tenements such as the gentlemen of this committee have seen, I believe, to some degree, and the sight of which, I understand, was so exceedingly offensive to their olfactory nerves that they abandoned that method of investigation—at least it has been so reported by the papers. The facts are that while there are hundreds and thousands and millions of acres of our lands, cultivated and uncultivated, in the hands of private owners, without a single fixed inhabitant upon them, we have here in the city of New York a population so dense that it is reckoned at the rate of 500,000 people upon a single square mile; a mass of people living in a state of wretchedness unendurable to the sight of gentlemen of this committee, and absolutely unendurable to the life of those people themselves—for we find that the mortality in those districts is double what it is in the other sections of New York.''

This testimony has been verified in the report of the Commissioner of Labor, in the fact that there are a million of unemployed people now in this country, in the fact that labor is disturbed and there is unrest everywhere, in the fact that there is among our people a disposition for change, for new legislation, or something that will cure the manifest evils that affect the family, that affect the comfort and well-being of the entire community. We are not at a loss to understand why that is when we understand that between three and four thousand millions of securities which have no consideration but, as was said by the Senator from Texas [Richard Coke], the ink and the paper upon which they are made, but which carry with them a taxing power upon every man, woman, and child to meet the gross amount of nearly $900,000,000 a year, that being the total gross earnings of these corporations, and between three and four thousand millions appears to be the most reasonable estimate of this character of securities bearing a proportionate part of this vast amount of tax paid for railroad transportation.

Mr. President, we have here this vast grant of something like thirty or thirty-two million acres which are involved in this question of forfeiture, which were not earned within the time specified in the granting acts, which were given upon the express condition, so specified in the law, that it should not be a grant unless that condition was complied with; and we find upon an examination of the reports that have been made to the two Houses of Congress and a careful estimate of the facts that between thirty and forty million dollars will be made from this land grant by the few projectors of this enterprise, those who hold and control its stock, over and above the entire cost of the construction of the road. We find that the indirect effect of this action of Congress is to tax the people who shall occupy these public lands not only with the actual cost of the construction of this road and then give it to a few individuals, but with thirty or forty millions above and beyond the cost of the road.

JAMES Z. GEORGE [Miss.].—Do I understand the Senator that the Government paid enough to build and equip the road fully from end to end and $30,000,000 besides?

SENATOR CALL.—That is the effect of it.

SENATOR GEORGE.—So as to make them a present of the road and $30,000,000 as a bonus for building it? Is that the idea?

SENATOR CALL.—That is the idea. I have been informed that there has been offered by an English syndicate an amount nearly equal to $300,000,000 for the land if the title can be confirmed.

Now, Mr. President, here is a great public question, a question involving the safety of the Republic, for both political parties have asserted, and it is plain to the eye of reason and argu-

ment that there can be no republican government if there be
several hundred millions of dollars in value of the public land
granted without consideration and as a gift to individuals.
Upon that proposition there can be no kind of doubt or question
that the people of this country will not sustain this Congress,
and that it cannot be covered up by any delusive and illusory
propositions and arguments in regard to the consideration of
the construction of a railroad. The necessity of railroads, the
advantage to the public, the necessity of them to the civilization
of the country is one thing in which all will acquiesce. The
construction of them even by donations from the Federal treasury is another thing, which does not concern that question. If
it be expedient that the public policy shall be established of
building these great public highways by donations from the
public treasury, none will contend but that it should be limited
to the cost of the road. None will deny that in the case of the
subsidy to the Northern Pacific Railroad it should be a lien
upon the property returnable to the people in some shape or
form. No one can justify the imposition by law (being the direct effect of a grant of the public lands) of the burden of building a railroad upon the settlers upon the public lands, taking
from them and their hard-earned toil the entire cost of a railroad, and then adding to it as much again as the cost paid by
them, and then give this enormous sum of from sixteen to forty
million dollars and the franchise and the completed railroad
built by the labor and toil of these people to a few individuals
who manipulate and control and own the stock of the road.
That is the question that is presented from which there is no
escape and no denial, and the question is how are we going to
deal with this condition of things.

I am in favor of a final settlement of this question. I have
no enmity to corporations. I recognize them as an instrument
of modern civilization. Associated effort, which can only be
effective in the form of corporate authority, is the great instrument of modern civilization; but it is a distinct question whether
they should be left without restraint, whether railroads should
be built by impositions upon the settlers and the hard earnings
of those who toil upon the public lands, and then give them
away with two or three times their cost with the power of taxation of those people. That is a different and a distinct question. That has nothing to do with the utility of railroads,
nothing to do with the policy of aiding them either by grants
of public money or otherwise. It is that question of abuse of the
legislative power of government in making donations of public

lands and increasing the power of individuals to impose unreasonable burdens on the country which we have to deal with.

It is no answer to this line of argument to say that the public in carrying into operation a transportation system has been greatly benefited, that freights have been reduced, that transportation has been made easy. We have a right to demand that it shall be done with the least cost to the people consistent with a reasonable and liberal profit to those who engage in these enterprises.

How did that distinguished man, whose great capacity none will deny, the lamented President of the United States, deal with this question when it came before him? I refer to the late President Garfield. What did he say to the American people, with the authority of his great name and reputation, with regard to that question which the Senate proposes to set aside and not deal with as demanded by the people—the question of this vast corporate interest unrestrained by law, the question of the donation of millions upon millions of acres of the public land without reference to the cost of construction? President Garfield, in his address upon "The Future of the Republic," delivered before the literary societies of the Western Reserve College, of Hudson, Ohio, on the 2d of July, 1873, said:

All railroad experience has verified the truth of George Stephenson's aphorism, that, "when combination is possible, competition is impossible."

*   *   *   *   *   *   *

It is easy to see that we are repeating the experience of Great Britain on a vast scale. We have doubled our miles of railway in the last eight years.

The process of consolidation of our leading lines of roads has been even more rapid than that of construction, and whatever dangers we may expect from the system are rapidly culminating to the point of full development. In antagonism to these and to similar combinations of capitalists are the combinations of laborers in trades unions and labor leagues. The indications are abundant that we shall soon see, set in full array, a conflict between capital and labor—a conflict between forces that ought not to be enemies, for labor is the creator of capital, which is only another name for accumulated labor. It is the duty of statesmanship to study the relation which the Government sustains and ought to sustain in this struggle, and to provide that it shall not be the partisan supporter of either combatant, but the just protector of both. The right to labor has not been sufficiently emphasized as one of the rights of man. The right to enjoy the fruits of labor has been better secured.

In view of the facts now set forth, the question returns, What is likely to be the effect of railway and other similar combinations upon our community and our political institutions? Is it true, as asserted by the British writer quoted above, that the state must soon recapture and control the railroads, or be captured and subjugated by them? Or do the phe-

nomena we are witnessing indicate that general breaking up of the social
and political order of modern nations so confidently predicted by a class
of philosophers whose opinions have hitherto made but little impression on
the public mind?

The analogy between the industrial condition of society at the present
time and the feudalism of the Middle Ages is both striking and instructive. In the darkness and chaos of that period the feudal system was the
first important step toward the organization of modern nations. Powerful
chiefs and barons intrenched themselves in castles, and in return for submission and service gave to their vassals rude protection and ruder laws.
But, as the feudal chiefs grew in power and wealth, they became the oppressors of their people, taxed and robbed them at will, and finally, in their
arrogance, defied the kings and emperors of the mediæval states. From
their castles, planted on the great thoroughfares, they practiced the most
capricious extortions on commerce and travel, and thus gave to modern
language the phrase "to levy blackmail." The modern barons, more
powerful than their military prototypes, own our greatest highways, and
levy tribute at will upon all our vast industries. And, as the old feudalism
was finally controlled and subordinated only by the combined efforts of
the kings and the people of the free cities and towns, so our modern
feudalism can be subordinated to the public good only by the great body
of the people acting through their governments by wise and just laws.

*   *   *   *   *   *   *

States and communities have willingly and thoughtlessly conferred these
great powers upon railways, and they must seek to rectify their own
errors without injury to the industries they have encouraged.

Now, Mr. President, these words of Mr. Garfield, who unquestionably, whatever may be said of him, was a man of great
thought, a man of profound reflection, come to us with great
force when we are considering the question of dealing in our
discretion with a grant of thirty-odd millions of acres of the
public land over which Congress has plenary and absolute power
for a railroad constructed outside the terms of the law with notice to everyone that the law giving that grant had expired,
for I undertake to say that there is not a single ground of argument to the contrary.

It has been said that no lawyer would express an opinion
that this grant was not vested up to the point of the present
completion of the railroad company. Why, there is not a decision of the Supreme Court and there is nothing but a single
decision of the district court in Oregon and one or two others
that Congress has abdicated its sovereign power of legislation
and created a vested right, in defiance of the power and the
duty of Congress, to an empire of public land under an act
which in express terms required that if a certain thing was not
done, to wit, the completion of the road by a certain time, it
should be without force and effect, or, as the Supreme Court

says, in the decision that I have before me, in words the law is a law as well as a grant and the grant is controlled by the law. Without the law it has no existence, and the law says it shall exist only upon condition, a condition which was never performed, and to this force and effect is every word of every decision, and the single fact that the Supreme Court has said that the words "there shall be and is hereby granted" create a present interest is the only foundation of an argument without reason and without countenance in the authorities which seeks to overturn the fact that the law controls the grant and that it is an act of sovereign legislative power for a great public purpose limited by time, because it is absurd to say that to do that hundred years hence which to do to-morrow would be of great public service would be a compliance with the public necessities and the public uses. Therefore time is of the essence of the law, made so expressly by the reason of the act itself, sustained by the reason of the law and by the public policy upon which it was based. Therefore I undertake to say that neither can there be an argument or pretence of an argument or reason for the assertion that the power of Congress is not absolute and discretionary over this subject.

I undertake further to say that it is a demonstrable fact that if we are to aid this railroad corporation, if this franchise to this great corporation of the road built by it does not furnish a compensation for its cost, we had better pay for it out of the public treasury and pay the reasonable and proper and just cost of the construction of the road than to impose upon the people of this country the burden of paying two or three times its value, or to impose it upon that portion of the people of this country who live in Oregon, who live in Idaho, who live in the States and Territories along the line of the road. The policy of this law was to say, before that country was occupied, "We will give this land if you will construct this road within the time limited," and in doing that from this enormous empire, greater than has been acquired by conquest almost at any period of the history of the world by the armies of one nation from another—from this great empire of public land, this act of Congress making the grant undertook to say there should be paid out of the labor and toil of the people who settled upon it whatever might be demanded as the cost of the construction of the road, which even at the present value of this land would realize to the grantees probably $100,000,000 more than the entire cost of construction of the railroad.

Certainly the intendment of the act was that it should be a

reasonable cost of construction, but, as Mr. Garfield said, these grants were made unreasonably, recklessly, without the limitations which sound policy would have imposed, and from the report to the two Houses of Congress the report of the president of the company, the report of the auditor, and in estimating, as the committee of the House did, the mean between the two reports they find that in addition to paying the entire cost of the construction of the road there was a difference of from sixteen to thirty or forty million dollars of profit over and above the estimated cost of the road, even taking the completed portion of it, and that was at the valuation of two dollars and a half an acre for the land.

Now, Mr. President, it cannot be disguised that what is proposed and what is sought to be done is a gift of an amount estimated from $16,000,000 to $93,000,000 to some few persons, and that this is sought to be covered up under the pretence of vested rights—vested rights under a law that gave notice to everyone that they should have no existence until the condition upon which the grant was made was performed. Now, what does the Supreme Court of the United States say on that matter? The law, as I have said, required the completion of this railroad by 1879. It has been said that there is an equity that arises against the United States because it was not enforced, because Congress took no action, that the law, which is mandatory, which by its very nature cannot be a law except it is absolute and is notice to everyone, was set aside and repealed. That is not the nature of law. It is not permissive, but it is commanding. It is an exercise of sovereign power; it admits of no distinction and of no qualification. The law said there shall be this grant made on condition that this road is completed by a certain time, and not otherwise.

JOHN H. MITCHELL [Ore.].—Suppose, after the time has expired for the completion of the whole road as designated in the act, that then the Congress of the United States, instead of declaring a forfeiture as they undoubtedly had the right to do at that time, proceeded to pass an act granting the same company further privileges in connection with the road by giving them the right of way through Indian reservations, and all that, what effect, if any, in the judgment of the Senator from Florida, would that grant have on the question now under consideration?

SENATOR CALL.—It would depend entirely upon the language used, and the purpose as declared for which such extension was made. The mere fact of perfecting its right to go through an

Indian territory would have nothing to do with the land grant. It would not touch the question. It could not destroy the effect of the exercise of sovereign, absolute legislative power in the original grant.

SENATOR MITCHELL.—Can there be such a thing as a waiver in law upon the part of the general Government in reference to a land grant by failing to proceed to take advantage of the failure to complete the road within the time and declare a forfeiture?

SENATOR CALL.—I think not. I think such a thing as that would be a clear denial of the force and effect of the law. Nothing can waive a law or repeal a law except the sovereign legislative power that enacted it, and which by constitutional authority has express power to do it. But that question has been decided in The United States vs. Clarke (8 Peters, 436), confirmed and affirmed by repeated decisions subsequently, and especially in the case from which I read, The United States vs. Thompson (98 United States Supreme Court Reports), where the court then said:

The United States possess other attributes of sovereignty resting also upon the basis of universal consent and recognition. They cannot be sued without their consent. (United States vs. Clarke, 8 Pet., 436.) If they sue, and a balance is found in favor of the defendant, no judgment can be rendered against them, either for such balance or in any case for costs. (United States vs. Boyd, 5 How., 29; Reside vs. Walker, 11 id., 272.) A judgment in their favor cannot be enjoined. (Hill vs. United States, 9 id., 386.) Laches, however gross, cannot be imputed to them. (United States vs. Kirkpatrick, 9 Wheat, 720.) There is no presumption of payment against them arising from lapse of time. (United States vs. Williams, supra.) They can maintain a suit in their own name upon a non-negotiable claim assigned to them. (United States vs. White, 2 Hill, N. Y., 59.)

The rule of *nullum tempus occurrit regi*[1] has existed as an element of the English law from a very early period. It is discussed in Bracton, and has come down to the present time. It is not necessary to advert to the qualifications which successive Parliaments have applied to it.

The common law fixed no time as to the bringing of actions. Limitations derive their authority from statutes. The king was held never to be included, unless expressly named. No laches was imputable to him. These exemptions were founded upon considerations of public policy. It was deemed important that, while the sovereign was engrossed by the cares and duties of his office, the public should not suffer by the negligence of his servants. "In a representative government, where the people do not and can not act in a body, where their power is delegated to others and must of necessity be exercised by them, if exercised at all, the reason for applying these principles is equally cogent."

[1] "No time lapses against the king."

That answers the Senator from Oregon. If no laches can be imputed to the Government, if the negligence of the servants of the Government cannot affect the law, but it stands until repealed, where can the waiver be? A law by your Constitution is repealed, is deprived of its force and effect, only by a certain exercise of sovereign legislative power. It cannot be modified, .. cannot be diminished, it cannot be altered in its force or operation except constitutionally by the exercise of the sovereign legislative power that enacted it. Therefore, if it cannot be altered or affected or qualified or repealed, there can be no waiver of it. Considerations of equity address themselves to the general legislative discretion of Congress.

But what did Mr. Garfield say upon the subject of this question of vested rights which are so often interposed to deny and qualify the exercise of the sovereign legislative power of the Government? The very existence of property depends upon its use in such form that it shall not burden the people of the country with such taxes and such impositions as will make life uncomfortable, as will deprive it of ease and comfort. The existence of corporate power and property depends, as he says, upon wise and just and temperate legislation by the Congress of the United States and by the State legislatures within their respective spheres. He says:

Since the dawn of history the great thoroughfares have belonged to the people—have been known as the king's highways or the public highways, and have been open to the free use of all, on payment of a small, uniform tax or toll to keep them in repair. But now the most perfect and by far the most important roads known to mankind are owned and managed as private property by a comparatively small number of private citizens. In all its uses the railroad is the most public of all our roads; and in all the objects to which its work relates the railway corporation is as public as any organization can be. But, in the start, it was labeled a private corporation; and, so far as its legal status is concerned, it is now grouped with eleemosynary institutions and private charities, and enjoys similar immunities and exemptions. It remains to be seen how long the community will suffer itself to be the victim of an abstract definition.

It will be readily conceded that a corporation is strictly and really private when it is authorized to carry on such a business as a private citizen may carry on. But when the State has delegated to a corporation the sovereign right of eminent domain—the right to take from the private citizen, without his consent, a portion of his real estate to build its structure across farm, garden, and lawn, into and through, over or under the blocks, squares, streets, churches, and dwellings of incorporated cities and towns, across navigable rivers, and over and along public highways—it requires a stretch of the common imagination, and much refinement and subtlety of the law, to maintain the old fiction that such an organization is not a public corporation.

In the famous Dartmouth College case it was decided, in 1819, by the Supreme Court of the United States that the charter of Dartmouth College is a contract between the State and the corporation which the Legislature cannot alter without the consent of the corporation; and that any such alteration is void, being in conflict with that clause of the Constitution of the United States which forbids a State to make any law impairing the obligation of contracts. This decision has stood for more than half a century as a monument of judicial learning and the great safeguard of vested rights.[1] But Chief Justice Marshall pronounced this decision ten years before the steam-railway was born, and it is clear he did not contemplate the class of corporations that have since come into being. But year by year the doctrine of that case has been extended to the whole class of private corporations, including railroad and telegraph companies.

But few of the States, in their early charters to railroads, reserved any effectual control of the operations of the corporations they created. In many instances, like that of the Illinois Central charter, the right to amend was not reserved. In most States each Legislature has narrowed and abridged the powers of its successors, and enlarged the powers of the corporations; and these, by the strong grip of the law and in the name of private property and vested rights, hold fast all they have received. By these means not only corporations but the vast railroad and telegraph systems have virtually passed from the control of the State. It is painfully evident, from the experience of the last few years, that the efforts of the States to regulate their railroads have amounted to but little more than feeble annoyance. In many cases the corporations have treated such efforts as impertinent, intermeddling, and have brushed away the legislative restrictions as easily as Gulliver broke the cords with which the Liliputians attempted to bind him. In these contests the corporations have become conscious of their strength and have entered upon the work of controlling the States. Already they have captured several of the oldest and strongest of them; and these discrowned sovereigns now follow in chains the triumphal chariot of their conquerors. And this does not imply that merely the officers and representatives of States have been subjected to the railways, but that the corporations have grasped the sources and fountains of power, and controlled the choice of both officers and representatives.

The private corporation has another great advantage over the municipal corporation. The jurisdiction of the latter is confined to its own territory; but, by the recent constructions and devices of the law, a private corporation, though it has no soul, no conscience, and can commit no crime, is yet a citizen of the State that creates it, and can make and execute contracts with individuals and corporations of other States. Thus the way has been opened to those vast consolidations which have placed the control of the whole system in the hands of a few and have developed the Charlemagnes and Cæsars of our internal commerce.

In addition to these external conquests, the great managers have in many cases grasped the private property of the corporations themselves; and the stocks which represent the investment have become mere counters in the great gambling-houses of Wall street, where the daily ebb and flow of the stock market sweeps and tosses the business and trade of the continent.

[1] Daniel Webster presented the arguments which were sustained by the court.

This is the answer which has been made by a great leader of the Republican party. This was the answer which the platforms of the Republican and Democratic parties gave to the question of leaving this vast unearned land grant in the possession of a few individuals. No proconsular power in the Roman Empire was ever so great as the dominion of the thirty-odd millions of acres of magnificently fertile land, to be inhabited by millions of the people of this country, in defiance of the public law of the country which dedicates that land to homestead settlement, to actual settlement, which recognizes the principle that the land of the country belongs to the people who toil and work upon it, which the public interest demands shall be in their hands with the least possible cost. This is the answer that is given to the proposition now made, which is involved in the Senate's turning its back now upon the proposition of forfeiture and attempting to appease the public mind by a forfeiture of an insignificant portion of the territory, not desired by the corporation, over which it has built no road, while the great practical question before the country, Shall the unearned grant, unearned within the time specified in the act, be forfeited, is answered by non-action and by indirect efforts to confirm it?

On June 15 Senator Van Wyck offered an amendment to the bill repealing the exemption of the railroads' right of way through the Territories. This was adopted by a vote of 26 to 20.

Senator George moved to amend the act by express statement that the Government did not waive any right to have any other land grant than the one in question forfeited for any failure, "past or future," of the company to comply with the conditions of the grant. This was adopted without division.

The opposition, with one exception, feeling that the rights of the Government were fully protected, did not oppose the bill, and it passed by a vote of 42 to 1, the negative vote being that of Henry W. Blair [N. H.], who believed that the way should be left open to restore to the people all the lands granted to the railroads.

The bill was referred in the House to the Committee on Public Lands, which, through Barclay Henley [Cal.], the chairman, reported a substitute measure declaring the forfeiture of all grants the conditions of which had not been complied with, and throwing them open to settlement.

The bill was passed on July 27 by a vote of 187 to 47.

The Senate refused to concur in the House substitute and a joint conference committee was appointed. It failed to agree, and was discharged during the next session, and a second conference committee was appointed. This also disagreed, and a third conference was appointed.

The subject came up again during the first session of the Fiftieth Congress (December, 1887-October, 1888).

On January 13, 1888, Preston B. Plumb [Kan.] introduced in the Senate a bill to forfeit all unearned grants of lands to railroads. It was referred to the Committee on Public Lands, which reported the bill on January 23. It came up for discussion on April 17, when various amendments were proposed, some of which had the effect of exempting certain lands from forfeiture.

FORFEITURE OF RAILROAD GRANTS

SENATE, APRIL 26-MAY 8, 1888

Joseph N. Dolph [Ore.] on April 26 charged the Democratic party in Congress with partiality toward the South in the matter of forfeiture of land grants to railroads.

I call attention to the fact that in one of the acts forfeiting railroad land grants there is excepted out of the provisions of it the grant to the Gulf and Ship Island Railway Company for the express purpose of allowing the company to earn those lands, and that in another that thing was done which has been the subject of so much discussion in the Senate and of which some Senators stand in such mortal fear. There were confirmed to a railroad company, not to the original grantee, but to the assignee of the original grantee, the earned lands, and their title was placed by the act beyond the power of Congress to reach them.

Can it be that the location of these grants had anything to do with the action of Congress and accounted for the silence of my friend from Florida [Wilkinson Call] and my friend from Louisiana [Randall L. Gibson]? If so, how can we account for the fact that the clarion voice of the then senior Senator from Nebraska [Mr. Van Wyck] was not heard protesting against such action? There was no protest. There was silence on that side of the chamber and silence on this side of the chamber; and in the year 1886, without a dissenting voice, the time was extended to enable this Southern railroad company to earn its grant by the construction of its road, and even the Democratic House of Representatives consented to it, and a year later consented to the great iniquity of confirming to another Southern railroad company lands which had been earned by the construction of road after the time limited in the grant.

On May 8 Henry M. Teller [Col.] spoke in the interests of settlers on the lands proposed to be forfeited.

Is it the Government that is to be benefited? Not at all. The moment it is declared that these are void entries, that moment the land is open under the settlement law, and Mr. Jones and Mr. Smith and everybody else jump onto it, and the man who had cultivated it for fifteen years and put fences on it and houses on it and had made it a garden, who has held it and paid taxes on it, is deprived of his property that some saloonkeeper who hung around the town and did nothing may go upon it and receive the benefit of the enhanced value by the labor of the former occupant.

What I mean to say is that, when the Government has by its decision misled its citizens and justified them in buying land of the Government or of a railroad company, the Government, while it is not in law, is in morals and in decency estopped from despoiling its citizens in that way.

JAMES H. BERRY [Ark.].—I want to say to the Senator that a very large portion of this land which we are discussing is not agricultural land; it has no houses and no ditches and no farms upon it. It is mineral land; it is iron land of great value. The Senator says that the Government would not be benefited. The law requires this land to be offered to the highest bidder. If it is offered to the highest bidder to-day it will bring from $25 to $30 an acre, it is said. If there is any reason why these men who purchased in fraud of the law, in the face of the instructions of the Commissioner of the General Land Office, shall be given by this Government the difference between a dollar and a quarter an acre and that which the land will bring at public sale to the highest bidder—if there is any reason why we should donate and contribute this to these corporations and these syndicates that do not occupy the land, I shall be glad if the Senator from Colorado would tell me what that reason is.

SENATOR TELLER.—I take issue with the honorable Senator. There is not any law that requires the land now in controversy in Michigan to be put up and sold at auction. It is discretionary with the department. They may withdraw it from the operation of the settlement law and put it up. The Senator knows that upon pretty nearly every one of these pieces of land there are now four sticks laid out in the shape of a basement of a house. He knows that there is a little something done upon it by some speculator, and it is not a question whether the Government of the Unitetd States is to get what the value of the land is, but it is a question whether somebody else who has not had anything to do with this land up to the present time shall step in and have the enhanced value produced, perhaps not by the labor that these men have put upon it in Michigan, but by the holding of it until circumstances have made it valuable, upon which they have paid taxes for fifteen or eighteen years, and some man who has no claim at all upon the Government, who has never been misled by the action of its officials, who never has paid a dollar in State tax or anything else, or paid for the land, is to come in and take it as a homesteader or preemptioner if he sees fit.

SENATOR BERRY.—The Senator has just admitted that it was in the power of the department to withdraw it from settlement and offer it to the highest bidder.

SENATOR TELLER.—So as to the men who bought the land in the vicinity of Denver, who bought it from a railroad company that had a patent to it, and, after there had been two determinations in the department that it was railroad land and not public land, it is in the power of the President of the United States to put up that land that has now enhanced in value, having passed through the hands of half a dozen owners, and sell it for a thousand dollars an acre; but it would be downright robbery if he should do it; and there has not been any President who has ever sat in the chair of Washington who would have thought of doing it. The people of the United States are not so poverty-stricken and so poor that they want the Government of the United States to engage in robbing the citizens. They are willing that the Government should do what any individual would be compelled to do by the decent and respectable people of the community in which he lived, and that is to make good his contracts and not to resort to technicalities of law. I say that the Government of the United States cannot afford to take from anybody the land it has conveyed to him when the purchaser believed that he was getting a title from the Government, there being no fraud on his part.

If there was a mistake, what is the rule of equity? That the man who made it must suffer for it, and not the man who acted in good faith. If it was ignorance on the part of the Government officers, then the Government should suffer. If it was fraud on the part of the Government officers, then the Government should suffer and not the citizen, unless the citizen participated in the fraud.

Now, Mr. President, it may be that you could save fifteen or twenty or thirty thousand dollars of money by these proceedings; it may be that by resuming control of the land I have spoken of that is covered with houses in the city of Denver the Government of the United States can add to its overflowing treasury; but does the Senator from Arkansas want that done? Does he believe the respectable people of this country want it done when it comes out of the pockets of some citizen of the United States who is himself without fault?

Mr. President, money of that kind would be a disgrace to us, and ought to bring misfortune to us as well.

SENATOR BERRY.—Mr. President, the Senator from Colorado is horrified at the idea that this Government should attempt to take lands because of a mere technicality, and he says the trouble arose from a mistake of the Government. I read six letters from the Commissioner of the General Land Office at Washington to the local officers at Marquette, telling them again and again, "These lands are not subject to private sale"; and in subsequent letters, "You have disobeyed the orders, and I again remind you that they are not subject to private entry." In the face of that the officers at Marquette went on and sold 800,000 acres of these lands, three-fourths of which were sold to twenty corporations and syndicates, and the same register of the land office is now in partnership with the parties who purchased; and yet the Senator from Colorado says that is a mere technicality, and it would be robbery on the part of the Government to claim the lands. That may be called a technicality in the courts in which he has practiced, but in those in which I have appeared that would be called fraud, and any man who would doubt that these corporations had full knowledge of the fact that the Commissioner of the General Land Office was instructing the local land officers not to sell these lands at private entry—I say the man who would doubt that knows little of the operations of the corporations of this country.

Mr. President, the whole history of land grants to corporations of every character and description has been that in every instance almost the corporation has failed to comply with the conditions contained in the grant. The history of it is that, wherever they have secured an advantage by the decision of any court over any poor settler, they have with merciless hand driven him from his home; and yet when they have made a mistake, when they thought they could purchase in the face of the law, when they knew they were violating the law, when this land would have brought thousands upon thousands of dollars if put up at public sale, when these favored individuals were permitted in the face of the law to take it up at $1.25 an acre and now come and make a pathetic appeal to Congress when they have possession of lands said to be worth to-day millions of dollars, the proposition that these men who paid $1.25 an acre for 800,000 acres of land should receive back only the money paid the Senator from Colorado thinks would be a great hardship, and he seeks to make an appeal to the Senate and to its sympathy in behalf of these syndicates.

I assert that no man can read the testimony taken before the House committee, no man can read the majority report, without coming to the conclusion that in nine cases out of ten these parties had knowledge of the fraud, and they knew they were gambling, they knew they were speculating, and they have no hold upon this land, but they have secured by paying a dollar and a quarter an acre lands of immense value, and that their hold is uncertain, and the department having decided against them they come here now and seek to foist it upon a bill known to be popular, a land-forfeiture bill forfeiting lands granted to railroads. They know they cannot get their claim through on its own merits, and their only hope is to tack it onto a bill that the whole country is in favor of, and then they hope by that means to confirm a title which was conceived in fraud and which was known to be a fraud at the time it was done.

I insist that this land-forfeiture bill, which we all protest that we want to pass, ought not to be clogged and loaded down with amendments which will have a tendency to defeat it, and then Senators go before the country and say the Senate of the United States passed the land-forfeiture bill, but the House of

Representatives did not agree to it when they are placing amendments on it which they know that no man who understands that testimony can conscientiously agree to.

The bill was amended and it passed without division on May 9.

FORFEITURE OF RAILROAD GRANTS

HOUSE OF REPRESENTATIVES, JULY 5, 1888

The House referred the bill to the Committee on Public Lands, which reported it three times, with amendments, the House recommitting it twice. The third report was debated on July 5. William S. Holman [Ind.], who presented it, explained its nature.

The House proposition would have the effect in the case of the Northern Pacific road and all the others to restore to the people a large body of land, an aggregate of lands double the area of the great State of Ohio, subject, however, to bona fide sales. Is there an absence of power in Congress to do this? Is it inequitable? This House has decided more than once that it was within its power to declare these forfeitures.

Here the speaker reviewed the debate on the Northern Pacific grants.

Can any person say it is unjust to restore those lands to the public domain, subject, of course, to the equities that might arise on behalf of the purchasers of land opposite to completed railroad?

The country was teeming with people and the great land grant increasing in value under their enterprise and labor before this railroad corporation thought proper to even take the first step toward completing in good faith its part of the engagement to construct this railroad. The facts were known to the corporation as to the nature of their grant and the object for which it was made, as well as to Congress or to the officers of the Government. No laches of Congress or of the Government officers can impair the rights of the people. They have a right to demand that if the contract was not carried out in good faith it should be declared void. I think the right and duty of Congress to declare this forfeiture is clear beyond question upon every consideration of law and justice, and I am confident it is sound upon the high consideration of public policy, for the grant was made without justification, to build up private fortunes, and not for the public good.

Indeed, sir, that grant cannot be defended. Can any just man defend any of these grants?

I admit that so far as the Union Pacific road is concerned it stands solitary and alone. Its construction was authorized for a purely political reason, in the midst of great public disorders, and when it was deemed essential for high public reasons that there should be closer relations between the Atlantic and the Pacific States. I admit that at the beginning there was some uncertainty whether the bond subsidy which the Government provided for the construction of that road would be sufficient, but when the act of 1864 finally passed, under which the road was completed, then all men knew that the grant of 28,000,-400 acres of land in addition to the enormous subsidy in bonds was without any possible justification, for it was well known at that time that the two series of bonds authorized were more than sufficient to complete the road. The land grant was a naked gift. That grant was opposed on this floor by Elihu B. Washburne [Ill.] with the great ability and marvelous energy of which he was master. I was glad to follow his lead. He opposed these grants as earnestly as the distinguished gentleman from the same State [Lewis E. Payson] has favored their forfeiture.

This Union Pacific grant was passed on the very heels of the homestead law, and was the beginning of that extraordinary system of land grants to corporations which has so fearfully reduced in a few years your public domain. Grants followed in rapid succession. This Northern Pacific grant was one of them. Look at the time when these events occurred.

While your people were watching with patriotic solicitude the movements of your armies, while those the most interested of all men in the public domain were rushing into the ranks of your armies to steady and uphold the tottering pillars of the Union, at that very time ex-governors of States, ex-members of Congress, men of high social and political standing were here upon this floor lobbying for these grants and securing by the favor of Congress vast portions of your national wealth—your public lands—of especial and inestimable value to the men— the laboring men of the country—who were then imperiling their lives in the national defence. In that unpatriotic and mercenary spirit these grants were obtained by which the people were robbed of their rights and imperial fortunes were secured.

Congress was engaged in the work of parceling out among mercenary capitalists your public domain when the clash of arms could almost be heard in this hall!

Are great grants of land obtained under such circumstances to be carefully guarded by Congress and the courts of justice? Will Congress refuse to declare their forfeiture when a just ground for forfeiture is presented? You have a right to declare the forfeiture of these millions of the public land wrongfully granted, and justice demands that it shall be done.

I do not wish to enter into a political discussion over this matter of the public lands, but gentlemen in a recent debate here talked as though the Democratic party had no special reason for championing measures for the annulment of these grants. I think the Democratic party have a special interest in the subject; that party can look back with great satisfaction to the record of its representative men on the land question.

Here the speaker reviewed the history of the Virginia Cession, the Louisiana Purchase, and the Homestead Law.

While the Homestead bill was pending in the House on the 18th day of December, 1861, I submitted a proposition that the act of March 3, 1855, which had secured allotments of public land to the soldiers of every successive war prior to that which was then waging, should be extended to the soldiers of the then existing war for the Union. That proposition was made in view of the uniform policy of our Government in all former wars, and because no act could be more becoming a Republic than to give the soldiers who fought in its defence a freehold in the soil of their country. The argument against it was that its tendency would be to monopolize the public lands, that bounty-land warrants assignable would certainly produce that result. That was the only argument that could be urged against it, for the public lands were then ample for the purpose; but it was successful, and my provision failed by the action of the gentleman who controlled the bill in the House. The debate on my proposition to grant bounty lands to the soldiers of the war for the Union, in view of the results, was one of the most interesting debates that occurred during the war. John F. Potter, of Wisconsin, who controlled the bill, indignantly declared, in his speech against my amendment, that "the issue of land warrants under previous acts has absorbed nearly 100,000,000 acres of our public lands and thrown nearly that amount into the hands

of speculators." William Windom, of Massachusetts, was still
more indignant, and declared, in substance, that it was mere
demagogy. James A. Cravens, of Indiana, a gallant soldier
of the Mexican war, was the only member who stood by me
with a speech. This debate will be found in the *Congressional
Globe*, second session Thirty-seventh Congress, volume 67.

But, Mr. Speaker, what an extraordinary result followed!
Within ten years afterward grants of public lands to an extent
unexampled in the history of any country were made to corporations, commencing with the same Congress. How does the
account stand?

It appears, therefore, that while it was not thought proper
on February 22, 1862, to grant bounty lands to the soldiers of
the Union army on account of its tendency to land monopoly,
yet, beginning with July 2, 1862, with a grant of 28,000,400
acres to the Union Pacific Railroad corporations, Congress
within ten years gave directly to corporations and to States for
corporations 181,419,569 acres of land, a territory eight times
greater than the State of Indiana. All this in ten years! While
from the year 1787 down to this day all the grants made by
Congress for common schools, the foundation of the grandest
system of education the world has ever seen, including the sixteenth section of every township of the public domain down to
the formation of the Territory of Oregon, and the sixteenth and
thirty-sixth sections in every township of every State and Territory organized since, including also all grants for universities
and colleges, and all grants for military services in all the wars
from the Revolution down to the war with Mexico, aggregate
146,678,061 acres.

A careful inquiry will reveal the fact that the present Administration has absolutely reversed the land policy of the Republican administrations. Instead of a policy that favored the
grants to railroad corporations, the Spanish and Mexican grants,
and the enormous claims under entries made for speculation,
every effort is now made consistent with justice to restore the
public lands to the bona fide settler. General Sparks and his
able successor, Colonel A. M. Stockslager, pursuing the same line
of policy under the earnest approval of the President, have restored by Executive order 52,437,373 acres to the public domain.

You have, gentlemen, at the present session of Congress
passed a bill for the first time classifying the public lands and
securing to actual settlers all the remaining public lands adapted
to agriculture, protecting your remaining coal fields and streams
of water from monopoly, protecting your forests from destruc-

tion, and repealing all laws under which speculation in the public lands is possible. You have declared in that bill that the public lands shall be held to secure homes for our people, and for no other purpose. Had that bill been passed as a part of the homestead measure of May 20, 1862, how many generations would elapse before the peril would approach that comes to a nation from a homeless, hopeless, and discontented people! The promise of a home on your public lands has through generations past inspired with hope the hearts of millions of laboring men of the United States. Every laborer at the forge, in the shop, and everywhere has been buoyed up with the hope that after a while by patient industry he might secure for his family an independent freehold upon the public domain. It has been not only the source of your greatness, but the ark of your safety. But, unfortunately, the spirit that inspired the homestead law died with its enactment; the vast body of your public lands were left exposed to speculation for the benefit of those for whom the homestead law was not intended.

In that bill you have passed a homestead measure which does not leave one acre of public land open to the speculator. By that bill you have set apart your public lands for homes for your people. If the Senate, yielding to just public sentiment, should pass that bill, and this measure now pending of public justice should become a law, much will have been done to retrieve the past.

Let this measure proposed by your Committee on Public Lands pass. Let it become a law. Restore the land to the people from whom it has been unjustly taken; restore to them these millions of acres which have been so unwisely and improvidently granted to favored parties; restore the land to its rightful owners and dedicate your remaining lands for homes for your people and then those whose praise is most to be desired, the unfortunate, the poor, the landless, will rise up and pronounce their blessings upon the Fiftieth Congress of the United States. [Great applause.]

William J. Stone [Mo.] defended the Democratic land policy.

The Republican party, forgetting or ignoring the history of the past, created corporations by congressional enactment, invested them with great privileges and powers, and put charters into their hands which authorized them to go out upon the fairest domain on the earth—the property of the American people, acquired and until then held by the Democratic party as the future homes of our fast-increasing population—and appropriate it by the tens of millions of acres; and, not content with that, they must issue them more than half a hundred millions of bonds, bearing a high rate of interest, to be paid out of the earnings of honest labor. Instead of having landlords among the titled nobility of Europe, holding by authority of the Crown, we have corporation landlords, holding by authority of a Republican Congress—corporations whose stock is largely owned and held in Europe.

This system of corporation landlordism is, if anything, more dangerous than the one against which our fathers drew the sword. It is full of menace and danger to every man who looks into the future of our country. The very idea of a single corporation, especially one whose stock and bonds are principally owned abroad, like the Northern Pacific, holding as the free gift of the Government of the United States a territory as large as the fifth State in the Union and capable of sustaining twenty-five or thirty millions of people, cannot but excite the gravest apprehensions in the minds of thoughtful men.

Our homestead laws were enacted with a view to serving the needs of actual settlement. They were intended to facilitate actual occupation of the public lands, and to promote the interest of those who should venture to establish homes upon the frontier and lay the foundations of great commonwealths. It is undeniably true that these well-intended statutes have been a great blessing to many thousands of poor men who have found homes under their provisions; but in later years they have also been grossly abused by the grasping and the vicious in a way totally at variance with the public right, the public interest, and the public weal.

Rich men, syndicates, and corporations have employed thousands of people to make fraudulent entries for their benefit under the preëmption, desert-land, and other laws, by means of bribery and perjury. The laws have been evaded and many millions of acres of the public domain have been literally stolen. Laws that were intended to protect the public lands from speculation and preserve them as free homes for the homeless have been so administered under administrations previous to the present one as to enable a favored few to acquire lordly estates amounting to tens of thousands of acres. I have not time to go into this phase of the question with anything like detail. It is sufficient to say that so startling and universal had fraud become, and such a storm of protest was rising from the people

SERVING TWO MASTERS

THE SORT OF THING THAT WILL CEASE WHEN SENATOR BECK'S BILL BECOMES A LAW

Cartoon by Joseph Keppler in "Puck"

281

against loose and dishonest methods of administration, that President Cleveland, after having had a thorough and exhaustive examination made into the subject, in his first message to Congress asserted that the tide of fraud and corruption had risen so high and become so strong that the only remedy was to repeal the laws under which such things were made possible.

Following the lead of the President, the Democratic House of the Forty-ninth Congress passed a bill, reported from the Democratic Committee on the Public Lands, repealing the commutation clause of the homestead law, the preëmption law, and other laws under which the public lands had been fraudulently appropriated during a long series of years, and holding whatever was left of the public domain exclusively for actual settlement.

That bill was sent over to the Senate, and that Republican house of lords refused to concur in the measure unless the House would agree to insert a provision confirming all entries, without regard to their character, which had been made up to that time. That the House refused to do, because it was a known fact, ascertained as the result of exhaustive investigations begun and prosecuted by the officers of the present Administration, that frauds upon a large scale had been committed. Many fraudulent entries, involving millions of acres, were then hanging up in the General Land Office, undergoing investigation, with a view to cancelation because of their fraudulent character. The House would not consent by an act of confirmation to sweep all of that work of the department aside, and permit the thieves to walk off with the plunder, bearing the sanction of our approval; and hence the bill did not become a law.

None the less the President, through his subordinates, has been going steadily on with the work of investigation, canceling fraudulent entries, eradicating evils of various kinds, and perfecting the methods of administering the laws. In addition to the forfeitures made by the Forty-eighth and Forty-ninth Congresses, the Interior Department, by executive action, during the present Administration has restored over 52,000,000 acres to settlement.

The land thieves had a harvest of twenty years, and they made hay while the sun shone. But the blizzard came with Cleveland. Under his administration the first staggering blow in twenty years was struck at this monstrous corruption. The wolves showed their teeth, snarled and snapped, but the "man of destiny" at the White House has been steadily beating them back.

I come now, Mr. Speaker, to consider briefly the bill immediately under consideration. At the beginning of this Congress a number of bills were introduced in the House to forfeit lands granted in aid of the construction of railroads, which have been favorably reported, and are now pending on the calendar of the House. Some six weeks ago the Senate passed a bill entitled "An act to forfeit certain lands heertofore granted for the purpose of aiding in the construction of railroads, and for other purposes." That bill has been considered by the House Committee on the Public Lands, and, as it is general in its character, it has been made the basis of the pending measure.

The Public Lands Committee have reported it back to the House with amendments. Indeed, there are three reports from that committee. It may not be inappropriate to remark that a consideration of those reports will forcibly illustrate the position of the Democratic and Republican parties on the subject of forfeiting these railroad land grants.

The bill, as it came from the Senate, proposes to forfeit and restore to the public domain all that part, and only that part, of the lands granted by Congress to aid in the construction of railroads which lie along that portion of the routes over which no road has been built up to this date. That is the bill our committee have been considering. Out of it three propositions have grown and are brought here into the House by the various members of the Public Lands Committee.

First. Four distinguished Republican members of that committee, namely, Lewis E. Payson, Joseph McKenna, Augustus J. Turner, and Binger Hermann, file a report in which they recommend the passage of the Senate bill.

Second. A majority of the committee, through Judge Holman, file a report in which they recommend an amendment to the Senate bill extending its scope so as to embrace and forfeit not only the lands where no road has been yet built, but also all lands across which no road had been built at the expiration of the period limited in the granting acts for the completion of the whole road.

Third. My colleague on the committee, Thomas C. McRae [Ark.] and myself have filed a separate repcrt, in which we recommend a forfeiture of the entire grant where there has been a failure of compliance by the corporations with the terms and conditions of the grant. We propose simply to go a little further than the majority recommend in the repnrt filed by Judge Holman.

If the Senate proposition should prevail, the forfeiture would amount to 5,627,436 acres. If the majority amendment should prevail, the forfeiture would amount to 54,323,996 acres. If my proposition should be adopted the forfeiture would amount to 78,503,088 acres.

As to most of the features of the bill proposed by the House committee we are all substantially agreed. We propose to except from the forfeiture the rights of way of the companies, and sufficient lands for depots, machine shops, and so forth. We also except from the forfeiture all lands appropriated for town sites, lands in the possession of actual settlers, and all lands held by bona fide purchasers for value. I am in favor of all that. The committee is in accord as to that. I would freely give to the companies whatever lands are reasonably necessary to the convenient operation of their roads. I would not disturb titles and create confusion where towns and cities have been built; nor would I disturb or distress actual settlers, or persons who have in good faith purchased lands from any of the companies for a valuable consideration. Whatever defect there may be in such titles I would remove by an act of confirmation. The reasons for such a course, I assume, are too manifest to require elaboration.

If the companies are protected in their rights of way; if town sites are left undisturbed because excepted from the forfeiture; if honest actual settlers and bona fide purchasers for value are protected from harm by having their titles confirmed; if all equities and all questions of this character are eliminated from the legislation proposed, then there is nothing left but a naked and unincumbered issue between the Government of the United States, representing the people on the one hand, and the railroad companies on the other. It is a simple issue between the grantor and the grantee, with all intervening rights protected.

If the corporations receiving the grants have any equities to urge in their own behalf, they have neglected their opportunities to do so, though they may expect to have it done for them upon the floors of the House and Senate. In the committee room they have combated the forfeitures upon purely legal grounds. They claim the lands as a matter of legal right, and deny the power of Congress to disturb them. And it is purely a question of law. I claim that the grants were made upon such conditions as vest in the Government the right to reenter and take possession after a breach thereof.

I shall not discuss the legal phases of the proposed forfeitures at this time. The *Record* is full of speeches made by the best lawyers in the House upon the subject. I shall quote but one authority, that of the distinguished gentleman from Illinois [Mr. Payson], who wrote the minority report on the pending measure, in which he advises the House to adopt the Senate bill. During the Forty-seventh Congress that gentleman was a member of the Judiciary Committee. A bill had been introduced and referred to that committee forfeiting the lands granted to the Northern Pacific. That was the pioneer forfeiture bill. That company was required to complete its road in 1879. Its grant was made upon the condition that it should do so. It did not construct its entire road by 1879. At the expiration of the period limited for its completion only a comparatively small part had been constructed. The road is yet unconstructed, and so the question of forfeiture was fairly presented in the bill to which I have alluded. The gentleman from Maine [Thomas B. Reed] was then chairman of the Judiciary Committee, and, acting for the majority of that committee, made an adverse report upon the bill. The gentleman from Illinois [Mr. Payson], acting with the Democratic minority, prepared and presented a minority report advocating the passage of the bill. From that report, made July 24, 1882, I quote:

We conclude, then, on the legal question of power in Congress, that it has the right to declare the title to all unpatented lands in the grant forfeited and revest the United States with it, so that it can be restored to the public domain, open to sale and settlement under existing laws.

On July 6 the bill was passed by a vote of 179 to 8.

The Senate refusing to concur in the House's substitute, a conference committee was appointed. It did not report during the session.

CHAPTER IX

PACIFIC RAILROADS FUNDING BILL

H. Henry Powers [Vt.], of the Committee on Pacific Railroads, Introduces Bill in the House to Remit Obligations of the Union Pacific and Central Pacific Railroads to the Government; Charles K. Bell [Tex.] Presents Minority Report—Debate: David B. Henderson [Ia.], James G. Maguire [Cal.], Mr. Powers, Joel D. Hubbard [Mo.], Mr. Bell, Galusha A. Grow [Pa.], Grove L. Johnson [Cal.], William C. Arnold [Pa.], John C. Bell [Col.], William P. Hepburn [Ia.], Henry A. Cooper [Wis.], William W. Bowers [Cal.]; Bill Is Defeated.

IN the session of 1895-96 H. Henry Powers [Vt.], of the Committee on Pacific Railroads, reported in the House a bill which declared in its title that its purpose was

"to provide for the settlement of claims growing out of the issue of bonds to aid in the construction of certain railroads, and to secure the payment of all their indebtedness to the United States."

The true purport of the bill will transpire in the debate upon it. The measure related particularly to the Union Pacific Railroad.

The measure was postponed to the next session.

In the ensuing presidential campaign the Democratic platform declared specifically against the bill as condoning and confirming a default by the railroads concerned of debts justly due to the Government.

On December 10, 1896, Charles K. Bell [Tex.] filed a minority report of the committee against the bill.

PACIFIC RAILROADS FUNDING BILL

HOUSE OF REPRESENTATIVES, DECEMBER 19, 1896-JANUARY 11, 1897

On December 19 the bill came forward. David B. Henderson [Ia.], of the Committee on Rules, brought forward the program for its discussion. He explained the situation as follows:

The subsidy bonds covered by the bill amount to over $61,-000,000. The amount of indebtedness on the 1st of next January will be, in round numbers, $111,000,000. The Government has a second lien for this on 2,293.4 miles of railroad, with the appurtenant property of the road. All of the prior liens upon the property remain unpaid, and hence the amount involved in the question to be considered is the Government claim, plus the prior liens, amounting in all to over $172,000,000.

The President tells us in his message that on January 1, 1897, there will be due on the bonds of the road $19,000,000, and by January 1, 1899, an additional amount of more than $41,000,000. It is contended—I do not know with what truth—that if a foreclosure is had the Government will realize but very little out of its claim. That, I trust, is a point on which we will have ample discussion and full light.

On March 3, 1887, an act of Congress was passed authorizing the appointment of three commissioners to investigate the whole subject of the relations of the bond-aided railroads to the Government. On January 17, 1888, President Cleveland transmitted the report of that commission, known as the Pacific Railroad Commission, to Congress, closing his message with these words:

The public interest urges prompt and efficient action.

To the second session of the Fifty-second Congress President Harrison said as to the subsidy bond debt:

We must deal with the question as we find it, and take that course which will, under existing conditions, best secure the interests of the United States.

And he renews his recommendation of the preceding year:

That a commission with full power be appointed to make settlement.

To the second session of the Fifty-third Congress President Cleveland, indorsing generally the department recommendation, transmitted the annual report of the Secretary of the Interior, wherein that officer recommended action by Congress on the subject, and referred approvingly to the report of the Government directors, calling attention to the approaching maturity of the subsidy bond debt and renewing the recommendation so frequently made by their predecessors for a prompt and complete adjustment of the financial relations between the railroad companies and the United States.

This he renewed in his subsequent messages.

The Committee on Rules, urged by the people's interests and by these different officers of the Government, have unanimously brought in this rule, so that the House might have an opportunity to determine whether or not it will take up this question and consider it. If they decide to consider it, then they must determine whether or not it is their intention to confess to the country that they have not the ability to bring forward a remedy by legislation. It may be that when this is considered no method can be pointed out that will show how the Government can save this vast sum of money. That is a matter for discussion, but at all events every Representative should have the courage to let this matter come up for full consideration and discussion, and see whether or not we can save these many millions to the country, or whether we must abandon them to the chance of foreclosure, knowing a prior lien is upon every dollar of that which we have a second lien upon. [Cries of "Vote!" "Vote!"]

JAMES G. MAGUIRE [Cal.].—Mr. Speaker, I am well aware that, under the rules of the House, clôture, which the committee invokes for the bill, applies to the consideration of the report, and I know also that a number of gentlemen who are opposed to the bill will not vote against the committee on this question.

But, sir, I cannot permit the statement just made by the gentleman from Iowa [Mr. Henderson] to pass unchallenged. Several of his statements are misleading and some of them absolutely erroneous. The Government is not menaced by any such danger as the gentleman suggests. It is not the interest of the Government, but the interests of the debtor companies that are to be promoted by the Powers bill. The Government is amply protected by the Thurman Act, under which foreclosure proceedings will shortly be instituted, unless Congress as a favor to the defaulting companies shall relieve them from their obligations under that act by extending the time for the payment of the debt.

That the companies interested should be anxious to have the bill brought on speedily for consideration is quite natural, because their interests are to be promoted by it, but the interests of the United States Government are now protected by the best safeguard of which existing conditions will permit, namely, the right of foreclosure and such rights as it may have to pursue diverted assets and the unpaid subscriptions of stockholders. The provisions of the Thurman Act are far better for the Government than the proposed refunding act. The Thurman Act was a settlement of the Pacific Railroad question. It presented the alternative to the companies to pay or submit to foreclosure. They did not pay, and this urgent proposition is to relieve them of the alternative. That is all. The only defect so far developed in the Thurman Act is that it does not vest jurisdiction in any particular court (nor, in my opinion, any court) over the interests of the United States Government in the roads.

If any change of existing law is needed, it is that jurisdiction be vested in the Supreme Court of the District of Columbia, or some other particular court, to adjudicate and determine the interests of the Government in the roads.

The gentleman from Iowa [Mr. Henderson] says that the question is how to get the most money for the Government. That question should properly be discussed when the bill is up for consideration on its merits. It is the question presented by the bill. That may be the ultimate question, but the gentleman is mistaken in stating that the Secretary of the Interior, Mr. Smith, suggested that refunding is the best method. He did not. He stated before the House committee and testified before the Senate committee that, in his opinion, foreclosure was the best means of getting the most money for the Government out of these roads. Messrs. Anderson and Coombs, Government directors of the Union Pacific Railroad Company, who have investigated the matter fully, in like manner stated and testified that, in their opinion, foreclosure is the best method of procedure for the protection of the Government.

Mr. Coombs, government director of the Union Pacific Railroad, testified before the Senate committee, and stated before the House committee, that $12,000,000 can be obtained by foreclosure sale of these two roads, which would net the Government about $60,000,000. This is about $40,000,000 more than it will ever get if the bill now proposed to be given consideration shall pass. Mr. Anderson, government director of the Union Pacific Railroad and author of the majority report of the Pacific Railway Commission, in which refunding was recommended, as stated by the gentleman from Iowa [Mr. Henderson], testified before the Senate committee, during its hearings last spring, that he had changed his mind on that subject, and that in his opinion foreclosure and not refunding was the best remedy.

The gentleman refers to the President's message to Congress

X—19

at the opening of the present session, urging action, or, rather, declaring that if action be not taken by Congress by the 1st of January next there would seem then to be no further reason for delaying foreclosure proceedings. It seems to me that neither this House nor the country has anything to fear from that alternative. The House and the country may well permit every reason which has heretofore influenced the President to delay foreclosure proceedings to be removed by the failure of further congressional action in the interest of these companies.

Let the course of judicial procedure ordinarily adopted in such cases among citizens be followed.

For my part, I am not only opposed to the bill, but opposed to the consideration of any such measure. It is neither necessary nor useful.

On January 7, 1897, Mr. Powers supported the bill.

If there be any attempt during the progress of this debate to make appeals to the prejudices of men, the opponents of this bill will have a monopoly of that privilege. It is a straight, simple, business proposition that we intend to submit to the consideration of the House. Very likely I can best serve the purpose that I am charged at this time with forwarding by calling attention for a few moments to the history of this Pacific Railroad legislation.

The act of 1862 provided that the two companies, the Union Pacific Company and the Central Pacific Company of California, should have, as substantial aid for the building of their respective portions of the road, a magnificent land grant of each alternate section of land on either side of the line for a distance of ten miles—five sections for every ten miles. These lands were granted to these two corporations for the purpose of enabling them to construct the railroad which the Government so much desired. In addition to that, Congress gave to these companies a subsidy. That subsidy consisted of this, that the Government should issue thirty-year 6 per cent. bonds and deliver them to the companies as fast as they completed the several sections of the road.

In the open country between the Missouri and the foothills of the Rocky Mountains the subsidy should be at the rate of $16,000 per mile. The act further provided that in crossing over the Rocky Mountains, and also in crossing over the Sierras on the California end, the subsidy of $16,000 per mile should be tripled, making $48,000 per mile, and that between the

Rockies and the Sierras, where the work of construction was more difficult than on the outside ends of the line, the subsidy should be twice the original amount, or $32,000 per mile.

Now, Mr. Chairman, it is important for us to remember that to-day the building of a transcontinental line of railroad from the Missouri River to the Pacific Ocean is not a difficult work. But when you go back to 1862 you find that this was looked upon as an almost impossible venture.

But these companies went forward. Under the act of 1862 they endeavored to enlist private capital in the enterprise. But it looked so chimerical—it looked to business men so practically absurd—that very little money was raised, and the scheme seemed to be paralyzed from the start. So those men came back to Congress in 1864 and said to the members of both Houses: ''We cannot raise the necessary capital to construct these railroads; we are hampered by the fact that the Government itself, under the act of 1862, is to have a bottom mortgage on the railroad; we cannot raise money ourselves to build the road. But we ask you to permit these companies to place upon the road a first mortgage underlying the claim of the Government; and with the sale of the bonds and the proceeds of that mortgage, plus the aid that is to be rendered by the Government, we can assure Congress that the road can be constructed.''

In 1864 Congress had the same patriotic ardor for the construction of these roads that it had in 1862. It very readily, therefore, granted this request, and the distinctive characteristic of the legislation of 1864 is the fact that the Government stepped back one pace in the lien which it was to impose on these roads and the securities for the repayment of the subsidy which had been given them, and allowed the companies themselves to place beneath the mortgage of the Government a mortgage of prior obligation upon which they could realize money for the prosecution of this enterprise.

Now, those two acts—the act of 1862 and the act of 1864—contain the charters of the Union and Central Pacific Railroads, so far as the provisions of these charters are important for us to consider to-day.

Now, the Supreme Court has decided that under this legislation the security of the Government rests upon that portion of the railroad line that was actually aided by the Government. As everybody knows, the Union Pacific Railroad is now or was until recently a great system of railroad lines embracing nearly 8,000 miles, whereas the original line as projected under the legislation of 1862 and 1864 embraced only about 1,800 miles.

The Central Pacific Railroad of California, as it existed under the original legislation, embraced only the line from Ogden, in the State of Utah, to San José, in the State of California, a distance of about 860 miles; but to-day the Central Pacific system embraces a large number of additional lines that have been brought into it by purchase and by new construction.

It is easy to see, Mr. Chairman, that with this magnificent land grant given to the Union Pacific and the Central Pacific system, as well as the subsidy granted to each, it became a question of rivalry between them as to which should get the largest share. It became a race of diligence between the Central road, building from the west, and the Union Pacific, from the east, to see which could get the most of this grant by the Government, because the land grant and the subsidy were paid to both of them by the mile, and the more miles that any road could get in, the more land and the more subsidy it would be entitled to. The result of it was that these roads built right by each other in the vicinity of Salt Lake for a distance of about 80 miles, which was graded by the Central Pacific east of Ogden, the present terminus of the road; and the Union Pacific had shot by where the work of the Central Pacific was going on; and then each of the roads came to Congress claiming the land grant and subsidy for the additional mileage thus constructed. Congress settled the matter by the act passed in 1869, which provided that the point of junction between the two roads should be at a certain point about five miles west of Ogden.

This diligence resulted in another strange fact. Under the legislation of 1864 the roads had up to July 1, 1876, to complete the line, a distance of more than 2,000 miles. They had to cross the Rocky Mountains, the Sierras, as well as to traverse the great intervening arid space between the two. But this race of diligence enabled these companies, under the most formidable obstacles, to build the complete roads to the satisfaction of the Government, and they were accepted by the Government on the 10th day of May, 1869, four years after they had struck the first blow in the work.

Now, why did the Government want these roads built? I will show you. They were paying for the transportation of the mails overland to California, as well as to other points or the Pacific coast, a sum total of between seven and eight million dollars a year. After the roads were built this was cut down from $8,000,000 a year to a little over $1,000,000. They were compelled, before the building of the roads, to incur very heavy expense in the transportation of their supplies for the Indian agencies, their munitions of war, their troops, and other matters of freight. By the building of this road they were enabled to cut down this expense in an equally large ratio.

Not only that. Prior to the building of these roads that great and almost boundless empire that lies between these two ranges of mountains, with millions of public lands for sale, was practically cut out from the world. No man wanted to go there and settle, and therefore no man would buy an acre of that land. But by pushing this line of railroad through it opened these lands to sale and to settlement, and thousands and millions of inhabitants are to-day living in that region that was opened up by the enterprise of these men that had this matter in charge. And I may say right here in passing that, if the Government of the United States should lose every dollar of its indebtedness against these companies, should make a free gift of it, it could still credit the companies and itself with more than ten times as much in dollars and cents as it has ever expended in the construction of these roads. Why, the building of this Union Pacific through Nebraska and Kansas has strung together towns and cities like beads, and has carried civilization out through that country and across the Rockies, through its open portals to that great plain beyond; and we to-day are enjoying the blessings of it, not least among which is the presence on this floor of the genial gentlemen from Colorado and Utah, and Nevada, and other States out there that we should never probably have heard of had it not been for the building of this road. It opened up the great silver-mining industries of the country. Colorado, Utah, and Nevada were opened up, and the mines of that country were worked. Why, we never should have heard of a free-silver party if it had not been for the opening up of that country. I do not know that that is any argument in support of the passage of this bill. [Laughter.]

Now, in short, this is the way in which the Government got into this fix. The Government away back, under the act of 1862, undertook to secure to itself the payment of these subsidy bonds, and the plan which they then adopted, in the light of the facts then existing, was undoubtedly a safe one to calculate upon. They provided that the issue of these subsidy bonds upon the completion of each forty miles of railroad—the delivery of these bonds to the companies—should *ipso facto* create a statutory lien upon that section of road, and to secure payment they provided that this statutory lien should be a first lien, and that the roads, in addition to that security, should pay into the treasury of the United States a sum of money equal to 5 per cent.

of its net earnings after the road was constructed. It was supposed that this 5 per cent. of the net earnings would be sufficient
to meet the current obligations of the Government as they matured.

At that time, as you will remember, this was the only line
in contemplation. Nobody dreamed that the Atlantic and Pacific, the Texas Pacific, the Northern Pacific, the Canadian Pacific, or three or four other competing lines that have since been
built, would ever be constructed. Everybody supposed that all
the freight and all the passengers that were moved between the
East and the West were to go over this line and that the business therefore would be immense. But, in the progress of time,
these promoters, having demonstrated that a road could be built
over the Rockies, other men interested themselves in competing
lines, and in a very short time four or five of these lines have
been constructed. Therefore the receipts of these two companies have been lessened by that active competition on the part
of other lines.

We are not to say that the Congress of 1862 acted in a short-
sighted manner, because as things then appeared to them it was
doubtless a sound piece of reasoning to say that the 5 per cent.
of the net earnings of these companies paid into the sinking
fund would pay off this indebtedness in the end.

Now, matters ran along in this way until 1878. Mind you,
the road was finished in 1869 and accepted by the Government.

It was soon seen, after the roads started in and these other
competing lines were projected and completed, that the provision made under the legislation of 1862 and 1864 would be insufficient to meet the debt at its maturity.

The Supreme Court of the United States had meantime decided that the interest upon the subsidy bonds was not due from
the companies until the maturity of the bonds. The provision
in the statute is that the bonds shall be issued running thirty
years, the interest thereon payable semi-annually, and that these
companies should meet and pay that interest. But the court
says, and I think it is a unanimous opinion, that under the
language used in that enactment the interest upon the subsidy
bonds paid by the Government could not be taken from the company until the principal of the debt matured. And the result
of that is the interest has been accumulating against these companies, and to-day we are confronted with a vast amount of
unpaid interest, as well as the balance of principal.

In 1878 this matter was again taken in hand by Congress,
and Judge Thurman, then a Senator from the State of Ohio,

prepared and secured the passage of a bill known as the Thurman Act, the essential provisions of which, so far as this question is concerned, are these: That instead of paying into the treasury 5 per cent. of its net earnings, which upon an actual experience had proved to be insufficient, that there shall be 25 per cent. of the net earnings paid in. I ought to have said, in passing, what the two acts of 1862 and 1864 provide. The act of 1862 provided that the whole amount of the indebtedness from the Government to the railroads for the transportation of mails, for the transportation of its troops, and for other purposes should be retained by the Government.

In 1864 Congress modified that by providing that of these transportation charges only one-half should be retained in the treasury and the other half paid to the company. You observe that the Government thus was one of the very best customers of these roads. It had to pay these roads an enormous sum, and they took care to provide in the act itself that they should not be charged any higher rate than that charged private individuals for similar service. These transportation charges, which were enormous in amount, were to be retained, under the act of 1862, altogether in the treasury; under the act of 1864 one-half only, and under the act of 1878, the Thurman Act, the whole was to be retained, but one-half of it should be applied to the current interest on the subsidy bonds, and the other half go to the sinking fund, the theory of the Thurman Act being that one-half of its transportation charge, plus some other reserve, would take care of the current interest on these bonds, and the sinking fund itself would at the maturity of the bonds be large enough, if well invested, to take care of the principle.

Now, I will restate these propositions, because it is a pretty important piece of arithmetic. Under the act of 1862 the security retained by the Government was a first mortgage on the road, plus 5 per cent. of the net earnings and the whole transportation charges; under the act of 1864 the security of the Government was a second mortgage on the road, plus 5 per cent. of the net earnings and one-half the transportation charges; under the Thurman Act of 1878 the security of the Government was 25 per cent. of the net earnings, made up in this way: First, the transportation charges that the Government would be owing to the road as a debtor; second, 5 per cent. of the net earnings; third, such a proportion of the aggregate sum of $1,200,000 in the case of the Central Pacific, and $800,000 in the case of the Union Pacific, should be paid into the treasury of the United States, which, with the other two reservations, transportation charges, and 5 per cent., would aggregate in the whole 25 per cent. of their net earnings.

Now, then, Judge Thurman, in one of the most elaborate discussions of this question that has ever been made in its entire history, practically demonstrated, as the reader will see, the facts that his provision amply secured the repayment of this money. Why did it fail? Why, it failed, Mr. Chairman, just as many times the best laid plans of men as well as mice fail. The reduction in the rates of transportation was a very important contributing factor to bring about this result. The freight rates from the East to the West have been going down, down, down, as time advanced, to such a point that they hardly pay the charge made necessary by that transportation. This, however, is not peculiar to the history of these roads. It is peculiar to the history of all railroads in this country. How many of these roads have gone into the hands of receivers from the same cause exactly? Not only that, but the Government itself has divided this patronage with the Pacific roads. Instead of sending all its freight, all its transportation business over this line, the child of its own creation, the child that it should nourish and encourage, especially if it expected a repayment of its debt, it has divided its patronage. Some of it has gone to the Central Pacific, much of it to the Santa Fe, and much of it has gone to the other roads, thereby reducing the receipts in the treasury of the company, and to a corresponding degree the receipts in the treasury of the United States have necessarily been cut down.

But that is no fault of the railroads. It was a wise policy that promoted the building of these other lines. Other sections of this country needed opening and development as well as that central portion, and therefore the Government was wise in encouraging it, and no man has a right to criticise that policy; but the necessary result of it was to diminish the earning capacity of these roads which the Government itself had assisted in building, and therefore that policy contributed very largely to bringing the road into its present insolvent condition.

The Thurman Act was based upon the theory that government money was worth 5 per cent. interest, and, if that theory had proved correct, no doubt the Thurman Act would have worked out the result anticipated by its author. But, instead of the Government borrowing money at 5 per cent. interest, it can borrow at a rate nearer to 2 per cent., and this appreciation in the credit of our Government, which ought to thrill with pleasure the heart of every patriotic American, has also contributed very largely to the disastrous result which has overtaken these roads.

The Government said to these Pacific road companies: "Gentlemen, we want a line of railroad constructed from the Missouri River to the Pacific coast; we want to open up our great possessions between the two great ranges of mountains; we want to lessen the cost of transporting supplies and munitions of war across the continent, and supplies for the Indians to the interior of our country; we want a cheaper mode of transportation. If you will take all the risk and peril of building the road and will construct it to our satisfaction, we will give you so much money, we will give you such and such a land grant, and we will lend you each $33,000,000 by way of subsidy, which you may repay according to the terms of contract. If these conditions are acceptable to you, go on and build the road."

Now, if those companies went on and built the road, what man is there outside of a lunatic asylum who will say that they have got rich out of the Government? They have gotten out of the Government just exactly what the Government contracted to give them; no more. Not only that, but under the provisions of the acts of 1862 and 1864, as well as the Thurman Act of 1878, they have paid into the treasury of the United States, notwithstanding the fact that the Union Pacific Company during the last three years has been in the hands of a receiver, every dollar that the Government required of them. Not a cent has been defaulted. Where, then, is the ground for saying, as my friend from Louisiana [Charles J. Boatner] will say when he comes to discuss this question, that the men who built this railroad ought to "disgorge" and pay this debt themselves? They are nothing but stockholders in a railroad company. If any of you gentlemen are stockholders in an insolvent bank, do you pull out your own pocketbooks and pay its debts, or do you insist that the bank itself must pay?

Why, gentlemen, the result of those requirements exacted of those companies has been this, that the Union Pacific Railroad Company has returned to the treasury of the United States the total principal of the subsidy bonds issued to it plus $5,000,000, and the Central Pacific has returned into the treasury under those various requirements a sum that lacks only about $10,000,-000 of the amount originally granted to that road. That leaves, therefore, this difference of $5,000,000, plus the accrued interest; and that is the subject-matter of this proposed legislation.

This Congress is confronted with this condition: These subsidy bonds have some of them already matured, and the balance of them mature on the 1st day of January, 1898, and the 1st day of January, 1899. The time for action has come. The Government must do something to close out its relations with these roads. The President of the United States under the act of 1887 already has authority to foreclose the lien of the Government, and, if necessary, pay off the underlying first mortgage. The first question, therefore, that presents itself to us is this: Is it wise business policy for the Government to foreclose its lien or to seize the property, as some gentlemen contend it may be seized under the act of 1862, and get out of it what it can by the foreclosure?

Supposing that these gentlemen are right—that the Government can seize this property; the act of 1862 provides that upon a default in the payment of this interest as it matures the Government shall be authorized to take possession of the property; but every lawyer knows that that does not mean at all that the Secretary of the Treasury can walk into the office of this company and demand possession of the road and its property, and by force of arms or otherwise actually take possession. It means that he can take possession only by judicial process. He must resort to some judicial process if his request is not granted peaceably. That implies litigation. That raises all the questions that the company might raise as to the right of the Government to do that. It does more: It would require that the Government pay off its underlying first mortgage in order to realize any benefit from the seizure. Suppose that the Government, instead of taking that course, should foreclose the mortgage by proceedings in the courts. Now, under the practice of the Federal courts, where this case would go, the Government does not have what is known in New England as a strict foreclosure; that is, when the mortgage upon the foreclosure takes the property itself.

Under the Federal legislature the procedure must be to expose the property to public sale. The Government, therefore, if it forecloses the mortgage, must put the road and its property up at auction subject to the lien of the first mortgage, or it must pay off the lien and sell the fee of the property. Is that wise? Now, let us consider that matter for a moment. What would it amount to? It will cost the Government, to pay off the underlying mortgages upon the road, between sixty and seventy millions of dollars. Does the condition of the treasury at this time, and the condition of the business of the country, warrant us in imposing on the treasury a burden of sixty or seventy millions of dollars for the purpose of trying an experiment—for the purpose of trying the experiment of foreclosing the mortgage, and trying to get something for the property or the land that is left behind? Is it a wise proceeding? Would we do that in our dealings with individuals?

Why, gentlemen, it seems to me that the absurdity of the proposition needs no illustration. Take a common case familiar in your own business experience and illustrated in everyday life. If you have a man who owes you a debt—and every man who hears me has undoubtedly some time in his business life had an insolvent debtor to deal with—if he had an insolvent debtor, and he held a second mortgage on the farm, a farm encumbered by an underlying mortgage big enough to sweep it all away, would he send for the debtor and say to him what you propose to say to these railroads? How would he conduct the business? Would he do it by pounding his debtor, swearing at him, calling him a thief, abusing him for the faults committed in the past; or would he deal with him on a business footing and proceed to get the very best settlement available? Would he say to him, "My dear sir, you are a gambler, or a thief; you are dabbling in politics, or, worse, you have been dabbling with Polly, and to punish you for your sins I decline to deal with you on a sound business basis or on ordinary business principles. I will sacrifice your property as a punishment for your past sins, although probably by the same operation I lose the amount of my debt." Would any sensible man act in that way? That would be the act of a child.

As individuals dealing with an insolvent debtor we would be very likely to say: "My dear sir, what I want to find out is your debt-paying capacity; the ability of your farm to meet the obligations. I want to know the average income of your farm under ordinary conditions." When we have ascertained that fact we will adjust the burden to his shoulders in such way as he can bear it. Now, if by reducing our rate of interest and extending the debt for four or five years, it will enable him to work out from under the load and permit him to pay in full, why, manifestly every man here would adopt that plan. We have adopted the same plan in all of our dealings heretofore. We say that a foreclosure would be unavailing; that the receipts of the property would be unavailing from the fact that the thing you seize or foreclose is nothing in the world but an interior or underlying property.

If we are going to foreclose the mortgages, it is important for us to consider what we are going to get under that proceeding. Instead of getting a road with terminals, and with these branch lines, a network of which, as you will observe, runs all along in connection with these roads; instead of getting a system that can be worked as a railroad, we get an empty trunk, without terminals anywhere, and we have got to take our chances in dealing with somebody else.

Not only that. This road would have to be put up at public sale under foreclosure proceedings. Who on earth would be likely to bid it off? Would you or I or any outside party take the risk of stepping in and bidding on that property that was nothing but an interior property, without terminals or anything else? Certainly not. We should not dare to. The ownership of these branch lines, the very ownership of these terminals, the very ownership of everything essential to make that railroad worth a copper is in the hands of other parties and probably hostile parties. Now, where will you find the man with capital, the man who has millions of money to invest, who will step into a hornets' nest of that kind and make a bid? What is the practical result? These very men whom you are now scolding about, the very men who own the terminals and own these connecting lines are the only ones who can safely bid on the property, and probably they will be the only bidders. They would get the property at their own figures.

Every man can see what that would necessarily lead to. So that the procedure of a foreclosure compels the Government to raise sixty or seventy millions more of money to put into this hopper, and also leaves the Government with an insecure property after they have got their decree.

Now, it struck the committee, and it has struck every committee that has ever considered this subject since the Pacific railroads have been built, it has struck all the railroad commissioners, everybody who has investigated the matter, and they have all reported with one voice, that the true way to solve this problem was to fund this debt by an extension at a lower rate of interest, get a security upon a line which, if we are obliged to take it, will be a railroad line and not a section of a railroad line.

This committee have therefore proposed this bill, the essential features of which are these: That the amount of the Government indebtedness shall be ascertained as of July 1 next. The present bill before you reads January 1; but, as I said before, this will have to be corrected, and I will ask for an amendment. On the 1st of July this indebtedness is to be ascertained by getting at the present worth of the subsidy bonds that have not yet matured, bringing them down to the 1st day of July, 1897, so that on that day we will know just exactly what is the debt from the railroad company to the Government; and that thereupon the companies themselves shall issue first-mortgage bonds, taking up the existing mortgage, not only on the aided portions of the lines, but on their entire system, issuing a first mortgage equal in amount to the principal of their existing first mortgage; and that the Government shall take a second mortgage, lapping over the same property, lapping over the terminals, the Omaha Bridge, worth $2,000,000, and lapping over the Denver and Pacific road that runs from Denver to Cheyenne, and lapping over the branches forming the Union Pacific. In other words, a blanket mortgage, resting upon all this property, from branch to branch, to the same extent as the first mortgage that we allow to be put on.

Now, will we gain anything by that? We get a mortgage on a system of roads. We get a mortgage on a railroad instead of a mortgage on a portion of a line. It covers the whole thing, the terminals at Council Bluffs, the Omaha Bridge, the Omaha terminals, and on the line clear through. Essentially it covers also this line from Kansas City out to the three hundred and ninety-fourth milepost, where it now ends, to Denver, together with all the branches and feeders that supply this line. So that, if the worst comes to the worst in the end and the Government is obliged to foreclose its indebtedness, it can then take a property that can be operated as a railroad.

Joel D. Hubbard [Mo.] opposed the bill in a long speech in which his statements were enforced by financial statistics. In conclusion he said:

This bill does not require the Union Pacific to mortgage its bonds and stocks. The bill further permits the Central Pacific Railroad Company to remain under lease to the Southern Pacific of Kentucky, which is certainly in violation of laws passed by several of the States, and in violation of a principle which has been recognized even by Congress, feeble as it has been in its effort to legislate to prohibit the consolidation of parallel or competing lines of road.

The time that the bonds are to run under this mortgage is eighty-six years for the Central Pacific and eighty-three years for the Union Pacific, taking a second-mortgage 2 per cent. bond, which is practically worthless, and giving away these properties, because if they should fail again it would require over a hundred million dollars to come in and clean off the underlying mortgage, whereas now it can be cleaned off for less than thirty millions and give the Government a clear road to sell. The bill is inadequate to guard the interests of the Government, delusive, and visionary, and the results of its practical application will be to destroy, not conserve, the rights it vainly assumes to protect. [Applause.]

Charles K. Bell [Tex.] opposed the bill.

I do not agree at all with the gentleman from Vermont that the owners of the stock of the Union Pacific and the Central Pacific railroad companies are in an attitude which entitles them to the least favorable consideration at the hands of this body. I did not suppose there would be anyone who would attempt to defend either the builders of these railroads or those who have subsequently operated them. The scandals that grew out of their construction, and particularly out of the construction of the Union Pacific, are a disgrace to the civilization of the age and ought to be a warning to all who might be inclined to loan the credit of our Government to the prosecution of private enterprises. I do not, however, intend to be diverted from a discussion of the real merits of the proposed settlement by questions of this kind, and would not refer to them except for the fact that it has been assumed that those who have been the beneficiaries of outrageous peculations and frauds had conferred some great favor upon our country, and especially upon that section of it which is traversed by the roads which they constructed and have subsequently wrecked.

It has been asserted that it should make no difference to us, and was none of our concern, if the Government of the United States was not directly defrauded, whether the manipulators who constructed the roads acquired a fortune or not. From this proposition I utterly dissent. I entirely agree that, if any man by his labor, or by his superior judgment, can accumulate a fortune honestly and honorably, he ought to do so, and that he ought to be commended for doing so; but I dissent entirely from the proposition that it is honest or honorable to accumulate a fortune in building railroads, or in other public enterprises, by watering stock or issuing bonds which do not represent an actual investment. I deny that those who accumulate fortunes in this way are public benefactors, and I particularly dissent from the suggestion that we, as representatives of the people, are not interested in preventing such transactions, or in preventing those who have been the beneficiaries of them from enjoying the fruits of their ill-gotten gains. If gentlemen see proper to build a railroad, and, if they issue stock or bonds in excess of the actual cost of the enterprise, the excess represents so much indebtedness which the public, who from the very nature of the thing are compelled to patronize the road, have to pay the interest upon.

Enormous land grants were made to the railroad companies, but it is unnecessary to discuss the disposition which has been made of those lands, as they were a gift and not a loan, but so far as the subsidy bonds are concerned the case is entirely different. It was not intended, and never was suggested, that these bonds should be given to the companies, but only that they should be loaned, and it was always understood that the Government was to be repaid the entire principal and interest upon them; but it has been suggested by the gentleman from Vermont that, inasmuch as there had been repaid to the United States an amount equal to the original amount of the bonds granted, therefore, the Government ought to deal more leniently with its debtors in collecting the remainder of its debt. It is a familiar principle of law that partial payments upon a debt must be applied first to the payment of the interest, and this was in contemplation at the time the bonds were loaned.

If those who constructed the railroads had used the money which they realized from the sale of the bonds secured by the first mortgage, as well as from those which had been loaned by the Government, in the construction of the roads, and had issued no stock except for the money which was used in the construction of the roads, the annual charges against the companies would not have been so great but that the amounts which were to be applied under the law of 1864 to the Government's debt would have been sufficient to have paid the interest on the Government's debt, and inasmuch as that was not done, and as those who constructed the roads made use of these moneys to accumulate immense fortunes, and did so, I think they at least are in no position to ask favors at the hands of this body.

Nor do I agree at all with the statement that these companies have built up and turned into a garden the waste places which formerly existed where the roads now run. It is a great mistake to suppose that the railroads make the country. The hardy and honest people who have settled up our frontiers have made the railroads possible, and the railroads have shared but not occasioned the prosperity, so far as it has prevailed. Prosper-

ous communities were planted on the banks of the Mississippi
and Ohio, and the fertile lands of Illinois and other Western
as well as Southern States were occupied before there was a railroad.

I maintain that, from the time the first contract was made
for the construction of either of the roads concerning which we
are now legislating, every step has been taken with a view of
rendering it more difficult, if not absolutely impossible, for the
Government to collect its debt; but at the same time we are not
in nearly as bad a condition as some of the gentlemen seem to
imagine. For instance, it was stated by the gentleman from
Vermont that, inasmuch as our lien did not attach to that part
of the Union Pacific road which was within three miles of its
eastern terminus, therefore we could not use it in the event the
Government should become the owner of the road, or that the
purchaser of that part of the road upon which the Government has a lien could not do so. There is an express provision
in section 15 of the original act chartering the road which covers this case, and no one need have the least fear of such a catastrophe as the gentleman anticipates.

The bill proceeds upon the theory that we ought to accept
the proposition made by the railroad companies themselves instead of making a proposition of our own for them to accept or
decline. No business man would ever make a settlement upon
that principle. When people are dealing with others, they get
the best offer they can, instead of taking the most favorable
offer from the other party to the proposed contract. We have
accepted, or it is proposed that we shall accept, the offer of the
railroad company, just as if they were entirely insolvent, and
as if all we could do is to take what they are willing to give us.
Now, I believe that by submitting a fair and reasonable offer to
the companies, with the distinct understanding that they may
accept or decline it, we can reach a satisfactory adjustment of
our debt; that is, an adjustment that will be satisfactory to all
those who are simply trying to collect the Government's debt,
instead of trying to secure legislation by which their particular
section would be benefited to the exclusion of other portions of
the United States. It is true that these roads have not been
making satisfactory earnings for several years past, but the reasons for this are very plain. It is not to the interest of those
who have managed and operated these roads that they should
make money.

There are two reasons for this: First, and one which by all
means should be considered, is the fact that if the roads had

been making a satisfactory showing this body would not be disposed to settle on so liberal terms as they otherwise would; and another reason is the one which I have explained—that is, that one-fourth of the net earnings of the roads would have to go into the sinking fund. But the settlement proposed by the committee proceeds upon the theory that we should take the present net earnings of the roads as a basis for settlement, and that we should fix only such charges as the present earnings of the road would meet. I think this is entirely an erroneous basis upon which to proceed. If those who own the stock in and the properties of the companies are not going to raise money in some way for the purpose of putting the corporations on a more solid basis than they are now, then we had better refuse to treat with them and let some other person get control of the property who will be disposed to do right by the Government. What is it that we propose to do for these companies? If they, or others who may be their successors, have to go into the market and borrow money, they would be compelled to pay probably 6 per cent. per annum interest upon it.

I do not discuss the proposition to extend the debt at the rate of 2 per cent. per annum, because I do not believe that proposition will meet with favorable consideration at the hands of any considerable number of the members of this body, but at the rate of 3 per cent. per annum there is a saving in round numbers of $3,000,000 per annum to these companies in interest charges alone. This is a bonus greater than has ever been conferred by any government upon any corporation. It is one which we ought not to be compelled to consider the propriety of extending, but we must face the conditions as we find them. Without any fault of ours the conditions exist, and if we do not act cautiously and wisely our Government may lose its enormous debt. So, then, it is proposed that we confer upon these corporations a privilege which is equivalent to loaning them the credit of the Government, and thereby saving them $3,000,000 annually for an average period of forty-four years. What is it we ask in return? According to the bill recommended by the committee, absolutely nothing. We do not ask that they materially increase our security and make our debt more safe; in fact, that they do anything that will place the Government in a better condition than it has heretofore been. But I assert that we are in a position which enables us by exercising some degree of firmness in dealing with these corporations to compel them to deal justly with the Government in settling its debt, and if they will not do so there are others who will.

X—20

I think the theory upon which the committee has proceeded—
that is, that we determine what the companies can pay and accept that—is entirely wrong. We must insist, if we are going
to confer the great favor of loaning our credit, and thereby
enabling these companies to obtain cheap money, money, in fact,
so cheap that no other company has ever been able to get money
at nearly so low a rate—we ought to exact something considerable of them in return. But if the theory of the committee
that the earning capacity of the roads affords a correct basis
for determining the amount of the debt which could be placed
upon them is accepted, then I maintain that what the roads can
earn is not properly shown by returns of recent years.

Mr. Chairman, I think the facts which I have stated show
that we would not materially improve the condition of the Government and not increase to any considerable extent the prospect of the collection of the Government's debt by adopting the
bill reported by the committee. For that reason I oppose the
legislation. But I do not wish to appear in the attitude of an-
tagonizing measures that others recommend without suggesting
some other remedy.

There are three courses which naturally suggest themselves
as those which ought to be pursued in attempting to settle the
Pacific Railroad debts.

First. That the Government should pay off the indebtedness which is secured by a prior lien, and should thus become
the owner of the roads. I do not desire to enter into a discussion of the merits of this proposition. I do not at all favor the
proposition that the Government should become the owner of
railroads or engaged in the railroad business. I am aware that
there are very few members of this body who favor that policy,
and so it is useless to consume any time in attempting to an-
tagonize it.

Second. A foreclosure of the Government lien and a sale of
the property. Of course, if the property would bring the amount
of the Government's debt, as well as that which is secured by
the prior lien, this would be the most satisfactory way in which
a settlement could be effected; but there has been no evidence
before the committee, and, so far as I know, no one believes,
that if the property should be sold at forced sale it would bring
anything like enough to satisfy the debt due us; that is, after
satisfying the debt secured by the first lien. Hence, if it can
be avoided, we ought not to adopt the second proposition.

Third. An extension of the debt due the Government by
the respective railroads for a long period of time, at a low rate

of interest. If it was likely that at a forced sale the property would bring very nearly enough to satisfy the Government's debt after paying off that which is secured by the prior lien, I should be in favor of having the Government take what it could realize and sever itself entirely from the railroad business; but the debt is so enormous that, if there is any possibility of our being able to secure a reasonably satisfactory settlement, we ought to forego our individual preferences and attempt by every possible means to preserve the Government from loss.

The bill recommended by the committee provides for funding the Government's debt at 2 per cent. per annum interest. Inasmuch as the Government cannot obtain money at this rate, but must pay 3 per cent. per annum, I do not think we ought to entertain any suggestion of a lower rate.

The other question then is, How can the company secure the Government in the collection of its debt? I have prepared a substitute for the committee's bill which I propose to offer at the proper time. This substitute provides that the moneys in the sinking fund shall be applied as a payment upon debt which is now due the Government, and that if the companies will pay off and discharge the debts which are secured by mortgage, which is prior to that of the Government, then the debt shall be extended for an average period of about forty years at 3 per cent. per annum interest.

Galusha A. Grow [Pa.] supported the bill.

Mr. Chairman, if I had my say, I would say to these people, "Pay the Government the largest amount of money that you can raise," and let us pocket the loss of the difference.

MR. MAGUIRE.—Is not that the thing to be done by foreclosure and sale?

MR. GROW.—The evidence is that foreclosure and sale will not give you your debt.

MR. MAGUIRE.—We have testimony that they will sell for $120,000,000, which would give the Government $60,000,000.

MR. GROW.—There are some more suppositions and beliefs. With the testimony before us that these roads are not worth the first and second liens, what is the use in talking about somebody giving more than that amount on a supposition or belief?

MR. MAGUIRE.—That testimony was unsworn statements.

MR. GROW.—What is your statement but an unsworn statement? [Laughter.] Your statement is just as good as theirs.

MR. MAGUIRE.—Exactly; and theirs is worthless and should not be acted upon.

MR. GROW.—You have not got the money and do not guarantee that any amount of money would be paid. Money is the most timid of all things; and there is nothing more timid than $1,000,000 except $2,000,000. [Renewed laughter.] Moneyed men do not invest their money in any kind of enterprise without knowing as to its value; and when they have the net earnings of a railroad they know how to invest. If the evidence as to the net earnings do not show that they are sufficient to pay the interest on the first mortgage and on our lien, which is second, at a rate of interest not greater than 2 per cent. on the bonds, why expect moneyed men to put their money into this property and give us a first lien and they take a second? There is no money circle in the world charitable enough to do that for our Government.

Should these roads be put up for sale on foreclosure, the Government would have either to take out of the treasury money enough to pay the first lien, or the owners of the first lien will make the same combination that was always made when we made a sale of public lands by the Government, fixing the price at $1.25 per acre. There would be no probability of the Government realizing anything unless the Government paid the first mortgage. Are we ready to raise money and pay off the first lien? Right here let it be distinctly understood the Government has no more right in this case than any other junior creditor that has invested his money in an enterprise, I do not care what it is. We are bound in good business faith to do the same as we would as individuals (without any vote or power to coerce a particular course of action) of a board of directors in reorganizing a road in which we had individual interests as junior creditors.

The question before us is not one that we can settle by the main strength of our votes if we propose to act fairly and justly with the men who invested their money in this great enterprise which originated in legislation for the unity and benefit of the country and of mankind. [Applause.]

On January 8 Grove L. Johnson [Cal.] supported the bill.

Mr. Chairman, when we are called upon to settle the question as to what the United States shall get out of its second mortgage, which is the only matter before us, we are met by the gentleman from Louisiana [Mr. Boatner] and other gentlemen with this old talk that the men who built these roads made money. All right; suppose they did make money. They did only what everybody else would do if they had had the chance. Just imagine! If these gentlemen who now denounce so fiercely the men who built the Pacific railroads had only been in their positions at the inception of that enterprise, how differently they would have acted.

Suppose that they had built the road, and after they had completed it, seven years ahead of time, and when all the nations of the earth were rejoicing that we had succeeded in binding together the East and the West, they had presented themselves before the then President of the United States, and the gentleman from Louisiana would have been the spokesman, and he would have said:

"Mr. President, we have built this road, and we have built it seven years ahead of time, but we find that by some strange miscalculation we have made some money out of it. [Laughter.] We have kept every agreement we have made with you, but, *mirabile dictu,* we have made money, and our consciences will not permit us to retain it; so we come now to pour it back into the treasury of the United States." [Laughter.]

The gentleman from Wisconsin [Henry A. Cooper] might have said that he would like to have some of the money saved for the improvement of the harbor of Manitowoc. [Laughter.] The gentleman from the Fourth district of California [Mr. Maguire] would probably have expressed a desire to have some of it appropriated for the propagation of the doctrine of the single tax. [Laughter.] And the gentleman from Louisiana [Mr. Boatner] might have asked for some to pay the expenses of his contested elections. [Laughter.] Some of it might have gone in the interest of my colleagues to Petaluma Creek, and some to erecting a public building at Oakland, Cal. [Laughter.] But the balance would certainly have been covered into the treasury of the United States. [Laughter.]

Now, Mr. Chairman, would those gentlemen really have done that? Why, if Adolph Sutro, who has been bombarding Congress with letters on this subject, or if that blackmailer, William Randolph Hearst, who runs the *Examiner* in San Francisco, had been connected with this great enterprise, they would not only have made all the money that the other men made, but they would have brought the Government itself into contempt and ruin, and would have usurped the entire control. [Laughter.] But, Mr. Chairman, the real question for us to

consider is, How shall we get back our money? It is purely a
business question with us. Abuse of the men who built the
roads, animadversion upon their motives, or denunciations of
their acts will not avail us. We must deal with the matter as
it is in 1897. Our ancestors made the mistakes, if any were
made, that resulted in the present status of the case.

Now, there are three ways to deal with this question. The
first is to sell these roads under foreclosure to the highest bidder; the second is for the Government to take the road and
run it; the third is to extend the time for the payment of the
indebtedness. I apprehend that everybody in this House is opposed to the government ownership of railroads. The next
question, then, is, Shall we foreclose? If we foreclose, how
much shall we get? Who will bid? I do not ask any of these
gentlemen from California to answer that question, because
they are all wealthy, and if they did not have the money themselves they could call upon the committee of fifty in San Francisco and get the money from them—from Sutro or from
Hearst—and thus they could bid on this property. [Laughter.]
But I ask gentlemen from other parts of the United States,
who would bid in these properties if they were offered at auction? There are just three parties that could bid. One would
be the United States. The United States could, of course, bid,
could pay off the first mortgage, and then carry on the railroads. But nobody wants that to be done. The Vanderbilts
could bid, because they own a line of road leading into Omaha.
But they say they do not want the property. The only other
parties that could bid would be the same men who now control
the Central Pacific and the Union Pacific roads. They might
bid the property in at their own price, and thus get rid of paying the debt due to the Government.

The next question is—and this I understand to be the agreement of all who have spoken—whether or not this debt should
be extended. It is said that the Government ought to get a
larger rate of interest. Let us examine that question. Every
man knows that a railroad is valuable only for the money that
it can make. Everyone knows that a railroad company can
only pay its debts out of its earnings. Everyone knows that
the United States Government itself could not pay its debts if
they were all presented at once. A railroad company in debt
is not in a different position from anybody else, nation, corporation, or individual, who is indebted. There is not a bank
in the United States, except one, I believe, that could pay its
debts if they were all presented at once.

Should we estimate that the companies can refund their old debt at 4 per cent.? I do not think so. Money is not plentiful for railroad corporations at such a low rate of interest. I think they would have to pay at least 4½ per cent., and, if so, that will use up all of the surplus and consume all the earnings of these roads.

The opposition in California to the bill is unreasonable and hollow. It makes up in noise what it lacks in solidity. It mistakes vituperation for argument, abuse for reason, caricatures for facts.

The traveler across the Western plains has frequently been deprived of needed rest and felt compelled to mount guard all night by hearing the most unearthly and hideous noises coming seemingly from every quarter of the horizon, and apparently from the lungs of a thousand wild animals anxious to rend his limbs and feast upon the bodies of his horses, his family, and himself. Often has he paced the weary rounds of his camp with heart quickly beating, rifle in hand, finger on trigger, nervously waiting an assault while praying for the morning to come that he might face and fight in daylight the fierce wild beasts that, as he thought, encircled him. When at last the glorious orb of day came rising above the eastern horizon, illumining the whole earth, driving darkness away and giving renewed vigor to man and beast and flower and shrub alike, he has carefully scanned the country round about him that he might see the hordes that he thought had all night watched and waited for his death, when lo! he found that two measly, gaunt coyotes had furnished all the noise and given him all the terror of his wasted night. So with this California opposition to this funding bill. If you turn the sunlight of truth upon it, destroy its secrecy, and show its true relations to the subject, you will find that all this noise, this opposition, this denunciation of the funding bill and its friends, all this fearful wail against Huntington and the railroad and the friends of funding comes from two persons gifted, like the coyote, with leather lungs, innate wickedness, and an infernal desire to injure all that they cannot control.

These two are Adolph Sutro, by some mischance the mayor of San Francisco, and William Randolph Hearst, by the gift of his parents the proprietor of the San Francisco *Examiner*— *arcades ambo*.[1]

Of Sutro but little need be said. He admits his opposition to be founded upon personal spite against Collis P. Huntington.

[1] "Pals."

Of the other of this precious pair of literary coyotes, William R. Hearst, much could be said.

He is a young man, rich not by his own exertions, but by inheritance from his honored father and gifts from his honored mother. He became possessed of the idea that he wanted to run a newspaper. Like the child in the song, "he wanted a bowwow," and his indulgent parents gave him the *Examiner*. By the reckless expenditure of large sums of money he has built up a great paper.

The *Examiner* has a very large circulation. It did have a great influence in California.

It has done great good in California. It has exposed corruption, denounced villainy, unearthed wickedness, pursued criminals, and rewarded virtue.

At first we Californians were suspicious of "Our Willie," as Hearst is called on the Pacific coast. We did not know what he meant. But we came to believe in him and his oft-repeated boasts of independence and honesty. Daily editorials written by "Our Willie's" hired men praising his motives and proclaiming his honesty had their effect. Besides, "Our Willie" through his paper was doing some good.

We knew he was erotic in his tastes, erratic in his moods, of small understanding and smaller views of men and measures, but we thought "Our Willie," in his English plaids, his Cockney accent, and his middle-parted hair, was honest.

We knew he was ungrateful to his friends, unkind to his employees, unfaithful to his business associates, but we believed he was trying to publish an honest paper.

We knew he had money, not earned by himself (for we knew he was unable to earn any money save as a statue for a cigar store), but given him by honored and indulgent parents; we knew he needed no bribes with which to pay his way, hence, while we knew all these things, we did believe "Our Willie" to be honest.

We thought that he was running an independent newspaper on a plane far above the ordinary altitude of newspapers, with a sincere desire to do good to the world, with an honest wish to expose shams, to speak the truth, and to establish a paper that, while it might be a personal organ, would still be an honest one. We came finally to admire "Our Willie" and to speak well of him and his paper.

When William R. Hearst commenced his abusive tirades against C. P. Huntington and the Southern Pacific Company and the Central Pacific Railroad Company and all who were friendly to them, and to denounce the funding bill and all who favored it as thieves and robbers, we thought his course was wrong, his methods bad, and his attacks brutal, but we believed "Our Willie" to be honest in it.

When C. P. Huntington told the truth about "Our Willie" and showed that he was simply fighting the railroad funding bill because he could get no more blackmail from the Southern Pacific Company, we were dazed with the charge, and as Californians we were humiliated.

We looked eagerly for "Our Willie's" denial, but it came not. On the contrary, he admitted that he had blackmailed the Southern Pacific Company into a contract whereby they were to pay him $30,000 to let them alone, and that he had received $22,000 of his blackmail, and that C. P. Huntington had cut it off as soon as he knew of it, and that he was getting even now on Huntington and the railroad company because he had not received the other $8,000 of his bribe.

We have lost on the Pacific coast an idol. We grieve over a dead and wicked newspaper.

If it be given to spirits of the departed to know the actions of those left behind them on this earth, the honored and respected father of "Our Willie" is suffering now from the blackmailing conduct of his son. [Laughter.]

And that is the man who has created all this furor in California. He has intimidated people.

Nearly if not quite nine-tenths of the newspapers in California outside of San Francisco favor a funding bill.

I ask every member of this House to drop everything except the common-sense, business view, and to accept the settlement of this question on a business line. Remove it from politics; remove it from Congress; remove it so that the blackmailer no longer can hold it *in terrorem* against men, but will be obliged to allow everybody to carry out their ideas as to them seems proper. [Applause.]

William C. Arnold [Pa.] supported the bill.

I simply wish to say to the House that we are not to legislate for the State of California. We are legislating for the entire Union. Let the fight as between Mr. Sutro and Mr. Hearst on the one side and Mr. Huntington on the other go on to the hearts' content of the combatants. But let us address ourselves to the question before us, which is not their fight, but the question how the Government can save its money.

The proposition to defeat this bill is simply in the interests of Populism pure and simple—the Government ownership of railroads. I might say, as I have stated before, that there are just two questions before this House—either pass this bill or have the Government ownership of railroads. I am opposed, as I believe the vast majority of this House is, to any Government ownership of railroads. We are trying to get out of the railroad business instead of getting into it. [Applause.]

John C. Bell [Col.], a Populist, advocated the Government taking possession of the roads by foreclosure, and running them.

There is no law in morals or elsewhere that requires the people to pay toll to outsiders on their own donations. It is not necessary that there should be any great machinery for operating these roads. They may be operated under a receiver; they may be operated by the Government directors, or they may be operated under a lease.

Mr. Larrabee says, in his excellent work on railroads:

A number of European states, notably Prussia, France, and Belgium, as well as Australia, British India, and the British colonies in southern Africa, have adopted government ownership of railroads. The motives which led to this step in the various countries differ greatly. . . . The experiment of state ownership and management of railroads has been longest tried in Belgium, and with the best results. With an excellent service, the rates of the Belgian state roads are the lowest in Europe. Their first-class passenger tariffs are, next to the zone tariff recently adopted in the State of Hungary, the lowest in the world, and are, for the same distance, lower than those of American roads. In Prussia the state service, upon the whole, is also superior to that of private companies, and is probably equal to the public demand. In France the government only owns and operates less important lines, but furnishes upon these a more efficient and cheaper service than private companies would either be able or disposed to furnish. The oft-repeated statement of those opposed to government regulation to the contrary notwithstanding, government ownership and management of railroads is a decided success in Europe.

William P. Hepburn [Ia.] supported the bill.

Its opponents, he said, do not want any settlement that does not look to the ownership of this road by the Government, and its operation as a great highway upon which the owners of trains can compete with each other. They propose that we shall inaugurate the new but not untried experiment of government ownership and operation of railroads. We have had experiences in that line. No less than seven of the States of this Union have, at different times, tried the burdensome and costly experiment, and in every instance the result has been loss to the public, dissatisfaction on the part of the shippers, and emancipation from the business at great loss to the State.

The gentleman from Colorado [Mr. Bell] tells us of the admirable manner in which this experiment is resulting in some of the European countries. I say that it has never been a success in any country as compared with proper management, or with the average management, of railways in the United States. In every instance it has been more expense and less satisfactory. The experiment generally has been a failure. In Belgium, with a dense population, with short roads having an immense traffic, the Government has been enabled to run its roads without loss, and there are two roads in Hungary of which the same may be said; but, with those exceptions, neither the gentleman from Colorado nor any other gentleman in this House can point to a single instance where satisfactory results have been secured.

JOHN C. BELL.—How about France?

MR. HEPBURN.—France has abandoned the experiment in a great majority of instances, though there are still two or three roads in which the Government participates in ownership and in operation.

HENRY A. COOPER [Wis.].—Do you assert that this question of Government ownership of these railroads in the United States is involved in the foreclosure of the Government lien on these roads?

MR. HEPBURN.—I said this was the entering wedge, and that the advocates of it were so persistent now because they recognized the fact that it is the beginning of what they desire. Ask the gentleman from Colorado [Mr. Bell], does he believe that this is the entering wedge? Does he not believe that it will be followed on and on and on, no matter at what expense, until every mile of railway in the United States is under the control and operation of the United States Government? Look at every platform, repeated over and over again as the years go by. If there is any one thing above all others that that somewhat whimsical Populist party is addicted to, it is to this proposition of railway ownership by the Government. Each year it changes, in part, "the fundamental and eternal" principles that underlie its organization, but never this. It is always consistent in insisting that railway ownership and operation by the Government are essential to the happiness and prosperity of the American people. Ownership and operation by the Government of the Pacific roads is what the gentlemen from California desire. It is because of that desire they fight the pending bill.

Now, Mr. Chairman, I believe that this proposition of foreclosure under the law as it now exists simply means the total loss of all the indebtedness due now from these corporations. Not only that, but it means the expenditure of $61,000,000, which, with delinquent interest, amounts to about $64,000,000, or nearly that, that we shall have to pay before we shall have the title. Now the Government has invested in the roads more than $100,000,000. Then it would have invested in the roads more than $164,000,000. We would have a railroad without terminals on our hands, that we could build or replace for less than the money—this $64,000,000—that we would have to advance.

On January 9 William W. Bowers [Cal.] opposed the bill.

Advocates of the bill seem appalled, and are trying to stagger the House on account of the magnitude of the first mortgage. Sixty-one million dollars seem a large amount of money, but it must be borne in mind that we have $33,000,000 actual accumulated cash in the sinking fund now at our command, available to apply on the first mortgage, and that the roads are actually earning about $15,000,000 a year over and over operating expenses.

The gentleman from Missouri has shown us that it will only be necessary to raise about $30,000,000 to pay off the first mortgage and buy all necessary terminals.

If we are afraid of the first mortgage now, how can we expect our successors to be any braver if we now add to it $47,-000,000 more and leave the way open to run it up to $500,000,-000 when the accumulated interest of nearly a century shall have done its work?

They tell us, sir, we are weak, but when shall we be stronger?

Never.
The Government directors in their report in 1895 advised foreclosure. In 1896 they renewed the same recommendation. They have never advised funding or extending in any such

way as proposed in this bill. They have from long years of training in the service of the Government become experts and specialists. Their advice should count for something. What are we to do, then? My answer is simply, Do nothing. There is nothing for us to do, unless we want to give away the rights and the money of the United States. The laws creating these railroads provided all the machinery for enforcing the rights of the Government when the fullness of time should come and the default occur. The time has come, and the default. The clock has at last struck the hour. We can now either foreclose or the Secretary of the Treasury can simply take possession of the property without foreclosure, as provided in the original act.

In neither event is Government operation necessary. We have of late years been too well accustomed to seeing the Government operate railroads through receivers to be scared at that.

The enforcement of our rights is now an executive function and not a legislative one, and I for one am willing to rely with confidence on any administration in the belief that the President of the United States will protect the rights and the property of the United States. There are laws enough now on this subject. All they need is enforcement, and if given a chance the President will do it. The Reilly bill of last Congress proposed to give us first mortgage and 3 per cent. interest. This bill offers a second mortgage and only 2 per cent. We who spurned that bill and rejected it by an overwhelming vote certainly can never vote for this.

MR. MAGUIRE.—Mr. Chairman, the bill under consideration is decidedly the worst measure for the settlement of the Pacific railroad debts ever offered to Congress, the worst proposition that has ever come from those companies.

This failure of evidence on the part of the company to establish any of the facts essential to this settlement should of itself cause the House to reject this bill. Yet, with amazing pertinacity, they still ask the House to be satisfied and pass the bill.

I say to you that this House will never be in a position to legislate intelligently for a settlement of these claims until a court of competent jurisdiction shall have tried and determined all questions relating to the validity of all alleged liens and the relation of all valid liens to each other. Such a decree is absolutely necessary as a basis for legislative action, if any legislative action shall then seem wise or necessary, but to legislate now in the dark—in utter ignorance—on a question of such importance would be monstrous.

The interests of the Government are not in any danger. The Government will have no payments to make on the first mortgages until foreclosure, nor after foreclosure, unless it becomes the purchaser at the sale. The Government must pay its subsidy bonds, no matter whether the debts are funded or not, and nothing more, except the expenses of the litigation, need be paid at any time, unless the Government buys the roads.

The Central Pacific Railroad Company will cease to exist on the 1st of June, 1911, by operation of the constitution and laws of the State of California, under which it was incorporated.

Its lease of life cannot be constitutionally extended unless it is expected to make an act of Congress override the constitution of the State in a matter of purely domestic concern, such as the life of an artificial person created under the laws of the State.

It is, therefore, absurd to contract with that company for payments to be made after 1911.

I am opposed to the whole refunding scheme. Foreclosure is the only sensible business method of dealing with these properties and claims as they now stand.

I cannot close these remarks without noticing some of the extraordinary statements made by the gentleman from California [Mr. Johnson] in his speech of yesterday. That speech is the most remarkable instance that has ever come to my knowledge of the resident of a glass house throwing stones, but I am concerned only about answering the attacks made and shall confine myself to that purpose.

The gentleman said that I, among other Representatives from California, would support and vote for the Powers refunding bill if left free to follow my own convictions and judgment in the matter, and that I am opposing it against my conscientious convictions solely on account of my fear of the San Francisco *Examiner* and its proprietor, Mr. Hearst. By that statement he sought to brand me before this House as an unfaithful Representative.

He further sought in the same speech to smirch my reputation by stating that I was the personal friend and official defender of Mr. William R. Hearst, whom he attacked in terms of foulest reproach.

With respect to the first statement of the gentleman to which I have called attention, I say that it is absolutely false and without the slightest shadow of foundation in fact. I am opposing the Powers bill, as I have opposed all similar bills, solely on my own judgment and because I am conscientiously convinced that it is a vicious measure.

As to the second statement of the gentleman to which I have called attention, I say that I am the personal and political friend of Mr. William R. Hearst. I have known him personally since his childhood and known him to be a man of honorable character and strong human sympathy. In his journalistic career he has shown himself a man of the highest genius and of sterling worth. He sympathizes with the afflicted and gives largely of his means to relieve distress. He loves justice and contends for it. He hates injustice and opposes it practically. He hates oppression and fraud and scourges them in high as well as in low places. He has done more than any other hundred men to purify the politics of California, and he is doing more to-day to purify the politics and the political institutions of the United States than any other man within its borders. But he has one grievous fault. He is not merciful to the tyrants or the corruptionists whom he assails. This fault causes bitter and sometimes powerful enemies (I do not refer to the gentleman from California) to rise up against him. Every human reptile that formerly reveled in the corruption with which his efforts have interfered hates him as it hates sunlight and spouts venom at him whenever it gets into a place of comparative safety. In their rage for revenge the vicious ones whom he has assailed are not restrained by any consideration of conscience or veracity. The worst falsehoods that polluted minds are capable of breeding are by them preferred to truth. I am speaking now of the sources of the gentleman's information against Mr. Hearst.

I will not further notice any of the contemptible falsehoods concerning Mr. Hearst's private life, but the charge that he levied blackmail on the Southern Pacific Company is tangible and requires some attention. The facts upon which this charge is based, as nearly as I can remember them, are these: About five or six years ago the Southern Pacific Company made a contract with the San Francisco *Examiner* for advertising, during the World's Fair period, for thirty months, at the rate of $1,000 per month.

The advertising matter was published and the agreed price paid by the company for twenty-two months. Then a controversy arose. The *Examiner* had occasion to editorially denounce some schemes in which the company was interested. The company insisted that because of its advertising patronage the *Examiner* should refrain from attacking its interests editorially.

Mr. Hearst, through his business manager, immediately replied, repudiating that principle of business, and stating that under no circumstances could the advertising patrons either affirmatively or negatively control the editorial or news columns of the paper. There the matter ended, until Mr. Huntington, a few months ago, in a moment of impotent anger, stated that he, or the company, had paid the $22,000 to the *Examiner* as blackmail. Mr. Hearst immediately published the contract and the correspondence concerning it. The gentleman from California [Mr. Johnson] said that Mr. Hearst had admitted receiving $22,000 from Mr. Huntington as blackmail. That statement is simply false.

The bill came to a vote on January 11, 1897, and was rejected by 103 yeas to 168 nays. The votes in the affirmative were largely Republican. Among the Democrats who voted for it were George B. McClellan, Jr. [N. Y.], and William Sulzer [N. Y.]. Since opposition to the bill had been specifically declared in the Democratic national platform of 1896, the Democrats who voted for the bill were severely criticised by the party organs. The New York *Journal* and the San Francisco *Examiner*, papers owned by William R. Hearst, charged that Richard W. Croker of Tammany Hall had gone to Washington, and, in the interest of Collis P. Huntington, ordered the Democratic Representatives from New York City to vote for the bill. Amos J. Cummings was one who refused to obey the boss, and was punished therefor, it was said, by Mr. Croker deposing him from his place as the candidate favored by Tammany for the next Mayor of New York, a position for which Mr. McClellan was subsequently nominated, and to which he was elected.

CHAPTER X

THE INTERSTATE COMMERCE COMMISSION

George W. McCrary [Ia.] Introduces in the House Bill to Regulate Inter-state Commerce (Railroads); Bill Is Passed; Not Acted on by Sen-ate—John Sherman [O.] Introduces in the Senate Bill to Regulate Interstate Commerce; It Is Committed—John H. Reagan [Tex.] Re-ports Bill from Committee on Commerce to Prohibit Discrimination in Rates by Railroads; No Action Is Taken—He Proposes to Establish an Interstate Commerce Commission; No Action Is Taken—He Intro-duces Bill in the House to Regulate Interstate Commerce; It Passes the House but Not the Senate—Shelby M. Cullom [Ill.] Introduces in the Senate a Bill to Regulate Interstate Commerce Through a Com-mission—Debate: Sen. Cullom, Thomas W. Palmer [Mich.], Leland Stanford [Cal.], Johnson N. Camden [W. Va.], Zebulon B. Vance [N. C.], George F. Hoar [Mass.], Samuel J. R. McMillan [Minn.], John E. Kenna [W. Va.], Nelson W. Aldrich [R. I.], E. C. Walthall [Miss.], William J. Sewell [N. J.]; Bill Is Passed—John H. Reagan [Tex.] Reports Substitute in the House—Debate: Judge Reagan, Charles O'Neill [Pa.]; Substitute Is Passed; Senate Refuses to Accept It, and Conference Committee Is Appointed; It Reports Bill Next Ses-sion—Debate in the Senate: Orville H. Platt [Conn.], John T. Morgan [Ala.], Richard Coke [Tex.], Isham G. Harris [Tenn.], William M. Evarts [N. Y.]; Speech of Robert M. La Follette in the House: "Honest Railroads Aided by Government Regulation"—Bill Is Enacted.

ON March 3, 1874, George W. McCrary [Ia.] brought before the House a bill he had earlier introduced from the Committee on Railways and Canals to appoint a commission to regulate interstate commerce carried by railroads.

The bill was ably discussed, and at great length, by the leading constitutional lawyers of the House, but as their arguments will be found in connection with the later establishment of the Interstate Commerce Com-mission they will not be presented here. It was passed on March 26, 1874, by a vote of 121 to 116. The Senate took no action on this bill.

On May 13 John Sherman [O.] introduced a bill in the Senate to regulate interstate commerce, which was referred to the Select Committee on Transportation Routes to the Seaboard. It was not reported from the committee.

On May 2, 1878, Judge John H. Reagan [Tex.] reported in the House from the Committee on Commerce a bill "to regulate interstate commerce and to prohibit unjust discrimination by common carriers." The debate on this bill was long and exhaustive, but as the main arguments were later presented in the discussion on the Interstate Commerce Commission they are here omitted.

No action was taken on the bill during this session.

During the third session of the Forty-sixth Congress [1880-81] Mr. Reagan reported in the House from the Committee on Commerce a bill to establish a Board of Commissioners of Interstate Commerce. It was extensively discussed, but finally the House refused to take action upon it.

In the session of 1884-5 Judge Reagan secured the passage of a bill by the House, by a vote of two to one, to regulate interstate commerce. The debate is omitted here for reasons given above. The bill failed to pass the Senate.

On February 16, 1886, Shelby M. Cullom [Ill.], from the Select Committee on Interstate Commerce, introduced in the Senate a bill to regulate interstate commerce through a commission. It came up for discussion on April 14.

INTERSTATE COMMERCE COMMISSION

SENATE, APRIL 14-MAY 12, 1886

Senator Cullom explained the provisions of his bill.

If the three propositions are correct, that the public sentiment is substantially unanimous that we should act, that the necessity for action exists, and that the power of Congress is

J.H.Reagan

admitted, the only question left is what kind of an act should Congress pass? The committee has unanimously reported a bill which is the best judgment that it had upon the subject.

The general legislation proposed in the bill is contained in the first seven sections, the remainder being devoted to the organization of a commission and to the details of its operation as a means of securing the enforcement of the act.

The general theory of the measure is that as unjust discrimination in its various forms is recognized as the chief of all evils growing out of the existing methods of railroad management it is the duty of Congress to strike at that evil above all things else. The bill has accordingly been drawn with that end in view. The first section defines and prescribes the scope and application of the bill. The second, third, and fourth sections specifically prohibit and declare unlawful the various forms of unjust discrimination between persons, between different commodities or particular kinds of traffic, and between places. The fifth section requires the publication of rates and declares it unlawful to charge more or less than the public rates. The sixth section provides that shipments shall be considered as continuous from the place of shipment to the place of destination, and prohibits combinations to evade the provisions of the act by breaking of bulk, carriage in different cars, transshipment, or other devices. The seventh is the general-penalty section. It makes the performance of any acts declared unlawful in the preceding sections a misdemeanor and fixes the penalty.

In connection with these sections I desire to call attention to section 20, in which it is expressly stipulated that the provisions of this act shall not in any way abridge or alter the common-law remedies now open to the shipper, but shall be considered as in addition to such remedies, except that the remedy at common law and that proposed in the bill shall not both be prosecuted at the same time. Under the terms of the bill no one is obliged to appeal to the commission, and two courses are open to anyone who may be aggrieved by the violation of any one of these general provisions which I have mentioned. He is simply obliged to elect which course he will adopt, and may at his own pleasure either bring suit in the courts on his own account for the recovery of overcharges or damages, or he may ask the commission to arbitrate the controversy, and, if necessary, to investigate his complaint, the advantage of the latter course being that in the event of a favorable finding by the commission his evidence is collected for him without expense to himself, and he can if it becomes necessary go into court with a *prima facie* case already established.

It is substantially agreed by those who have investigated the question of railroad regulation that publicity is the most effective remedy for the evils most seriously complained of, so far as it is possible to remedy them by legislation. There are two directions in which a greater measure of publicity is essential and can be secured by legislation. The first is as to the rates actually charged, in order that every shipper may know whether he is treated fairly and without unjust discrimination. The second is as to the methods of management and financial operations of the railroad corporations, in order that the net results of their business may be accurately known, and that the public may be placed in a position to determine the reasonableness of the charges made, which are in the nature of a tax upon commerce. The publication of rates as provided in the fifth section is intended to meet in part the first requirement I have mentioned, and the bill proposes to meet both the first and second by the creation of a commission authorized to secure the enforcement of the law and with ample power to investigate every detail of railroad management, and to enforce the making of complete and accurate reports by the corporations. If the railroads can be compelled to let in the sunlight of publicity upon all the operations, personal favoritism and the chief causes of complaint will to a great extent disappear, and the accurate information obtained will enable the law-making power to devise any further remedies that it may be possible to apply by legislation.

Thomas W. Palmer [Mich.] of the committee supported the bill.

The necessity for the enactment of this measure recalls an Oriental tale: Some fishermen one day drew to the shore in their nets a chest from which sounds proceeded, and on listening the sounds became articulate and intelligible. In reply to their questions a voice told them that its possessor was a dwarf endowed with wondrous powers, that he had been imprisoned by a wicked Genie, and if they would release him he could and would labor for them and enrich them. They forced open the lid and there emerged a misshapen being, black, feeble, and unattractive. Its docility and intelligence were remarkable. It showed the greatest eagerness to serve them. As its strength increased it brought coal, precious stones, and fragrant woods from the mountains, and fish and amber and coral from the sea. It evinced such capacity, tact, and tractability that they reasoned if he did so well as he was what would he do if they could increase his strength and stature.

Acting on this idea, they fostered him, brought the most nutritious food for him, and did everything they thought would conduce to the desired end. He thrived and grew apace. He expanded, became erect, and in time towered above them all. Then there came a change in his demeanor, and instead of being their servant and benefactor, showing them hidden sources of wealth and teaching them how to cheapen the necessaries of life and multiply its luxuries, he proclaimed himself their master and compelled them to bring to him for his use gems, spices, and costly bales, and assumed all the pomp, circumstance, luxury, cruelty, and rapacity of an Indian prince.

Among the servants of our civilization none have approached in efficiency the railway. It has annihilated distance; it has not only made the wilderness blossom as the rose, but also has enabled the rose to be readily exchanged for the products of cities. It has conducted to the widest diffusion of labor and rendered nations measurably homogeneous. In our own country the cost of transportation of a year's food from the agricultural West to the seaboard has been reduced to the price of a day's labor, so that the mechanic of the manufacturing centers may by the sacrifice of a single holiday be said practically to live by the side of the farm.

It has rendered possible the establishment of great manufactories at centers of population, where labor is abundant and capital present to superintend, instead of the former necessity of placing the manufactory at the point of supply of raw material. The natural advantages of production in each locality have, by minimizing the cost of transportation, been allowed to be exercised to their utmost, and values added to cereals in remote and isolated districts. The surplus corn of the Northwest, which was formerly so cheap as to be used for fuel, has, by reduced transportation, been enabled to compete with that raised near the seaboard. Ores are profitably shipped from the mountain fastnesses, where a plant is undesirable, to St. Louis, Detroit, Philadelphia, and Pittsburgh, for reduction.

Railways are improved highways, not a new, but a developed, feature of the advancement of the race. The question at the front to-day in this country and in Europe is not how to cripple or restrict railroad building or railroad operations; is not how to do away with the vast commercial power, extending over 265,000 miles of rails laid through developed and developing territory, but how best to promote them, that they may continue to serve rather than to rule the interests of individuals and communities.

That the experience of a little more than half a century under various conditions and under every civilized form of government has not been sufficient to remove the regulation of railways from the field of experiment is shown by the various methods of to-day on trial in Europe and America. In Belgium the government has either built or purchased the main trunk lines of the kingdom. Branch lines are allowed to be built and operated by private capital, the government guaranteeing 4 per cent. interest upon the investment and retaining the practical supervision of the management.

It is reported that the roads are managed satisfactorily to the people, that the rates are fixed and stable; but an early absorption by the government under provisions in the charters of the private lines is predicted, which would indicate a dissatisfaction on the part of private capitalists.

In France the main trunk lines were originally assigned a district or field supposed to be profitable without competition on condition that they should build branch lines into the less productive districts. This proved impracticable, and the government was obliged to lend its aid for the development of the territory. The charters provide that at the expiration of ninety years all railways shall revert to the state, the state purchasing the rolling stock at an actual valuation. Already the government has advanced 600,000,000 francs to the railways, and its policy looks toward an earlier appropriation than that nominated in the charters.

Already a perpetual committee supervises the management, arranges the tariff of charges, and settles disputes between competing lines and between the public and the railways. Rates and time-cards are required to be published, and no change against the interests of forwarders or passengers can be made without thirty days' notice and the consent of the commission. No private arrangements with individuals or corporations are permitted.

In North Germany all concessions are made by the minister of commerce, unless there is to be a largess or guaranty of interest when an act is required. In Prussia, at the commencement of its railway system, each railway chartered was given a field without competition, the state reserving the right of purchase of the road after the lapse of thirty years. In 1882 there were 9,500 miles of state lines, 1,320 miles of private lines under state management, and 2,400 miles of private lines. The control of the government may be considered practically absolute, and is given over to a special board at the head of which is the minister of public works. Special tariffs are prohibited, correspondence in time-cards in railways insisted upon, persons and merchandise conveyed in the order in which the application is made. No variation in rates or time-table can be had without the consent of the board.

Austria followed the course of France in allowing concessions for the period of ninety years, and in addition the government built several trunk lines, which it retains. It also maintains supervision over passenger and freight traffic. Switzerland has no state lines, but an effectual system of supervising the tariff charges and a perpetual commission to regulate the relations of the corporations to the stockholders and the public, and provide for the constant publicity of railway transactions. Italy owns a portion of its railways and is in negotiation for the remainder. The policy of the government is ownership by the state.

In the history of English legislation on railroads and its results we find the closest resemblance to our own. In 1836 England had, next to Holland, the most complete canal system and service in the world, and its restrictive endeavors were guided not by a proper conception of the problem before it, but by its experience in dealing with oppressive methods in canal management. The popular belief in the power of competition to cheapen rates and control commerce in the public interest was accepted, and in spite of the warnings of the astute Morrison and the terse axiomatic statement of George Stephenson, that "where combination is possible competition is impossible," their early legislation was bent to increase competition between capitalists.

The natural consequences of combination, discrimination, secret rate making, preferences, the building up of seaports, and the oppression of non-competing points followed in spite of the most stringent legislation, until, in 1872, after over 3,300 acts had been passed and the expenditure of about £80,000,000 imposed upon the companies, a joint select committee recommended and Parliament provided for a railway commission, which has since become permanent and been increased in executive and judicial power. Some progress has been made in the regulation of the interests of the general public.

According to the statement of H. R. Hobart, editor of the *Railway Age,* made before the Senate committeee, the railway mileage of the United States and Territories at the commencement of 1885 was about 125,500 miles. In 1828 there were three miles of railroad. The capital stock and bonded indebtedness now show a value of $7,795,000,000, or more than four times the national debt, and 20 per cent. of the estimated wealth of the entire country. They employ about 725,000 persons, and thus support directly more than 3,000,000 of men, women, and children; and indirectly they aid in supporting many millions more concerned in the manufacturing, mercantile, and other interests of which the railways are very large patrons.

These roads are the modern highways for commerce, and should differ only in extent and facilities from their predecessors back to the days of the Roman roads. The laws governing the Roman highways were the bases of the laws of the road to this day. They were built by sovereigns having the right of eminent domain, and their use was common and equal to all. They were supported by taxes upon the bordering people, or by tolls upon those who made use of them.

Under our somewhat complicated system of government the railroads were chartered by States, who bestowed upon them the right of eminent domain, and they were builded wholly or in part by contributions directly from the State or by the people along their lines, and they were intended for the common and equal service of all who chose to make use of them. In their inception they were supposed to bear an analogy to the canal, and traces of this mistake appear in almost all of the early charters. It was believed that the railway, like the toll roads of that day, would be built by one company and used by any and all who chose to prepare suitable carriages.

Liberal legislation and a speculative spirit among our people led to overbuilding and misbuilding, and upon emerging from the crisis of 1857 many railroads found themselves embarrassed and the mortgages upon them were foreclosed.

At this time, under a system of reorganization which appeared plausible and just to the people, to the stockholders, and to those holding other than first-mortgage claims, bankruptcy was given a novel and dangerous turn in railroad financiering, and "additional capitalization," discounted upon the markets of the world, paved the way for the absolute control of this vast value and interest by a handful of men irresponsible to the people for the condition and conduct of their highways.

To-day it is represented that half a dozen gentlemen meeting in an office on Wall street may, by the power derived from ownership in these railway and wealth not obtained by the development of the country or improved transportation but by financial jugglery, dictate the profits or losses of men and communities throughout the land. By their fiat Rochester must stop milling that Minneapolis may thrive. All manufacturing establishments at Niagara Falls save one must suspend that the one may become wealthy. The capital and labor invested in thousands of oil wells and refineries must be lost that one combination may be made powerful. Villages and cities as well as individuals have been selected for development or for destruction.

The Senate committee, whose investigations have resulted in the presentation of this bill, present in their report eighteen specific causes of complaint against the railroad system, which may nearly all be epitomized as "discrimination" in one form or another. They cite among the many instances the case of the Standard Oil Company, which has been enabled by railroad discrimination practically to control the oil supply of the continent, and is reported to have realized $10,000,000 in a single season from diminished freights alone.

A single instance is sufficient to condemn the system. It appears that the company operates the Macksburg pipe line which carries oil to the Cleveland and Marietta Railroad. This road was in the hands of a receiver, who was removed by Judge Baxter upon the investigation of the rates charged for the transportation of oil. It was found that he was charging all independent shippers 35 cents per barrel, and the rate to the pipe line was but 10 cents. It appears that the Standard Oil Company owned the pipes through which the oil is conveyed from wells owned by individuals, with the exception of certain pipes owned and used by one George Rice, carrying oil from his wells, and to get rid of this competition the assistance of the receiver was sought and obtained.

The company offered to give the railroad three thousand dollars' worth of business each month, while Rice could give but three hundred dollars' worth. If its demands were not complied with it threatened to extend its pipe line from Macksburg to Marietta, on the Ohio River.

I do not expect that the passage of this bill and the appointment of any five gentlemen who might be named under its provisions for its enforcement will at once bring the millennium to American transportation. For forty years a constant struggle of wits has been going on between the grasping corporations and legislatures endeavoring to restrain them, and to-day we are confronted with successful, legalized wrongs remaining uncontrolled and unredressed. But we shall have done our duty when we shall have done our utmost for the future security of the people. I do not believe that this bill will accomplish radical results, but it is a step in the right direction, both for the people and for honest railroad management. For many years a contest between the safe maker and the burglar has been waged. Each failure of the safe to withstand its robber has begotten improvements believed to be final, and each in turn has yielded to human cunning and ingenuity. But it is not for the safe maker to stop in his endeavors. If this bill, becoming a law, should fail utterly to supply a remedy, another attempt must be made. If it is partially successful, we shall have accomplished something and new remedies will be suggested by its partial failure.

An examination of the report and testimony will not show that railroad corporations are making too much money, or that the average rates of transportation are too high. On the other hand, they have been in the main unprofitable, and transportation between competing points in America is the cheapest in the world. The complaint of the people is of discrimination, uncertainty, and secret injury. The complaint of investors is that two-sevenths of the capitalized investment is water, and that through inside combinations the masters of Wall street are able to realize vast profits upon railroad wreckage and the depreciation of railroad property, as well as upon their prudent conduct and honest management. A great stride toward personal liberty was believed to have been made when our Government was organized with the prohibition of entail; but the sovereignty of trunk lines and railroad system, imperishable as they are, present a more dangerous *imperium in imperio* for our consideration than the largest entailed interests of the world.

Railroads are beneficent servants, but they must not become masters. The dwarf has grown large enough for us to impose restrictions upon his growth, else the old fable will be illustrated in practical life. If unchecked he bids fair to develop into an Afrite of gigantic stature and overwhelming and malignant influence. Railroads are no longer dull, insensate things. They are imbued with intelligence, and in intelligence that neither slumbers nor sleeps. They are no longer joint stock companies alone; they are dynasties.

They are already outlined, and in a few years if not supervised and controlled by legislation they will have become as firmly fixed in their grasp upon continued power, commercial, social, and political, as the Hapsburgs, the Hohenzollerns, or the Guelphs. These reigning houses were born of force. They were the triumph of the strong over the weak. These modern dynasties will have been born of law and of concession and will be the triumph of the creature over the creator.

The old cry of the mayor of the palace when he appeared at the window of the Tuileries, ''The king is dead, long live the king,'' may well be proclaimed when the railroad magnate goes to his long home. Not a schedule is changed, not a locomotive puffs less fiercely, not a sardine less is sold in the restaurant. The same intelligence, fortified and intensified possibly by new blood, wields the scepter and utters its mandates.

The fact that the stock changes hands does not detract from its power or alter its purposes. It is more remorseless than man, for the responsibility is divided. The cabinet or ministers who shape its policy and carry out its behests justify their course by the plea of necessity, and feel no tremors of conscience from the fact that their personality is merged in that of the corporation.

Hitherto content has come to the plain people of our land, to the mechanic, to the farmer, to the artisan, because, as he sat by his hearth noting the progress of his fellows who had outstripped him in life's race, his eye turned to the bright boy and the laughing girl with a knowledge that to them America offered every possibility of culture, wealth, and power. He knew that the history of the men whom America had delighted to honor had shown that from the humblest beginnings nothing restricted or directed the development of the American citizen outside of himself. To-day he sees the price of his labor determined not from his surroundings. He sees his village built up or destroyed by a foreign will. He sees the value of his little property decreased and that of the property of his fellow in an adjoining village increased without the action of either and beyond the control of any. He sees his neighbor, by secret arrangement with the railroad company, increasing his store with no extra labor or display of energy or ability, while his fellows are correspondingly depressed.

These things it is the object of this measure to correct.

All the American citizen has asked in the past or will ask in the future is a fair chance; no odds of the Government, but its protection, for which his life is pledged, and its schools, for

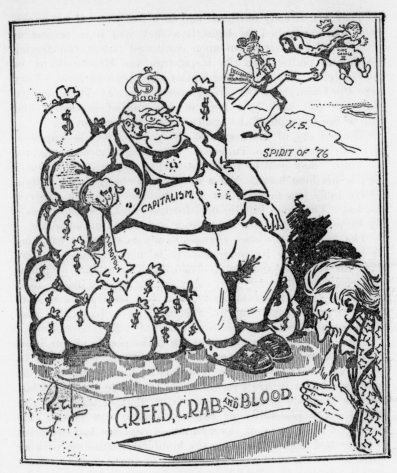

"AMERICAN IDEALS"
Cartoon by Ryan Walker in "The Comrade"

which his money is paid. Special privileges for none, equal rights for all.

On April 26 Leland Stanford [Cal.] opposed the bill.

This bill purports to be an act to regulate commerce between the different States. But everything in it is as to the carrier only. The word commerce has a well-defined meaning. It means interchangeable commodities, with which the carrier in the transaction of his legitimate business has no concern whatever. I therefore think the title of the bill, instead of reading "A bill to regulate commerce," should be "A bill to regulate carriers."

If it were a bill to regulate shippers and owners, whose material the carrier moves, the title would be more appropriate. I may be told perhaps that there are judicial decisions that the regulation of the carrier is the regulation of commerce, but here when we propose legislation it is entirely legitimate to discuss the question as to the original matter and to determine it upon the principles which seem to be involved. There is a great difference between the possession of a power and its exercise.

Of course the Constitution plainly gives Congress the right to regulate commerce between the States. But as the carrier has nothing to do with the control of the shipment of goods, wares, and merchandise, with their ultimate disposal or destination, therefore regulating him or determining the price he may receive for his services can have no relation in determining the commerce between States. As a national question why should the price fixed for carrying freight across a non-physical line between the States be different from what is charged for the same service on either side of that line? Would it not be making of our State lines more or less obstacles to free intercourse? Would it not be converting every State line into something very nearly akin to a frontier? What do my friends say who have been always so anxious to claim that we are of right one great family with free business intercourse between ourselves, and what do my State rights friends say to the general Government interfering and controlling their local institutions?

It has been said that the right to regulate the railroad carrier is peculiar, in that the corporation operating the railroad is the creature of the State.

If there is anything in this argument it cannot apply here in Congress, as Congress has had nothing whatever to do with creating the corporation. Its existence is entirely by virtue of State laws and has under those laws the right only to operate within the jurisdiction of the State. Of course I except some Pacific roads.

It is pertinent for us to inquire into the wisdom of this kind of legislation, assuming that the authority for it exists. The right of association is a natural one and it is the duty of the national and State legislatures to aid that natural right, and that I contend is what legislation by the various States providing for the incorporation of railroad companies has done. The incorporation is made by individual incorporators as much so as a partnership between individuals is established by the partners themselves. The character of railroad investment as compared with others is set forth by the fact that States can and do exercise the right of eminent domain in order that railroads may be constructed.

The State cannot exercise this right for the benefit of the railroads. It only exercises it because the investment is of that peculiarly beneficial character to the public that it may be said to be a public good. The rule is, moreover, that the railroad companies must pay individuals deprived of the control of their property under the right of eminent domain whatever may be the value of that property. The State pays nothing.

Now, then, if the investment in railroads is so beneficial to the public, why should not the investors be permitted to reap the same full rewards of the wisdom of their investment and of their industry and the management and direction thereof as though the same capital, the same wisdom, and the same industry had been employed in a business so much less important to the interests of the State that the State could not, if solicited, exercise the right of eminent domain in its behalf?

In discussing this question of the right to regulate railroad fares and freights in a manner which will necessarily impair the earning capacity of these roads we should not forget that the investments were made by individuals. If the railroads are so important to the public, surely these individual investors ought not to be discouraged by the apprehension that the value of their investment may be lessened by adverse legislation.

Furthermore, inasmuch as labor enters very largely in the construction of railroads and continues in their operation, any attempt on the part of Congress to fix the rates of railroad companies tends to fix the price of labor.

Further, in all these efforts at regulation I find no protection to the railroad companies, no guaranty against impairment of income. Therefore, if legislation interferes to decrease income, surely the value of the property is affected to the extent of the diminution of the income. This is taking property without compensation. It is confiscation.

I think there never has been a bill introduced into any legislature purporting to regulate railroads against which the owners of the roads did not find occasion to protest on the ground that it diminished the income-producing quality of their property.

Now, then, the investment being a legitimate one and a desirable one, as is established by the exercise of eminent domain not in behalf of the railroad company, for the State has no right to do that, but in behalf of the people, and the State being justified in regarding railroads as public benefits, why should they after their completion have less protection from the laws than other property, or why should they be made the objects of direct and injurious legislation? And in this connection I think it proper to remark that railroads have no legal monopoly of business, since they have no exclusive privileges.

Practically this bill denies to the various railroad companies the right of competition. It precludes the shippers from reaping their rightful advantage of competition, and causes to them and to the railroad companies absolute loss. If the low rates for the long distance mean a reduction of the shorter, the carrier must submit to a loss from the usual rates on the shorter distance, or else abandon the business at the competing points.

Under the force of competition the carriers are often compelled to take business over their roads long distances at a lower rate than they receive for shorter distances. No railroad company would do this if the rate to be charged was a matter under its control.

For this reason rates are oftentimes below the average cost of transportation, and freight of a low value in the market is often moved at less than average cost. Low rates, if they pay anything above the direct expenses consequent upon movement, aid to sustain the railroads and the better enable them to move the traffic at non-competing points. Railroad companies cannot ignore the various circumstances that establish competition, much of which depends on the geographical condition of the country. The shipper for a short distance is not charged more, but the shipper for a long distance is charged less because the carriers cannot help themselves.

All will admit that no legitimate enterprises should be discouraged, particularly those that add most to the convenience and comfort of the people, and to the wealth, strength, and dignity of the nation.

The chief discussion upon the bill was in reference to an amendment offered by Johnson N. Camden [W. Va.] prohibiting a railroad charging *more* for "short hauls of freight than for long hauls."

Zebulon B. Vance [N. C.] on May 6 expressed his

opinion that the prohibition ought to have been more drastic; that the railroads should not be permitted to charge the *same* amount for the two hauls. Nevertheless he accepted the provision as a step in the right direction.

It falls far short of doing justice, but we have been so often warned of the danger of attempting to interfere with commerce, which we are told should be left to its own devices and to work out its own salvation according to the laws of political economy, generally resulting in damage to the people—we have been, I say, so often warned of the danger of interfering, that it seems that legislators are afraid to set the coulter very deep at the beginning, and, instead of saying by the bill that a corporation should not charge as much for the short haul as for the long one, we stop short on the first proposition, to see if the world is going to come to an end before we try something more.

It reminds me very much of the story of a man who went into a saloon in some Western country where they sold a quality of liquor which used to be known in your country, sir [William J. Sewell, of New Jersey, in the chair], as Jersey lightning. [Laughter.] He called for two glasses, which the saloonkeeper accommodatingly poured out for him. He saw an antiquated, odoriferous, and oleaginous African standing near by, and he called to him and asked him if he did not want to take a drink. With a tragic air which would have done credit to an actor, he said, "Boss, I'll tell you no lie about it, I would"; whereupon the colored gentleman drank his spirits, and the white customer who had called for the two glasses went and took a seat. The saloonkeeper asked him if he was not going to drink his spirits. He said, "Please wait fifteeen minutes, and if that nigger don't die I will try mine." [Laughter.]

The proposition here is admitted on all sides that it is not only wrong, but it is an outrage to charge a man who lives 100 miles from Chicago as much for hauling his freight from Chicago 100 miles as is charged to the man whose freight is hauled from Chicago a thousand miles to New York. But so fearful are we of disturbing commerce, so terrible are the dangers which overhang us if we undertake to control a ring, that we have concluded to try the effect of limiting the charge to the same for the hundred miles that is charged for the thousand miles, and then if there is not a great cataclysm and nature is not convulsed we may perhaps yield to the demands of the shippers

of the country and after a while say that the corporation shall not charge quite as much.

Senators on the other side, I believe, do not pretend to justify it upon abstract principles of right and wrong, but they say that it would operate against the man who has the long haul, it would increase his freights, and it would increase the rates from the great West to the seaboard.

Mr. President, what does that admit? It admits that under the influence of competition the railroads are hauling freight from distant points in the great West at rates by which they make no money, and that they are maintaining their roads by an extortion upon the men who live at the intermediate points and whose shipments come within the meaning of the short haul.

So long as Senators give us the reason that we cannot maintain these great lines, that we cannot afford facilities to that great and boundless and fertile West which would enable it to throw its products upon the markets of the seaboard and into Europe without this extortion upon the short haul, then it is a very respectable argument founded upon necessity, and would come well within the meaning of the terms which are usually applied to a high protective tariff.

GEORGE F. HOAR [Mass.].—Will the Senator allow me to make a question to him for his answer?

SENATOR VANCE.—Certainly.

SENATOR HOAR.—I do not myself in my vote agree that the charge for the short haul is an extortion, whether it be less than the charge for the long haul or not, necessarily. I do not understand that that is admitted by any considerable number of persons in the country. There have been such times in the past, but it is not claimed that the railroad rates to-day are such anywhere, unless there may be very few exceptions indeed, that they can be construed as an extortion.

As I understand the proposition, it is exactly this, which I might illustrate by a very simple instance of a stage-coach. Suppose you have got a stage-coach running from a point 20 miles out of Elizabeth City, or any other town in your State, and it can take eight passengers a day, who are dropped on the way, and it charges them a dollar apiece. That charge just pays the entire expense and cost of the line, the drivers' wages, supporting the horses, and repairing the vehicle and harness, and that is all; there is no profit. At the end of the road the stage is competed with by a railroad, which takes passengers from end to end of that road for half a dollar apiece. If the

X—22

stage charged the passengers who went the whole length the full dollar which it charges the others, which is a fair price, it would not get any of them; but still by taking in competition with the railroad at half a dollar the few passengers it can get to go through, it enables it to make a little profit and that keeps the line out.

That is precisely a very homely and simple illustration of this railroad problem as it appears to us who vote against the amendment of the Senator from West Virginia; and it does not answer our argument or help us to be won over to the other side to call it a comparison of extortion committed on one set of people for the benefit of another. These railroads are built primarily for the use of the localities through which they go. The land is taken, the right of eminent domain exercised, through these localities, and the railroads are to be compelled by the bill to deal with them at reasonable rates without extortion; and, if they undertake any extortion on a single locality in the United States which is affected by interstate commerce, here is a mechanism which will cure that defect, as we hope and believe.

That being done, and the rights of these parties being secured, here is a railroad running from Chicago to New York or Boston which says: "If I undertake to charge the same reasonable rates for the wheat which I take from point to point, I cannot compete with the water way, I cannot compete with the Canadian railroad, and I cannot get it at all, because the farmer, on paying me that same rate, cannot sell it in the European countries, he cannot afford to raise it, and the community will stop. But having this apparatus of cars and railroad track and so on, running for the benefit of these localities, I can take on this through business at a less rate than I am charging them, and still make something on the whole."

SENATOR VANCE.—Mr. President, I yielded for a question and I got a speech. I yielded for a short haul and I got a long one. [Laughter.] That is another instance of the extortion which is practiced upon short-haulers.

SENATOR HOAR.—If my honorable friend will haul that proposition of mine any distance whatever, I should like to look on at the process.

SENATOR VANCE.—If I were to haul that proposition far I should think I had made a water-haul. [Laughter on the floor and in the galleries.]

I should like to know if my friend from Massachusetts objects in a matter of morals to the proposition that all men

should be charged according to the service which is rendered them; that all men should be taxed according to their ability to pay? I am sure he would not; he has not.

Mr. President, if you will pardon me for giving an illustration in my homely way, I was down in the lunch room but a short while ago. I took a sandwich and a glass of milk, which was a very short haul. A Senator not far from me took a porterhouse steak and accompaniments. That was a long haul. Now, do you not know that if the keeper of the restaurant had charged me more for that short haul than he did my neighbor for the long haul there would have been a disturbance of the peace in this Capitol before many minutes. [Laughter.]

Those of us who favor this relief to the people of this country, who favor this proposition, admit that the Senate of the United States, or Congress, or even the legislatures of the States for that matter, having railroads wholly within their States cannot resolve themselves into a board of directors and determine every individual item of charge that a railroad shall make. Nobody is attempting to do that; but we are attempting within bounds, and within safe and reasonable bounds, to place or limit upon the power of a railroad corporation to charge whatsoever it pleases without regard to service or distance. That is what we are attempting to do by this amendment.

Samuel J. R. McMillan [Minn.].—The bill makes a provision that the short hauls shall not be charged more than a reasonable and just price. Now, is there any objection to permitting the same road to haul a longer distance for the same sum if it so pleases?

Senator Vance.—Who is to say what is reasonable?

Senator McMillan.—The commissioners under the bill and the courts can determine that question. Now, you deprive the communities of the benefit of all the competition for long hauls where the roads would be compelled to charge a lower price where there is competition.

Senator Vance.—If the Senator will excuse me, that is precisely what I desire to do. I desire to deprive any portion of the American people of the benefits of competition which competition is maintained at the expense of the rest of us.

Senator McMillan.—But the competition is not so maintained; the short-haul people have the limitation of the law that they shall not be charged more than a reasonable sum, and the courts can enforce that law. Then the only provision of the bill is as to a long haul, that where competition exists the communities can have the benefit of it; and by placing this limitation upon it you destroy competition on commerce throughout the country.

JOHN E. KENNA [W. Va.].—The proposition of the Senator from Minnesota, like the proposition of every Senator on this floor who urges opposition to the amendment, that the railroad should not only be allowed, but should be required, to charge reasonable rates, involves us in the old geometrical question as to the size of a lump of chalk. What constitutes a reasonable rate is precisely the thing which the people of this country are unwilling to leave to the arbitrary discretion of the railroad commission.

I do not want to interrupt my friend the Senator from North Carolina in his speech, but I do want to reiterate the fact that in the amendment of my colleague which was adopted yesterday, and which seems to be the bone of contention here, the simple principle is announced that without interfering with railroad rates—I dislike to hear the term "rates" mentioned in the line of this discussion, because there is no question of rate involved in it—without reference of any kind or character whatever to interference with the traffic of railroads or their freights, it has been deemed by the friends of this measure a reasonable limitation that they should not be allowed to charge in gross more for a shorter haul, even if that shorter haul be ten miles, than for a longer haul, even if that longer haul be a thousand miles. It is an equalization which is essential to restoring to Congress a prerogative which has heretofore been usurped by the railroad companies of this country to control its interstate commerce and to give to the West or any other section the great markets of the East, giving to the one to the exclusion of the other. That is the real principle involved in it, after all.

Here Nelson W. Aldrich [R. I.] engaged Senator Kenna in a controversy on the subject; he twitted him upon not carrying his "principle" to its logical conclusion and advocating compulsion of the railroads to make a less charge for a short haul than for a long one.

Senator Vance resumed.

Mr. President, it has been so long since I was on the floor that I have forgotten what I intended to say, I believe. I was going to say something, I think, on the subject of all freights having to be reasonable and just, and to comment somewhat upon the difficulty of coming to a conclusion as to what was reasonable and just, and at the same time practicable. A witty man once remarked that a man and his wife were one it is true, but which one was a big question. [Laughter.]

What enters into the elements of a just freight charge? Will you compare with the charges that were once made by the wagoner on the dirt road? How will you arrive at it? Will you take into consideration the interest upon capital; and, if so, how much and what profit shall be allowed? It seems to me that much the most practical way to remedy this defect is not to trust to the commissioners, whoever they may be, for arriving at a conclusion, however reasonable and just, but to fix a boundary at least beyond which they shall not pass by saying that they shall not charge more.

On May 10 E. C. Walthall [Miss.] spoke on the bill. He advocated dealing directly with the railroads rather than through a commission.

To my mind there are grave objections to such a commission. Congress acts only under delegated powers; and where is the warrant to be found for their delegation by Congress to a commission? Congress may undoubtedly create a commission and confer upon it given powers, if they be so precisely and narrowly described and limited as to leave the commission no discretionary authority in any matter where its action would be final; but they would leave the commission no field for any useful work. Does any Senator feel safe in announcing that Congress can confer on a commission the power to regulate the rates of transportation so as to bind the railroad companies? And, if it cannot fix rates, what good purpose that is practical can a commission serve? But, if the power be conceded, the work is beyond the capacity of any commisison that can be appointed. There are more than fifteen hundred railroads in the United States, stretching over about 140,000 miles of territory. Some of them cost millions to construct a single mile, and, by comparison, some were built for inconsiderable sums, and the cost of none of them is the true test of their present value.

These shipments vary in value, in the difficulty of handling them, in the necessity for speedy transportation and prompt delivery, and in the measure of responsibility for loss, damage, or delay. They may consist of coal worth $40 a carload or silks or laces worth thousands of dollars a case with hundreds of cases in a car. They may consist of ice, or live stock, or fruits, which must go through with speed; or of lumber or brick, which would neither waste nor perish by delay. The variety of freights is endless, and so is the variety of the questions which the commission must consider, as affecting the rights of hundreds of railroads and millions of people, before it could arrive at a tariff of charges which the commission itself would say is even approximately just to shipper or carrier.

How long would it take the commission to perform even imperfectly the duty of gathering the necessary data on which to proceed advisedly, and then determining, on the material collected, what rates would be reasonable on all the "interstate" roads in the Union? So long, I venture to say, that before the completion of the work the changes in business in this active age and in the conditions of the railroads would make necessary a reëxamination of the subject and a readjustment of the rates.

There are other objections to an interstate-commerce commission, growing out of the fullness of its powers, the disastrous consequences of its mistakes, and the dangers and temptations incident to the position of its members; but those will suggest themselves, and I need not now discuss them. It is enough that such a scheme seems impracticable, even if clearly constitutional, to lead me to prefer a simple one whose constitutionality is beyond dispute.

Judge Reagan, an able, an earnest Congressman from Texas, who for more than ten years has been laboring to master this great question and has been pressing its importance upon the attention of Congress and the country, at the last session secured the passage of a bill through the lower House by a vote of 2 to 1 to regulate interstate railroad traffic. In advocating that measure he expressed the opinion that "no law fixing rates of freight could be made to work with justice either to the railroads or the public," and the same conclusion has been reached by others who have maturely considered the subject from a wholly impartial standpoint. To me this seems clear, and the reasons for it are equally forcible when applied to rates fixed by an interstate commerce commission.

The Reagan bill, as it passed the House, has in it the idea which seems to me the correct one for practical legislation embodied in general provisions, prohibitory and mandatory, to restrain and direct the railroad companies and protect shippers from all unfair, unjust, and unreasonable dealings, with stringent and specific remedies for a violation of these provisions. I think a system built on this idea would be far better than a commission.

I prefer a law which requires that all freight charges between all interstate points as to all persons, all distances, and all kinds and quantities of freight shall be reasonable, and provides speedy redress in case of violation, and imposes penalty, if the violation be willful, in any court of competent jurisdiction, whether State or Federal. Details should be prescribed having preference to the grievances most complained of, such as requiring rates to be published, prohibiting unjust discriminations between persons and places, and forbidding oppression in any mode, direct or indirect. But there is, I think, no longer room for doubt that arbitrary rules which are inflexible as to long and short hauls, or as to shipments in bulk or small parcels, are injudicious and dangerous. It seems now almost agreed, at least in this body, that such iron rules are likely to defeat the object we aim at, the relief and protection of the people.

The objections I have offered to a commission under congressional law do not apply, except perhaps in a very small measure, to commissions under State laws where there is constitutional warrant for their creation. The sphere of action of such commissions is comparatively small, their duties are far less complicated, and their powers are limited and restricted. In a number of States such commissions are working well. For want of a better measure I am ready to vote for the bill in its present shape, though I do not approve the creation of a commission.

William J. Sewell [N. J.] opposed the bill.

If business is going to be demoralized by this legislation, if adopted by Congress, we ought not to pass it. The Senator from Michigan [Mr. Palmer] is perfectly correct in saying that the railroads have brought the price of transportation from 35 cents a bushel charged by water transportation down to from 6 to 9 cents. It has been forced down by railroad competition. Instead of relieving the situation, when you adopt the amendment of the Senator from West Virginia [Mr. Camden] you destroy the whole fabric that we have been building up for fifty years.

It is within the recollection of myself when the extreme limit of transportation by rail was to the Ohio River. By reason of the energy and the genius of our people it has been from time to time, and day to day, and year to year pushed mile after mile westward by the building of railroads, by the advancement of science, and the laying of tracks, and the running of locomotives, until to-day we present the spectacle to the world of having accomplished what no other nation and no other people ever has done, of bringing grain, cattle, and other products of that kind two thousand miles to the seaboard, and allowing the community to have the benefit of competition.

The capital invested in the railroad transportation lines of this country is enormous when you come to look at the figures—125,000 to 130,000 miles of railroad, from eight hundred to a thousand million dollars of the absolute savings of the people of the country for forty years invested, because it has been probably the best field of investment when applied to bonds, although that does not apply to stocks.

We are told by some gentlemen in the Senate that there is a great deal of water in this. Mr. President, when I had the honor to address the Senate on this subject at the last session of Congress, I admitted that there was water, but that water is limited to a very small percentage and limited to the lines constructed in late years, and with the approval, as we saw here a few days ago, of those very complaining Senators about water who voted deliberately to allow a company chartered lately to issue any amount of securities for the building of its road. The Senate voted on it on the basis that company should have the same privileges as those that preceded it, and that they could not compete with the previously organized and chartered and running railroads unless they were allowed to have water, as though transportation was absolutely to be by water and not by rail. In other words, that the more indebtedness you piled on a corporation the easier it was to run it and pay expenses! It is hardly necessary to talk about it, but such was the argument and such was the vote.

Mr. President, the railroad men of this country as a class are about the best merchants and the brightest minds we have to-day, and necessarily so. They have the best education of any set of men in the country. Gentlemen who occupy seats in the Senate mostly belong to the legal profession. Coke, Blackstone, are the same, and the classics have not changed. You will never build great railroads on them; you cannot follow the progress of the age; you cannot settle this country with them.

It takes all the elements of a great man to be a successful railroad manager; and we have a great number of them who have grown up in the last twenty-five years. They must have all the education that any gentleman on this floor gets in order to equip himself as a lawyer or as a Senator; and it is but the starting point of what he has to acquire of professional knowledge in order to fit himself for his position. After he has graduated at Yale or Princeton or Harvard he has to go for four or five years to a special institute for the purpose of learning the science of mechanics, chemistry, metallurgy, and then he rolls up his sleeves and goes into a shop and applies himself to the mechanics about which it will be necessary for him to have perfect knowledge in his business as the manager of a railroad.

At thirty years of age that young man, never having up to that time probably earned a dollar, preparing himself in every way, spending money to acquire this knowledge, enters upon his career in a subordinate capacity as a railroad man; and if he has the talent and the brain necessary he rises rapidly, because in our country a man of thirty years of age has practically but twenty years of active business vital force in him. That man applies himself to the business of his life. He has all the knowledge that books can give him; he has all the knowledge that practice can give him. He is not a moneyed man. He does not enter upon the business of railroads for the interest of the community in which he lives, but as a matter to furnish for himself a position, and for his family, if he has any, their bread. He has no prejudice, no feeling. He is as well equipped as any man can possibly be to do as near right as any one man can. And this is the class of men you have to-day in the active management of the railroads of this country.

It is not fair to say that those men, absolutely working for a salary without any interest in the railroads, without any dealing in a share of stock or ever going into Wall street, are going to oppress the people. They are the men to-day who have built up this country to be the great nation that it is. Without the genius and the money and the labor and the education that have been applied to getting these men into the positions they hold, your railroad transportation, with the movement of the products of the mines and of the crops, would not have been what it is to-day, and you would never have been able to reduce the cost of the movement of a ton of corn or a ton of wheat from three cents a mile down to four-tenths of a cent a mile or three mills a mile as has been done within the last two or three years and is being done probably to-day.

Senator Camden's amendment was adopted on May 12 by a vote of 26 to 24. The bill was then passed by a vote of 47 to 4.

It was referred by the House to the Committee on Commerce which reported it back on May 22 with an amendment of the nature of a substitute, which was along the lines of the Reagan bill passed by the House during the previous session. The bill came up for discussion on July 21.

INTERSTATE COMMERCE COMMISSION

HOUSE OF REPRESENTATIVES, JULY 21, 1886

John H. Reagan [Tex.] of the majority of the committee stated the differences between the Senate bill and the House substitute.

The Senate bill related to passengers as well as freights, and to water as well as land transportation; the House bill related only to freights and railroads.

The Senate bill provided for specific damages, the difference between the just and the unjust charges. These, said Judge Reagan, were inadequate.

This is no improvement on the common-law remedy which may now be invoked. The common law furnishes no practicable remedy for the abuses of power and the unlawful conduct of the managers of railroads. Claimants for small sums as damages cannot as a general rule afford the expense of litigation to establish their claims, while the railroad corporations as a rule protract such litigation to such an extent as to wear out the claimants and defeat the ends of justice.

The House bill provides for the recovery of full damages and requires the court in each case of recovery to tax the corporation with a reasonable fee for the plaintiff's counsel or attorney fees. This is an improvement of the common-law remedy in that, in case of recovery, it requires the defendant to pay the plaintiff's reasonable attorney's fees. The remedy should go further and require the payment of double or treble damages. Besides this, the railway corporations have the power by discrimination and unfriendly delays to punish any of their patrons who may attempt by litigation or otherwise to prevent their discrimination and injustice.

The Senate's bill contains the provision that "no common carrier shall be required to give the use of its terminal facilities to any other carrier engaged in like business."

This is a clear attempt at congressional regulation of the corporate rights and franchises of the railroad corporations, and is not within the powers of the constitutional provisions which authorize Congress to regulate commerce among the States. It is a power which clearly belongs to the States as to roads not situated in the Territories and in the District of Columbia. It is also evidently put in the bill to subserve some private purpose and not for the public good. A note to page 82 of Hudson's "Railways and the Republic" shows how the Standard Oil Company got possession of the terminal facilities for handling oil in Philadelphia and Baltimore. This clause may have for its object to invoke the authority of Congress to preserve to it the advantages it then gained. And there may be other like cases. But as the enactment of this clause would be in violation of the Constitution it could afford them no protection in their wrongdoing, and would not avail to establish or perpetuate monopolies.

The fourth section of the Senate bill, the one which deals with the question of the long and short haul, is simply meaningless. To the casual reader it would seem as if it meant to prohibit charging more for the carriage of a like amount and kind of freight for a shorter than for a longer distance, but it does not do this. It does not define or designate the original point of departure. Where is the original point of departure on any railroad? Is not every depot from which freight is sent an original point of departure for that freight? This section can only mean that one person cannot be charged more than another for a like amount and kind of service, and is but a reënactment of other provisions of the bill. It does not prohibit charging more for a short than for a long haul.

The fourth section of the House bill is plain and specific on this subject.

The Senate bill, said Judge Reagan, provides that the commission may exempt railroads from the operation of this section. This is an unconstitutional delegation of the law-making power of Congress to the commission.

The object of this important provision is to protect the people at noncompetitive points from paying for the carriage of the freight shipped from competitive points. It was found difficult to provide a rule which would be entirely equitable. It would not be right to charge the same rate per mile for a long as for a short distance; as the loading, unloading, preparation of trains, and handling would be the same in both cases. In adopting the provision that no more shall be charged for a shorter than for a longer distance, which includes the shorter, we in the House did discriminate in favor of the long haul to the extent of providing that no more should be charged for the shorter than for the longer distance, thus leaving the provision so that if the transportation companies find it necessary they may charge as much for the short as for the long haul. This rule recognizes the territorial extent of the country and the character of shipments to be made.

It enables the transportation companies to carry grain and flour and meats from the productive fields of the West as cheaply as from Illinois, Indiana, Ohio, West Virginia, or from the western parts of Pennsylvania or New York to the seaboard.

Justice and fair dealing could surely require no more. And in preventing charging more for the short than for the long haul it conforms to the rule adopted in the State constitutions of Pennsylvania, Missouri, Arkansas, and California and by the statute laws of Massachusetts and other States.

Besides the injustice and the ruinous consequences to shippers of charging more for a short than for a long haul, the power to do so enables the transportation companies to control the manufacturing interests of the country and to drive them from noncompetitive points and from the rural parts of the country, where living is cheaper and health better, to the great commercial centers, where there is competition in freight rates. This is a power which no government of a free people would dare to exercise, and which no wisely administered government would think of exercising, and yet the railroad companies demand and insist on the right to exercise this vast and dangerous power. And under it they are impoverishing some cities, towns, and communities, without any fault of theirs, and enriching others having no other merit to this favor than the arbitrary power of the transportation companies.

The House bill, said Judge Reagan, requires common carriers, under penalty, to post schedules of kinds of freight, termini of hauls, freight rates, with itemized statements of "terminal facilities," etc., the last being to prevent extortion under cover of a general term.

The Senate bill does not make such requirement.

It also only requires the schedule rates to be made public so far as may in the judgment of the commission be deemed practicable, and that said commission shall from time to time prescribe the measure of publicity which shall be given. This is a serious defect in this bill. Publicity, as provided for in the House bill, is the one essential means of protecting shippers against unjust discriminations by means of rebates or other secret means of discrimination. Can anything more humiliating and demoralizing be conceived than this practice of secret frauds by transportation companies, constantly inviting so large a part of the people to seek to make themselves parties to fraud of this kind? No government and no people ought to submit to such a condition of things.

Another reason for the publication of freight rates, which should be controlling, is that, in questions before the courts involving the reasonableness of such charges, when the rates are not authoritatively published it is not difficult for railroad experts in the interest of the companies to defeat just demands for damages by confusing juries with artful statements of what they term all the elements which enter into the questions as to the reasonableness of rates. Posted schedules of rates would not only advise the people what they would have to pay, but would furnish evidence of what reasonable rates are.

The House bill, continued Judge Reagan, defines what "pooling" is; the Senate bill merely orders the commission to investigate pooling and recommend legislation concerning it.

Pooling by railroads is prohibited by the constitution of the States of Arkansas, Michigan, Missouri, Nebraska, Pennsylvania, and Ohio. It is prohibited by the laws of other States. Pooling is a violation of the common law, because it is a restraint upon the freedom of trade and a conspiracy against the public welfare. And this doctrine is maintained in the following American cases: 8 Mass., 223; 1 Pickering, 450; 35 Pickering, 188; 19 Pickering, 51; 35 Ohio State Reports, 672; 68 Pennsylvania State, 173; 5 Denio, 343; 4 Denio, 349.

Judge Gibson, in the case of the Commonwealth of Pennsylvania against Carlisle (Brightly, 40), says:

I take it that a combination is criminal whenever the act has a necessary tendency to prejudice the public or to oppress individuals by unjustly subjecting them to the power of confederates. "The object of these combinations is to raise the rate of freight, and the means adopted is to suspend competition and place the traffic under the exclusive control of the combination."

In the early history of railroad construction the anxiety of the people of this country to secure their construction induced them to grant charters without much reference to those safeguards necessary for the security and welfare of the people. It was understood then, as now, that each railroad would have a monopoly of the business of transportation on it. The people relied on three means of protection against monopoly prices:

First. On transportation by water and by other ordinary means of transportation.

Second. On the ultimate increase of the number of competing railroads; and

Third. On the exercise of legislative control and regulation.

Experience has shown that the first two of these means do not protect the public against the unjust exercise of these monopoly powers; and that if not controlled by law they will defeat competition with each other by pooling combinations.

The railroad managers recommend a universal pool, or federation of all the railroads in the country, and its recognition and the enforcement of its provisions by law. This Congress has no power to do under the Constitution. If this could be done it would be the creation of one vast and overpowering monopoly out of the many which now exist, and such a course would enable it to control the transportation and commerce of the country, and soon perhaps to control the legislation of the country, and to become the masters of the people and of their liberties.

As evidence that there is real danger of this, I will refer briefly to four notorious pools in this country, which have each exercised vast power, and inflicted great injury on individuals, on other corporations, and on the whole country.

Here Judge Reagan instanced (1) the live-stock pool, which granted a rebate of $16 per car to a single Chicago firm, giving it a monopoly; (2) the Standard Oil pool. which received in sixteen months rebates amounting to $10,000,000, enabling the company to crush out competition; (3) the anthracite coal pool of six railroads, controlling 195,000 of the 270,000 acres of anthracite coal lands in Pennsylvania, and by this monopoly increasing the price of its product and decreasing the wages of its miners at will; and (4) the transcontinental railways and Pacific Mail Steamship pool, absolutely controlling passenger rates and freight charges, limiting sailings, etc.

As illustrative of the methods by which the railroad companies defeat just competition, establish monopolies, and levy unjust tributes on the commerce of the country, I have before me the printed form of a contract which was to be executed between the Union Pacific, the Atchison, Topeka, and Santa Fé, the Missouri Pacific, and the Galveston, Harrisburg, and San Antonio Railway Companies, and such persons as they might carry merchandise for.

By this agreement shippers were required to bind themselves, in order to avoid excessive rates, to ship all their merchandise during the term of the contract, which, it is understood, was not to be for a less time than one year, by the above-named roads; and the shippers were required to bind themselves, in substance, that if they should ship any part of their goods by any other route it was to be held as *prima facie* evidence of default on their part, and it was then to be optional with those railroads whether they would cancel the agreement and charge their higher rates on shipments, "or collect as liquidated damages a sum equivalent to the charges said goods would have been subject to if shipped by rail in accordance with the terms of this agreement."

This pool, not content with its extensive combination, adopted this extraordinary means of forcing shippers to contract in advance to send all their merchandise over their lines, or pay the penalty of not doing so by paying much higher rates of freight than those specified in the contract. And the terms of the contract, which I cannot take time to read, show that two of the objects which the railroads expected to accomplish by these contracts were to prevent the competition of other railroads and of the Pacific Mail Steamship Company.

The Transcontinental Association of Railroads, in the exercise of its powers as a monopoly, conferred on another great and odious monopoly, the Standard Oil Company, a complete control of the oil trade on the Pacific slope, in the great plains, and in the Rocky Mountain region.

I quote an editorial paragraph from the Washington *Post* of April 8, 1886, going to show how these corporations enrich themselves by the dishonorable means of watering their stocks, and overtax the commerce of the country, and oppress the laboring people, in order that they may increase the value of their stocks or obtain dividends on this fraudulent stock.

There is a very general belief that the laboring classes are subjected to much injustice at the hands of the monopolizing capitalists who employ them. There is not a railroad corporation in the country which has not watered its stock to such a degree that its ostensible capital is largely fictitious. To create a market value for these fictitious shares a profit must be earned and a dividend declared, which can only be done by reducing wages to the lowest possible point. There results from this necessity a grinding pressure downward upon labor, which is grievance enough.

It will thus be seen that these corporations boldly enter into conspiracies in restraint of trade, in violation of the principles of the common law, and that with reckless audacity they defy constitutional provisions and statute laws, while they impudently set at naught the great fundamental principle imbedded in all our State constitutions denouncing monopolies as being contrary to the genius of liberty.

Yet these corporations now ask that pooling be sanctioned by law, and claim that the adoption of a universal pool is the remedy for all grievances on this subject.

I trust this House will show a higher appreciation than the Senate of constitutional principles, a firmer purpose to see that the statute law and the principles of the common law shall be respected and enforced, that these corporations are not greater than their creators, and that the interests of the people shall be upheld and their rights respected, by forbidding pooling in unmistakable terms.

The Senate bill, said Judge Reagan, provides for an interstate commission at high salaries with power to hire assistance, etc. Yet it does not order this expensive commission to fix rates.

The House bill does not provide for a commission. It proceeds on the theory of abridging the monopoly powers of the railroad companies, and of prohibiting the greater and more manifest violations of right by them, without attempting a detailed regulation of freight rates, and provides for the enforcement of its provisions through the courts of ordinary jurisdiction, which are within convenient reach of the people, and with whose methods of procedure they are familiar.

The Senate bill proposes to enforce its provisions by bureau orders and the proceedings of courts combined. The American people have as a rule great respect for law and for the action of the judiciary, but they are not accustomed to the administration of the civil law through bureau orders. This system belongs in fact to despotic governments; not to free republics. And I submit with due respect that the House bill will secure more ample, prompt, and perfect protection to the rights of the people, with less friction and embarrassment to the railroad companies, than the Senate bill, if it should be executed honestly and in good faith. The Senate bill is, however, preferred by the railroad corporations, because under it they see greater chances for trickery and evasion; with whatever chances there may be for their controlling in their interest the appointment of the commission, or of controlling the commission in their interest after it shall be appointed; and because the Senate bill puts the commission between the complaining citizen and the railroad, instead of allowing the citizen to appeal directly to the courts for the redress of his wrongs, as the House bill does.

When we remember that this commission is to be composed of five persons only, that all their judgments are to be rendered in Washington city, though it may send members of the board to different parts of the country to make inquiry and to take testimony; when we consider that it will have at least 130,000 miles of railroad to look after and to extend its supervision to, and that the roads cover over the thirty-eight States and eight Territories of the Union, with their 60,000,000 of population, and transport not less than $15,000,000,000 worth of interstate commerce annually, we may be better prepared to understand how futile the attempts will be to attend to all the controversies growing out of railroad management in this country.

But I have other objections to the appointment of a commission. I shall fear that the railroad interests will combine their power to control the appointment of the commissioners in their own interest. The notorious facts as to how railroad managers have corruptly controlled legislatures, courts, governors, and Congress in the past give us sufficient warning as to what may be expected of them in the future. It is not to be supposed that they would directly approach any President of the United States and corruptly propose to secure the appointment of commissioners in their own interest; but they have influential men at command to appeal to the President on account of capacity to appoint such commissioners as would serve their purposes.

Instead of such a system as that of a commission, the House bill provides that any citizen aggrieved by a violation of its provision may appeal directly to a court and jury for redress, and that he may proceed both by civil suit and by criminal prosecution.

The question as to which of these plans should be adopted has in three different Congresses in the last few years been passed on by this House, and on each occasion the House by a large majority declared in favor of the plan presented by the House bill as best for the general welfare.

Charles O'Neill [Pa.] presented the minority report of the committee on the Reagan bill.

It will be seen at a glance that commercial and agricultural products form the great bulk of the interstate commerce of the country, and it is universally conceded that through the system pursued by the railways in the past these industries have been extensively developed, and the United States brought into a position where a very large portion of its debt has been paid off and its prosperity enormously increased. That this could not have been accomplished except for the extraordinary reductions made by the railways in their rates upon traffic, which reductions have enabled the products of the most distant portions of our country to be transported by rail to the seaboard and thence by water to foreign countries, must be very clear. Certainly no serious ground of complaint can exist when figures show that in the last thirteen years the rates upon traffic have gradually been reduced from about $2\frac{1}{2}$ cents per ton per mile to about 7 mills, and when dividends and interest upon the capital invested in railways during the year 1884 did not exceed $3\frac{1}{2}$ per cent.

It can readily be seen how, in the management of so enormous a traffic, it is absolutely necessary that there should be entire flexibility in the adjustment of rates to meet the varying circumstances presented, and it is not believed that any "cast-iron" rules can be laid down for the regulation of this enormous traffic without seriously interfering with it and directly and vitally affecting the prosperity of the country.

The minority of the committee, therefore, have not favored the insertion of the provision preventing, under all circumstances, the granting of drawbacks or rebates, because cases were cited before the Committee on Commerce, in hearings, in which drawbacks or rebates were absolutely necessary to enable the domestic shipper to meet his foreign competitor on equal terms; always, however, in the opinion of the minority, having the system of drawbacks or rebates open to all under similar conditions and circumstances.

Nor do the minority favor the provision prohibiting a greater charge for a shorter than a longer haul, as it was shown to a satisfactory degree, as we think, in the hearings, that, where two competing points were connected by water as well as rail, it was impossible for the railways to secure the traffic unless they made their rates as low as the water rates, and that, while they might be able to do this on a portion of their traffic, it would be destructive of their interests to reduce all their rates to those which were forced upon them between certain points by the competition of the water routes. The minority consider that in this, also, unjust discrimination should never be made, but that the idea of charging the same rate for the haul under similar conditions and circumstances should be adhered to.

The minority also differ from the majority upon the subject of "pooling." They believe its absolute prohibition is unnecessary. There should be legislation imposing restrictive provisions, for shippers should not be placed at a disadvantage or competition in freight charges lessened so that transporters only should be benefited. If fairly carried out and not done by secret and private arrangement, if resorted to for the purpose of preventing what is called injudicious "cutting down" of rates, so that reasonable and just charges should be permanently adhered to, "pooling" would not be open to many of the objections made to it.

Past experience in railway transportation has satisfied transporters that the "pool" is the nearest and fairest device yet used to enable them to place shippers upon an equality and prevent grievous discrimination in favor of the large shippers as against the smaller ones.

But we appreciate the difficulty of satisfactorily legislating upon this subject, and would prefer to leave it to the consideration of a board of interstate commerce commission, which tribunal we hope will be created. So much for what the minority suggest as to the drawback or rebate, the longer and shorter haul, and the "pooling" systems. Proper notification of the changing of rates, with the limitation of a reasonable time, publicly posted in stations judiciously selected in accordance with the amount of freight offered, upon an equitable annual average, might also be conducive of confidence of the shipper in the transporter. A carefully digested section might be incorporated in the law to meet this point.

The conclusion of the minority is, however, unfavorable to positive legislation other than the above suggested. We believe that it is impracticable for Congress to deal directly with the roads, necessarily limited as it is in practical knowledge of railroad movements, and prejudiced perhaps against the railway system by some local disagreements not yet settled, being led to think that an occasional instance of what appears to be unfair dealing with the shipper is the transporter's general course; and we beg leave to suggest that the most available present remedy for imaginary as well as real grievances is the creation by law of an interstate commerce commission.

It is the province of legislators to ascertain by intelligent experience the legislation required, and that experience can best be secured through the proposed commission. It should be a permanently established bureau of an appropriate department; should be composed of the ablest men of the country; salaries should be large enough to attract men from the very highest and most lucrative positions of the varied business life of our citizens. This board should have power to investigate all complaints connected with the management of interstate commerce; power to secure their redress through the voluntary action of transporters or through legal proceedings instituted by it through the proper legal officers of the United States.

We desire to impress the House with our implicit belief in the present advantage of a board of interstate commerce commissioners. We ask you to defer radical legislation until we have tried the commission, which, with powers to hear grievances, will also be required to report annually to Congress, and to suggest from time to time the legislation necessary to create harmony between shippers and transporters.

Mr. O'Neill supported the report with an extended speech at the close of which he said in reply to Judge Reagan:

I assert that in the broad State of Pennsylvania, with her six millions of people, with her vast railroad interests, with her immense volume of freight requiring to be carried from one end of the State to the other and to all parts of the country, there is scarcely a complaint to-day about what the gentleman from Texas [Mr. Reagan] calls the excessive charges and discriminations of these "monopolies." The matter regulates itself. The railroads themselves have worked it out, so that within a few years the rate of freight charges has been reduced from 2½ cents per ton per mile to less than seven-tenths of a cent per mile.

On all important subjects of legislation we hear a great deal through the petition box. Now, the petitions to this House on the one side or the other of this question come from only twelve or thirteen different sources; and almost all of these petitioners, be they commercial associations, supervisors of counties, boards of any kind, or individuals, recommend generally in so many words the Cullom bill, and there is but one of those petitions, and that coming from an almost insignificant town of this country, I mean in population, which recommends the passage of the Reagan bill.

I believe that a commission of suitable men properly selected can better settle these questions than can members of Congress with their crude ideas. Certainly five men as fit, as virtuous, as incorruptible, and as able as the men who compose the Supreme Court of the United States can be selected by the President. Just as the country confides in the decisions of the Supreme Court of the United States, so will the decisions of a carefully selected board of commissioners of interstate commerce satisfy the public mind.

The question was extensively debated by the House along the lines laid down by Judge Reagan and Mr. O'Neill. On July 30, 1886, the Reagan bill was adopted by a vote of 192 to 41. The Senate refused to accept the House substitute, and a conference was ordered between the two chambers.

The following were the members of the joint conference committee:

Senate: Shelby M. Cullom [Ill.], Isham G. Harris [Tenn.], Orville H. Platt [Conn.]; House: John H. Reagan [Tex.], Charles F. Crisp [Ga.], Archibald J. Weaver [Neb.].

The committee reported during the next session on December 15, 1886.

On January 5 and 6, 1887, Senator Platt presented the provisions of the conference bill to the Senate, while opposing its anti-pooling provision.

THE CONFERENCE BILL

SENATE, JANUARY 5-13, 1887

SENATOR PLATT.—The discussion upon this bill is narrowed
to two issues, and I think the committee and the Senate may be
congratulated that the work of the committee has been practically adopted by both branches of the national legislature, with
the exception of these two topics which still excite discussion.
These two questions are, first, whether the Senate will adopt
the modification proposed by the conference committee in the
short-haul section, and, second, will it prohibit pooling instead
of leaving it for the present to the investigation of the commission.

With regard to the change in the short-haul clause I have
this to say: I do not think as an original proposition the
change was a wise one. I do not think it is an improvement of
the bill as it left the Senate. I think the Senate bill recognized a principle which was sound, and that principle was that
the question of what is a reasonable charge upon freight to a
station or from a station is not to be determined by the question of what is charged for freight to or from another station.
In other words, the question of reasonable freight charges must
vary with the location of the place to or from which the freight
is shipped, the volume and character of the business to be
transacted going to and from that place. I believe that was a
wise provision based upon a sound principle, and I do not think
it was wise to depart from it; and I think that these words
which have been inserted about the shorter distance being included within the longer distance are uncertain and ambigu-
ous. I do not think any man knows to-day what they do mean.
I think it will greatly trouble courts and commission to decide
what they mean.

It is certain that the introduction of these words makes an
exception to the rule. It is certain that the bill, as it stands
reported by the conference committee, implies that there are
some shorter distances for which more may be charged than for
longer distances. It is for courts and the commission to find
out what those shorter distances are, for, mathematically
speaking, every shorter distance is included within the longer
distance. But this bill says on this subject that it shall not be
lawful to charge more on the same line in the same direction,
under similar conditions and circumstances, for a like kind and
amount of freights, for the shorter than for the longer distance

which includes the shorter. Mathematically speaking, we should say that was impossible. Speaking of the words when put into a statute, we know they must have a construction. I have never yet seen the man who was able to say what those shorter distances were in which railroads were to be permitted to charge more than for longer distances. They are there in the bill if it passes, and the courts will have to say what they mean.

But, notwithstanding all this, I stand by the short-haul clause for the purpose of getting legislation on this subject. I am willing to surrender, so far, my judgment as to what is wise and best. Right here I want to allude to an objection based upon a possible construction which I have heard urged against this short-haul clause.

I am told that there is fear in many quarters that this construction will be put upon it: that where two or more independent lines of railroad (independent in ownership and operation) contract with each other to forward freight over the entire line so made up, and for each independent link the railroad company owning and operating it to accept a certain proportion of the through freight as its share, that portion which it so agrees to accept under these circumstances will be made the measure of the charge upon freight shipped over its own road or any portion of it. I do not think that such can be the construction of the bill.

Every road must stand by itself. It is upon ₒne company's own road that the short-haul clause takes effect. If a number of independent companies, having independent lines which together form a continuous through route, contract as to the freights which shall go over those routes, then they, as contracting parties, are bound as to freight which is shipped over those roads as to the price, and may not charge more on freight sent under contract between those points for the shorter than for the longer distance; but the share which each road may receive for carrying such through freight does not, in my judgment, furnish the measure by which any one of those independent and independently operated companies is to measure the rate for other freight upon its own road.

I have said this much to explain the fact that, although I do not think we have improved the Senate bill on this subject, I still take it and stand by it.

But the section of the bill proposed by the conference committee which prohibits pooling under criminal penalties I cannot consent to. I would for the sake of getting legislation assent to it if I did not believe in my inmost mind that it was impolitic, unjust, and calculated to embarrass and possibly defeat the beneficial operation of the bill.

I do not think that to justify my dissent I must hold affirmatively that pooling contracts are legal and right. I think the burden of proof is upon them who would make such contracts criminal. Can it be that in the Senate of the United States and in the House of Representatives of the United States crimes are to be made and penalties of $5,000 a day are to be inflicted, and the parties who propose it are not to show why the contracts for which those fines are imposed are illegal or wrong? And, to give reasons why I cannot assent to such legislation, must I prove affirmatively that such contracts are right and are according to the common law? It is for those who say that pooling between railroads shall be criminal to show that such arrangements are either opposed to the common law, condemned by the common law, or they are so far wrong in principle, as being opposed to public policy, that it is just and wise legislation to make them criminal offences.

Mr. President, we must get back to definitions. I apprehend that these contracts, which are known as "pooling contracts," are entirely misunderstood in character, in purpose, in results, and it is the evil significance which attaches to this unfortunate word "pool," which railroads never apply to these contracts, which has created an unreasonable prejudice in the minds of the people of the country, upon which it is supposed that, without investigation and without affirmatively showing anything wrong or improper in these contracts, we are to brand the making of them as criminal. It is said that "that which we call a rose by any other name would smell as sweet," but the converse of that proposition does not hold true. These contracts under other names would never be supposed to be against the public interest. Railroad companies have tried to escape from the fateful influence of that name. They have called such contracts what they more properly are—coöperation—contracts for traffic unity—but without avail; that unfortunate name is fastened upon these contracts. But I do not propose, therefore, to strike at what cannot be shown to be wrong, improper, or against the public welfare or opposed to public policy.

What is a pool? What is a pooling contract? It is simply an agreement between competing railroads to apportion the competitive business; that, and nothing more. I repeat it—it is an agreement between competing railroads to apportion the competitive business. It does not touch the local business; it does not reach it; it has no reference to it. The local business is left to each individual company. It is non-competitive. A pool has nothing to do *per se* with making rates.

And right here I want to call attention to a glaring inconsistency in this proposed legislation. The proposed prohibition of pooling does not prohibit the railroad companies from making rates. Indeed, the whole bill compels agreements between competing roads for the making of rates. The section does not propose to prohibit a hard and fast agreement between railroads to maintain rates. Indeed, it almost compels it. It does not propose to interfere with any other means which railroads may adopt, which are inducements to the railroads themselves to maintain rates. All that it does propose to do is to make criminal the apportionment of freight between competing railroads, or the division of earnings by competing railroads. With that criminal clause in the bill, it would still be open to railroads to enter into any other kind of contracts which they might invent for the purpose of maintaining rates agreed upon. It would be open to competing roads to put a sum of money in the hands of a commissioner or an arbitrator to be used as penalties, as liquidated damages to be recovered by the other companies of any company that should violate the agreement to maintain rates. It does not apply to a hundred means by which railroad companies may in some way make it for their interest to maintain the rates which they themselves have fixed and have legally agreed to maintain under this bill. Is it not pretty remarkable legislation that there should be left the right of competing roads to fix rates jointly for competitive business; that there should be left the right to agree to maintain those rates and not cut or vary from them; that there should be left free to them every means to protect themselves against the violation of those agreements, except just this matter of apportioning between them the competitive business of the roads or the division of joint earnings?

It may be said that perhaps it is not so bad a measure, after all, if it leaves all those things open to the railroads, but the inconsistency of it is intensified many times.

I say, then, that the thing which it is proposed to make criminal is contracts for the pooling of freights of different and competitive railroads or the division between them of the aggregate or net proceeds of the earnings of such railroads. Now, I want to read a word from John C. Nimmo's report, which is called the report on the Internal Commerce of the United States in 1879. showing what a pool really is. Mr. Nimmo said:

The use of the term ''pool'' as a designation of the agreements entered into between railroad companies for the apportionment of traffic, or the receipts from traffic, is of recent application. The term has usually been applied to a game of *chance*, in which all the players contribute toward making up the stake or pool, and the winner in the game gets the whole, whereas what is now known as a railroad ''pool'' is simply an agreement entered into between companies for the apportionment or division of the traffic between roads engaged in competitive traffic. By this arrangement they take no chance, but seek to escape the chances that, under unrestrained competition, they may be able to secure less than what they deem to be their equitable share of traffic and reduce to a certainty the share of the traffic which they shall secure. The main object, however, is to avoid the great losses inevitably resulting from wars of rates. In its application to the apportionment of division of railroad traffic, the meaning of the word ''pool'' appears to be, in a double sense, the reverse of its ordinary significance in its application to games of chance.

Sometimes the same authority which apportions or divides the traffic agrees upon and fixes the rates, and sometimes it does not. The maintenance of rates is in no sense *per se* part of the pooling contract, and it is not so treated in the bill which prohibits and makes criminal only a thing independent of and distinct from the making of rates and the agreeing to maintain them.

Now I call attention for a moment to Judge Cooley's explanation of a pool, which is to be found upon page 2 of a pamphlet by Judge Cooley in 1884, originally published in the *Railway Age* of Chicago, entitled ''Popular and Legal Views of Traffic Pooling.'' He says:

The avowed purpose in pooling is to avoid ruinous competition between the several roads represented, and the unjust discrimination between shippers which is found invariably to attend such competition.

Would you believe that in a bill largely and mainly aimed at the prevention of unjust discrimination a clause would be found making criminal that practice to which railroad companies have resorted to prevent unjust discrimination?

A pooling contract is based—that is to say, the percentage of freights or the portion of freights which each company agrees to be satisfied with—is based upon the results of traffic for several years under free competition; and it is a strange thing that, however little or great the competition, the amount of competitive traffic which a road secures remains practically the same.

It may be said that the purpose of pooling is to maintain and establish equal and stable rates. What is this bill for? What has been the purpose of the committee in this bill? They have heard from all over this land that one of the chief and greatest causes of complaint against railroads was the fluctuation of rates, rates which were up to-day and down to-morrow, up for the retailer and down for the wholesaler, and fluctuating up or down as the caprice of the railroads or the emergencies of the competitive strife should require. Look at the report of the committee, look at the testimony before the committee, and you find that one of the main objects of this bill is to make rates stable and permanent when they have been found to be reasonable. I challenge any man to show that the object or purpose or faithful observance of a pooling contract can be anything else except the maintenance of stable and reasonable rates.

I challenge proof of it. There is not a man who ever studied pooling contracts but will tell you that the main purpose of them is to prevent discrimination; and yet here we have a bill in which we propose to make criminal the means which the railroad companies adopt to prevent discrimination. Others may agree to it for the sake of getting legislation. I will not.

I know this is no place to discuss a legal question thoroughly and exhaustively, but I say the advocates of the prohibition of pooling cannot maintain that these contracts are objectionable under the common law, certainly not that they are illegal at common law; nay, more, I would with confidence stand before the Supreme Court of the United States, or the supreme court of any of the great States of this country, and undertake to maintain that, one thing being assumed, such contracts are legal and would be enforced by the courts, and that one thing to be assumed is that the rates shall be reasonable.

A pooling contract—a contract to apportion between competing roads the competitive business for which reasonable rates have been agreed on—I undertake to say, in my judgment, will be held valid at common law.

I am not unmindful of the general principle that contracts in restraint of trade are held to be illegal—that is, in the sense that they will not be enforced by the courts. I am not unmindful of the fact that combinations wholly to prevent competition in trade would be held illegal by the courts to the extent that they would not be enforced, that courts would say to the parties to such contracts, "these are voluntary agreements of yours; you can get no sanction from the courts, because we think they are against public policy." That is what is meant when it is said such contracts are illegal.

But contracts in partial restraint of trade have been held to be valid for the last one hundred and sixty years in all the courts of England and America. And I hold that combinations for the partial prevention of competition are governed by the same rules as govern contracts for the restraint of trade, and that contracts only for the partial restraint of competition will never be declared to be illegal and void unless it clearly appears that they are injurious to the public interest. (See remark of the commentator in Smith's Leading Cases, commenting on the great case of Mitchell *vs.* Reynolds, which was decided, I think, in 1711.)

And Judge Bradley, of the Supreme Court of the United States, held, in a case reported in 20 Wallace, that that was the doctrine of the common law as it exists in this country.

The common law of England and America is the same. And yet the English courts, law and chancery, each hold just such contracts as it is proposed to declare illegal and criminal to be valid, and enforce them. I want to put this question to the Senate of the United States: England has had as much experience in railroads as we have; it has had the experience of thirty years of legislation; it has experienced all the evils; it has tried all the remedies for abuses; and does the Senate of the United States propose deliberately to-day to say that arrangements which English courts with all this experience hold to be legal and valid shall subject the parties practicing them to criminal penalties of $5,000 a day?

Judge Cooley, in a very exhaustive work, from which I have already quoted, "Popular and Legal Views of Traffic Pooling," goes thoroughly into the question. He says:

The suggestion of pooling, though likely, perhaps, to occur anywhere, comes to us from England, where pooling contracts in the railroad business and others of a semi-public nature have been held not to be illegal, both when they were made on the basis of an equal division of profits and where the basis was a division of business between the contracting parties.

Judge Cooley in his argument clearly maintains that such contracts ought not to be held illegal in this country, but he says it is impossible to tell what the courts may do on the subject, as the question is still an open question.

Contracts for the division of competitive business of railroads, or of the earnings thereof, are not agreements to enhance or depress prices—are not agreements to control production, or the market for certain products—as in case of agreements to limit the output of coal or iron, or the supply of coal, or iron, or salt, or other commodities.

I must not omit a *dictum* of Judge Deady in the circuit court in Oregon upon this very point, for, although a *dictum*, it is significant.

The State of Oregon passed a law conforming—as nearly as State jurisdiction would admit—to what is known as the Reagan bill in Congress. It was called in Oregon the ''Hoult law.''

Upon this law Judge Deady of the circuit court gave the following opinion to a railroad receiver:

Pooling freights or dividing earnings is resorted to by rival and competing lines of railway as a means of avoiding the cutting of rates, which, if persisted in, must result in corporate suicide. It is not apparent how a division of the earnings of two such roads can concern or affect the public so long as the rate of transportation on them is reasonable.

Sound common sense, if not sound law. I apprehend it will be found to be sound law.

But I want to refer to the report of this very Committee on Interstate Commerce on the subject of pooling. The majority of the committee when this report was made believed that to prohibit pooling would endanger the success of the methods of regulation proposed in the bill. What new light has dawned since? How is it that the views of the minority of that committee come now to be the recommendation of a majority of the conference upon the bill? There is but one answer, and that is that what has been believed to be a wise principle has been surrendered for the sake of not imperiling legislation on this subject.

I have taken the testimony of the witnesses before the Interstate Commerce Committee; I have analyzed the testimony of two hundred of them who testified on the subject of pooling, and with what result? About three-fourths of the witnesses examined say: ''Do not prohibit, but legalize pooling.'' I admit that a good many of them were men of vast experience in railroad business. I know that whatever a railroad president may say in this country, no matter how justly it reflects the light of his experience, will go for nothing with a certain portion of the people. But every railroad commissioner and every ex-railroad commissioner who testified before the committee, with one single exception, said, ''Do not prohibit, but legalize and regulate pooling." A large proportion of shippers and business men said the same.

Among the fifty men, more or less, who said "prohibit," there are not three to be found who claimed that pools resulted in unreasonably high rates, and it was manifest that these did not know very much about it when they claimed it.

About a third (fifty men out of two hundred) of those who would prohibit pooling, put it on the ground that it was against public policy to restrain competition, that the pooling contracts were in restraint of competition, and therefore they were against public policy and should be declared criminal.

As I have suggested, there is a class of people in this country who hold that any competition between railroads is for the public interest. It comes from men usually who want this whole railroad question to revolve around their city, or their farm, or their store, their mine, their manufactory, or their bank. There are men who would be glad to have their wheat and their cattle and their coal carried for nothing. There are shippers who would rejoice to get secret rates, or pass rates, if I may use the word, for their freight, and they welcome all competition which puts down prices to unremunerative points. Such individuals gain by such competition, but it is to the injury of every other citizen of the United States; it is to the demoralization of all business; it is the breaking down of all business honesty and lawful trade. There is a competition which is worse than the combination and coöperation of railroads.

I challenge denial when I say that the rates for competitive business in this country are not unreasonably high. It is not true, as the petitions presented this morning stated, that pooling makes excessive rates.

There is a world of figures which might be introduced for the purpose of proving the fact that under pooling arrangements all kinds of rates have steadily on the average diminished in this country. I remember in the testimony before the Interstate Commerce Committee that question came up as to the Union Pacific. It was admitted that the through rate, the competitive rate, was as low, perhaps, as could be asked. It was shown that it had been going down steadily, year by year, until the managers of the road said they did not know what they were going to do. But it was urged that the local rate had not been reduced as the competitive rate had been reduced. The superintendent of that road, by figures, showed that about the same ratio of reduction had taken place in local freight as in competitive freight.

I might turn the attention of Senators to the statement of Mr. Edward Atkinson in the *Century* for the present month, where he gives in a table the charge per ton per mile for moving merchandise over the New York Central and Hudson River Railroad in each year from 1855 to 1885. In 1855 it was 3¼ cents per ton per mile in gold. In 1885 it was 6 8-10 mills per ton per mile. This, of course, includes noncompetitive as well as competitive business.

I do not deny that discriminations exist. It is one of the reasons why this bill should be passed. Discriminations exist in spite of pools by the breaking of pooling contracts, not by the observance of them. Do not, in the name of common sense, declare that a practice is criminal which has for its end the very object which you avow is one of the main purposes of the bill.

I want to look this bugbear of so-called free competition, which it is claimed must not be limited, in the eyes for a few minutes. I have heard the maxim that "competition is the life of trade." I have heard much talk of the so-called law of nature and social life and economic life, "the law of competition and the survival of the fittest." In the sense in which they are invoked, I deny and repudiate them both. There is a competition which is not lawful, which is not legal, which is not honest. There is a competition which degenerates from true competition, and becomes simply war and strife—war carried on and conducted upon the old maxim that "all is fair in love and war." If by "competition and the survival of the fittest" is meant competition and destruction of the weakest, I say it is anti-Christian; it is anti-republican. I say that that kind of competition which results in the destruction of the weakest, the survival of the fittest, if permitted, would draw us back into barbarism. It would be the old pagan idea—the old despotic idea—that "might makes right"; that men are ruled by the strong hand, and not by regard for the moral law. It is expressed in that common phrase, "Every man for himself and the devil take the hindmost." Talk about such competition being demanded on the grounds of public policy! The sooner governments put an end to such competition the sooner humanity will be free to advance along that upward pathway by which it is to reach its final glorious elevation; the sooner governments will come to that beneficent standard designed by the Creator for the happiness of mankind.

You cannot stop competition. Pooling arrangements do not tend to stop it. Their only province is to regulate it. The regulation of competition is not only not against public policy, but is really in furtherance of the public welfare.

Let me quote a gentleman whom I regard to be the most thoroughly informed student of the railroad problem in the United States, a man who is beyond the suspicion of having an interest in railroads, a man who is so close to the industrial interests of this country that he was selected as labor commissioner of the State of Connecticut. I refer to Professor Arthur T. Hadley, of Yale University. I wish to read a little of what he says about this kind of competition. I read from the May number of the *Popular Science Monthly,* from an article entitled "The Difficulties of Railroad Regulation":

> While railroad competition has been in some respects a beneficent force it cannot be trusted to act unchecked. To the business community regularity and publicity of rates are more important than mere average cheapness. Business can adjust itself to high rates easier than to fluctuating ones. And railroad competition of necessity makes rates fluctuate. It tends to bring them down to the level of operating expenses regardless of fixed charges. If it acts everywhere as in the case of the New York Central and West Shore it leaves little or nothing to pay fixed charges, and means ruin to the investor, followed by consolidation. If it acts at some points and not at others, those points which have the benefit of competition have rates based on operating expenses, while the less fortunate points pay the fixed charges. Then we have discrimination in a dangerous form.
>
> As long as competition exists, there is no escape from this alternative. If it exists at all points, it means ruin; if it exists at some points, it means discrimination.

I read from Professor Hadley's book on "Railroad Transportation," published in 1886, a book which I commend to every student of the railroad question. Referring to combinations to prevent competition, mainly of combinations among laborers, and incidentally of combinations by way of pools to prevent indiscriminate and illegal railroad competitions, he says:

> While the experiments in State socialism have been so often bad, there has been a tendency in a great many cases to go too far to the opposite extreme, and to call everything bad which restricted competition in any way.

That is the only ground upon which you propose to make these pooling contracts illegal.

> Courts and legislators have tried to stop the growth of industrial monopoly by shutting their eyes to industrial facts. They have tried to prohibit such combinations altogether, the courts saying that they would not enforce contracts in restraint of trade, the legislators trying to render it illegal to make such contracts.

They could not stop such combinations because they were a necessity of business. The result of trying to prohibit them was what always happens when you try to prohibit a necessity; the worse features of the system were intensified. Secret combination was substituted for open; short-sighted and arbitrary policy was encouraged. By prohibiting the whole system the courts deprived themselves of the power of dealing with specific evils, such as secret favors or arbitrary discriminations.

Competition in railroad transportation differs from every other kind of competition in the world. I do not say that it is not to be judged by the same legal rule, but I say in essence and character it is different from competition in any other business. In the first place, it is not competition in trade. The railroad buys nothing of the producer; it sells nothing to the consumer. It simply carries—it distributes; that is all. Contracts in restraint of trade may operate the same with reference to contracts between common carriers as between merchants; but the two kinds of business differ in character. Ricardo is a great advocate of the doctrine that competition is the life of trade; but he writes from a banker's standpoint. In banking, capital is circulatory. If competition drives it out of the banking business it may go into the manufacturing business. But the railroad stays, whatever the result of the competition. If "competition and the survival of the fittest" means the physical removal of the weakest, the pretended law is inapplicable, for you cannot remove the railroad. However many companies may be bankrupted by competition, for each there stands another company ready to take its place and to be bankrupted in turn.

Mr. President, I have heard it suggested in reply to all this that we can pass this law and then pass another law directing the commission to investigate; and, if the commission shall, on the whole, conclude on its investigations that pooling arrangements are not injurious to the public welfare, then we can repeal the section prohibiting pooling. That is after the fashion of what is known in Scotland as Jedburgh justice, for border marauders, "hang them first, try them afterward." That is not a correct principle in legislation. We had better investigate first.

I do not believe that the legislation will fail if this bill goes back to a conference with an indication that the Senate will not consent to brand as criminal practices those arrangements which railroads have made to accomplish the precise object which is intended to be accomplished by legislation in this bill. I believe we may trust to the good judgment of conferees and

X—24

of legislators not to do a thing which, upon reflection and investigation, they must be satisfied will probably, I may say almost invariably, break up and demoralize the existing conditions of railroad service in this country.

Nine-tenths of all the interstate commerce business done to-day is done under those arrangements which are sought to be damned because of the evil meaning which has been given the word "pooling."

Whatever of stability has been given to the railroad business, and through it to other business of the country, has been secured by these traffic arrangements, and in my judgment a bill which breaks them all up ruthlessly within sixty days, which invites the competition which is to demoralize business, will be far-reaching in its injurious results. For one, I prefer to stand by my judgment. I will try to do what I believe to be right, and I cannot assent to a bill which, though I accept its other provisions, contains a provision which I regard as positively vicious and wrong.

John T. Morgan [Ala.] opposed the bill.

I cannot subscribe to the doctrine that interstate commerce can receive protection against the wrongful acts of private persons, or public and private corporations, only through the action of Congress in providing laws and tribunals for their regulation or punishment.

This bill is based solely on that false premise. It opens the door to the interference of Congress with every regulation of trade and commerce, whether sanctioned by universal custom or by express or implied agreements between the parties concerned. It exposes the charter rights of every railroad company given by the States to modification and repeal by acts of Congress.

It multiplies indefinitely the list of crimes punishable by statute in the Federal courts, and correspondingly narrows the power of the States to punish their own citizens for crimes committed within their borders, because the commerce against which the crime is directed is interstate commerce, and is therefore within the exclusive jurisdiction of Congress.

This claim of the exclusive power of Congress to legislate, whether for the freedom of commerce or against it, is made in this bill to depend on the interstate character of the traffic, and that is made to depend on the will of the shipper. The States can make no regulations touching the subject or objects of interstate commerce, according to the theory of this bill and of the Supreme Court. If they should enact statutes for the punishment of crimes against interstate commerce committed by their own people, in the very language of this bill their laws would fall to the ground because, as this bill assumes, they could not touch the subject.

The States, it appears, can take an officer from the army or navy or from one of the civil departments of the United States and hang him for murder; but they cannot, on the theory of this bill, punish a man for killing an engine or kidnapping an engineer who is about to cross the line of a State and enter another State if he is engaged in interstate commerce, and is for that reason under the sole jurisdiction of the United States.

Congress has power to regulate interstate commerce, but there is a limit to this power, and it is not so far an exclusive power as to annul all acts of the State legislature, as well in the absence as in the presence of laws of Congress, through which this power may be exerted.

For a hundred years the States have assisted and protected interstate commerce by their many statutes and by many hundreds of judgments in their courts. Congress, doubting the extent of its powers, has permitted this assistance and protection on the part of the States, and, in doing so, has blessed the country by its silence and inaction. In that time commerce has hewn its own highways through the mountains and built its grand structures across great rivers and chasms; the arid deserts have bloomed under its footsteps, the wilderness has bowed a welcome to its coming, and every river and bay opening into lakes or oceans has floated the burden of its wealth out among the nations of the earth.

When these laws were enacted they were valid, because the commerce over these lines was, as to the railroads, necessarily commerce within the States; when the lines of railway were extended by consolidation the laws became invalid according to the theory of this bill, because they then applied to interstate commerce. Thus, if the theory of this bill is true, the States, by consenting to such consolidation, gave new powers to Congress and made sudden havoc of all laws enacted by them for the protection of their railways and the commercial traffic they were engaged in. I do not accept the verity of this legislative romance.

If there is any limit upon the power of Congress to regulate commerce among the States, it is not to be found in the nature of the commerce, the points of shipment and destination, or the special character of the business in which the carrier is engaged; for every regulation by Congress based on these circumstances detracts from the power of the States reserved to them in the Constitution over their commerce.

But there is a limit to this power of Congress, and it is found in the purpose for which the power was given. That purpose, I repeat, was to protect interstate commerce in absolute freedom from the power of the States to control it within their own limits by any law or regulation that would operate to the detriment of the people of other States. A State law that imposes no such restraints or burdens on interstate commerce, but increases its freedom and security, is a valid law; but a State law that does impose any such burdens or restraints upon interstate commerce falls under the denunciation of the Constitution; and Congress, as well as the courts, would have the power to annul the offending law and to free commerce from its burdens.

The power of Congress under such limitations is benign and useful. Without such limitations it is dangerous, and will become aggressive and uncontrollable. It will end in making merchandise of politics, while it rules and ruins the commerce of trade.

I dread to set in motion a doubtful and dangerous power which will soon become a factor of immense influence in the party politics of this Republic. It is urged that the railroads will absorb and corrupt the State legislatures if we leave to them the duty of checking their enormous powers. The thirty-eight legislatures number more than four thousand men.

Is it easier to corrupt four thousand men, scattered through thirty-eight States, than it is to corrupt four hundred who are assembled in Washington? Or, is it easier to corrupt these four hundred representatives than it is to corrupt five commissioners intrusted with very broad discretionary powers?

If Congress, instead of holding the States in check by a constant distrust or denial of their powers, will open their way to the full and free control of the men and corporations engaged in domestic commerce, through civil and criminal laws, and will hold over the States its corrective authority, so as to prevent any of them from doing injustice to the other States or their people, the States will soon settle all the knotty problems about long and short hauls, pools, drawbacks, bribes, and bonuses.

As I read this bill, the interpretation of which is so uncertain that everyone must needs adopt his own, it necessitates an increase of rates on long hauls of freight in every case where the roads cannot sacrifice a large part of their income and still live. In Alabama we have four great staples of commerce. They are cotton, timber, coal, and iron. Each of them must find a market far distant from home. High prices for long hauls on railroads are the best inventions for the destruction of these industries. If I had no other reason for disagreeing to this bill that one would determine my vote.

On January 11 Richard Coke [Tex.] supported the bill as a step in the right direction.

A brief glance at the leading points will, I think, justify this assertion. They are:

First. That all charges shall be reasonable and just.

Second. That there shall be no discrimination between persons or firms, either directly or indirectly, by special rates, rebate, drawback, or any other device, but that all shall be treated equally and alike for like and contemporaneous service.

Third. That no undue or unreasonable preference or advance shall be given to any particular person, firm, company, corporation, or locality.

Fourth. That no greater compensation shall be charged for the short than for the long haul, where both are made under substantially similar conditions and circumstances over the same line and in the same direction, provided that in special cases, upon application to the commissioners, they may upon investigation relax the rule; and provided, further, that nothing contained in the bill shall be construed to authorize the charge of as much for the short as the long haul.

Fifth. It declares unlawful any combination, contract, or agreement between railroad corporations for the pooling of freights of different and competing roads, or to divide between them the earnings of such roads, provides penalties, and declares each day of the violation of the law a separate offence.

Sixth. It requires all schedules of rates plainly printed, and posted at all depots and stations for public inspection. It forbids any advance in rates as published except upon ten days' notice duly published. Reduction of rates may be made without notice.

These are the leading, salient points of the bill, the remainder of it being mainly administrative in its character and devoted to the methods of enforcing the provisions named.

Now, Mr. President, I assert, without the fear of successful contradiction, that these provisions are in substantial if not literal accord with the common law governing common carriers as known and practiced in the States of the Union so far as the rights of the public and the duties and obligations of the carriers are concerned.

The penalties for violation of the law and the means of enforcing it involve some departure from common-law methods, but this is rendered necessary by the inadequacy of ordinary remedies in the hands of a citizen for the enforcement of the law or the vindication of his rights against powerful railroad corporations. It is this consideration which justifies the appointment of a commission and devolves upon it the important part it is to perform in securing an enforcement of the law.

This bill, except as to remedies, is in substance and legal effect, so far as they are applicable to conditions here, a substantial epitome of the English statutes, which confessedly are only a codification of the English common law of common carriers, the source of our common law on the same subject. There is but one substantial exception to this proposition, and that is as to combinations and agreements between railroad corporations, which, in some cases, are permitted under the English law, but forbidden under this bill. As this fact has been adverted to in the debate in justification of the pooling system here, I will read from an able argument of Mr. Simon Sterne, of the New York bar, made before the House Committee on Commerce, extracts from the English statutes and some of his observations thereon, which show how this phase of the subject has been met in England, from which it will be seen that no argument in favor of the American system of pooling can be drawn from that in England.

Here the speaker read extensive extracts.

The rights of English subjects are guarded and protected and the iron hand of the law placed upon the power of great corporations. English law does allow railroad combinations made, but under its own eye, its own supervision, its own dictation, its own regulation, and its own control. This system grew from a small beginning, and has been perfected as time and experience have suggested, as ours will be if we will only commence it by the passage of this bill. The English Government represents the public and stands between the people and corporate rapacity, as the American people have heretofore demanded, and do now demand, that our Government shall do, instead of leaving them, as they are now, absolutely defence-less and without appeal, the prey of the unbridled power of railroad pools and combinations, which destroy all competition while they are unregulated and unrestrained.

Pooling builds up some cities and towns, and destroys others. It terrorizes merchants and shippers and traders, who submit quietly to being plundered, because it is in the power of the pool to destroy their business, by advancing their freights and by giving reduced rates to their competitors. They dare not seek redress against the roads over which their freight-ing is done and with which they deal every day, and upon which they are dependent for the successful prosecution of their business, for there are a thousand ways in which they may be harassed and injured. Under the pooling system there is no uniformity, no stability in rates, so necessary for all legiti-mate business. The system of rebates and drawbacks, which are secret concessions to favored and preferred shippers, under-mines confidence in commercial communities, for no man can tell when his competitors may be thus enabled to undersell him, and subject him to loss in his business.

Without reason, except that the corporations desire more money, and generally when such action cannot be anticipated, rates are advanced. There is now but one limit to the power of pooled roads to tax the products of industry in this country; and that limit is found when to tax higher will stop produc-tion and transportation—how much will a given product bear in the way of tax for transportation and leave a pittance for the producer so as to keep him at work producing?

These pools are operative only where there are competing roads. Wherever only one road is found, it may fix its own rates to suit itself. That territory belongs to that road, and is out of the jurisdiction of the pool.

The pools are all for the corporations and nothing for the people. Mr. Albert Fink, the head and chief, or president, of the great New York pool, who is generally admitted to be the ablest man in America in railroad affairs, in one of his argu-ments before the House Committee on Commerce admitted the illegality of pooling, in this language: ''The first step to this end (speaking of pooling) should be to legalize the management of railroad property under this plan, and to abandon the anti-quated notion that a government or combination, as it is called, of this kind is against public policy.''

Of course pooling would not need to be legalized if it were not now unlawful. The law as it stands now is a dead letter as against the powerful corporations who violate it, though vital and forceful against weaker trespassers like the canal boatmen, and the railroad men object to an invocation of the power of the Government for its execution and enforcement upon all alike, the strong and powerful as well as the poor and weak.

These people are contending for a vast stake. No greater ever hung upon the chances of human effort. Learned experts estimate the annual commerce of this country at three thousand millions of dollars' worth, three-fourths of which is carried by rail; and three-fourths of that carried by rail is interstate commerce, over which Congress alone has regulating jurisdiction. They are seeking to defeat this bill, as they have defeated all such bills heretofore, because that result will leave them unmolested to handle as they please, and levy such tolls as their avarice may prompt upon twenty billions of dollars' worth of commerce annually.

While this bill is being fought on every clause and section in it, the chief assaults are made upon the section which prohibits pooling, and upon what is known as the "long and short haul" clause. The rule established by this clause is that more shall not be charged for the short haul than is charged for the long haul, but a discretion is vested in the commissioners in special cases to relax this rule and allow more to be charged for the short than for the long haul. I confess that I would greatly have preferred the rule established by the clause made absolute, and the discretionary proviso left out. This clause recognizes that the short haul is attended relatively with greater expense than the longer haul by reason of unloading, detention of cars, etc., in that it does not forbid as great a charge for the short as for the long haul.

It does not seem possible, with the discretion vested in the commissioners to reverse the rule, when upon investigation in special cases it may be right to do so, that it can work any hardship. The objections to this clause amount to this, when reduced to their simplest form, that when the roads find it to their interest to make the long haul for less than a reasonable compensation they should be permitted to recover the deficiency by a higher charge on the short haul. This is the method of discriminating between localities, tearing down some towns and cities and building up others by unjust and unreasonable discriminations.

Railroads are public highways, and railroad corporations are common carriers. "Common carriers" (says the court in Munn *vs.* Illinois) "exercise a sort of public office, and have duties to perform in which the public is interested; their business is therefore affected with a public interest.'' Their charges are required everywhere to be reasonable, and to be so must be based on the cost of the service rendered. Their duty to the public in virtue of their ''office'' demands equality in the treatment of all of whatever locality, subject only to the difference in the cost of the service rendered. It is impossible that the cost of making the short haul, under similar conditions and circumstances, with the like kind of property, in the same direction on the same line, the shorter being included within the longer distance, shall be greater than that of making the longer haul, and this bill simply recognizes this fact, and provides that greater compensation shall not be charged for the short than the long haul.

Railroads are, in their nature, essentially monopolistic under the freest possible system of competition. Competition such as obtains between merchants, mechanics, traders, and others, which regulates prices, is not possible in its fullest sense among railroads. They exclude all other methods of carrying. The vast amounts of capital required to build and maintain them, and the large areas of territory necessary to support them, and over which they are supreme in all matters of transportation and commerce, exclude the numbers which in other cases are necessary to promote active competition; while their terrorizing influence over those whose business is within their power—their power to punish enemies and reward friends—creates such a monopoly as should not be permitted to exist except under the regulating control and active, vigilant supervision of the Government for the protection of the rights of the citizen.

The States are powerless. Congress alone can respond to the great popular demand for relief. The repeated passage through the House of the well-known Reagan bill, a much more radical measure than that now before the Senate, establishes beyond doubt or cavil the will and demand of the American people who support and maintain this Government, and in whose interest it is supposed to be administered, that a law regulating interstate commerce shall be enacted. The Senate has heretofore defeated this plainly expressed popular demand. It remains to be seen if corporate power is so intrenched in this body that the pending bill is to share the fate of its predecessors.

IshAM G. HARRIS [Tenn.].—When all provisions of this bill are considered, and each fairly construed in the light of all the others, I cannot see the possibility of injury to any carrier who proposes to deal fairly and justly with the public, and be satisfied with the reasonable income of a legitimate business.

Every carrier should be permitted to earn legitimate fixed charges, operating expenses, and a reasonable interest upon the actual value of its plant, but the public should not be required to recognize or pay interest upon either stocks or bonds which originated in the process known as watering, and which represent nothing but the avarice and cupidity of the speculator.

The producer and the carrier are dependent upon each other, and neither can afford to cripple or embarrass the other in a legitimate business, but each has the right to demand justice at the hands of the other.

On January 13 William M. Evarts [N. Y.] opposed the bill.

Pooling, which is equalizing matters as to receipts, is in the same nature as equalizing lineally, and is right or wrong, useful or mischievous, according as unification, stability, equality, and reasonableness are accomplished. Though pooling is assumed to be unpopular, and the name may carry a measure of disfavor by force of the phrase, really the effect of pooling is to give reasonable stability and equality. The legislators of the great State of New York have refused to control pooling, and, instead, by advisory intimation of the State commission and advisory intervention of the chambers of commerce and of boards of trade at manufacturing centers, as well as at the seaports, they have obtained a rate of transportation that at present meets with very little objection from all the interests in our State. But here in the national legislature the intervention of an authority peremptory, conclusive, and permanent is proposed.

Mr. President, everything is tending, as everything should tend in this country, to unification and equality in all the intercommunication, the passing of property, of exchange, of commerce in every direction, so that within the periphery of our now vast country there should be no line of discrimination known that the law tolerates, and certainly none that the law defends. We may talk about the mischiefs that have grown out of the exaggeration of wealth and the distribution of wealth under the railroad system; one person has been pinched here and one has been inflated there; but I put it to the scope of consideration of the Senate that, with all the infirmities, with all the burdens, by whatever phrases they may be described, which the system has caused, progress has gone on in the sense of dispersing population and bringing lands into our fertile and productive system, and the commerce *ab extra* has not been affected injuriously. It has grown and flourished without the aid of intervention, certainly without intervention to constrain. Who shall desire that without investigation we should attempt so vast a disturbance of this equality and these flattering commercial prospects?

Mr. President, to this fortunate land of ours we may apply the description *armis potens terra et ubere glebæ;*[1] and it is this railroad system, pushed on rashly, losing so much to its investment, which has conveyed to the homes of the consumers that which the land produces so abundantly.

And now this very question of ours is at the bottom of the political agitation of Europe: restrained by all sorts of legal impediments the landed aristocracy of Ireland have been brought to the necessity of yielding to the tenants; and in Germany the soldier can no longer prescribe the terms for holding lands, but these are fixed by their productiveness and that is determined by our competition. In view of the rivalry of these vast equals in freedom who shall say that the Congress of the United States desires to lay impediments on transfers between the States or burdens on their foreign commerce? No, Mr. President, whatever we can see in the future, whatever we can read in the past, the greatest and the most classic examples all warn us to beware of entering on the path now proposed to us.

The report was agreed to on January 14 by a vote of 37 to 12. The House, after an extensive debate, agreed to it on January 21 by a vote of 219 to 41. President Cleveland approved the bill on February 7, 1887.

In the debate on the bill in the House Robert M. La Follette [Wis.] made a significant prophecy concerning the greater regulation of railroads, and the acceptance of this by the corporations themselves.

Honest Railroads Aided by Government Regulation

Robert M. La Follette, M. C.

If we can judge the operation of this law from the experience of States in the administration of similar legislation af-

[1] "A land powerful in arms and in the fertility of the field."

fecting corporations, we must be prepared for some sharply
contested litigation in the beginning. The railways will insist
on their own construction of it; the people upon theirs. But
the cool, determined administration of the law in a few test
cases settling pivotal points will change the whole aspect of
affairs, will bring order out of chaos. The railways will alter
their management to conform to the decisions, and the benefits
of the law will soon be secured without further strife or opposition. The judicial functions of the commission will cease to be
arduous, and will become chiefly supervisory and executory.

Mr. Speaker, I know little of railway management, but I
think it is no injustice to suppose that some of the fear and
alarm expressed in railway circles concerning this bill is but the
exaggerated apprehension with which conservative men always
regard any radical change in the method of conducting their
business. The prosperity of this country and of railways are
interdependent. Any measure that would permanently injure
railways, that would cripple their usefulness, would certainly
be against public interests. But this legislation has been under
consideration many years. All sides have had a hearing. It is
no hasty expedient adopted to meet some sudden emergency or
popular demand of the hour. It pursues no short-sighted, sui-
cidal policy. And all railways that are sincerely anxious to put
their business upon a firm and stable, an honest and enduring
basis will share the benefits of this law equally with the public.

It is urged in vindication of these discriminations as to different kinds of traffic that they are the result of custom and
that railways are not to blame for the practice. If railways
maintain incongruous rates upon dry goods and groceries simply because dealers in the one insist upon a long-established low
tariff while transporters of another submit to a relatively exorbitant rate because of long usage, if managers dare not make
new classifications because of the responsibility that the consequent strife and contention and business disturbance would
place upon them; if this is true—and it is the reasoning of men
who ought to know—then in this instance the law will surely
be a great benefaction to railways. They will secure the benefit
of a reasonable and just standard of classification without being
in any degree made answerable for any of the unfortunate consequences that may result from the change. If the enforcement of the provision that all rates must be just and reasonable should necessitate a readjustment of the charges on different kinds of traffic, surely no one could complain nor hold the
railways answerable for any temporary business unsettlement

that might occur, because the classification would be made in accordance with express law.

So if discriminations in favor of places are, as is claimed, necessary under existing conditions of competition, and if the provisions of this law, operating as they do upon all railways alike, relieve them from the pressure of that necessity, they will profit accordingly. If the publication of rates, the obligation to give notice of any advance in them, together with the restraint of the long and the short-haul clause, operate to make their business certain and stable, railways are as much the gainers as the public. While it may cut off a few sources of large profit, it acts as a preventive of great losses.

And so, sir, while it may be difficult for men of the present school of railway management to adapt themselves to the new conditions; while it may be impossible for them to understand how any other practices than those which have been long established can succeed, still I believe the time will come when even they will recognize the wisdom, from a business standpoint, of the principles of this law; when they will wonder how a management ever flourished which permitted such disproportional rates and acts of favoritism involving so many conflicting ideas.

And, sir, the time will come when it will be a marvel how such abuses ever arose and why they were so long tolerated; when all parties alike will wonder how the just and simple provisions of this initiatory measure ever created such bitter and uncompromising opposition.

It may take years of supplemental legislation to accomplish it, but I believe the time will surely come, and I hope it is not far off, when railways will be limited to their legitimate sphere as common carriers; when they will conduct their business upon the same principles of impartiality toward persons, places, and things as govern the United States mail service; when they will have but one standard of regulating rates, the cost of transportation; when they will seek but one object, perfect service to the public and fair profits upon the great capital actually invested.

CHAPTER XI

FEDERAL CONTROL OVER RAILROADS
[THE CHICAGO STRIKE]

''Coxey's Army''—Coal Strike; Government Protects Railways—Pullman Strike; Government Troops Suppress It—William A. Peffer [Kan.] Introduces in the Senate a Resolution Endorsing Federal Control of Railways, Coal Mines, and Money—Debate: In Favor, Sen. Peffer; Opposed, Gen. Joseph R. Hawley [Ct.], Cushman K. Davis [Minn.], Gen. John B. Gordon [Ga.]—John W. Daniel [Va.] Offers Substitute for Sen. Peffer's Resolution; It Endorses the President's Actions in the Strike—Debate: Sen. Daniel, Joseph M. Carey [Wyo.], Joseph N. Dolph [Ore.], Orville H. Platt [Ct.]; Substitute Is Passed—James B. McCreary [Ky.] Introduces Resolution in the House Endorsing President Cleveland—Debate: Opposed, Lafe Pence [Col.], Richard P. Bland [Mo.], Thomas C. Catchings [Miss.]; It Is Passed.

D URING the winter of 1893-4, while Congress was in session, "armies of the unemployed" were organized in various parts of the country which proceeded to march toward the national capital, there to demand aid of the Government. Instead of gathering forces as they advanced, as was expected, the armies disintegrated on the way, and only one of them, that headed by "General" Jacob Coxey [O.], a well-to-do manufacturer who had espoused their cause, entered Washington, and this was reduced to 350 men. The only result of this demonstration was to afford Congressmen an illustration to enforce their opposing claims, the Democrats declaring that the poverty and lack of employment in the country were due to the McKinley tariff, and the Republicans replying that these were produced by manufacturers limiting production and even shutting down their factories in view of the passage of the Wilson bill.

In April, 1894, a general strike of the coal miners

'occurred. In five of the States, extending from Pennsylvania to Illinois, the militia were called out to sup-

LAW AND LABOR

By Ryan Walker in "The Comrade"

press violence. The Government employed Federal marshals and troops to protect the railways, finding justification for such intervention in the claim that the Government's business of carrying the mails was interfered with. In May the employees of the Pullman Company of Chicago struck against a reduction of wages, and in their support the American Railway Union, of which Eugene V. Debs was president, ordered a boycott of all Pullman cars (sleeping coaches). As these coaches were used generally by the railroad companies throughout the country the prospect was most alarming. The first effect of the boycott was to interfere seriously with the railway traffic between Chicago (the great point of departure from the East) and the Far West. In this interference rioting took place, occasioning destruction of railway property and even loss of life. Against the protest of John P. Altgeld [Dem.], Governor of Illinois, who declared the State troops were sufficient to restore and maintain order, President Cleveland, on the ground that the mails were interfered with, sent Federal troops to assist the militia, and proclaimed a state of insurrection, first in Illinois, and subsequently in railroad districts further west. By these energetic measures the strike was brought to an end on August 3.

The President's action was discussed in Congress, and endorsed by both chambers.

FEDERAL CONTROL OF RAILROADS

SENATE, JULY 10, 1894

On July 10 William A. Peffer [Kan.], a Populist, offered the following resolution in the Senate:

In view of existing social and business conditions and by way of suggesting subjects for remedial legislation—
Be it resolved by the Senate of the United States—
First. That all public functions ought to be exercised by and through public agencies.
Second. That all railroads employed in interstate commerce ought to be brought into one organization under control and supervision of public officers; that charges for transportation of persons and property ought to be uniform throughout the country; that wages of employees ought to be regulated by law and paid promptly in money.
Third. That all coal beds ought to be owned and worked

by the States or by the Federal Government, and the wages of all persons who work in the mines ought to be provided by law and paid in money when due.

Fourth. That all money used by the people ought to be supplied only by the Government of the United States; that the rate of interest ought to be uniform in all the States, not exceeding the net average increase of the permanent wealth of the people.

Fifth. That all revenues of the Government ought to be raised by taxes on great wealth, incomes, and real values.

Senator Peffer supported his resolution.

While the resolution is made up of four or five distinct parts, they all relate to one fundamental error that our country has fallen into, and I wish to direct the attention of Senators and of the people of the country at large of all classes to that fundamental error. We have permitted a few men here and a few men there, one man here and one man yonder, to usurp governmental functions. So the resolution begins with the proposition that all public functions ought to be exercised by public agencies.

In order that we may understand the situation which now confronts us, I want first to call the attention of the Senate to a statement of a man named Debs, of whom we have heard a good deal recently and may possibly hear more in the future. This man Debs, by reason of his being the official head of a great organization of railway employees, is the recognized mouthpiece of that body. On the 6th day of June Mr. Debs made a written statement of the condition from his standpoint.

Mr. Debs goes on to say that, in the first place, the American Railway Union had no connection whatever with the Pullman difficulty, as it is known. Then he describes what the Pullman difficulty was. Without going into all the details, I will state by way of preface that the Pullman Company established what most people in this world believed to be an ideal community, in which all the citizens should have equal rights, in which none should have special privileges. The object was to build a community where the best modern scientific principles of hygiene, drainage, sewerage, grading, lighting, watering, and every other convenience should abound.

But while the company was doing that, while the world was looking on applauding, the company, like every other corporation of which I have ever known anything, held all of the power,

X—25

all of the reins within its own grasp. That is to say, while there was sewerage, while there was light, while there was water, while there were parks, and all those desirable things, at the end of every month or of every week, as the case might be, when pay day came around, the charges that were set up against the residents of the town of Pullman for their lots and for their conveniences were deducted from their pay (just as the clothing of a soldier or extra rations or a lost gun were deducted from his pay) and the balance found to be due was paid to these people. Among these charges were rents and stated dues for the purchase of property.

After a while hard times began to pinch the company as it did everybody else, and it began to reduce the pay of the men. The men submitted patiently. Another reduction came and the men again submitted, only asking, however, that their rent charges should be reduced, that their taxes should be reduced to correspond to the amount of reduction in their wages.

Then it was found that these poor people were absolutely defenceless, absolutely powerless in the hands of a corporation that had no soul. They asked to have a reduction of their rent charges and of other charges; they asked for a little time to turn around.

All these things were denied them. Finally the Pullman citizens came to the conclusion that they might as well starve in defence of their rights as to starve while the proprietors of the town, the organizers and controllers of the corporation, were feasting on the fat things that these men had made for them. Now the trouble is on hand, and the leader of this great corporation [George M. Pullman] is off at the seashore, refusing to entertain even a newspaper man, except to say, ''I have nothing to say; the company at Chicago will look after the company's interest there''—heartless, soulless, conscienceless, Mr. President, this tyrant of tyrants.

Mr. Debs then states to the public that the Railway Union took no hand in this matter until after the grievances of the Pullman men had been submitted to them. These grievances were submitted to the local assemblies, and a national assembly of the union was held in Chicago, and the local representatives came up instructed, many of them, and a resolution was adopted unanimously that the American Railway Union should make the cause of these Pullman men the cause of the American Railway Union.

After having done that, a committee was appointed to present their conclusions and their request to the Pullman Company. Their request was that these troubles between the employees and the Pullman Company might be submitted to an impartial arbitration. This was denied. The committee again went with the same request, and that was denied. Then came a very general dropping of tools, a dropping of employment, so that the men might go out of the traces and let the railway companies go ahead without them if they could do so. Their object was—and it was so stated to the railway managers—to boycott the Pullman cars.

At the close of his statement Mr. Debs said:

If the corporations refuse to yield and stubbornly maintain that there is "nothing to arbitrate" the responsibility for what may ensue will be upon their heads and they cannot escape its penalties.

Then, after this conclusion had been reached upon the part of the American Railway Union, the general managers of the railways held a meeting at Chicago for the purpose of considering the situation. They came to a unanimous agreement likewise, and their agreement was published, and it was to the effect that they would stand by the Pullman Company, let the results be what they might; and we have seen in the newspaper dispatches several times important telegrams from New York City and from other points to the managers at Chicago, "Stand firm; to yield now is to lose everything"—substantially that.

GENERAL JOSEPH R. HAWLEY [Ct.].—I should like to have the Senator put all the facts in. Is he not quite aware that the railway companies have contracts with the Pullman Company under which they are absolutely bound to use their cars, and is not Pullman under a corresponding obligation to them?

SENATOR PEFFER.—The railway companies are under no greater obligation to Pullman than Pullman is to the men who make the cars. There is the sticking point in this controversy, I say to the Senator from Connecticut in all kindness and frankness. These men have nothing to do with the railway contracts with the Pullman Company, and the contract the railway has with that company has nothing to do with interstate commerce. That is merely a matter of personal convenience.

But I was surprised, almost startled, the other day by the venerable and distinguished Senator from Ohio [John Sherman] introducing a resolution that Congress should overhaul the Pullman car business—a private matter between the Pullman Company and the railway companies. However, I was delighted as well as surprised to see the resolution coming from such a source at such a time, even if it do savor of paternalism.

But, Mr. President, we have no time to talk about the contract of the railroad companies and the Pullman Company, and it is strange in this presence that a Senator of the United States should bring this in between these men and the great question that confronts us, more especially from a Senator who is now and who has many times been the champion of American labor. Oh! from such friends, Mr. President, God save us.

GENERAL HAWLEY.—The Senator ought not to misrepresent me. He talks about the railroad companies declaring that they would stand by Mr. Pullman. I know nothing of the kind, and have never heard anything of the kind. I called the Senator's attention to the undeniable fact that there were certain things that they are bound under the law to do.

SENATOR PEFFER.—Let them go along then and do the things.

SENATOR HAWLEY.—I say with the Senator that the relation between Pullman and his men has nothing in God's world to do with the rioters and murderers in Chicago.

SENATOR PEFFER.—It has not only a great deal to do with it, but things that may yet come will grow out of this strike, unless employers will hear and unless legislators will hear.

I do not wonder sometimes that there is a growing feeling against the condition of things at Washington; I do not wonder sometimes that men write me and say, "Would to God that the Senate were abolished." I wrote to a friend the other day that I was ready for its abolition and would be willing to vote for it, and I would go still further and vote for the abolition of the House of Representatives, and I would favor that the personnel of the Government should be confined to a few men, not to exceed one from each State, and let them select a presiding officer from their own number. The fewer governors we have in this country the better, Mr. President, as it seems to me; at any rate a few men could do no worse than a few hundred men have done.

One of the grandest, and yet most dangerous, in one sense, of spectacles that could be presented to the human sight would be the stoppage of every workingman's arm for just ten days.

These things teach us, Mr. President, the brotherhood of men; they teach us the necessity of one man to another; they teach us the interdependence among people. The time has come for employers themselves to learn that the best way to handle these situations is by fair treatment of their men, and, if they cannot do that, it is time for the people in their own sovereign capacity to interfere and say, "This thing has gone far enough; thus far and no farther."

This morning the dispatches brought us news of great importance. Citizens of Chicago met with the officers of that city and requested some official interference in the interest of peace, good order, and law. A committee was appointed. The committee visited the Pullman Company and asked that the matter be arbitrated. They were received by Vice-President Wickes, of the Pullman Company. Mr. Wickes said:

"The Pullman Company has nothing to arbitrate."

Then there was a painful silence. Finally Alderman McGillen said: "Am I to understand that the Pullman Company refuses this slight request, made at so grave an hour, and upon which so much depends?"

"The Pullman Company has nothing to arbitrate," reiterated Mr. Wickes.

Mr. McGillen said: "Mr. Wickes, your company demands the police protection of the Federal Government, the State of Illinois, the county of Cook, and the city of Chicago, and yet you utterly ignore a fair request made by the city—a request, the fundamental idea of which is the preservation of the peace. We have come to you as conservers of the peace, and you have assumed grave responsibility in thus refusing the request we make—a responsibility greater, perhaps, than even you are aware of."

"There is a principle involved in this matter," replied Mr. Wickes, "which the Pullman Company will not surrender. It is that employers must be permitted to run their business in their own way, and without interference from their employees or from anybody else."

Not even from the city of Chicago, I will interject, nor from the State of Illinois, nor from the United States Government. Pullman, and Pullman alone, is king. Great is Pullman!

It is an axiom of the common law that when anything becomes a nuisance it may be abated, no matter what it is. Everywhere the hands of the law, and properly so, are about the people in order that the public good may be conserved.

On Sunday before the 4th of July this year some of Christ's ministers in this city undertook to discuss existing conditions. One of them [the Rev. Dr. Hamlin] used this language, so the reporter says:

He said that there was a chance in this country for demagogism, and he thought that it was making headway in our State and national politics and now musters a formidable array of votes in both branches of Congress. "Populism," he said, "is simply an incipient, ignorant, and unorganized socialism. Its political capital is the arraying of the poor against the rich, the improvident against the thrifty, the idle against the industrious. Coxey is its typical product; the mob violence which is disgracing so many sections of our country its legitimate fruitage. An income tax which, it is estimated, will fall upon only one out of 800 of our citizens is its conception of equitable legislation.

I should like to know what that man's income will be when he goes up where coin of heaven is used. He proceeds:

All this is the protoplasm of anarchy. It proceeds upon the assumption that political power can level moral distinctions; that government is bound to make everybody comfortable and happy. When these delusions are exposed it will be ready to lay violent hands upon government and upon the human lives that represent it.

If that preacher does not know anything more about the doctrines of Christ than he does about the doctrines of the Populist party, he, with a good many more of us, will have to pass through the eye of a needle before he gets into heaven.

Mr. President, the Populist idea is exactly the opposite of anarchism. The Populist is the antipodes of anarchy. The Populist believes in government. He believes in the government of the people. He believes in the doctrine taught in the Declaration of Independence, which is not a doctrine at all, but simply a terse statement of a fundamental truth, that all men are created equal, and that flowing out of that equality of birth there are certain rights of which even the individual himself cannot divest himself—the right to life, the right to liberty, and the right to pursue his own vocation in his own way, unmolested, so long as he does not interfere with the right of his fellow-men.

The Populist not only wants government, but the very highest form of government. The Populists are ready to take the great prototype of my excellent friend who sits in front of me [Roger Q. Mills] as their leader and their guide in political philosophy. I can now recall nothing that Thomas Jefferson ever said which does not find a warm, responsive heart-throb in the breast of every Populist.

Mr. President, the birth of the Populist party came about naturally. It came because of the conditions of which I have just been reading. Its Republican members believed what the Democrats said in their convention about the Republican party. Its Democratic members believed what was said by the Republicans against the Democratic party.

We had sense enough to know that things were out of joint and that some persons somewhere were responsible for it. We made up our minds that conditions must be changed; that

politics must be purified; that the old parties must be converted
or they must be destroyed, and that the Government must be
restored to the people for whose happiness and safety it was
established. That is what the Populist party has set out to do.
We have some isms—yes, we have some isms, and it would
have been a good deal better for our political enemies if they
had had some of those isms, ten, fifteen, twenty, or thirty years
ago.

We would not to-day find ourselves in the condition we are
in. The truth is that existing political machinery is corrupt,
no matter who pronounces the arraignment. We have seen its
effects in our own action here in the Senate within the last
three months. We have seen the politics of the country corrupted by the use of money, by the patronage and influence
of corporations. The Populists are trying to remedy the evil,
faintly, feebly, it may be, but after a while we shall succeed,
because we represent the people, and either we, under our present name or some greater popular movement under a broader
and a better name, if a better one can be originated, will do
the things we are aiming at. The American people have too
much sense, too much patriotism, too much loyalty, to allow
their Government to go down in anarchy.

I come back to this point: The Government is now managing nearly one-half of the railway mileage of the country
through its courts. The Government, State and national, interfered when the coal strike was on six weeks or two months ago.
The Government is now interfering and, for the first time in
the history of the American Republic, the President has sent
the army into one of the States without the request of
either a State or a city officer. I am not criticising the action
of the President. I am simply calling attention to the fact
that we now have actual, active, earnest, and effective Federal
interference in what many wise men are pleased to call State
concerns.

A few mornings ago, when it was noticed first that the
President had sent troops to Chicago, a distinguished citizen
in public life was reported to have used language something
like this: "If I were governor of the State of Illinois I should
take the State troops and drive the Federal soldiers into the
lake."

My view is this: Railroads are a matter of Federal concern.
The busy people of the United States have no time to stop
with a surveyor to point out where the State line is, that they
may inquire what the laws of this new domain are upon which

the railway train, running at the speed of fifty miles an hour, has just entered.

The American people have grown too big for that, and State lines, except for purposes of local government, are of no manner of account in the polity of the Republic. When the time comes for the Government to interfere, whether it be in Chicago, or Boston, or New Orleans, or Galveston, the power of the Government will go there, and the people will say amen, provided always that the movement of the Government is in the interest of the people.

That brings to mind a thought. I think it was in yesterday evening's paper it was stated that some distinguished personage now in public life is asking that the army be increased. This is not a good time to increase the army. This is a time to decrease the army. This is a time for the weapons of peace; this is a time for reason; this is a time for cool, deliberate judgment, not passion, not prejudice, not bayonets, but consciences, tongues, and pens, and brains. There is a kind of military mania taking possession of the people. We now detail army officers to teach military tactics in agricultural colleges. What a splendid idea it is to teach the farmers' boys the military art in order to fight grasshoppers and chinch bugs, and crows and blackbirds. We find that in our private colleges there are classes studying military tactics, borrowing arms from the Government and from the State. The same is done even in our high schools, which are the acme of the country district school, the crowning glory, the ambition of the country boy and girl. They are having military science taught in some of the country schools, and in some of our public schools here in the capital of the American Republic I have seen the boys go out and drill on the public streets. More than that, even in our Sunday schools there is a military air.

It is time that this military idea, the idea of quelling every little disturbance by force, should cease, and that brings me to the vital point in this whole controversy. What are you going to do when disputes arise between employers and employees? Keep your hands off, Mr. President. That is my advice.

The parties in interest will settle the matter themselves, and they will do it without bloodshed. They will do it without using the torch; they will do it without getting angry; they will do it justly, safely, wisely, promptly. But the instant that you begin to call out the military arm in order to protect one side and send the other one to prison, just that soon you arouse a spirit of animosity which cannot be quelled by force.

That was tried about two years ago, on the 6th day of this month. Pinkertonism died an inglorious death in its own blood on the battlefield of Homestead. Some day there will be a monument erected to those brave men who, standing upon the shores of the Monongahela, defended their right to work in that great structure which their hands had builded.

CUSHMAN K. DAVIS [Minn.].—At a time when in the second city of the United States, and the fourth or fifth city in the civilized world, order is suspended, law is powerless, violence is supreme, life is in danger, and property is in the very arms of destruction, I am appalled to hear the trumpet of sedition blown in this Chamber to marshal the hosts of misrule to further devastation.

Mr. President, this question does not now concern the issue between the Pullman Company and its employees. It has got beyond that. It does not concern the sympathetic strike of the American Railway Union. It has got beyond that. It does not concern any strike which may hereafter be ordered. It has gone far beyond that. A simple strike as to a local organization not directly connected with the transportation instrumentalities of this country grew into another strike of far more comprehensive proportions. That grew into a boycott. That boycott took the liberty of the American people by the throat, and then grew into a riot, and from thence into an insurrection which confronts this Government to-day with all the dormant and latent powers of revolution, and speaks here in the voice of its advocate, threatening and advising the dismemberment of the Government by the abolition of its executive and legislative departments.

The Senator from Kansas affects to speak for the people of this country. Who are they? For his present purposes it is the mob which has obtained control of a strategic point in this country, the city of Chicago, which has paralyzed the means of intercourse, and interrupted the sources of supply of food and traffic over several States of the Union.

The Senator from Kansas has not a single word of reproach for the blood that has been shed in Chicago in the last ten days, for the millions of property which have been destroyed. The red light of arson against the sky in that city has caused him no pang and elicited from him no word of disapprobation. He insists that we shall go back to the cause of the strike, as he alleges, the difficulty between Pullman and his men, and arbitrate that, when everybody knows we have got far beyond that transaction for the present. It is as futile, it is as foolish, as if some one coming from the caves of the past when the battle lines were drawn at Gettysburg had insisted that the impending conflict should be delayed until Meade and Lee could have argued out between the lines the question of the rights of slavery in the Territories.

Mr. President, the people are interested in this controversy —and by "people" I mean the entire body of the American people. I do not mean that segment of the people who, acting under delusion, have sought by force to overthrow not only the functions of civilization and intercourse, but also the rights of all the other people and the very existence of government itself.

The Senator from Kansas says that these instrumentalities of commerce and government should be controlled by public officers, and in that I agree with him to a certain extent. Are they controlled by public officers in Chicago now? Can the United States marshals execute the process of the courts? Can that great function of interstate commerce, that great system of railroads upon which the people depend for commerce, for everything which beautifies and adorns and makes enduring our civilization, and upon which the messengers of commerce come and go like the angels whom Jacob saw upon the ladder of his dream—can that be carried on, and is it carried on now, with the best aid of the public officers of this country?

Not at all. They are impeded in Chicago, at Hammond, and surrounding places by riots which have grown into insurrection, disturbing the stability of the Government itself, and drawing from the lips of the Senator from Kansas the expression of the opinion that now is the time to annihilate the legislative and executive departments of this Government and to change its form into that of its prototype, the Committee of Public Safety during the Reign of Terror in the days of the first French Revolution.

This whole proceeding, which has grown to a movement which I have inadequately described, has come from the illusion that a fraction of society, useful in itself, of course, and indispensable, I admit, can by force dominate every other portion of the body politic.

Mr. President, what is society? It is all the members thereof taken together. The railroad employees of this country number some five or six hundred thousand men, perhaps, indispensable, useful, valuable citizens in ordinary times, when not misled, but, compared with the great mass of the American people, how few they are in number! Why will they not learn, and why will not their self-appointed teachers teach them, the doctrine of community of interest and interdependence of all upon the whole?

Does anybody suppose that by burning cars, destroying property, disturbing security, wrecking credit, taking life their means of employment are to be increased hereafter? They are destroying everything from which they derive their employment; the very thing which they, so much to their credit, have helped to upbuild, it is true, an act of which they would have never thought unless it had been for the self-appointed dictators who have placed themselves at the head of their organizations.

People prate about liberty, and define that liberty as the liberty of the particular class they are speaking for. The only liberty worth having in this country is the equal liberty of all men alike. Liberty in its philosophical and common-sense definition consists in that right of each individual to exercise the greatest freedom of action up to, and not beyond, that point when it impinges upon the like exercise of freedom of action of every other man. Beyond that it is the destruction of the liberty of the weak by the strongest, a subversion of the very theory of a republic, and a return to primeval anarchy on the one hand, or, as an alternative, to despotism on the other.

Mr. President, this boycott business—not a little incidental boycott in some little community, which, while it works great local inconvenience, works no particular harm in general—but a universal boycott is spoken of as something perfectly feasible and perfectly justifiable, to be put in force in the operations which are now going on. All men may stop work, all men of a certain class may stop work, and the Senator from Kansas calmly depicts here without a word of censure or disapproval, without a single temperate admonition to the men who are looking to him for leadership, the terrible and disastrous consequences of that step.

But the people for whom he pretends to speak are repudiating the strike. Through every avenue of public communication and by private letter—by telegraph, in the public press, and through the pulpit—they are crying aloud in denunciation of this most wicked, monstrous, and cruel attack upon every function of our civilization.

Mr. President, who has conferred this authority upon Mr. Debs? Where is his patent of right to say to the city of Chicago that it shall not be fed, to say to the people of the Northwest that they shall not leave their homes, or that they shall not be able to get to their homes if they are away? What signature is subscribed to that patent of popular right or of popular consent?

No, Mr. President, this Masaniello of a day,[1] drunk with power, has unloosed agencies which he can not chain, has set at work destructive forces which he cannot recall; his own disciplined men have gone beyond his control, and it is a notorious fact that their violent action has called from the caves and dens of Chicago the professed criminal, the idly vicious, the anarchist. Everybody who is conspiring to put down modern civilization is now moving under the mask of this strike and taking life and destroying property in its name.

Mr. President, the Senator from South Dakota [James H. Kyle] introduced into the Senate the other day a resolution, the substance of which is that no process, civil or criminal, shall issue from any court of the United States in regard to acts affecting interstate commerce by the obstruction of trains, unless such acts involve the delay of the mails, and that the detaching of Pullman cars from any train shall not constitute an offence. At the time that resolution was introduced interstate commerce was arrested at Hammond, Ind., it was in collapse at Chicago, and freight and common passenger cars and Pullman cars were being destroyed in that city. The meaning of that resolution is that, while these acts were flagrant and being committed, the United States was to be called upon to make itself an accessory to the crime while it was in the act of perpetration.

Mr. President, consider the importance of the relations of this Government to interstate commerce. A clause in the Constitution, contrived by the wise foresight of our forefathers, has become efficacious and widespread in its operations a hundred years after it was framed.

The railroads of this country, 176,000 miles in length, belting this land, and laid over it like a network of iron, an armor of defence, are the daily convenience and the indispensable necessity of every man, woman, and child in the United States, and this movement is aimed at this great instrumentality, this great necessity, this indispensable convenience of our civilization, necessary to support life, to move troops, to move supplies, to carry on the Government itself—this strike is thus aimed, that has grown from a strike to a boycott, and from a boycott to a

[1] See Masaniello in Index of Proper Names.

riot, and from a riot to an insurrection, and has suspended and paralyzed the powers of this Government in the second city of the Union.

And by what acts? Tearing up the tracks, derailing locomotives, overturning cars across the tracks, burning them, robbing trains of provisions, disarranging switches, all with the result of the loss of human life, and yet the resolution of the Senator from South Dakota proposes to take away from the United States courts the power to follow, repress, or punish these flagrant offences against everything which goes to make up civilization and security.

The effect of that resolution as to any Territory of the United States or as to the District of Columbia would be that if any such act there committed, where the United States has ample and plenary jurisdiction, should result in death, constituting murder at common law or under the statute, no warrant of the United States courts could issue, no indictment could be found, no judge or jury could try the criminal.

Mr. President, the sea, the Great Lakes, the rivers, everything within the admiralty jurisdiction of the United States, were once the main instrumentalities of commerce, and there is a stringent code of laws applicable to them and to the ship, as security for persons and passengers and the means of conveyance. I say here, without fear of successful or even attempted contradiction, that if any one of the acts which have been perpetrated in Chicago in the last ten days against persons and property of this great means and necessity of land communication had been perpetrated upon the waters within the admiralty and maritime jurisdiction of the United States those acts would have been piracy and punishable with death, under the statutes of the United States.

In the eye of reason, humanity, and common sense the acts which have been perpetrated at Chicago, involving the safety of a great city, not as on shipboard the safety of a single vessel or those who are in it, constitute a much more flagrant offence than any piracy which is defined by the statutes of this country or by the law of nations.

The authority of the United States can not be denied, Mr. President. Within the limitations of the Constitution it is supreme. The duty of the President of the United States is to see that the laws are faithfully executed; the duty of the courts is to declare those laws and their consequences, and to execute them through their process. Those limitations are plainly drawn and settled, not only in the original instrument, but by comment after comment in recorded decisions. Why should the hand of the Government be kept off these insurgents under the circumstances? Is the interstate commerce of this country to be held in suspense and paralyzed, property destroyed, food cut off, conveniences taken away, necessity thwarted, until some remote disagreement as to wages between a private corporation and its employees can be adjusted? Is there any such reserved right as that to any of the citizens of the United States, or is it the mere usurpation of a mob, commencing in riot and tending toward anarchy?

Speaking of the people of the United States—a large, mouth-filling phrase that we have heard so often here—let us consider a moment that there are 5,000,000 farmers in the United States, with their families, constituting 45 per cent. of the population. I suppose, Mr. President, if anybody is entitled to be distinctively called "the people," the bone and sinew of this country, it is the farming population. They supply the great cities. They represent the land; without them the country would be nothing. They have been its invulnerable and loyal arm of defence in all times of peril.

How are they affected by this strike of that segment of the people in Chicago? Have the farmers of this country called out to have commerce stopped until the question of wages can be settled between a few employees and a company constructing cars? Has any Illinois, or Minnesota, or Wisconsin, or Iowa farmer cried aloud for this remedy and been ready to pledge his life, his fortune, and his sacred honor until the desired end can be brought about? Not one. How has it affected them? How does it affect the constituents of the Senator from South Dakota or the constituents of the Senator from Kansas? They cannot market their wheat if this thing continues; they cannot market their wheat to-day.

The early product of the farms of Illinois, the fruit, the early vegetables, have been rotting throughout the fields. The early fruitage of California has become a crop perfectly value-less under existing conditions. The beef of the country can not be marketed in New York or Washington. It is rotting in Chicago, and prices rise to the people. Mothers go from place to place in the city of Chicago seeking for milk for their children, and can scarcely find it.

I say, Mr. President, that no interest in this country is stricken such a deadly blow by this cruel, remorseless, unreasonable, merciless, and finally treasonable attack upon the liberty of the American people as the farming community of the United

States, and they will find it out some day by the stern logic
of events teaching them the lessons which I have endeavored to
impart. It will not be necessary for them even to learn that
lesson by experience to array them, as they always have been
arrayed, on the side of law and order and the perpetuity of
this Government.

Do not people realize that the Constitution itself is upon
trial and that the country itself is in danger? The military
power, the last resort in a free government, has necessarily been
called into action. The President of the United States, to whom
is committed the commandership of the army and the navy in
the execution of the laws, has declared the danger by a
proclamation which every citizen is bound to respect. He says,
"I have sent the troops there"; the Senator from Kansas says,
"Take them away." What shield does the Senator propose to
interpose between the innocent people of Chicago and their
property and the men who to-day are only held in awe and
suppressed by the presence of troops, if they are taken away?
Can Debs recall the force that he has unloosed? He can no
more do it than by word he can reconstruct the burned cars
or give back life to those from whom it has been taken away
as the result of his operations.

The Senator from Kansas cited the common law that a
nuisance may be abated—abated by force. What is Mr. Debs?
Does he fall within the definition of a nuisance, or is his office
more comprehensive? Is the power of the State or of the
individual greater against a mere nuisance than it is against
an agency which threatens the very destruction of the Government?

Let us hear what Mr. Debs is reported in a morning paper
to have said:

President Debs, in speaking of the situation to-night, said: "The
Pullman Company is certainly responsible for any blood that may flow
from now on. If honest labor is not entitled to recognition, the worker
cannot be blamed if he tries to commit some acts of violence against
the man who spurned him."

Will the Senator from Kansas indorse that?

The Senator from Kansas took occasion to bring into this
debate the ministers of the Christian religion here in Washington who have preached the gospel of law, order, and peace, and
to teach them their duty from a loftier plane than he conceives
them to occupy. He wishes to introduce into the church a

Christianity from without, to revive its spirituality and restore it to its pristine apostolic purity.

Mr. President, the Senator from South Dakota is also a minister of the Prince of Peace on earth and good will toward men. He is here as a Senator, and before the public he is an evangelist of the meek and lowly Nazarene. He is the author of the resolution to which I have adverted, making lawlessness lawful and murder unpunishable under certain circumstances in any court where the United States has jurisdiction.

I would adjure him to withdraw it from the consideration of the Senate in the interests of humanity and good government. I would ask him to take that bomb from the Clerk's desk whereon he has laid it, but if through pride of opinion, or mistaken sentiment, or incapacity to see the right, he should refuse, I say to him that he has attempted to inflict upon the body of the Commonwealth a wound as deadly as that given by the dagger of Santo.

Mr. President, these are troublous times. The time will come in the new order of events when these matters will be satisfactorily arranged, for this Republic has always been adequate to every emergency, and these disturbing questions between capital and labor—and they exist with strong equities in them, I admit—will be settled. I think that time is now upon us. But they will not be settled as the result of any such proceedings as those against which I speak to-day. Something more than capital, for which I care nothing; something more than the wages of the laboring man, for whom I care much; something more than a railway corporation, for whom I care nothing, is at stake here. National existence is at stake.

It is the very condition of the existence of republics that they are subject to continual attacks from within and require continual assistance from their citizens to perpetuate themselves. That is the meaning of the maxim that "Eternal vigilance is the price of liberty." Kings, like Saturn, devour their children. The children of republics devour their parent. That attack is nearly always from within. France is subject to it to-day; the short-lived Republic of Spain succumbed to it; the Republic of Mexico fell, and only rose again when it shed the blood of an immolated monarch upon its plains.

The same dangers and difficulties environ this Republic, and they are upon us now. It is not a mere question of disagreement or dissension. The ship of State, which two weeks ago was floating securely and proudly through untroubled waters, is now buffeted by contrary winds and is driven headlong over the waves of an exasperated sea.

I have not said a word about parties in this discussion. I shall expect the Democrats, the Populists, and the Republicans to join hands in this emergency, which Mr. Debs and those who are acting with him proclaim to be of supreme and perilous exigency to the Republic, and which the Senator from Kansas asserts demands the dissolution of the most important functions of this Government, to the end that a secure and peaceful rest to our troubles may be attained at last, to accomplish which the best efforts of the legislative department of this Government, and of all the departments, will be bent to bring about the only solution of these difficulties which possibly can be attained.

GENERAL JOHN B. GORDON [Ga.].—Sir, what matters it to any lover of his country—of his whole country—at such an hour whether this or that party be in power; what matters it on which side we stood in the mighty and bloody conflict of the past? If we would save our country from anarchy we must stand now shoulder to shoulder for the enforcement of its laws, for the preservation of its peace, the support of its dignity, and the perpetuity of its freedom.

Our system is to govern through representatives chosen by the people, who make the laws which are declared and enforced through the orderly processes of courts of justice, and whenever the people fail to support the law the Government fails. We have no government except that recognized and upheld by the free will of the people.

Our Government was ordained by the people to protect property, public and private; to protect popular rights, among which is the right of the laborer to sell his labor at such price and in such employments as he pleases, and whenever that right is invaded it is a blow at personal liberty, and not only threatens the principles which lie at the foundation of our institutions, but is an inauguration of a system of slavery never known in the past history of the country.

There was a time when the Southern master had the right to order his slave to desist from labor, but that day has passed. The institution to which that right attached was recognized in the fundamental law of the land, and the master ordered the slave according to law. That institution has gone down in revolution. Liberty and the rights of organizations involve no such power or privilege as that now assumed to force others to desist who wish to labor. Such a claim is so utterly abhorrent

X—26

to our American ideas that it is impossible to treat it with any patience.

Standing in this law-making body and considering the law-breaking mobs at Chicago, I recall, with some misgivings I confess, that woeful prophecy of Lord Macaulay, that in some great public upheaval, like that which confronts us, this free Republic would either lose its civilization through mob law or in putting it down by the strong arm of power would lose its liberty. Sir, I do not believe that prophecy, but, if such doctrines as we have heard on this floor this morning are to become popular among us, well may we pause and consider whether Macaulay's prophecy may not yet be realized.

I prefer to agree, however, and I do agree with the great Gambetta of France, that at such times the liberty-loving people of this country, without distinction of party, would unite and save the Government, however they might differ about its policies. These lawbreakers will so find it, Mr. President. The day is not distant, it is upon us now, when they will realize this truth. There will be no divisions among us when the constituted authorities call upon the people. Their response will ring through the land as a warning to those who defy the laws. The men who wore the gray from 1861 to 1865, under strong convictions, will be found side by side with the men who wore the blue, following the same flag, in upholding the dignity of the Republic over which it floats, and in enforcing every law upon its statute books. [Applause on the floor and in the galleries.]

ENDORSEMENT OF THE PRESIDENT

SENATE, JULY 10-11, 1894

John W. Daniel [Va.] offered the following substitute for Senator Peffer's resolution:

Resolved, That the Senate indorses the prompt and vigorous measures adopted by the President of the United States and the members of his Administration to repulse and repress by military force the interference of lawless men with the due process of the laws of the United States, and with the transportation of the mails of the United States and with commerce among the States.

It is within the plain constitutional authority of the Congress of the United States "to regulate commerce with foreign nations, and among the several States, and with the Indian tribes"; "to establish post-offices and post-roads"; and to ordain and establish inferior courts; and the judicial power extends to all cases in law and equity arising under the Constitution and laws of the United States.

It is the duty of the President under the Constitution to "take care that the laws be faithfully executed," and to this end it is provided that he shall be "commander-in-chief of the army and navy of the United States, and of the militia of the several states when called into the actual service of the United States."

It is treason against the United States for a citizen to levy war against them, or to adhere to their enemies, giving them aid and comfort.

Those who combine to use force to assail or resist the constituted authorities of the United States, civil or military, should be warned of the magnitude of their offence; and those who earn honest bread by honest toil can do nothing more detrimental to their interests than to show them any sort of countenance in their lawless course.

The action of the President and his Administration has the full sympathy and support of the law-abiding masses of the people of the United States, and he will be supported by all departments of the Government and by the power and resources of the entire nation.

MR. DANIEL.—I am a State rights Democrat, who would not like to see the muniments of local self-government overridden. But I am also a national Democrat, who would not like to see the muniments of national authority and national safety destroyed.

Anarchy is no remedy for anything. It intensifies every evil that exists. It impedes every remedial process. It should be stamped out wherever it shows itself.

The President is commander-in-chief of the army and navy. He has the plain right, and it is his plain duty, to employ them whenever and wherever the Constitution and laws of the Federal Government are forcibly resisted by combinations of men.

The establishment of post-offices and post-roads and the transportation of the mails through and by them is a Federal matter. Commerce among the States—interstate commerce, as distinguished from local intrastate commerce—is a Federal matter.

The due process of law in the Federal courts is a Federal matter. And in all three of these matters the President, having imposed upon him the constitutional obligation to "take care that the laws be faithfully executed," has the right and duty to use the army and navy to that end, and to oppose force by force.

I am the friend, and have often been the champion, of those who work for their daily bread. My sympathy is with them. But they can have no lot or share with anarchists, the destroyers of property, the destroyers of life, the breakers of law, the enemies of peace, order, and civilized existence. They have no place in the ranks of incendiaries, and they have no enemy who can be so fatal to their every interest as those who seek to fire them into defiance of law.

The President is right in dealing promptly with lawbreakers. He ought to be upheld and cordially and unstintedly supported here, as he will be throughout this land, by upright and law-abiding citizens.

Sections and parties disappear in the face of society imperiled. We should know only the country, the Constitution, and the laws, and, as the President says, in such an emergency discussion may be well postponed. Peace, order, and obedience to law are the conditions precedent to discussion; with them assured, grievances will be heard, rights protected, and wrongs redressed.

On July 11 Senator Daniel added another resolution to his substitute.

2. *Resolved,* That while the Senate thus explicitly declares its determination to support the Executive in the enforcement of the laws and in maintaining the supremacy of the Constitution, it deems it proper also to declare its adhesion to the principle of the arbitration of differences or controversies between the employers of labor and their employees, as recognized in the laws of the United States; and to express its condemnation of the refusal of any party to such controversies or differences connected with the late disturbances in the city of Chicago and its vicinity to submit such differences or controversies to fair and impartial arbitration. And the Senate also expresses its determination to use, in promotion of the arbitration of such differences or controversies, whatever constitutional power it may possess.

JOSEPH M. CAREY [Wyo.].—As I understand the resolutions which were introduced yesterday by the Senator from Virginia [Mr. Daniel] they were for the purpose of upholding the hands of the President of the United States in the enforcement of the laws and maintaining the Constitution of the United States in Chicago. Now, the purpose, it appears to me, of the resolution of to-day is to lessen the effect of the resolutions of yesterday.

The Senate has nothing whatever to do with the settlement of difficulties between employers and employees. The Senate is now making resolves with reference to the disorder that exists in the city of Chicago and elsewhere in the United States.

SENATOR DANIEL.—Briefly, let me say to the Senator who has just spoken that by an act approved October 1, 1888, the Congress of the United States and the President gave their sanction and approbation to the principle of arbitration and provided machinery for a peaceful settlement of such controversies as we now have to deal with, and the settlement of peace ought to be commended and put before all, in order that force may not be resorted to any further than may be absolutely indispensable. That is as much a part of the law and Constitution of the country as any of the laws which provide for the use of the military force, and it should receive equal consideration and be equally impressed upon the attention of the people.

SENATOR CAREY.—So far as the law is concerned, to which the Senator from Virginia refers, it has been inoperative; it was passed, as many things are passed by Congress, to please somebody or other, but it has no effect whatever. It can not be enforced, and never has been enforced.

JOSEPH N. DOLPH [Ore.].—I am not quite pleased with the statement contained in the third clause of the resolution introduced by the Senator from Virginia, as follows:

It is the duty of the President under the Constitution to ''take care that the laws be faithfully executed,'' and to this end it is provided that he shall be ''commander-in-chief of the army and navy of the United States, and of the militia of the several States when called into the actual service of the United States.''

If that means in case of insurrection and a proper case made for the interference of Federal troops it is the duty of the President as commander-in-chief of the army and navy to interfere for the protection of life and property, I have no objection to the statement. It is correct.

But if it means that the President is made commander-in-chief of the army and of the navy for the purpose of enforcing the ordinary execution of the laws or enforcing the law by process of the courts, I do not believe that that authority is conferred upon the President of the United States. It is his duty, in the first place, to see that the laws are enforced through the ordinary means of courts of justice and officers of the courts of justice. The law has provided how the process of a court of justice may be served and enforced, and it is only when there is an insurrection, as I have said, when there is organized treason against the Government, State or national, that the President is authorized to put into motion and to exercise the power conferred upon him as commander-in-chief of the army and of the navy.

Heretofore it has been supposed that in case of insurrection in a State it was not the duty of the President to act, if the legislature was in session, until the legislature had called for the interference of Federal troops or, if the legislature was not in session, until the governor of the State had called for them. We have taken a new departure I think. I am not prepared to say that it is not right. I stand here and commend it, and say that what has been done by the Executive would be done by me under the same emergency if I had the authority, and I stand here to commend the President for his action and to say that it was fortunate for the country that there was a chief magistrate who had the backbone to do what he has done.

But I repeat that heretofore it has been supposed that the President could only use Federal troops in a State to suppress an insurrection or riot when the legislature, if in session, called upon him or, if the legislature was not in session, when the governor called upon him for Federal troops.

But, as I understand the present condition of affairs, the Administration started out to protect railroads which were in the hands of receivers, and now the protection is extended, without the request of the governor of Illinois at least, or the legislature of Illinois, to railroads engaged in carrying the mails and railroads engaged in interstate commerce. I am not entirely certain and I have not examined the question critically enough to know whether the declarations contained in the resolution as to the legal aspects of this question are correct.

It looks as if the Senator from Virginia had this morning become afraid of the resolution he introduced yesterday, and, having introduced a resolution yesterday sustaining the Administration in what it has done and commending it for what it has done, he proposes to add another clause to the resolution and throw a sop to those who are engaged in defying the laws, in destroying property, and in committing murder.

If I read the amendment aright it is a covert condemnation of the Pullman Company for its refusal to arbitrate. I want to know more about the facts of that matter before I undertake to give an expression as to the merits or demerits of the case. If I am going to make any declaration upon the subject, I want to do it squarely; I do not want to do it by implication; I do not want to do it by a resolution which has any double meaning. I hope that the Senator from Virginia will withdraw the amendment or stop with the declaration that the Senate still adheres to the principle of arbitration.

SENATOR DANIEL.—I think we all seek a common purpose in the right spirit. I propose to drop all of my resolution except the first clause, which goes at once to the root of this matter, and the last clause, which is to the same effect.

This proposition met with approval from a number of Senators and with dissent from none, and was agreed to.

Orville H. Platt [Conn.] then said:

Mr. President, we are confronted with one supreme question, and that is who is President of the United States and whether we have any United States? The question is whether the person whom we elected to be our Chief Executive is the Chief Executive of the United States or whether a man who calls himself President Debs is the President and Chief Executive of the United States?

Any other question injected into this discussion seems to me entirely out of place. The Senate should express its approval of what its lawfully elected President has done; and our views about arbitration and all those matters can be discussed hereafter. They are in the form of law. I object to anything except the straight, square, manly indorsement of what President Cleveland has done, and I shall vote against anything else.

The amended resolution was then passed.

Endorsement of the President

House of Representatives, July 16, 1894

On July 16 James B. McCreary [Ky.] introduced in the House the following resolution:

Resolved, That the House of Representatives indorses the prompt and vigorous efforts of the President and his Administration to suppress lawlessness, restore order, and prevent improper interference with the enforcement of the laws of the United States, and with the transportation of the mails of the United States and interstate commerce, and pledges the President hearty support, and deems the success that has already attended his efforts cause for public and general congratulation.

Lafe Pence [Col.], a Populist, opposed the resolution.

Mr. Speaker, the citizens of this country, and certainly the member of this House who would withhold from the Administration proper praise in a time of great emergency would be a public enemy. But this resolution, in my judgment, is broader than this House, if guided by its conscience and its better judgment, is willing to adopt. It goes certainly further than the old line State-rights Democrats of the House will want to record themselves. It certainly goes further than the Republican side of this House can want to go, because the framer of the resolution rests the indorsement not only upon the orders made by the President himself, but in terms it is drawn so as to indorse the efforts of the President "and his Administration."

Mr. Speaker, there may be proper times in this country, in case of dispute between striking laboring men and the corporations which employ them, for calling out the strongest arm of the Government. We all admit that. It may be proper to issue injunctions of the Federal courts. It may be proper to demand indictments by Federal grand juries. It may be proper to call out the military, but, Mr. Speaker, in my humble judgment, the American people will never believe that the Attorney-General who orders the indictments, who orders the injunctions, who orders the military, should be either the attorney of one of those corporations, a stockholder in any one of them, or a member of the board of directors of any one of them. It may be that emergencies may arise where all that the President has done in this case would be proper and right.

Do the Democrats of this House stand ready to indorse the course of the Attorney-General [1]? Is there a Democrat here who believes that it was the right, decent, meet, and proper thing, when the Attorney-General came to name and designate a special deputy to take charge in Chicago, that he should designate the attorney of railroad companies there? I think not.

Is there a Democrat upon this floor who stands ready, of record, to say that it was the meet and proper and decent thing, calling for our praise and our congratulation, that a gentleman who has been an attorney of trusts, who was one when he was appointed, who has continued so to be for a year, and is so to-day, according to the charges made in the New York *World* and other leading Democratic papers, should be the leader, in the Administration which they now seek to praise, in calling into force the strong arm of the Federal judiciary, the strong arm of the military?

Richard P. Bland [Mo.] opposed the resolution.

I believe every member of this House, no matter to what political party he belongs, will indorse the State government

[1] Richard Olney.

and the Federal Government in all legitimate efforts to preserve our institutions, to put down riots, and preserve the majesty of the laws of this country. I have no sympathy, Mr. Speaker, with any man who raises his arm in violence to destroy property to enforce what he may consider his rights of work, and try to prevent others from working. No principle of that kind can find indorsement on the part of anyone who has a proper conception of the rights of the people of this country to liberty.

But, sir, in these great disturbing times, such as we have passed through, it often occurs that acts are done under an assumption of authority that we may be called upon to indorse by a sweeping resolution of this character. I am, as a Democrat, to-day where I have always been, and that is for the rights and the dignity of the people of the States. I believe in local State government, and that the whole arm of the State authority should be used in suppressing violence before the Federal Government should interfere, except to protect its own property and to protect its mails.

I am aware, Mr. Speaker, that throughout this country, even in States where there was no violence, and where if violence occurred at all, the State authorities were ready and able to deal with it without any instructions sent out by the Attorney-General, the whole country was flooded with deputy marshals; sheriffs were arrested, State authority was overthrown, and the strong arm of the Federal Government took possession of matters properly belonging to the States. Against that, sir, I protest. I protest against these blanket Federal injunctions. I protest against the omnibus injunction. I object to sending deputy marshals all over the country to take the place of State authority; and that in a measure like that resolution, in the excitement of the times, we are as a party, as a Democratic party, liable to do violence to every Democratic principle and to surrender here, in these halls, as representatives of the people of our States, the essential Democratic principle of local self-government. If this Union is to be maintained, it is to be maintained by maintaining and respecting the rights and the authority of the people of the States.

If we are to have imperialism, let it not come with the assent of the representatives of the people in this House.

THOMAS C. CATCHINGS [Miss.].—Mr. Speaker, there is no question of State rights involved in the proposition embodied in this resolution. No man believes more sincerely than I do that it is necessary for the future prosperity and greatness of this country that due observance shall be given to those limitations in the Constitution which define the rights of the States on the one hand and of the general Government on the other. But, Mr. Speaker, it must not be forgotten that it is written in the Constitution that it and the laws made in pursuance thereof constitute the supreme law of this land, and, when it comes to executing the Federal authority, let it always be remembered that the shadow of the national flag obscures and obliterates all State lines. There is not a nook or corner or crevice in all this broad land of ours where the power of the Federal Government may not lawfully go when proper occasion arises.

Mr. Speaker, no man who has spoken here, and no one who will speak, will undertake to point out a single thing that has been done by the President and those who have acted with him that has not been for the purpose of maintaining the Constitution and the laws that have been enacted in pursuance thereof. So far as the matters are concerned which the gentleman from Colorado has commented upon as against the Attorney-General, I wish to say here, speaking not only as a Representative, but as a member of the legal profession, that in my judgment the course of the Attorney-General has been such as to command the admiration and inspire the confidence of every good citizen. He is an able lawyer, a brilliant and distinguished member of his profession, and he could not have done less than he has done and at the same time have discharged his duty to the country.

Mr. Speaker, it is not to be tolerated that any class of citizens in this country shall take the law into their own hands. It can not be permitted that commerce between the States shall be paralyzed and that loss shall be inflicted by the millions of dollars upon the people of this country simply because a dispute has arisen between one class of our citizens and another. I say that the President has commended himself to the favorable judgment and the kindly and thoughtful consideration of the people of this country by the lofty, the determined, the courageous attitude which he has assumed in this dreadful controversy, and I hope it will have taught a lesson to men like Debs and others who choose to organize within the body of our citizenship a special class which claims the right to lay its heavy hand upon the business of the country and disturb and paralyze it.

The resolution was adopted without division, at least two-thirds of the Representatives voting for it.

CHAPTER XII

Regulation of Railroad Rates

[THE HEPBURN BILL]

The Elkins Interstate Commerce Act—President Roosevelt on ''Rebates''—
William P. Hepburn [Ia.] Introduces in the House a Bill to Regulate
Railroad Rates—Debate: Varying Views by Charles E. Townsend
[Mich.], Robert L. Henry [Tex.], Charles E. Littlefield, Joseph C.
Sibley [Pa.], Henry A. Cooper [Wis.], Ollie M. James [Ky.], Augustus
O. Stanley [Ky.], Theodore E. Burton [O.], Charles H. Burke [S. D.],
Samuel W. McCall [Mass.], James R. Mann [Ill.], William C. Adamson
[Ga.], Gordon Russell [Tex.], John J. Esch [Wis.], Oscar W. Under-
wood [Ala.], William Sulzer [N. Y.], W. Bourke Cockran [N. Y.],
John Sharp Williams [Miss.], Mr. Hepburn; Bill Passed by the
House—Speech in the Senate on ''Physical Valuation of Railroads''
by Robert M. La Follette [Wis.]; Senate Amends Bill—Compromise
Bill: Speech on It in the House by James S. Sherman [N. Y.]; Bill
Is Enacted.

O N February 25, 1903, a supplementary act to the
act of February 4, 1887 (which had created the
Interstate Commerce Commission), and the
Sherman Anti-Trust Act of July 2, 1890 [see Volume XI,
chapter i], was approved by President Roosevelt. It was
known as the Elkins' Act, from the mover, Senator
Stephen B. Elkins [W. Va.]. Its character will transpire in the following debate.

In his annual message of December 6, 1904, President Roosevelt made the following observations and
recommendations upon the subject of rebates:

REBATES

PRESIDENT ROOSEVELT

Above all else, we must strive to keep the highways of commerce open to all on equal terms, and to do this it is necessary
to put a complete stop to all rebates. Whether the shipper or

the railroad is to blame makes no difference; the rebate must be stopped, the abuses of the private car and private terminal track and side track systems must be stopped, and the legislation of the Fifty-eighth Congress which declares it to be unlawful for any person or corporation to offer, grant, give, solicit, accept, or receive any rebate, concession, or discrimination in respect of the transportation of any property in interstate or foreign commerce whereby such property shall by any device whatever be transported at a less rate than that named in the tariffs published by the carrier must be enforced. For some time after the enactment of the Act to Regulate Commerce it remained a mooted question whether that act conferred upon the Interstate Commerce Commission the power, after it had found a challenged rate to be unreasonable, to declare what thereafter should, *prima facie*, be the reasonable maximum rate for the transportation in dispute. The supreme court finally resolved that question in the negative, so that as the law now stands the commission simply possess the bare power to denounce a particular rate as unreasonable. While I am of the opinion that at present it would be undesirable, if it were not impracticable, finally to clothe the commission with general authority to fix railroad rates, I do believe that, as a fair security to shippers, the commission should be vested with the power, where a given rate has been challenged and after full hearing found to be unreasonable, to decide, subject to judicial review, what shall be a reasonable rate to take its place; the ruling of the commission to take effect immediately, and to obtain unless and until it is reversed by the court of review. The Government must in increasing degree supervise and regulate the workings of the railways engaged in interstate commerce, and such increased supervision is the only alternative to an increase of the present evils on the one hand or a still more radical policy on the other. In my judgment the most important legislative act now needed as regards the regulation of corporations is this act to confer on the Interstate Commerce Commission the power to revise rates and regulations, the revised rate to at once go into effect, and to stay in effect unless and until the court of review reverses it.

In the following annual message (December 5, 1905) President Roosevelt returned to the subject, making more specific recommendations, which were largely incorporated in a bill introduced during the session. He closed by saying:

Let me most earnestly say that these recommendations are not made in any spirit of hostility to the railroads. On ethical grounds such hostility would be intolerable, and on grounds of mere national self-interest we must remember that such hostility would tell against the welfare not merely of some few rich men, but of a multitude of small investors, a multitude of railway employees, wage-workers, and most severely against the interest of the public as a whole. I believe that on the whole our railroads have done well and not ill, but the railroad men who wish to do well should not be exposed to competition with those who have no such desire, and the only way to secure this end is to give to some Government tribunal the power to see that justice is done by the unwilling exactly as it is gladly done by the willing. Moreover, if increased power is given to some Government body the effect will be to furnish authoritative answer on behalf of the railroad whenever irrational clamor against it is raised, or whenever charges made against it are disproved. I ask this legislation not only in the interest of the public, but in the interest of the honest railroad man and the honest shipper alike, for it is they who are chiefly jeoparded by the practices of their dishonest competitors.

This legislation should be enacted in a spirit as remote as possible from hysteria and rancor. If we of the American body politic are true to the traditions we have inherited we shall always scorn any effort to make us hate any man because he is rich, just as much as we should scorn any effort to make us look down upon or treat contemptuously any man because he is poor. We judge a man by his conduct—that is, by his character—and not by his wealth or intellect. If he makes his fortune honestly, there is no just cause of quarrel with him. Indeed, we have nothing but the kindliest feelings of admiration for the successful business man who behaves decently, whether he has made his success by building or managing a railroad or by shipping goods over that railroad. The big railroad men and big shippers are simply Americans of the ordinary type who have developed to an extraordinary degree certain great business qualities. They are neither better nor worse than their fellow-citizens of smaller means. They are merely more able in certain lines and therefore exposed to certain peculiarly strong temptations. These temptations have not sprung newly into being; the exceptionally successful among mankind have always been exposed to them, but they have grown amazingly in power as a result of the extraordinary development of industrialism along new lines; and under these new conditions, which the lawmakers of old could not foresee and therefore could not provide against, they have become so serious and menacing as to demand entirely new remedies. It is in the interest of the best type of railroad man and the best type of shipper no less than of the public that there should be governmental supervision and regulation of these great business operations, for the same reason that it is in the interest of the corporation which wishes to treat its employees aright that there should be an effective employers' liability act, or an effective system of factory laws to prevent the abuse of women and children.

All such legislation frees the corporation that wishes to do well from being driven into doing ill, in order to compete with its rival, which prefers to do ill.

We desire to set up a moral standard. There can be no delusion more fatal to the nation than the delusion that the standard of profits, of business prosperity, is sufficient in judging any business or political question—from rate legislation to municipal government. Business success, whether for the individual or for the nation, is a good thing only so far as it is accompanied by and develops a high standard of conduct—honor, integrity, civic courage. The kind of business prosperity that blunts the standard of honor, that puts an inordinate value on mere wealth, that makes a man ruthless and conscienceless in trade and weak and cowardly in citizenship, is not a good thing at all, but a very bad thing for the nation. This Government stands for manhood first and for business only as an adjunct of manhood.

The question of transportation lies at the root of all industrial success, and the revolution in transportation which has taken place during the last half century has been the most important factor in the growth of the new industrial conditions. In the old days the highway of commerce, whether by water or by a road on land, was open to all; it belonged to the public and the traffic along it was free. At present the railway is this highway, and we must do our best to see that it is kept open to all on equal terms. Unlike the old highway it is a very difficult and complex thing to manage, and it is far better than it should be managed by private individuals than by the Government. But it can only be so managed on condition that justice is done the public. It is because, in my judgment, public ownership of railroads is highly undesirable and would probably in this country entail far-reaching disaster, that I wish to see such supervision and regulation of them in the interest of the public as will make it evident that there is no need for public ownership.

The opponents of Government regulation dwell upon the difficulties to be encountered and the intricate and involved nature of the problem. Their contention is true. It is a complicated and delicate problem, and all kinds of difficulties are sure to arise in connection with any plan of solution, while no plan will bring all the benefits hoped for by its more optimistic adherents. Moreover, under any healthy plan, the benefits will develop gradually and not rapidly. But, while I fully admit the difficulties in the way, I do not for a moment admit that these difficulties warrant us in stopping in our effort to secure a wise and just system. They should have no other effect than to spur us on to the exercise of the resolution, the even-handed justice, and the fertility of resource, which we like to think of as typically American, and which will in the end achieve good results in this as in other fields of activity. What we need to do is to develop an orderly system, and such a system can only come through the gradually increased exercise of the right of efficient Government control.

On January 24, 1906, William P. Hepburn [Ia.] introduced in the House a bill along the lines of the President's recommendations amending the act of February 4, 1887. It was referred to the Committee on Interstate and Foreign Commerce, of which Mr. Hepburn was chairman. He reported it back on January 27 as unanimously approved by the twelve Republicans and six Democrats on the committee.

REGULATION OF RAILROAD RATES

HOUSE OF REPRESENTATIVES, JANUARY 30-JUNE 29, 1906

Charles E. Townsend [Mich.], of the committee, explained and supported the bill.

Like the Esch-Townsend bill of the preceding Congress, he said, the present bill was in response to the public demand for a larger and more satisfactory regulation of interstate carriers.

The bill passed by the House in the Fifty-eighth Congress sought to do two things—first, to invest the Interstate Commerce Commission with the power to fix a reasonable and just

rate or regulation, after complaint and hearing, in place of
one found to be unjust and unreasonable; in fact, to confer
by law the power which the commission actually exercised for
the first two years of its existence, and until the supreme court
declared such power had not been conferred by the law of
1887, and, second, to speed the orders of the commission to
a final determination. It was a simple bill, and its friends did
not claim that it remedied all existing evils, but they did claim
that it would bring great relief to the people, and that it was
wise at that time to take one step and from that vantage
ground view the situation before taking another. The advocates
of that measure felt that delay would simply increase the demand for more radical railroad legislation.

The bill passed the House almost unanimously and was
presented to the Senate, whose committee took it in charge and
proceeded to have hearings upon it. President Roosevelt remained firm in his advocacy of the principles of the measure
and suggested that he would call the Fifty-ninth Congress in
extra session in case the Senate failed to pass a reasonable
bill on the subject, but it continued its hearings until the
Fifty-eighth Congress expired and then on into the summer.

A year has passed since the prophecy was uttered, and yet
business has not been disturbed; railroading has extended its
operations, increased its mileage, and improved its facilities
and equipments in an almost unprecedented manner, thus furnishing conclusive answer to the carriers' own arguments.
To-day we offer a new bill, and I present it to you now, as I
did the one of last year, with the statement that it is probably
the least the people will accept. It confers wider powers than
its predecessor, for the reason that the demand is for a greater
exercise of the Government's control over public carriers. It
may not remedy every defect in existing laws to which every
complainant has called the commission's attention, but it is
believed that it will be sufficient to cure every defect against
which any considerable objection is made.

The committee, or at least a majority of it, believes that
this bill is not only within the constitutional powers of Congress, but that it is clearly an expression of the duty of Congress
to the American people.

When the Fathers established the Government of the United
States and adopted the Constitution as its bill of rights they
wisely delegated to Congress control over all commerce among
the States. As a legal basis of procedure in the exercise of
government the common law was adopted, and that law treated

common carriers as public servants and subject to governmental control, and provided that all rates and regulations charged or imposed by them should be just and reasonable.

At first the Government, recognizing the need of common carriers, entered into the business of carrying products for the benefit of the people; highways were built, boat lines established, and canals dug. These were operated either without charge to the people or by imposing a charge upon the user of the means of transportation. Then the railroad was born, and regions remote from navigable waters were opened up to settlement. The luxuries of yesterday have become necessities of to-day. Inventive genius has revolutionized past ideals and ancient methods; ignorance, superstition, and religious fanaticism and bigotry, which once blocked the way of progress and blinded the eyes of genius, have been ruthlessly crushed to death beneath advancing civilization, which has strengthened with contest and grown wise and audacious with experience, until to-day nothing is sacred but eternal right and nothing impossible to him who wills. [Applause.]

Under such conditions the most progressive government in the world is required at this time to deal justly and fairly with the transportation problem, justly and fairly to the people and to the carriers—to the people, because the Government exists for them; to the carriers, because, being necessary for the general welfare, they are included in it and an injury to them would be an injury to the people.

When population was scattered and business small, strict regulation was not so imperative. When carrier actually competed with carrier for traffic, the shipper did not suffer so much, but when the country became settled and business increased to vast proportions; when individuals, trusts, and combinations grew to such power that the railroads were in a measure at their mercy; when in looking for business the traffic manager was actuated by the sole desire of obtaining every cent the traffic would stand and would prefer, and therefore favor, one shipper who could give 100 cars of freight rather than 100 shippers who could provide only one car each; when carriers combined to eliminate competition and manipulate schedules in ways past all finding out; when at a time when business commissioned every car of every carrier; when railroad facilities had become so improved that a dollar's worth of labor or coal would earn more money for the railroads than ever before [applause]; when traffic sought the railroad instead of being solicited; when under such conditions hundreds of

X—27

articles of commerce were subjected to an advance in freight rates; when these public servants were demanding tolls from the people to pay dividends on fictitious capital representing nothing but graft; when the railroads were assuming to say how the country was to be developed, what men should prosper, and who should fail, which cities should grow and which should not, then the people affected by such conditions—and who were not?—insisted that the servant should not be the master and that the Congress should pass a law to enforce their rights under the contract between the carriers and the public; the right to impartial treatment and to just and reasonable rates and regulations, for "it is so nominated in the bond." [Applause.]

In response to this demand the present bill has been prepared and presented to Congress.

The bill attempts to place under the supervision of the commission every form of interstate and foreign commerce, all instrumentalities of commerce and transportation. We have declared that cars, vehicles, and instrumentalities of shipment or carriage, irrespective of ownership of any contract, express or implied, and all services in connection with traffic, such as elevation, ventilation, refrigeration, or icing, shall be considered as being furnished by the carrier, and therefore under the supervision of the Interstate Commerce Commission. We have also stipulated that terminal, icing, and other similar charges shall be published as separate items, so that the shipper may understand just what he is paying for each particular service, and then we have said that all such charges shall be just and reasonable, that any other is unlawful.

Some of the most serious complaints have been those against these special services. Private car companies have been organized to do the people's work; the railroads have loaned their tracks to these companies, and while they have presented the charge to the shipper these private companies have really imposed them, and it is claimed that they were outside the jurisdiction of the Interstate Commerce Commission. It is not necessary for me to detail to the House or the country the gross injustice which has been done the people through these instrumentalities. We believe the bill effects a complete remedy for these evils. Hereafter any car hauled for an interstate carrier and any charge imposed upon a shipper, whether by a carrier or any direct or indirect agent of the carrier, must be just and reasonable, and in case it is not the commission has power to make it so.

The same argument applies to elevator and terminal charges. We believe it will no longer be possible for a great manufacturing corporation to build a spur or siding up to its factory and then use it as a basis for obtaining rebates prejudicial to its competitor. The bill also aims to prevent the custom so common and so detrimental to honest competitive business followed by many large shippers, *viz.*, of notifying the carrier that such shippers are on a certain date to have a large amount of traffic for shipment and at the same time demanding that the published rate shall be reduced on that date, so as to give them the advantage over other shippers.

This evil is known as the "midnight-rate" evil, and is one of the most effective means of violating the law against rebates known in the commercial world. We have attempted to cure this by enlarging the time in which a rate can be changed. If the bill is enacted into law, any change made in the schedule of rates hereafter must be published at least thirty days. It is thought this will give all shippers sufficient notice of a change to prepare to meet it.

ROBERT L. HENRY [Tex.].—If that thirty days' clause is violated by the common carrier, what specific penalty is provided in the act for a violation of the kind, and how is the penalty to be enforced?

MR. TOWNSEND.—The penalty provided in this bill is in case of a violation of an order. For instance, if an order of the commission is made in the first place it is $5,000 for each violation, and each day of the continuance of that subjects the road to an extra penalty of $5,000. It is also subject to the law we have now for enforcing orders—the right to compel by mandamus or other summary writs the observance of this rate, and the road would have no right under the law to carry any freight or indulge in traffic unless it had complied with the provisions of the bill.

MR. HENRY.—And then, under the present law, there would only be a fine and there would be no imprisonment of any official who violated that provision of the statute?

MR. TOWNSEND.—The law makes no provision for penalties of imprisonment except in cases of making false reports or in violating the publication feature of the bill.

The main feature of the bill, the one about which the greatest controversy has been had, and the one, I believe, which lies at the foundation of the whole matter, is that which gives the commission power, upon complaint and after full hearing, to substitute a reasonable maximum rate in place of one found to be unjust or unreasonable. Heretofore the commission has had power to declare a rate unjust and unreasonable and to order its discontinuance, but it had no power, under the decision of the supreme court, to substitute a just rate in its place. This has resulted in making the law absolutely nugatory, so far as positive relief to the people is concerned. It is known that ten or twelve railroad men can and do get together and arbitrarily, overnight, as it were, change hundreds and hundreds of rates, and the remedial power of the commission should be as large as the evil to be remedied. [Applause.]

CHARLES E. LITTLEFIELD [Me.].—I would like to make this inquiry: Whether the gentleman's understanding of the bill as it reads confers upon the Interstate Commerce Commission the power to eliminate or correct or affect what is known as the preferential or differential rate—that is, the differential between the long haul and the relatively short haul?

MR. TOWNSEND.—I am sorry to say that it does not. I stand practically alone with one or two other gentlemen of the committee on this matter. I had hoped that we might give the commission powers to fix the differential.

MR. LITTLEFIELD.—I have an apprehension that it does produce practically that result indirectly. Does not this bill authorize the commission to fix a maximum rate upon the short haul, and thus eliminate in that way the differential, and indirectly accomplish what they might otherwise be authorized to do directly?

MR. TOWNSEND.—I do not think it does. The commission has no power to raise the rate, so that is eliminated, and it has no right to reduce a rate unless that rate in itself is unjust and unreasonable.

MR. LITTLEFIELD.—Yes, but that is the whole question before the commission.

MR. TOWNSEND.—If it is unjust and unreasonable it should be reduced, but it does not have anything to do with the relation of rates.

MR. LITTLEFIELD.—But my point is, does not this bill indirectly confer upon the Interstate Commerce Commission the power to control or eliminate the preferential or differential? Of course the assumption is that they would act properly, and would not change any condition unless there was an undue or unjust rate, but do they not get the power?

MR. TOWNSEND.—They do not unless, in the case you assume, one of the rates is too high in itself. If there is simply a difference in rates, and the higher rate is reasonable and the lower rate is unreasonable because it is too little, the commission can give no remedy in that case.

This power to fix a contested rate is not a new principle, nor is the exercise of the power without precedent. For years many of the States in the Union have had commissions created by legislative authority of the States and invested with full power, not only to adjust and establish rates about which complaint has been made, but in some instances to fixe entire schedules for the carriers. The Interstate Commerce Commission during the first years of its existence assumed it had power to fix maximum rates in contested cases, and it exercised that power, and with most of its orders the carriers complied, and not until the decision of the Supreme Court in the maximum rate case did it discontinue the exercise of that power, and during all of that time the railroads were uninjured and the business of the country undisturbed. It was also claimed by the opposition that Congress had no authority to confer upon the commission the power to declare a reasonable rate in place of one found otherwise, for the reason that it was a delegation of legislative power, and this claim has been made notwithstanding the fact that the Supreme Court of the United States has held, where the question was squarely before it, that the legislature of a State—and therefore that the Congress of the United States—had power to appoint an administrative board and confer upon it full authority to fix rates as proposed in this bill. [The Stone case, in 116 United States.] In the Reagan case, from Texas, the Supreme Court of the United States held the same thing. The reasoning in these decisions is this: The legislature having passed a law declaring that all rates must be just and reasonable, it has authority to create a board to execute that law, otherwise the legislature would be absolutely futile to regulate rates effectively in the State or among the States.

But this is not the only constitutional objection which has been urged against the exercise of this power. It was insisted, more formerly than now, that, if a commission fix upon a contested rate from any interior point to a seaport, such action would be a violation of the so-called non-preference clause of the Constitution, which provides that the ports of one State shall not be preferred to those of another. This question was squarely raised in the Wheeling and Belmont bridge case. That was a case where the Government had allowed the construction of a bridge across the Ohio River, and it was authorized to be constructed so low that large vessels which had been engaged in commerce with Pittsburg were unable to pass under, and thus Pittsburg had no trouble in showing that she had been injured, but the court held that Congress had not violated the Constitution in exercising power of regulating commerce by the construction of the bridge, as it had exercised a conceded power, and the injury to Pittsburg was incidental and not a violation of the fundamental law of the land.

The opponents of regulation have also urged that the enactment of this provision would result in an injury to widows and orphans dependent on income from railroad investments. Taking the two classes together, we have this argument: Railroad earnings will be reduced, the expenses of the road must stand the loss, hence the widows and employees must suffer.

A double-barreled argument—one used to kill stockholders, another to destroy the laborer. But what are the facts in the matter? During all the period in which rate legislation has been exercised by the States these direful predictions have not been realized. When the Interstate Commerce Commission exercised the power, securities remained undisturbed and labor was happy. The history of railroading during the last year is interesting reading in connection with this subject. When the Esch-Townsend bill passed the last Congress almost unanimously, one holding the views of these calamity prophets would naturally believe that some disturbance would occur in the railroad world, and especially when it was known that the President of the United States [Theodore Roosevelt] was insisting that the measure should become a law and had said that in case it failed to pass the Senate an extraordinary session of Congress would be called. But, instead of railroad stocks declining, they continued to rise in value. Furthermore, railroad managers throughout the United States proceeded to build 7,200 miles of new railroad, and up to June, 1905, they had placed orders for more than $200,000,000 worth of new railroad equipment.

It is simply begging the question to say that the establishment of just rates will injure the railroads. One of the most serious wrongs at present is the custom which the roads have of reducing rates to certain individuals and places below what would be a fair rate, or one that would produce a dividend, and then imposing an unjust and unreasonable charge upon other individuals and places to offset the apparent loss. The country demands that all the people shall be treated alike, and that only just and reasonable rates shall be imposed. If that is done, the carrier will not necessarily be injured or its revenues reduced; the burden will be equally distributed. Frequently the establishment of a just rate, even if it is lower than the one theretofore existing, produces more revenue. This was clearly demonstrated in what is known as the "Michigan Central charter case."

The State legislature exercised its power under the railroad charter to reduce the fare from 3 to 2 cents per mile.

Immediately after the reduction of the fare the passenger receipts increased enormously, so that it is doubtful now if the roads would go back to the 3-cent fare if they had the opportunity. We should also understand that, while in some cases railroad labor has had its wage increased during the last few years, the carrier's ability to earn has also been increased by the substitution of the mogul engines for the old ones, of the large cars for the smaller ones, by the reduction of grades and the straightening of tracks. Railroad operations have been materially economized.

There is absolutely no danger to labor, and I conclude, if the gentleman who used these arguments had not so repeatedly declared that they were honest, patriotic, and high-minded citizens, the charge of demagogue and agitator which they make against us would react upon themselves.

There is still another phase of this question which should not be overlooked. Originally railroad securities were not eagerly sought as investments; to-day such investments are most attractive, and the disposition of promoters and managers has been to increase the capital out of proportion to the real assets of the companies, and now when gentlemen are asking that dividends shall be maintained they do not simply mean dividends on bona fide capital, but upon inflated capital, and I submit it is a proper question for Congress or its duly authorized commission, when determining the question of just and reasonable rates, to inquire into the capitalization of these carriers. I know it is claimed that these stocks have been issued in many instances and placed in innocent hands and that if anything were done—and I do not consider that it will be—to injure the value of these stocks such bona fide holders would suffer. I simply answer this argument by saying that we legislate for the whole people. It is our duty to so regulate interstate and foreign commerce as to deal justly with all of our people, and if it should be demonstrated that some few holders of fictitious capital should fail to get an exorbitant return on their holdings the law should in justice be enacted, for we have no business to "rob Peter to pay Paul." [Applause.]

The bill also provides for the widest publicity of railroad affairs. This, I believe, is one of the most potent influences for good. The carrier being a public servant, its methods should be subject to scrutiny; therefore we provide the method by which its accounts shall be kept. We provide for publicity of the contracts and agreements, written or otherwise. We provide that government experts shall have the right, not simply the permission, to inspect all railroad accounts and business methods at all times, and we impose heavy penalties for violation of any provisions of the law. False reports or a refusal to make full disclosure subjects the carrier and its agents not only to a heavy fine, but imprisonment. We also provide in the bill for the speedy determination of matters submitted to the commission. After an order has been made that order shall go into effect within thirty days from the time the same has been served upon the affected carrier. If at any time during the thirty days the carrier is dissatisfied with the order, he can institute proceedings in the district court of the United States wherein the complaint was made, and thereupon it becomes the duty of the Attorney-General to serve notice on that court that the case is of great public importance, entitling it to consideration by the expedition court. Such notice is served upon three circuit judges of that district, if there are three; if not, upon two circuit judges, and those two shall select a district judge from the district, and the three shall proceed at once to the determination of the lawfulness of the commission's order.

This, I believe, has the following advantages over the old law: It permits three judges to pass upon a question instead of one, and their judgment will have more weight than would the opinion of a single judge and more cases will end with a decision of the expedition court. In case, however, either party objects to the decision of that court an appeal can be taken to the Supreme Court of the United States, which under the law is obliged to consider it in preference to any other case pending before it, except criminal cases. The expedition court will simply pass upon the lawfulness of the order, and under the decision of the Supreme Court that means whether such order is confiscatory or whether it imposes a rate which does not yield a fair return upon the carrier's investment. In deciding interstate commerce cases the Supreme Court has passed through several stages of opinion.

Originally it held that there was no relief from the commission's order except by an appeal to the voters. Later it decided, and I believe wisely, that even the legislature could not impose a rate which was confiscatory, and still later, in the Nebraska case, it suggested that a rate which was not fairly remunerative to the carrier was unlawful.

It seems to me that a commission of seven men familiar with railroad matters, knowing all of the complexities which enter into rate making, are better able to determine what is a fairly remunerative rate than any court which only occasionally passes upon the subject, and I would prefer to leave it with the commission. But I bow always in proper submission to the decrees of the Supreme Court, and when it announces a decision I yield it obedience until at least it has had time to study public opinion sufficiently to reverse itself.

MR. LITTLEFIELD.—Do I understand the gentleman's position to be, as a matter of law, that the Supreme Court could interfere by injunction to restrain the carrying into effect of an order of the commission whenever they were of the opinion that the rate was unreasonably low, or is it based upon the confiscatory proposition?

MR. TOWNSEND.—My judgment until I had read the Nebraska case [Smythe *vs.* Ames] was that it would simply be on the confiscatory proposition. In this case the court undoubtedly is trying to stretch the doctrine of confiscation to cover "reasonable return." It is easy to imagine a relation between the two. The court can be trusted to include in the word "lawful" all that ought to be included. I have no doubt the Nebraska case will be used as a precedent in support of the doctrine that unless the returns are sufficiently reasonable the carrier must go out of business, therefore the rate imposed will be considered confiscatory.

For myself, I am satisfied that the proposed legislation will not harm honest carriers engaged in lawful business; all others will be and should be in imminent danger. I readily admit that there is an honest difference of opinion as to the policy of the measure. Some believe that the carriers will solve the problem if let alone, but it seems to me that such have not taken sufficient time to read and understand the history of railroading during the last few years. Gradually, but surely, rates have been raised, and during a period when there was no possible excuse for such a course except the desire to satisfy greed. Business has increased, and the net results of operation have shown that expenses have not increased in proportion to the enlargement of traffic. Railroad consolidation has been so complete that a few men, about six, control the great bulk of the railroads, and more and more the people are being placed at the mercy of these great corporations. Complaints have come up to Congress from all over the country against the growing and insolent power of great consolidations of capital, and it is not sufficient to say, as some have said, that the complainants are demagogues and agitators, for already members have discovered among the number their most patriotic and intelligent constituents.

From the millions of farms between the oceans, whereon the bone and sinew of the Republic produce its true and substantial wealth; from the million factories which transform beneath the magic hand of enterprise and genius those farm products into myriad forms of beauty and usefulness; from the millions of tradesmen who disseminate the output of factory and loom among the people; from the professions which minister to the wants of others; from forest and mine comes up the demand that the servant shall not be above the master.

This question is not and ought not to be a political one; but as a partisan I could hail with delight the disposition of my party to take it up, for it is everlastingly right, and the people, having recognized it as such, will not be much longer put off. They demand real, positive remedial legislation, and ill will fare the legislator who offers a serpent instead of a fish.

Some say that this legislation is born of a prejudice against corporations, and with such an ancestor must be an instrument of oppression and wrong. I reply that the great mass of the people are fair and honest and acknowledge that the railroad honestly managed under the law is a great necessary blessing. They know it was chartered to serve them, and, desiring its service, they will not knowingly weaken it or lessen its ability to serve.

That the people have become suspicious of some of these great corporations there is no doubt, but there is a great excuse for it. As a rule, these organizations have resisted every effort to regulate and control them even when it was known that such regulations would be beneficial; lobbies, rich and powerful, have been maintained at the capitals of State and nation, and many seemingly unwarranted interferences with the people's rights have been experienced. They have entered the domain of politics, and in many instances seemed to have dictated the nomination and election of legislators. They have assumed that they were too strong to obey and the people too weak to enforce the law. [Applause.]

Temporizing will bring nothing but disaster. Already we hear the rumbling of discontent, and socialism smiles in satisfaction with every delay. Regulation of a public servant is not a departure from the principles of popular government; but disregard of a righteous law and indifference to legal restrictions imposed to protect the people's rights are more than socialism—they are anarchy—and were I a railroad agent instead of a people's Representative I would hail the proposed legislation as a salvation to my master from the fate which an indignant people is sure to visit upon the corporations who, believing that they are above and beyond the law, seek to become a law unto themselves.

Let the bill pass, and let the railroads heed its provisions, and, instead of retarding its execution, aid in its operation, and then, instead of being the objects of suspicion and hatred, they will be recognized as the instruments of progress and prosperity. Rate legislation will enter into history, and its entry will not be marked by any business disturbance, but rather it will indicate the beginning of an era of better feeling between the railroads and the people—an era of equal rights and opportunities under a just and impartial law. [Prolonged applause.]

On February 1 Joseph C. Sibley [Pa.] opposed the bill.

He declared that if the Esch-Townsend bill were now before the House only the men who had given title to it would vote for it.

If one year is sufficient to show you the absolute incorrectness of your position on the other measure, why may we not with confidence hope and believe that if you will take one more year for the consideration of this measure there will not be two found in the House who would vote for this one?

Two years ago, I think, I might probably have doubted that there could be found upon this side of the chamber ten men who would have voted for a proposition to take from the business interests of this country the power to fix the price of transportation and confer it upon a body appointed by political power. This year, with this measure pending, the Republican side seem to have surrendered everything. They gave away, and gave away in order to get a unanimous report from the committee and get for its support the unanimous Democratic side of this chamber, and so I think our Democratic friends are entitled to a great share of the credit which they claim in bringing this resolution into the House. [Applause.]

Two years ago, or following the strike in the anthracite coal region, William Randolph Hearst, a distinguished member of this House, declared for the immediate government ownership and control of all coal mines. David Bennett Hill, another distinguished gentleman, who wore a feather on his hat always labeled correctly,[1] declared for the same measure; and no less a distinguished character than the chairman of the Judiciary Committee of the House of Representatives, the gentleman from Wisconsin [John J. Jenkins], introduced a bill into this House, drafted by himself, for the immediate ownership and control of all coal mines and the railroads leading therefrom and appertaining thereto. That measure at that time could not have commanded the support of this side of this body, but we have progressed rapidly. We have got to a joint pretty nearly where we are ready to declare for municipal ownership and municipal control of everything and everybody, and that vision which came to Jack Cade in the old days may yet be realized, when he declared that upon his accession to power "then should seven half loaves be sold at the cost of a penny, and every three-hooped pot should have ten hoops, and in all England it should be felony to drink small beer." [Applause.]

We are coming by rapid steps of progression to government ownership. Government control has not exhibited in that portion which has heretofore come under our observation such marvelous performances as to commend it to us. Here in Washington we have presented the best examples afforded of it. We have the Government Printing Office, and there is not a gentleman here who does not know that he could have a speech printed —and I could have this one printed if I wanted to—very much cheaper in a private printing office, probably at a third less than at the Government Printing Office. I am not going to have it printed though at any price. [Applause.]

In our Government Gun Factory here in Washington testimony has shown over and over again that 70 per cent. of the work upon those guns is done by contract and 30 per cent. of the work is performed by the Government, and yet 70 per cent. of the cost is represented by the 30 per cent. of the work done in the department here in the navy yard.

While there have been abuses under the present system of railway control and management, I believe that for twenty-five years they have been steadily diminishing. Since the passage of the interstate commerce act, supplemented by the Elkins Act, any man who has given a secret rebate or a rate to one man

[1] The caricaturists always pictured Governor Hill with a feather in his cap labeled: "I am a Democrat."

which was not open to another is a criminal, and if his punishment has not followed it has not been because of the lack of the law, but the lack of courage or the inattention and dereliction of the man whose sworn duty it was to punish and to correct that evil.

For the system of rebate no man can offer a defence. It is indefensible in business, it is indefensible in good morals, because, if the right be granted to give one man or corporation a rate that is not accorded to every other man or corporation, it is granting to that man or corporation that power to destroy that which never should be granted or permitted to rest in their keeping. That there have been abuses to be corrected I will grant you. If the law has been derelict, how shall those whose sworn duty it was to obey the mandate of the law be held under this measure to stricter accountability than they are to-day?

Mr. Chairman, in this measure now under consideration it seems to me we are invading the realm of socialism. This bill should be properly termed "A bill to fix rates by political agencies," and, in the language of another, "To establish the business of transportation by lawsuit." You have got to commence with a legal decision at the beginning, and you have got to take it at every point along to the very end of the chapter. If I construe it rightly that is the effect of it. If you yield to the sentiment that is coming up to-day—and we have had the warnings that worse is to follow—if you yield to-day to Mr. Hearst and Mr. Bryan, who declare that they support this measure, not as a panacea, not as a cure for all evils, but that they have indorsed it as a step in the right direction toward government ownership—if you yield to this sentiment, you must realize in what direction you are going.

This current of socialism has become so rampant in this country that within the past week Mr. Jack London, whose books we have all read with interest, is reported as having said from a public platform in the city of New York that the time had come for the division of all property and the use of so much force and the shedding of so much blood as should be necessary thereto. I am not to be stampeded by the desires of men who are looking at it merely from the standpoint of State socialism. And without any disrespect to my friends who favor this bill, because I guess you all do [laughter], I want to paraphrase the language of Horace Greeley.

"Not all men supporting this bill are socialists and anarchists, but every socialist and every anarchist in this nation does indorse this bill, the product of your creation."

HENRY A. COOPER [Wis.].—The gentleman is using the term "socialism" quite frequently. I should like to ask him this question: In the case of the street-car system of the city of Washington, does the gentleman believe that Congress ought to say what that street-car system shall be allowed to charge for fares; that it ought by statute to say that the street-car company shall give transfers at certain points; that they shall give commutation rates—that is, if you buy six tickets you shall only pay a quarter for them? Do you think that the use of the epithet "socialism" and the application of it to the men who vote for that sort of thing ought to deter them from voting for it? And if it is right in the case of a street-car system, which is essentially monopolistic in so far as the municipality is concerned, wherein does that sort of legislation differ in principle from the Government regulating interstate commerce over railroads, which are in themselves monopolistic of that traffic?

MR. SIBLEY.—I believe Congress is really the town council of the city of Washington, and in that capacity the regulation of street-car fares within the District of Columbia has been committed to it, and I presume that it is within the province of this House and its right to establish whatever conditions it sees fit to impose that are legal and constitutional.

OLLIE M. JAMES [Ky.].—The gentleman has told us that this measure tends to socialism and that Bryan is its leader. It is also said that his party is quite near unanimous in the support of this measure, and therefore he stands almost single and alone. I wish to ask him to enlighten this House as to the means employed whereby the whole Republican party has right about faced and is following William J. Bryan—the one you hailed as an anarchist, seeking to destroy. [Applause on the Democratic side.]

MR. SIBLEY.—Will my friend excuse me for putting the responsibility of answering onto broader and abler shoulders than my own among my colleagues? [Laughter.] I will say to the gentleman from Kentucky that he need not shake his gory locks at me. [Laughter.]

MR. JAMES.—I want to say to the gentleman that my locks are nearly as absent as his. [Laughter.] I might suggest to the gentleman that if he wants the burden taken off his shoulders perhaps the Republicans have had their ears to the ground on this great railroad question and heard from the people.

MR. SIBLEY.—Mr. Chairman, it would seem that all representatives of the highest ideals of development of our civil life who represent the civic virtues could be guided by these monuments, these beacon lights which human history and experience have erected all along the shores of time. It seems unfortunate, but nevertheless it is a fact, that never yet was the child born on all this earth that would ever believe the fire was hot until it stuck its fingers into it.

Mr. Sibley then recounted the socialistic experiments of New Zealand, such as government ownership of railroads, government employment of the otherwise unemployed, government loans to the poor, old age and indigent pensions, government establishment of local industries, such as creameries, etc., and declared that they led to waste of public moneys, corruption of the civil service, etc.

And when there came to the prime minister the people protesting that under their progressive land tax and their progressive income tax they were being denuded of all their possessions, the prime minister, Mr. Seddon, said, in answer to them, these words: ''That is the object of this legislation—that there shall remain in all New Zealand neither a rich man nor a poor man.''

So the forces have swept on until they are in the throes of state socialism, and they are going to make a glorious success of it just as long as there remains in pockets of thrift and industry one dollar to be wrung out in the form of taxation. Then there comes, as the sequence to the socialistic state, the state of anarchy, and then the reign of terror, and then the swing of the pendulum to the other side, and the strong man on horseback. In all human history that has been the experience, and society has been forced to rebuild its shattered superstructure upon those foundations which guarantee the rights of persons and of property.

Let us look at Germany—Germany, the most highly educated nation perhaps upon the globe, having a bright people, a progressive people, and an industrious and sober people. In 1878 Bismarck declared that it was necessary that the Government should take over the ownership of the German railways in order that through control of rates it might be possible to decentralize and unify the German Empire. Under the operation of that law communities have been built up and cities have been destroyed. Bremen, once a prosperous port, has seen her wharves rotting or idle and her freight and commerce transferred to Hamburg.

Von Miquel, one of the greatest ministers of finance Germany has ever had, said:

Summing up the situation, it would appear impossible to retain state ownership of the railways unless it should be made practicable to make rates in accordance with hard and fast rules such as those made upon the cost of service.

This was supplemented by a report of the commission appointed by the ministers to investigate railroad affairs, where they say in the report:

Any system which takes into account anything but the cost of service will precipitate a measureless conflict of interest and put the whole system into the domain of politics and array section against section, farmer against trader, and trader against manufacturer.

So Germany, instead of being unified, has been divided and they have been building and developing their canal system. Last year they voted ten millions to build a canal from Berlin to Stettin, 100 miles distant, already connected by a railroad with abundant facilities for transportation; that railroad last year transported but 200,000 tons of freight, less than is sent by one concern from my home town in Pennsylvania.

What has been the experience in France? Practically the same. The French commission, in order to protect their canals and their waterways, by ministerial decree ordered that the railroads should not fix rates within 20 per cent. of the price of water tolls. They had to have a law to prevent the railways competing with the canals.

In Italy, where the control of rates is fixed, and the Government controls all of the railways and owns a majority of them, the Italian commissioner summed up the conditions in that country by saying:

It is a mistake to expect lower rates or better facilities from government than from private companies. The actual results are just the reverse. The state is more apt to tax industry than to foster it, and when it attempts to tax industry it is even less responsible than a private company. Second. State management is more costly than private management, and a great deal of capital is thus wasted. Third. Political considerations are brought into a system of state management in a way which is disastrous to legitimate business and demoralizing to politics.

To-day, under the development of the American railway transportation system, a carload of wheat is shipped from the

Mississippi River and laid down on the docks at Liverpool cheaper than the English road charges for taking it from London to Liverpool, a distance of 210 miles. Under this development it has been said by no less an authority than Professor Hadley, of Yale, that the cost of transporting the wheat in a loaf of bread from Dakota to New York City is less than the cost to the baker delivering it from his shop four blocks distant to his morning customer.

This American railway system is not perfect, but it is working so far toward perfection that it is the admiration of all of the railway men of the world. This system, while it has not been responsible for all our growth and progress and development, is entitled to its fair share of credit as one of the chief factors incident thereto.

I know it is an unpopular thing to say, "We will charge what the traffic will bear," but that has been the foundation and keynote of our commercial and industrial development. The railroad has been ready to meet the producer more than half-way in finding an outlet for his products. Upon what principle has the Interstate Commerce Commission decided all of its cases? I want to quote the language exactly. Not once, but over and over again, this has been the exact verbiage of their opinions:

Each locality or section is entitled of natural right to the advantages of trade or industry accruing to it by reason of its geographical position.

That is the Interstate Commerce Commission which is going to interpret and execute your law; to whose hands you are committing this tremendous power. They are to emphasize the experience of France and Italy and Germany and Australia and every country and people of the globe where a rate-making policy by government has been attempted.

I can see no justice in a system that does not take into consideration the cost of the service. Living, as I do, 500 miles from New York, is it just to me, when I ship to New York at the rate of 16 cents a hundred, that a man who lives three times as far away, on the Mississippi, or four times as far, on the Missouri, or six times as far, out in Dakota, should expect and get the same rate that I, through my proximity to market, receive?

I would complain at once to the Interstate Commerce Commission under this law that that was an unjust discrimination against me, living in Pennsylvania in close proximity to the market. The Interstate Commerce Commission would be bound to declare that it was unjust and discriminatory that a man living in the Dakotas or Mississippi Valley should have an equal

X—28

rate, and would order my freight to be reduced in proportion, say, to 4 cents a hundred. The Supreme Court would declare that confiscatory. But say they will establish it at 10 cents a hundred—for certainly that is not unreasonable, for grain has been shipped from the Mississippi at 14 cents a hundred—then what happens?

A struggle between rival sections of this country which will make the struggle between the North and the South over the slave question seem insignificant. Then we will have Senators from Pennsylvania contesting with Senators from New York for the power that they can exercise to control the commission. So with Louisiana and Texas; so with South Carolina and Georgia. The Senators that represent those different commonwealths will be found in competition with each other. If you commence to apply any rule, you have got to apply a rule that is absolutely just. What is the cost of service and what is the distance traversed? You cannot apply a rule and make the American people conform to a rule which is not based on absolute and equal justice to all.

Augustus O. Stanley [Ky.].—Is it not a fact that this bill attempts to do that very thing, to give to some commission the right to review the action of a railroad company when it makes a ruling and makes a rate that is not dependent upon the distance and the cost, but upon some other consideration?

Mr. Sibley.—Mr. Chairman, in my judgment the inexorable laws of trade and of competition will establish at last either a *modus vivendi* or it may be a *status quo;* I do not know the exact term, but your lawyers and diplomats can figure that out. But somewhere there comes an armed neutrality after the war and rate conflict and struggle for supremacy between rival corporations and rival communities; there comes a fixed price for charges established either by common consent or by common experience, and they have got to make the best of them.

Now, I profoundly and sincerely hope that I am mistaken and unduly alarmed about the consequence of this bill. I hope that it does not open the door of socialism; that it is not responsive to a clamor that is going up and down the nation and which has resulted in almost giving the political control of New York City to one who declares for municipal ownership [Mr. Hearst]. I hope that this is not a step in the development of the theories so magnificent and glorious as outlined by Mr. Jack London; but I fear that it is a step in that direction. And therefore I trust through the orderly processes of courts of law, commanding the respect and confidence of all men, there may be the judicial determination of the reasonableness of a rate rather than by a body of men who have exercised such power in the past.

Theodore E. Burton [O.] spoke on February 2. While he supported the bill he nevertheless had a word to say in favor of the railroads.

There have been no organizations in this or any other land which have done more to increase wealth and build up a country's prosperity than the railways of the United States. They have made unoccupied areas to teem with population and abound in wealth, and by low charges on food products and raw materials they have made possible the capture of foreign markets and a phenomenal increase of manufactures. If I were to make any one criticism upon their management it would be that they have too eagerly observed the rule, "Get business." While they have shown liberal and broad-gauged ideas in measures adapted to develop the country, yet in the hurry and competition to get traffic they have oftentimes disregarded that which was best for great localities and paid too little respect to the rights of individuals. Perhaps almost anyone engaged in the business would pursue the same course. I especially deprecate the indiscriminate abuse of them. No profit can be gained by the violent declamation which in some places is indulged in against corporations. I hear speakers whose eyes are filled with visions of the octopus; a legion of monsters surrounds them intent upon taking the lifeblood of the people. Such talk as theirs will lead to no salutary reform. No glittering generalities will answer the purpose. We must descend to details and work out these problems with care and soberness, with an understanding of all their varied aspects which will enable us to act wisely and well. In saying this I would say not one word in extenuation of the discriminations and violations of the law which have characterized the fixing of freight rates. There have been many plans to discriminate and grant rebates, which have originated in that unexplored mysterious realm, the traffic managers' conscience—plans and schemes which would not bear the light of day; but if we compare the railway management with that of other great enterprises I think we may say without fear of contradiction that it has been characterized by a progressiveness, by a desire for the development of the country, and by a liberality unsurpassed.

And we should especially hold the shipper who holds a club

over the railway manager alike culpable with the railway manager himself. [Applause.] If necessary, impose upon him the
same penalty by bringing him before the court and subjecting
him to the same punishment.

As a remedy for ruinous competition Mr. Burton
said:

Possibly it would be best to give to each railroad of this
country an exclusive field of its own to work in. In France
they have five or six railway systems, each supreme in its own
sphere, which no other railway enters. Thirty years ago in
America there was almost ruinous competition between the railways. Freight was occasionally carried at very much less than
cost. This did not benefit anyone particularly. The large shipper gained the benefit of the low rates and the smaller shipper
took his turn when they were restored to normal figures. Then
there were "gentleman's agreements," made to be observed for
a time and then broken; made to give out to each other as if
they were to be maintained, but to be broken in secret. Now, we
are coming to a time of combination. Not only are there several
great railway combinations under one management, and these
combinations include railways which are in competition with
each other, but there is a general disposition all along the line
to act in concert. I may remark, in passing, that this bill will
diminish the influence of competition, because competition feeds
upon rebates and discriminations, but if the force of these factors in reducing rates is done away with it is all the more necessary that some governmental agency should control charges and
make them reasonable and fair to the people.

In explaining the misdeeds of the railroads and trust magnates, I would say that if we seek for the most responsible
source of the evil we shall find it in the ideals of our people. As
a people we have enthroned financial success. In these days a
boy who is coming to manhood now is brought up to admire the
great railway magnates and the managers of great corporations,
and his pathway is pointed out in that direction rather than
in the way of statecraft and of those thousand employments
where a real benefit to the people is possible, though from an
humbler station. It will be impossible to tear up the evil at
the root, except by a long process of education by which it shall
be shown that life has prizes infinitely more valuable than the
gaining of a great fortune. But by legislation we can do much
to bring about the desired result by providing for publicity in

the management of these great organizations; by checks and safeguards which shall remove temptation; by enforcing the law in such a manner that offences of colossal magnitude will be regarded as just as worthy of condign punishment as those which are small and mean. [Applause.]

The control of these corporations is a work that has hardly begun in the States of this country. In some they run riot at will. The national Government must correct the evil. It has set a good example in the national banking laws, which, while not perfect, are a great advance upon previous banking laws.

This is a great country of ours. We have gained a material development, in which the railroads have had much to do, beyond any other country on the globe. But is this all? Is it not well for us to consider whether a development less rapid, especially a development in which there shall be a greater degree of equality, would not be a better one? Is it not true that the benefits of wealth and increasing prosperity do not bring their best results unless they spread all over the land, bringing blessings to the humblest cottage, bringing plenty to the poor as well as to the rich and to the millionaire? [Applause.]

We should not lay all the blame upon those who have gained these great fortunes. They have been prompted in their course by the superabundant vitality of our industrial and commercial life and spurred on by the admiration of the people. But we can condemn and punish them for wrongdoing. We should labor to secure greater equality of opportunity. And along these lines, whatever defects there may be in this bill, however doubtful it may be whether it will work out as is hoped or not, it is, at any rate, a step in the right direction. It is a declaration of the principle that aggregate wealth must submit to the law. It enforces the idea that no combination can be so strong or so great but that the Government shall place its strong hand upon it to restrain and control its operations. [Applause.] And, I believe, there are none who will be more substantially benefited by this measure than the railways themselves, at least those roads in which the management is honest and straightforward.

Charles H. Burke [S. D.] supported the bill. Replying to the arguments of Mr. Sibley he began by good-naturedly referring to the repeated changes from party to party of the "distinguished gentleman from Pennsylvania."

It would seem, Mr. Chairman, that he of all members at this particular time ought to at least agree with one side of the House, but he states that he cannot agree with either, and therefore he is opposed to the bill. He says that the Townsend bill, which passed this House a year ago, if it was up for consideration at this time, would not receive two votes.

I desire, Mr. Chairman, to challenge that statement and to reiterate what I have already said, that if that bill was pending now, and it was the best thing that we could get on this subject, we would do substantially what we did in the last Congress, and that is to pass it practically unanimously. He says that if this bill had been up for consideration before this House two years ago it would not have received ten votes. Why, Mr. Chairman, this proposition was up for consideration in this House about thirty years ago. It was discussed in the House during a period of about ten years at intervals, particularly in the Forty-eighth and Forty-ninth Congresses, when, in 1887, was passed the present interstate commerce act, which it was believed contained the legislation that is proposed here, so far as conferring the limited rate-making power is concerned. So, if it is socialistic now to consider this legislation, it was socialistic twenty years ago. Why talk about socialism? Somebody might very properly ask what is anarchy. If it were not for the fact that the railroads have disobeyed the law we would not at this time be called upon to legislate compelling them to observe the law.

The gentleman from Pennsylvania assumed a false premise. He assumed that this was a proposition of government ownership. But I say, Mr. Chairman, that this bill does not propose government ownership. It is not a step toward government ownership. Indeed, it is a step away from government ownership, for just as sure as we do not get this legislation, or something very closely akin to it, then just as sure as anything can be it is only a matter of time when there may be legislation that will go to an extreme and go away beyond what any person would wish for or want to see happen.

The gentleman in the opening part of his speech took the position, substantially, that we did not have the right to enact this legislation, that it was an interference with private property rights. But, Mr. Chairman, I do not think that any person will seriously contend that dealing with the common carriers of the country and their regulation can be considered for a moment as dealing with private interests. Before the gentleman from Pennsylvania finished he practically indorsed every word in this bill with the one exception of the power to clothe the commission with the right to make a rate after finding a rate complained of unreasonable. The gentleman said, on the subject of rebates, that if there were rebates being practiced now it was because some officer charged with a duty of seeing that the law was enforced was not discharging that duty. Mr. Chairman, the report of the commission, all of the evidence upon this subject of rebates, shows that rebates are being indulged in quite generally throughout the country without any violation of the Elkins Act whatever by means of practices or instrumentalities, such as refrigerator cars, icing charges, elevator charges, terminal and side-track facilities; that rebates are given that are in fact rebates just as if the Elkins law had never been enacted. This bill makes it impossible for those practices to be continued if it should become a law. Why, the gentleman said that he would make a fine, I think, of a hundred thousand dollars for a carrier to give or any person to receive a rebate. Why, apply his argument in the early part of his speech; he would not have any legislation at all governing or regulating the railroads of the country.

Mr. Chairman, I have heard it stated by some that they were for this bill because it was a step toward government ownership. I have heard others say that they were in favor of this legislation because it is a step away from government ownership. Mr. Chairman, speaking for myself, I want to say that I am for this bill because I believe it is honest, because I believe it is right, because I believe that Congress twenty years ago thought they had conveyed to the commission the power that is sought to be given by this bill. It not only gives that power, but it goes further, and regulates many abuses that are now being indulged in by the railroads, and will, I think, make, with existing laws, a law that will be all that is necessary for many years to come; a law that will be not only fair to the railroads but do justice to those who have to do business with railroads. [Applause.]

Samuel W. McCall [Mass.] opposed the bill.

Mr. Chairman, if the pending bill made an effective response to public opinion upon the railroad question, it would deal in the most comprehensive and the most particular terms with rebates or favored rates, whether given directly or in any of the indirect forms in which they have been extended. A secret rate lower than the rate which is published for all or valuable concessions given shippers, under whatever subterfuge, are obnoxious to the law, which contemplates not merely a just and reasonable but an equal rate. What is demanded to meet the real evil, and what was demanded by public opinion until its attention was diverted to an utterly irrational and haphazard remedy, is legislation making clear beyond question the right of every man to equal treatment and giving him the amplest remedy for every violation of his right. The private car, refrigerator car, the industrial switch, receiving a part of the through rate as if it were an independent line, every instrument of favoritism and injustice, had justly received public condemnation. These evils were dealt with in general terms by the amendment known as the "Elkins Act." But that act needed to be broadened; it needed to be made more specific, so that it should prohibit unequal treatment under whatever guise, and then it needed to be enforced, not merely by a fine, but in clear cases of evasion by imprisonment both for the giver and the receiver of the secret rate. If a law had been passed upon these lines one year ago, every demand of what can justly be called "public sentiment" would have been satisfied. The Republican national convention in 1904 made no declaration whatever regarding railroads. The Democratic convention declared against rebates and discrimination. Rebates and discriminations in all their protean forms were the real evil. President Roosevelt in his annual message declared against them, but he promulgated as a remedy that authority be given the commission to fix railroad rates whenever a complaint should be made.

The leading authority upon railroad economics in the British Empire said, not long ago, of the bill passed by the House last winter in line with the President's recommendation, that it would have done no more to stop rebates than would the reenactment of Magna Charta. I endeavored to point out at that time upon this floor that there was no possible relation between the giving of rebates and the fixing of rates by a commission, and that a railroad could as easily give a criminal rebate from a rate fixed by a commission as from one fixed by itself. And the advocates of this legislation have refrained from penetrating the awful mystery and have discreetly permitted the relation between rebates and commission rate making to remain a secret until this day.

The issue of political rate making in the Congress of the United States is not the result of any evolution or of any expression of public opinion, but it is a mere fungus growth. It sprang up in a night. It grew out of the presidential *non sequitur,* and I am very willing to concede that a *non sequitur* is something in which a busy man may sometimes indulge. If teachers of logic are looking for a perfect example of a *non sequitur* for their classes, I commend them to the statement of the evils and the statement of the remedy contained in the President's annual message to Congress in December, 1904.

And at once political rate fixing became a burning issue—I mean in Congress, but not before the people, for there has been no election since it was so suddenly and so illogically sprung upon the country. Mr. Bryan, the once idolized leader of his party, for a time dethroned, but summoned back again by the overwhelming exodus of Silver Democrats at the last election, Mr. Bryan, who might have brought action for infringement, generously hailed political rate making as a decisive step toward his cherished dogma, government ownership, and he fixed upon it the stamp of his emphatic approbation. He looked upon it as his own child, and not long ago, as he was starting around the globe, in almost the last words he uttered upon American soil, with a paternal solicitude he commended the bantling to the tender care of the President.

The Democratic party followed its leader and took up the cause of rate making with enthusiasm and unanimity. As for the Republicans, rate fixing had been made party policy by our just elected President, and, logic or no logic, we were expected to get in line. This is the genesis of the public opinion upon this point. If any political platform adopted prior to the President's message by either of the great parties suggested any form of rate making by the national Government as a remedy for discrimination or for any other purpose, I trust some gentleman will cite it.

So far as favoritism is concerned, in every one of its forms I am opposed to it. I would have you enact against it the most drastic law which ingenuity could devise. And I would have the right of every man to a just, reasonable, and equal rate taken to the courts at the expense of the Government, in the first instance, and ultimately of the railroads, if they were held to be in the wrong, under every effective species of remedy, taken to that forum where Anglo-Saxon freedom has won its noblest triumphs. For my part I prefer the natural and beneficent liberty of the courts to the cast-iron regulations of a commission. I would encourage proceedings such as that in Scotland, which, for a differential given in good faith, took from a railroad company in damages and costs about $700,000. But in this measure we are neglecting to follow the vital line and paltering with the highest interests of the country. I am for every feature of your bill aimed at discrimination, and I would favor far more stringent features; but your rate fixing, which is the substantial part of your bill, is economically as vicious as it is illogical and I propose to submit to you some reasons why I cannot give my support to a measure which I fear you have already almost unanimously determined to enact.

And I shall at the outset dispose of two or three preliminary propositions. It is claimed that it was intended to confer the rate-making power when the interstate act was passed, and that the commission for ten years exercised it. The facts are that the framers of the act declared in the debate that it did not confer the rate-making power; the courts as early as 1890 decided that the power did not exist; there was no general belief that it had been conferred, and, although the commission assumed to pass on the relative reasonableness of rates in a few cases, when it attempted to exercise the power in a really important case, its authority was challenged, and the Supreme Court finally decided that the act did not confer the power of fixing a rate.

Of the same character as the misapprehension which I have referred to is the pretence that the rate-fixing power in this bill is altogether exceptional in its character—not for everyday use, but likely only to be exercised upon rare and great occasions. Gentlemen simply run away from their proposition, and it is little cause for wonder. Their bill confers the power to revise all the rates in the country and to substitute other rates for them upon the happening of a mere formality. In the maximum-rate case thousands of rates were involved, and there is the testimony of a high officer of one of the railroads concerned that the reduction ordered by the commission in that case would have cost the railroads $3,000,000 a year. It would have meant bankruptcy to some of the railroads.

It is clear that the present bill gives the commission, upon the mere formality of somebody's filing a complaint, power to set aside great groups of rates and to substitute other rates for them. The pretence that it contemplates only the challenging here and there of a single rate demonstrates clearly that the advocates of this measure do not understand it or that they do not dare avow its purpose. On the theory that a mere isolated rate is to be tried here and there your bill amounts to nothing from your own standpoint, for, as was said by a railroad president the other day, it would take hundreds of years for your court to sit in judgment upon each of the billion or more rates in the country. Indeed, the new rates would increase faster than your commission could decide them. I shall therefore assume that this measure is a rate-fixing scheme of the most sweeping character.

The fundamental question, then, involved is, Do we want rate making by a Government board? The burden of proof rests upon the man who contends that such a system should be substituted for the system at present in force. It is upon the advocates of this bill to show that we should set aside the American system of fixing freight rates which has given us rates hardly half as high as are paid by the other great countries of the world, although our railroads pay their labor twice the wages paid in the other countries. The burden of proof, I say, rests heavily upon those who would radically substitute for our present system the foreign system of fixing rates by the Government. Magnificent platitudes about eminent domain and our duty to exercise the great commerce powers of the Constitution will not sustain the burden. Give us a reason why we should discard a system which has been a success for a system which has been a failure.

The experiment has been thoroughly tried. We have the result of the experience of other nations and of our own. You will find the experience of the great countries of the world admirably set forth in a book by Professor Meyer upon Government Regulation of Rates. If Professor Meyer is wrong in any of his important statements, I have not observed that those who differ with him have pointed out his errors. And my friend from Pennsylvania [Mr. Sibley], in his masterly speech yesterday, left little to be said upon this point.

In all of these countries we see a rigidity to the rates established by the Government, and we see, too, the lack of constant supervision of detail, due to the enormous task of revising the great mass of rates, and a lack of responsiveness to the temporary conditions of business which an army of traffic agents, scattered over the country at the sources of freight supply, would keep in touch with and fully recognize in the making of rates.

The experience of Australia, where the government controlled the railroads, said Mr. McCall, was a warning to those who, by the bill, would destroy "basing points"—centers of distribution receiving better rates than the communities surrounding them.

The Australian system adopts a mileage rate, as our commission would be compelled to do, and what is the result? A road is built, say from Melbourne 100 miles into the interior, and at its terminus a town springs up which becomes a center for supplying the still farther interior. But the road is afterward extended, and the manufacturer or the jobber in the once flourishing interior town is obviously at a disadvantage with his competitor at Melbourne, because he has two shipments to make. He must either retire from business or go to Melbourne, and the result is that the commercial and banking and great industrial business of Australia is done at the four or five ocean termini of the railroads.

The destruction of "basing points," so called, in the United States, would take away a great part of the business of Atlanta, Memphis, and Kansas City, and scores of other interior centers, and would transfer it to New York and Chicago and St. Louis. If you think our industry and trade should be centralized in a few great cities instead of being diffused throughout the States of the Union, then you will support this bill, because, if it permits the adjustment of relative rates, it is an admirable instrument to accomplish that purpose.

Now, what is the American system which, without any consideration worthy of a great economic subject and upon mere generalities, you are airily proposing in this bill to set aside for the policy which I have been describing? In this country the interstate rates have been made by the railroads with practically no check, so far as governmental interference is concerned. It has been the prime policy of the railroads to develop a vast continental traffic drawn at low rates and between the most remote sections of the country. It has been to make of America a common market. The "natural-right" theory has more than once been involved. The low long-distance rates brought the agricultural products of the West in competition with the farms of New York, New England, and Pennsylvania, in markets which, on the "natural-right" theory, belonged to the farmers of the last-named States. And while your lands have gone up enormously in value the farms of New England and the East have greatly decreased in value. Yet on the whole the East has benefited because it concentrated its energies upon manufactures and trade and the railroad took its products to the West at low rates in the cars which bore your produce East, and which would otherwise have returned empty.

If we had had since 1865 a railroad commission with the power in this bill to fix railroad rates it is a moral certainty that many now civilized portions of the West would be unsettled regions, and as a necessary consequence your great cities would not be the magnificent affairs they are to-day. The Interstate Commerce Commission has more than once affirmed the "natural-right" theory, and if it is to pass upon the conflicting claims of sections it cannot escape from that theory. The elevator and dock owners and great merchants of New York protested against a rate from the West to New York on wheat destined for export lower than the rate to that city on wheat for internal consumption. The low rate for the export wheat was directly for the benefit of the farmer, but it took from the men of New York certain profits that they claimed the "natural right" to have, because their city was the gateway to the continent, and the Interstate Commerce Commission ordered that the rate on the wheat destined for export should be the same as that for New York. The question involved was of vital importance to the farmer, and it is significant that the railroads were fighting his battle, which the commission decided against him in effect upon the natural-right theory. The Supreme Court supported the railroads and overturned the decision of the commission.

The American railroad rates, in the mass, are not the arbitrary, fiat rates such as would be ground out by a governmental machine, but, in a sense, they are self-made rates, and result from the free play of commercial and industrial forces. Even such a differential as that established in favor of Baltimore and Philadelphia against New York and Boston, which would at first sight appear artificial, was the result of one of the fiercest and most expensive commercial wars ever waged upon this continent, and when a few months ago the Interstate Commission was called upon to arbitrate, under an agreement between the cities, as to this differential it reached the very conclusion that was the outcome of that war.

The rate making of our railroads is done by an army of tens of thousands of men, picketing every part of the country. Often cars have to be returned empty over a long route. A rate that would pay the difference between hauling a car loaded and hauling it empty in such a case would pay the railroad. The traffic agent will often discover a commodity of low value in one part of the country that can be used in another part, and which, unless carried at a very low freight charge, cannot be carried at all. The transportation will pay the owner of the commodity something; it will also pay the railroad, and the commodity will be used to advantage by a distant consumer.

That traffic would be at once set in motion. The nicest curve, the strain of a swift train upon a bridge, the building of tunnels, can present no more technical questions to the engineer than are often faced by the thousands of traffic men who, in their eager search for tonnage, must consider rival markets and the relative demands of localities.

The flexibility of this system, where rates are fixed by economic laws, is infinitely preferable to the wooden system established by this bill, where, after a rate has been determined, you walk off and leave it a fixed and immutable fact for three years, unless a decree can be obtained from an overworked commission changing its decision and establishing a new rate. And by the time the authority would be conferred the necessity for a change of rate would probably have passed away.

The editor of the London *Statist,* in writing recently of a typical report—that of the American Great Northern Railroad —said the results shown in that report would fill the shippers of Great Britain with envy, in which country he declares that, notwithstanding the density of traffic, the people under tariffs directed by government have had very little reduction in a quarter of a century.

I have not understood that a popular government was adapted to carrying on to advantage, even on its own account, a business ordinarily conducted by private enterprise. From the time when the Pilgrims saved themselves from starvation only by abandoning the practice of raising corn in common and permitting each family to raise its own corn to the time when Massachusetts built the Hoosac Tunnel for about thirty millions, which it afterward sold for ten millions, or when Illinois completely bankrupted itself in building railroads and canals and conducting the banking business, the experiments of government on this continent in running business enterprises have uniformly been attended with great waste, if not uniformly with failure. But what may not be expected when a governmental agency manages business for which private individuals pay the bills? The pending measure not merely confers upon a commission the power of establishing a rate, but it makes them in important particulars general managers of the railroads.

The commission may by an order destroy the prosperity of a section of the country and may, in effect, impose restrictions upon commerce between States which it was the prime purpose of the Constitution to prevent. With the Government fixing rates, constituencies would inevitably carry their grievances into politics. You will have the different parts of the country knocking at the door of the national Government for favors, and intrigue and politics will rekindle the sectional jealousies that have now been happily allayed.

The railroads are not even permitted by this bill to give excursion rates between interstate points without first publishing a schedule thirty days in advance, or unless the commission makes a special dispensation or a general regulation permitting it. If that does not make a legislature of the commission, then the hitherto accepted notions of the function of legislation will need to be radically revised. The "Be it enacted by the Philippine Commission," which gives vitality to the laws of a people who are neither a citizen nor a foreign people, will be matched by the "Be it enacted by the Interstate Commerce Commission" in laws passed for the government of the people of the United States. If the making of railroad rates is a legislative function which can be delegated by calling it administrative, why may we not in a bill originating in the House confer upon a commission the power to fix tariff rates?

You propose to confer upon a mere human agency a practical task that would be superhuman. It is made their duty upon complaint to revise any and all the thousand millions or more freight rates in the country and an untold number of passenger rates. In addition to administrative functions, in defiance of the Constitution, you confer upon them, as I have said, judicial and legislative powers. They are to be vested with authority over a dozen billions of property and nearly a million and a half of employees. The enormous magnitude of the task is admitted, but there is to be an easy solution for it all.

We are to have a commission made up of prodigies and paid splendid salaries. The first Canal Commission were paid magnificent salaries, and yet they were unceremoniously deposed from office in scarcely a year after the President had appointed them. And the present Canal Commission, even with the aid of the $10,000 press agent, does not seem to command the admiring approval of the country. [Applause.] The President will be compelled to discover a new field if he finds the remarkable men that he undoubtedly desires to appoint. But, even if he should find them, he cannot endow them with immortality, and some day another President will appoint their successors, provided the board should not be abolished beforehand, and these successors may be made of common official clay.

But the difficulty will be not so much with the men as with the system. They will be unable to perform those impossible duties, and then their work is near the political line, across which they will inevitably drift, and, as has been attempted already in some of the most enlightened States in the Union, some day, acting under pressure or under the spur of ambition or of a desire to "do things," some great schedule is liable to be broken into atoms, and the commerce and industry of one section may be arbitrarily transferred to another. I believe that it is vastly better for the interests of the country, so long as rates can be fixed under the operation of economic laws, to reject the artificial method proposed by this bill, which makes of a commission a sort of Providence with power to create one city and destroy another.

A railroad rate is a fluctuating thing in the cost of its production, and from an economic standpoint no law can fairly fix a future rate which does not fix those material elements upon which the rate depends. As was pertinently asked by Mr. Benton, an able lawyer of my own State, if the States fixes the price that railroads are to receive for transportation, would it fix also the prices that go into the making of the cost of that transportation?

Will it fix the price of coal and ties and iron, the wages of labor, and those other varying elements of the cost of service, all of which absorb by far the greater part of the rates they receive? What prudent man would care to conduct a business with the Government fixing the price at which he should sell his product and leave him subject to the laws of supply and demand for everything he was compelled to buy? A rate that is reasonable to-day may be unreasonable to-morrow simply from the standpoint of the cost of production, and, under the present law, what is a just rate can always be determined at any given time by a court and jury whenever an individual claims that an unreasonable rate has been exacted. The question of unreasonableness can be tested in the courts. The juries will not hesitate to do as they have done in England, and the public will be protected. Is that not far more rational than the method you propose in this bill?

I cannot find an economic authority worthy of the name who, prior to one year ago, supported the theory of government-made rates for this country. After the President had promulgated the notion of rate making as a cure for rebates and discriminations, there appeared a crop of economists whose names had previously escaped the attention of the country, each with a patent nostrum guaranteed to work a cure on the President's plan. It was the heyday of the economic quack. We have even had it proposed, on high authority, that if it were discovered that one of many competing railroads, say, between Chicago and New York, had given low, secret rates, those rates should immediately be declared to be the reasonable rates although they would be forced upon the competing railroads, who were entirely innocent, and might be made bankrupt by them. That is a fair illustration of some of the economic theories that have been evolved upon this question.

It is said that the sentiment of the shippers is behind this rate-making proposition. With the exception of isolated individuals, whatever sentiment has been expressed in favor of this policy did not appear until it was proposed fourteen months ago and was authoritatively put forth as the remedy for the evils of discrimination and the giving of rebates. Even then, few complaints were made that the rates were too high, but that they were unequal. The great national convention of the boards of trade of the country, the most representative convention of business men that is held upon this continent, held in the city of Washington during the last month, adopted by a vote of ten to one a resolution with regard to rate fixing where the proceeding was to begin with the courts and end with them and was, in effect, a most emphatic condemnation of this policy.

And let me say to members on the other side of the House that this rate-fixing policy found no more uncompromising opponents in that convention than were found among the delegates from the great cities of the South. They saw its viciousness not merely from the traditional Democratic standpoint, but also from the position of self-interest. They saw the South standing exultant upon the threshold of a brilliant era of prosperity, just entering upon her career of industrial glory, and that the railroads will do for her what they have already done for the North and West unless the capital which would naturally be invested in them should be frightened away by this populistic hullabaloo in which you are joining.

It is contended that the policy of national rate making is necessary in order to avert governmental ownership. Either governmental ownership is an evil or it is not. If it is a wise policy, we should embark upon it, but, if it is an evil, the way to avert it is certainly not to take the first long step from economic rectitude that lies in its direction. Some very vicious policies have threatened our country and have been made dangerous by our taking the first step as a compromise. That is true with reference to inflation. It is emphatically true with reference to the coinage of silver, when the reason was given for taking repeated steps in coining or buying that metal that they were necessary to avert free coinage, until finally we had thousands of tons of silver stored in the treasury, and it was only by an almost unexampled act of presidential heroism that we did not go to the silver standard by the mere force of gravitation.

You do not propose to have the Government take the railroads by this bill, but you propose to have it take away from the control of the owners their only beneficial interest, which is the rate. It is said by the advocates of the bill, for purposes of prejudice or extenuation, that the securities of our railroads are bountifully watered. If true, that would be a relevant matter, perhaps, for the courts to consider when a shipper claimed that an unreasonable rate had been exacted. Certainly it furnishes no argument for the passage of this bill. It must be considered as a matter of denunciation and indulged in for the purpose of exciting prejudice. But let us see what the fact is. There is no higher authority upon the subject of railroads in the United States than President Hadley, of Yale, who first won distinction as professor of railroad economics in that university.

Last year he made the statement in a letter published in the Boston *Transcript*—and the letter was by no means generally in favor of our railroads—that the railroads of the country could not be duplicated for $50,000 a mile. In other words, counting their franchises as of no value, the material and labor necessary to duplicate them would be in the aggregate not less than ten and a half or eleven billion dollars, which is substantially the amount of their outstanding capitalization. Probably it would cost the Government, if it undertook to duplicate the work, twice that amount, and that would not include the enormous sums that have been thrown away in reconstruction, where, in order to do away with curves and grades, much original construction has been abandoned. If you count the franchises as nothing—and your railroads cannot be duplicated today by private enterprise for less than substantially the amount of the capitalization—how can you say that there is any material amount of water in their securities? In the capitalization of some railroads the nominal capital is not equal to the amount actually paid in. In some cases the stock was sold by the railroad at a high premium and the premium went into its treasury. Undoubtedly there are cases where railroads were built over a new country at great risk, where business was not developed, and the men furnishing the capital received stock bonuses.

These bonuses were offered openly in order to attract capital necessary for the work. I fancy you will hardly deny that the investor was fairly entitled to a chance for extra profit to pay him for the risk he assumed. If the railroad should turn out to be unprofitable, he might lose his entire investment. The man who paid $2 an acre for his land saw it increase, in many cases, by the building of the railroad, by the jeopardy of the money of other men, to $100 an acre. Are we to call the $98 water? Gentlemen are not heard to advance that theory.

JAMES R. MANN [Ill.].—The total amount of stocks and bonds is something over thirteen billion dollars, with a railroad mileage of over two hundred thousand miles. In Great Britain, together with continental countries, the total amount of mileage is considerably less than two hundred thousand miles, with a total capitalization of over eighteen billion dollars, so that the amount of capital we have invested per mile in this country is far less than the amount of capital per mile invested in the roads owned by the European governments or by private ownership there, notwithstanding the prevalent opinion that everything here is watered and everything there is not watered.

MR. McCALL.—Then it is said that money bonuses and land grants were given to encourage railroad building. That bonuses were given does not now impress me as of the greatest consequence, because the Government, or the people who gave them, did so from the standpoint of their own self-interest, and in many cases they profited richly by the building of the railroad; but I believe I am entirely within the truth when I say your bonuses and grants from national and local governments and individuals would not all combined pay 5 per cent. interest for a single year upon our railroad capitalization.

The great factor in the advancement of America has been the free play given for individual action. If at the outset we had tied up the energies of men by statutes and removed the spur of ambition from the inventor, the railroad builder, and the man of business, the progress of our country would have been far less marked than it has been during the last century. The American railroad managers, not through altruism or philanthropy, but by their individual genius, called into play by the beneficent influence of our free institutions, have been working out the destiny of the American people. They have helped powerfully to mold a vast and naturally diverse continent into one people. They have, in a double sense, bound together the most remote parts of the country by cords of steel. They have interwoven our interests and our hearts inextricably with the meshes of the iron net. And, if they are to receive your denunciation instead of your gratitude, then there is no species of property in the country which may not be plundered by law. There is a prescription that will almost infallibly work in forcing through such legislation. Fiercely denounce some Wall street magnate by name and then add some lurid declamation about insurance, and you could successfully rob any business in the country except farming, and if farmers were not so numerous they, too, would not escape.

We often make a mistake, I venture to say, in thinking that there is a genuine public opinion. Quite too often here we think there is a raging popular sentiment when it is only that we have a tendency of blood to our heads. The people do not send us here to enact every popular noise into law. [Applause.]

The fundamental question here, stripped entirely of sentiment, is whether we shall continue the American system, where the rates have inevitably sprung from the action of economic forces, or whether we shall adopt the expensive foreign system of government-made rates and have the management of your railroads thrown into politics, as if there were not already enough in this country upon which the politician can lay his felonious paws. [Applause.]

The Government may, if it desires, provide and operate at its own cost highways over which its citizens may travel and move their property, but it has not been a commonly exercised function to require citizens, at their own cost, to carry the persons and property of other citizens. It certainly has been a no less common function of government to fix the price of bread and to establish public granaries for corn. And, if either of these functions must be exercised, it should be under the most careful safeguards or it will be attended with grave danger. Burke says that certain of the Pope's territories, being obliged to furnish Rome and the state granaries with corn, were utterly ruined. Burke's illustration applies to the pending bill. It is not the least weighty of the objections against the bill that it will tend to corrupt the American people. It implies no defamation, but only a slight knowledge of human nature to see that you are holding out to them a temptation dangerous to their morality and dangerous also to the rights of private property. Your railroad securities are held in a comparatively small portion of the country, and the great mass of people scattered over the rest of the country, with little interest of ownership, will be interested in cheaper transportation. Will not the pressure of the greater mass of what you call public opinion have the same effect upon the national commission as it has had upon State commissions, against whose rates the courts have felt compelled to intervene? If so, you must remember that the constitutional safeguards against the national Government are fewer and less effective than against the State governments.

Can anyone justly say, in view of the history of our railroads and the splendid service they are rendering, that the time has arrived for our Government to embark upon so venturesome a policy? The great organizations of labor, with their admirable sense of self-preservation, clearly see the danger.

Your bill pretends to grant a judicial review of orders of the commission fixing rates, but it adopts the device of permitting this to the railroad on the peril of its life. If the railroad avails itself of your inestimable privilege of review and the courts decide in its favor, it costs the Government nothing and the railroad has the enjoyment of its former rate; but if, as has happened in two cases out of thirty-four, the court sustains the commission, the railroad, if it has not adopted the commission's rate, which may prove to be confiscatory, must pay a penalty to the Government of $5,000 per day, multiplying each day by the number of times the rate is enforced, a penalty that in some cases would mount into the millions. Do you call this a fair judicial review? Would there be any taint of a "square deal" in saying to a man whom a police justice had fined, "Yes; the justice may be wrong, as justices usually are, and you may appeal; but, if the higher court happens to sustain the justice, you shall lose your life?"

WILLIAM C. ADAMSON [Ga.].—Does not the gentleman think that the carriers can avoid all such risks by putting in force the rates fixed while they litigate to set them aside?

MR. McCALL.—Certainly; and that illustrates the point. You are trying to coerce the carrier on penalty of his life.

There may be evidence of a sense of justice in all this, but, if so, it is the sense of justice not of man, but of the hyena and the bear. The philosophy of it is that you may run for your life, but you are eaten if you stand, and you will be eaten if you are caught. Compared with the scheme of this bill there is a certain nobility in the policy of government ownership, wrong as I believe that policy to be. You carve our magnificent railroad system not as a feast fit for the gods, but hew it as a carcass fit for hounds.

We pass laws here with an easy optimism and a profound faith that, so great are the American people, their prosperity is proof even against vicious government. And so the two great parties, in playing the game of politics, sometimes vie with each other in pandering to the popular passion of the hour, and court the roar of the galleries rather than history's approving voice. Undoubtedly the splendid strength and youth of the American people are well-nigh unconquerable, but no state was ever yet so great that a persistence in evil courses could not lay it low. We may presume too far. If we are guilty of reckless and impulsive action here we may wreck the nation. If you will pardon an old fable: As the boy Phaëton, driving the horses of the sun, but lacking Apollo's darting glance and unerring touch of rein, did not follow the safe middle course, and thus wrought havoc to both the earth and sky; so by impulse and unsteadiness in driving this Washington chariot of ours, now steering too high and now too low, we may put our American constellations to flight, dry up the courses of our iron rivers, and make of our fertile prairies the sands of another Libya. [Applause.]

In some remarks which I submitted on this floor one year ago upon a similar measure I dwelt upon what I regard as much more important aspects of the proposed legislation than its economic features. I shall not repeat what I then said, but content myself with the barest reference. This bill makes an enormous contribution to what I regard as an evil of the times —the steady encroachment of the legislature upon liberty. Our boasted American freedom is being construed to mean the power to weld statutory fetters upon the individual—to impose upon our own selves a species of slavery. We sometimes say that we are restraining the individual in the interest of the other eighty millions, and we thus take away the rights of every individual man in the whole mass and sacrifice liberty to a mere abstraction. This is a condition abhorrent to the idea of the founders of the Republic, who knew that men had suffered as greatly from too much as from too little government; that they had thousands of times been punished by law for actions essentially virtuous, and so, taking care to safeguard that high kind of liberty which would protect the individual against the encroachments of the Government, they set our State upon the middle course that lies between anarchy and despotism. This tendency to too much government is not confined to one party, for I have observed that gentlemen who delight most in quoting the immortal Jefferson are sometimes the fondest of imposing those fetters upon the people. The aggregate achievement of individuals has made America. To my mind, American freedom is individual freedom. Give men as much liberty as you can grant consistently with order, and under this stimulus of freedom and order, and the right to enjoy what they accomplish and what they gain, this nation will keep magnificently moving on.

And then there is centralization. At the rate we are now moving it will not be long before we regulate everything and everybody from Washington. You cannot govern the whole universe from a single point and have a shred of liberty survive.

Instead of chasing every will-o'-the-wisp that shows itself upon somebody's horizon, let us then guide ourselves by the great first principles of the American Government. And, to return to this bill, you will have, in my opinion, a better railroad system and a better people if you safeguard in the courts the fundamental right of every man to a reasonable and equal rate and permit those rates to respond, as they have hitherto, to economic forces. In the conditions existing to-day I believe the people would shrink from governmental ownership, because of the expense and danger incident to governmental management. But that expense and that danger would certainly not be less when you make our Interstate Commission general managers of railroads built and owned and operated at the risk of private capital. [Loud applause.]

Gordon Russell [Tex.] supported the bill. He presented typical instances of the producer paying the freight, and remarked in conclusion:

The producer always pays the freight wherever he cannot fix the price of his product in the market.

It is the producers of this country who are complaining of the situation of affairs that now prevails. The producer has been the most patient of all the classes in this country. He has stood aside while others have received relief and has rarely complained.

He generally quietly shoulders his burdens. It may be that these people have not complained because their lives have been too much filled with toil to leave them time to investigate. But they are complaining now. Wrought to a pitch of indignation by years of wrong they are now demanding relief. It is the producer who is demanding it—the cattlemen of the West, the farmers of the South and great Middle West, the fruit growers of California, of Florida, Georgia, and Texas. They are the people who pride themselves upon our national power and grandeur.

The producer is entitled to our consideration. The agricultural producer is the man who converted this country from a borrower nation into a lender nation. It was of the producer that Mr. Secretary Wilson said that in the last sixteen years he had wiped out an adverse trade balance of $543,000,000 and had piled up five thousand million dollars to the international trade credits of the country. [Applause.] The producer does not believe that a fair share of this stupendous sum has remained in his hands. He knows he has labored, he knows he has made wealth, he knows he has economized, and now he comes to this body and asks us under the Constitution to exercise such efficient regulatory powers over the transportation companies as will protect him from rapacity and extortion. He has a right to ask it. He has stood aside while others had their day in court here. This House has protected labor in the cities from competition with the Chinese. This body has listened to the demands of labor for the eight-hour law, so far as Government works are concerned. This body has listened to the railway employees, and has given them the safety-appliance law. And now the producer claims his day in court. He has made out his case on the law and the facts, and, with malice toward none and charity for all, he relies upon the inexorable logic of the facts and appeals to the integrity of the people's representatives. [Prolonged applause.]

Robert L. Henry [Tex.] supported the bill.

Mr. Chairman, I would not do violence to property rights in this country by my vote or my voice. It is realized that these railway interests own and control property worth more than $12,000,000,000. At the same time they assess their property at less than $3,000,000,000. These great interests are given the right by law to tax the people on shipments of interstate traffic. Interstate traffic amounts to almost 80 per cent. of the freight shipped in America. These gigantic institutions are authorized to directly tax 80,000,000 people on these shipments. There is now no one standing between them and the shippers to control their avaricious greed. The people are being burdened by them without representation. Here in this bill we propose to pass a temperate law to control them, and to say that the people who are being thus assessed and oppressed are entitled to representation and hearing in some way. These great companies are not private institutions. They are not private property in the commercial sense of the word. These corporations are creatures of the law, having the breath of life breathed into them by the representatives of the people. They have no right to rise above the power that made them. We, as representatives of our constituents, should stand between them and these artificial beings, and see that justice is done to both. [Applause.] Better expression of the nature of their public franchises cannot be found than to quote the strong language used by Justice Harlan in the Nebraska case:

A railroad is a public highway, and none the less so because constructed and maintained through the agency of a corporation deriving its existence and powers from the State. Such a corporation was created for public purposes. It performs a function of the State. Its authority to exercise the right of eminent domain and to charge tolls was given primarily for the benefit of the public. It is under governmental control, though such control must be exercised with due regard to the constitutional guaranties for the protection of its property. It cannot be, therefore, admitted that a railroad corporation maintaining a public highway under the authority of the State may fix a rate with a view solely to its own interests and ignore the rights of the public. But the rights of the public would be ignored if rates for the transportation of persons or property on a railroad are exacted without reference to the fair value of the property used for the public or the fair value of the services rendered, but in order simply that the corporation may meet operating expenses, pay the interest on its obligations, and declare a dividend to its stockholders.

We are willing to square our conduct here to-day in enacting this law by this temperate and just language of the Supreme Court. If we are anarchists, communists, and socialists, as the gentleman from Pennsylvania says [Mr. Sibley], so are the judges of the Supreme Court. [Applause.] Well may we be thankful that we live in a government where the representatives of the people can read the plain language of the Constitution and see that it confers upon their servants the power of authorizing a commission to stand between them and these creatures of the law that have grown so powerful that they defy the very mandates of the constituted authorities. And we can congratulate ourselves that those representatives are brave enough to do their duty in the face of criticism and slander. [Applause.] Neither in my individual nor representative capacity would I lay violent hands upon the railroads. Their benefits are too great, their services have been too useful. We realize what they have done for this country, and also we know what we have done for them. They have aided in building up the waste

places all over the Republic. In my own State, the great State
of Texas, they have been joint pioneers with the hardy citizens
who went to that empire when it was but a wilderness. Still,
we have helped them there and given them millions of acres
of land and hundreds of thousands of dollars as donations.
We have never mistreated them in our State, but our people
have undertaken to control them in Texas, and have succeeded
as far as their domestic operations are concerned, and we have
not injured them. We established a railroad commission and
placed at its head the author and founder of the Interstate
Commerce Commission idea, the old Roman, John H. Reagan,
who has gone to his reward and left a name that is a household
word not only in the State of Texas, but throughout the length
and breadth of the land wherever patriotism is revered and
purity of purpose appreciated. [Applause.]

Mr. Chairman, there were dire predictions made in my State
when we established the commission, and it was said that we
had retarded the building of railroads, that we were standing
in the way of progress. But since our commission was established we have not laid violent hands upon the railroads of
Texas. The records show that since our commission was created
Texas has constructed more miles of railway than any other
State in the Union, and they have prospered more than ever
in all their previous history there, thus exhibiting the beneficent
effect of such legislation. [Applause.] We did not confer
upon the commission merely the simple power of establishing
a reasonable rate where one was found to be unreasonable.
We gave the commission the broad power to establish tariffs
upon the whole body of railway rates in Texas. The railroads
contested the law and said that Texas was confiscating their
property. They took their cases to the Supreme Court of the
United States. They litigated every point and contested every
inch of the ground.

The Supreme Court of the United States, in deciding in
favor of the Texas law, never once referred to the constitution
of Texas, but announced its decision on the broad proposition
that the State had the right to create a commission to perform
an act purely administrative. Mr. Chairman, from the Granger
cases, which were decided in 94 United States Reports, on
down to the last commission case, it has been favorably decided,
and in every instance all the appellate courts in the various
States of the Union and the Supreme Court have marched right
ahead, dismissing the proposition that such laws are confiscatory,
anarchistic, socialistic, and have unhesitatingly decided that such

power resided in the State legislatures and the Congress of the United States and was as old as the governments exercising it. If it has come to pass in this country that these great combinations, owning more than $12,000,000,000 of the property of the nation, are above the Constitution and the Supreme Court of the land, it is high time that we were reforming our Government and adopting an amendment to the Constitution in order to protect ourselves from these gigantic corporate agencies. [Applause.]

Mr. Henry, indeed, thought the bill not sufficiently drastic.

We should amend this bill, restoring the penalties of the interstate commerce act which inflicted the punishment of imprisonment for its violation. We should so amend it as to make it possible to punish the great railway officials, corporation officers, and agents who wilfully and flagrantly violate the law and put them in the penitentiary, as well as the small clerk who happens to make a false entry in the books, perhaps at the dictation of his chief. Wide-open prison doors alone will deter them. Every man on the other side of this House says that rebates are criminal. If we believe what we say, why not enact a law that meets the demands of the people? Why do we hesitate to go as far as conservatism and justice demand? Are we afraid of the influences? If they have grown so powerful that the Representatives who breathe the breath of life into them cannot control them, it is high time that our system of government be reformed. With patriotic voice let us say that we are ready to do our duty. [Applause.]

John J. Esch [Wis.] supported the bill. He recounted the results which followed the establishment of the Interstate Commerce Commission:

Under the interstate commerce law of 1887, with the powers which that law gave to the commission, great good was done and many of the evils which had existed theretofore were in large part abated. Business became more stableized, because rates became more fixed and certain. The railroads themselves, conscious that the commission had the power, did not violate the law, but evinced a desire to obey it in spirit and letter.

In 1897 the commission lost its power to fix the rate for the future, but it did not on that account become a worthless body. It still had duties to perform, and still had the power of investigation; it still could hear complaints as to rates and determine as to their reasonableness, but had no power to make its orders effective. Its investigations of the Joint Traffic Association, the Northern Securities merger, of the coal strike, of the beef trust, and numerous other unlawful combinations have resulted in focusing public attention upon them and securing the evidence for their successful prosecution. Although it suffered a loss of power, it has justified its cost to the Government. Even the decision in the maximum rate case did not result in a useless body. But, Mr. Chairman, it is true that the fact that the commission lost its power to fix the rate for the future and to enforce the execution thereof diminished the respect and wholesome fear which railroad companies had for the commission. They no longer put their entire case before the commission in the event of a complaint and a hearing. It has been said on this floor, and has been often repeated, that the Interstate Commerce Commission rarely if ever has hit the mark in cases of appeal to the Supreme Court.

Mr. Esch replied to the criticisms made by Mr. McCall of President Roosevelt's message on fixing railroad rates.

I wish to say that the President's declaration of a year ago asking Congress to confer "on the commission the power to revise rates and regulations, the revised rate to go into effect and stay in effect unless and until the court of review reverses it," was not a *non sequitur*. There were members of the Committee on Interstate and Foreign Commerce who for a year before that message had been urging upon that committee and upon Congress legislation to increase and enlarge the powers of the commission. In the Fifty-sixth Congress Senator Cullom introduced a bill giving to the commission enlarged powers practically along the line of the bill under discussion to-day. His bill was succeeded in the Fifty-seventh Congress by the Nelson-Corliss bill, upon which hearings were had. That, in turn, was succeeded by the Quarles-Cooper bill in the Fifty-eighth Congress, upon which hearings were had; to be in turn succeeded by the bill which my distinguished colleague from Michigan and myself had the honor to present at the last session. That, in turn, is now succeeded by the bill which we are now considering, presented by the able and distinguished chairman of our committee.

Does all this show a *non sequitur?* Was it a chance thought of the President when he called the attention of the American people to the necessity of this legislation? No; this question had been agitating the minds of the people in various sections of the country for years. The President knew, and for some time must have known, the nature, extent, and volume of this agitation. He knew, as some people of the East do not even yet know, how, especially in the Middle West, the birthplace of national ideas, the birthplace of Republican policies, rate legislation was a burning question, and one which the people, through their legislatures, were settling in the form of law. [Loud applause.] Is it a *non sequitur* to say that the President "suddenly saw a great light" and therefore inserted this recommendation in his message of December, 1904, when all the papers of the land, when more than a thousand industrial, commercial, and shipping bodies throughout the land had sent petitions, and when more than twelve State legislatures had sent memorials to Congress asking for this identical legislation? No. The President well knew the sentiment of the American people and well knew the extent of the demand back of this legislation. The President of the United States is not narrow; his knowledge of the wants and wishes of his countrymen is not confined to the Atlantic seaboard. He is not "cribbed, cabined, and confined" in his ideas. He knows the United States; he knows every State in the Union as no other President ever has; he became conscious of the popular will, and so made that declaration in his message of 1904. [Loud applause.] And great good did the message do. It gave life to the whole subject of rate control; it gave hope and courage to the friends of this proposition. The first definite results came in the last Congress, when the House took favorable action. The President is with the people in the demand for this legislation, and this House is about to put, so far as it can, his recommendation in the form of a law. He will sign this bill if it reaches him.

On February 5 Charles E. Littlefield [Me.] opposed the power given in the bill to the commission to fix rates and compel the railroads to accept them.

Do I want to turn over to the tender mercies of a political commission of seven the existence of the cotton industries of New England? Within two weeks I have had it stated to me by distinguished gentlemen who believe in this legislation and are anxious to see it prevail, that they hope under its terms to destroy the preferential charges existing in favor of these New

England industries in order that the industries located near the raw material can have the benefit of what they call their natural proximity thereto. They conceded that by this indirect method they expect to transfer the cotton manufacturing industry from the North to the South. I do not propose by my vote to put in the hands of seven men the question as to whether there shall still be a Fall River, a Lawrence, a Lowell, a Manchester, a Biddeford, or a Lewiston.

Mr. Littlefield also called attention to other, and more autocratic, powers granted the commission, in the case of mining, agriculture, manufacture, or merchandising, where there was no appeal from the decision of the commission.

Only the railroad can interfere. Manufacturers, farmers, miners, and merchants do not exercise any public franchise. The Constitution does not guarantee them a reasonable return for the amount of money invested in their industries or ventures. They have to fight for their lives in the open market, and this commission is to sit on the valve that controls the circulation without which they cannot live. I submit to the candid consideration of this committee, Mr. Chairman, that all of these interests are vastly more vital and more potent than the mere interest of the transportation companies themselves. Our industries furnish the vital lifeblood. The railroads simply the veins and arteries through which it circulates. The railroads have an opportunity to go into the court and protect their rights and preserve their existence under the power of injunction, but these industries have not.

Mr. Littlefield criticised the bill as making the commission a political one, dependent wholly upon the President, removable by him at any time, without cause, and without review of his action.

Let me submit this proposition. Theodore Roosevelt may not always be President of the United States. According to his repeated declarations, he will be President for the balance of this term and no longer. And after that some other gentleman will be President of the United States. What is possible? I can imagine some man as President of the United States in whose hands I would not want to see vested the power to control this commission of seven men, four to be members of one political party. How long would it take a President with a complacent Senate to remove enough to make four of his political party? And what if that political party happened to be the Populist party?

I have in my mind the name of a gentleman that I would not want to leave the Constitution of this tribunal in the hands of. It would be perfectly open to him to have four that represented his peculiar views and his extraordinary vagaries in connection with the Government of this great country. More than that, it would be open to him arbitrarily to remove the other three. But he would not need to do this. Three is a majority of a quorum, and your act is so constituted and the possibilities are such that it is open to have three men, viciously inclined, take the mining, manufacturing, and agricultural and mercantile interests of this country, and, through the medium of that vital transportation upon which they exist and without which they can not live, throttle them until they either waver and die or render the tribute to Cæsar which is necessary to enable Cæsar to control the political destinies of the Republic.

To-day we have agitation and excitement and prejudice arrayed against the great transportation interests of this country. Our friends of the West, inspired by their exasperation and out of just resentment, cry out, "Crucify him! Crucify him!" and the more extreme this legislation the greater the gratification.

I warn you that, if we weakly quail before this storm and turn over these vast interests bound hand and foot to this fallible political tribunal without recourse or appeal, when the disastrous results which are well-nigh sure to follow the exercise of this tremendous uncontrollable power shall be visited upon a helpless people, that same people will turn again and rend you because you have been false to your trust as representatives of the American people. Inspired by passion, prejudice, smarting under the sting of resentment, because there are wrongs that have not been redressed, they may now bless us, but then, with equal facility and vastly greater zeal, they will rise up and curse you. They now applaud. Then we shall be *anathema maranatha.* [Loud and long-continued applause.]

Oscar W. Underwood [Ala.] supported the bill. He opposed particularly the argument that it would result in the decrease of wages of railroad employees.

The wage per hour of the average workman in the United States since 1895 has increased about 19 per cent. The average of the increase in wages paid trainmen in that period has been less than 15 per cent. In 1895 the purchasing power in the retail price of food of the weekly wages of employees was 100.6 and in 1904 was 100.4, a decrease of 0.2 per cent, and, as railroad wages have not increased in that period as much as general wages, it is demonstrated beyond cavil that railroad employees are not receiving as great a wage, measured in the purchasing power of their money to buy food, as they did ten years ago, and yet within that time the railroads have experienced an era of prosperity never before known in the world.

Now, what I contend is this—that the railroad employees, so far as their wages are concerned, will not be affected in any way by this legislation; that the wages of railroad employees in this country are maintained solely by their safe and conservative labor organizations; that the only real interest that railroad men have in the pending legislation is that of the general public in its opposition to present conditions, which allow the great monopolistic corporations of this country special privileges in the way of rebates, private car rental, switch-track pooling, and other devices, through which they receive the benefit of discriminating freights, whereby they are enabled to drive their competitors from the country's markets and absolutely control the prices the public must pay for many of the necessities of life.

Mr. Chairman, I am not in favor of the Government interfering with the business of the country. I believe every man should be allowed freedom to work out his own destiny, but I do believe that the railroad highways of the country are as necessary to the life of commerce as the air we breathe is to the life of the human body. I believe the air should be free to all, and I believe the opportunities of commerce should be free to all. This can be only when every man has equal rights and equal opportunity to seek his markets along the public highways with every other man. That is not the case to-day. This bill seeks to abolish discrimination and injustice. It provides a fair tribunal to see that all men are given an equal chance, that only just and fair rates are charged. The bill is not all I want, but it goes in the right direction and I support it for that reason. It stands for fair play, it stands against monopoly, it stands for the right against the wrong, it stands for the people against the trusts. It means the dawning of a new day in our commercial prosperity, when industry and thrift may march unshackled to the marts of trade. [Applause.]

On February 6 William Sulzer [N. Y.] proposed to organize a new department of government—that of transportation—with representation in the Cabinet, and empowered to investigate railroad conditions, fix rates, etc.

On February 7 W. Bourke Cockran [N. Y.] supported the bill.

Mr. Chairman, if gentlemen would only pause to realize the exact scope and purpose of this bill, they would see at once that many of the objections urged against it are both irrelevant and extravagant. The object of this measure is simply to compel companies engaged in railroad transportation between the different States to render the people whose franchises they operate efficient service—which means impartial service—at reasonable rates. To accomplish that result, any citizen who considers himself aggrieved by excessive charges is authorized by this measure to complain before a board empowered, after full inquiry, to decide whether the rate charged him is fair or unfair, and if unfair to substitute a rate which will be proper and just for the one found to have been onerous and oppressive. That is the entire scope and purpose of the measure which has been denounced with such brilliant rhetoric from the other side of this Chamber as a step toward the public operation of railroads, leading inevitably to socialism. Sir, this plain statement of the object and purpose of the proposal now before us must be enough to satisfy anyone not wholly captive to prejudice and passion that, far from this being a measure tending to establish public ownership of railways, it is the only means by which public ownership of them can be averted. [Applause.] Far from its being a socialist demonstration, it is an effective barrier against the rising tide of socialism which gentlemen seem to discern and to dread, because it takes from the socialist the most plausible argument that he can advance to impeach the existing order of society and to support his own theory of government. [Applause.] Far from its being an attempt to reduce the earnings of railroads, it is a measure to increase them, and at the same time provide that these steadily increasing revenues will reach owners of capital by which railways are operated, instead of being diverted largely

X—30

to the pockets of faithless managers, who plunder stockholders and people with cheerful but rigorous impartiality. [Laughter and applause.]

Mr. Chairman, the misapprehension of this bill which has so largely marked this discussion springs mainly, I think, from confusion of thought as to the precise relations between companies engaged in transportation and the State. Some gentlemen speak of railroads as if they were private enterprises. Other gentlemen seem to consider railways purely public enterprises, with which the State has plenary powers to deal as if they were public property. If either assumption were sound, the argument based upon it would be unanswerable.

Gentlemen who regard railways as public property are not wholly right; neither are those who consider them private property wholly wrong. Railroads are neither exclusively public nor exclusively private enterprises. They partake of both characters.

Under our industrial and political system there are two elements entering into a railway service. One is the right to operate it—the right sometimes to use public property; the right always to take private property for corporate purposes— what is known as the franchise. The other is the capital, in the form of lands, rails, locomotives, buildings, and other property by which the franchise is placed in operation. The franchise, the power to take anything I possess which may be necessary or useful to the operation of a great enterprise— the power to drive me from the house in which I was born, from the hearthstone near which I have lived, from the place where I had hoped to die—that power is an attribute to sovereignty. The right to control it must, therefore, always remain with the sovereign, that is to say, with the State—the Government. On the other hand, the capital by which the franchise is operated is the property of individuals who contribute it. It is private property dedicated to a public service. A railway, then, is a public function, the administration of which is intrusted to a private agency. But, whether it be administered by a private agency or by government directly through its own officers, a railway never ceases to be a public function. [Applause.]

Now, from this what follows? What are the reciprocal rights and duties of the capital by which railways are operated, and of the people whom the railways are chartered to serve— of the sovereign whose franchise is the basis of the enterprise and the individuals who own the property by which it is made

effective? Clearly, the railway, in return for the special opportunities of profit which it enjoys, owes to the sovereign efficient
service, and the sovereign—that is to say, the people—are bound
in return by every principle of justice, of prudence, of self-
interest, to protect, preserve, and maintain in absolute security
the capital—the private property—dedicated to this public
service. Stated in the narrowest compass, the railway owes
the people the most efficient service within the reach of human
endeavor, consistent with the security of the capital—the private
property—embarked in it.

Now, what is meant by security of property? What does
it involve? What are its essential features? What rights
does it embrace? While it appears to be conceded on all sides
that a rate which compelled a railway company to do business
at a loss would impair the value of the capital embarked in
it and therefore would be a taking of property without due
process of law, which the courts must condemn as confiscatory,
some gentlemen opposite appear to think that a rate which
did not entail actual loss in operation, but which nevertheless
was so low as to prevent any possibility of earning profits on
the capital by which the railway is operated would be within
the constitutional powers of Congress (acting directly or through
a commission) to impose, and therefore beyond the power of
the courts to correct. A little reflection will show these gentlemen that they misconceive radically and underrate grievously
the nature and extent of the security guaranteed by our Constitution to owners of property. Security of property means
not merely the safety of its body—the right to hold its *corpus*
intact—it means the right of the owner to employ it for a
profit, or what he conceives to be a profit, provided the specific
purpose be not in itself illegal. Unless property can be employed at a profit it won't be employed at all, and unless it
can be employed it is not worth holding. A right of property
which did not embrace the right to employ it for the profit
of the owner would be a mere right of custody, utterly value-
less, a burden rather than a benefit, a penalty rather than a
privilege, a hollow mockery, a trap for the unwary, baited
by delusive and misleading words. Such a conception of
property is at utter variance with all our jurisprudence, and
any law based on it that we might pass would most assuredly
be set aside by judicial decree. [Applause.]

A rate which even though it did not entail a loss in operation—that is to say, an actual impairment of the property
invested in railways—yet was so low as to prohibit profit, would

be confiscatory—confiscatory of an essential element—the most important element in the right of property. The idea that such a rate would be tolerated by the same courts which, uniformly and without exception, have set aside confiscatory rates is not a conclusion reached by logical processes, but a figment of the mind, a delusion of ardent imaginations, of fervent patriotism, and other excellent qualities stimulated to extravagance by improvident use of sonorous but misleading and sometimes nonsensical phrases. [Laughter and applause.]

A more serious criticism, Mr. Chairman, is that advanced by gentlemen who, conceding the right of the Government to exact from railways efficient service at reasonable rates, yet question the power—the intellectual capacity—of an administrative board or of any body not composed of railway experts to determine intelligently what constitutes a just and reasonable rate. This, of course, is equivalent to recognizing the existence of a right in government which it is powerless to assert and of a duty imposed on it which it is powerless to discharge. Mr. Chairman, I have never yet found myself compelled to admit incapacity or imbecility in government—at least, in this Government. [Applause.]

To ascertain and determine what is a just rate in every instance we have only to bear in mind the essential nature of the relations between these agencies and the public whom they serve—what the corporation owes to the people and what government owes to the corporation.

The rate which insures to every man the service for which he pays at the minimum cost consistent with safety of the property employed in rendering it—the rate which allows no man to enjoy any service at the expense of another—that is the rate which must ultimately be held the fair and the reasonable one. No other is consistent with justice, and therefore no other can be permanent in this country. [Applause.]

Mr. Chairman, in the light of these principles, I ask the committee to examine the actual operation of these corporations and measure the difference between the service to which the people are entitled and the service which they have actually received.

It is a matter of universal knowledge, not questioned here or elsewhere, that this service, which should be impartial, has been governed by favoritism and discrimination. I do not think there is a single locality in the country where rates have been excessive to everyone. Wherever charges for transportation have been unreasonably high to the general public, they have

always been unreasonably low to some favorite of the railway.
And this, sir, is not to benefit the corporation, but to benefit
some dishonest manager at the expense both of the railway
and of the public. Between a railway honestly administered
and the people there never can be a conflict of interest. A
railway cannot prosper except as the country through which
it passes prospers. Its revenues and earnings depend on the
volume of business in the community that it serves. Anything
that restricts the volume of business restricts the revenues of
the company and impairs the value of its capital. But the
interest of the company is not necessarily the interest of the
manager, who often profits by betraying it, and at the same
time oppressing the community. The means most usually employed for this plunder of the stockholders and the public is
the fixing of high charges for transportation to the community
and then secretly giving lower rates to favored individuals. The
business of the favorite is increased enormously, but the whole
volume of transportation is diminished. The railway would
reap larger profits from serving a hundred men, each doing
a business of $1,000 a week, than in serving one man doing a
business of $50,000 a week. But if the rates are made high
to the general public, and, at the same time, one man be afforded
transportation under such favorable conditions that all his
rivals will be crushed, his business will, of course, be multiplied
several times in volume, but, at the same time, the general
business of the road will necessarily be diminished. His
profits would be swelled enormously, while the revenues of the
company available for dividends would be reduced. The railway manager who shared the profits of the favorite would be
enriched, while the railway would be injured, and the stockholders who trusted their property to him would be plundered.
And this, sir, explains why this species of favoritism has been
so widely prevalent. It is safe to say that no rebate has ever
been enjoyed by one man at the expense of competitors where
the fruits of the plunder have not been shared by the railway
officials through whose corruption the favors have been obtained.
[Applause.]

The men who control transportation facilities and abuse
their authority have established a power greater than the
Government. The favor of a railway manager is more important to a man engaged in commerce than the favor of the
President, of both Houses of Congress, of the judiciary, of the
army, of the navy, and of all combined. Government, exercising all the power of all its departments, can only protect

a man; a corrupt railway manager can enrich him. Larger
fortunes have been established by illegitimate railway favors
than by the highest ability in legitimate industry ever possessed
by any man in the world. As all these favors are granted to
favorites at the expense of victims, as they are tributes levied
on the industry of many for the benefit of a few, this railway
corruption has resulted in the demoralizing spectacle of plunder
made more profitable than industry. Where discrimination has
been grossest, corruption the most depraved, the most cynical,
the most unblushing, there the profits of the criminal have
been most extensive. And the courts have signally failed to
prevent this corruption, while they have been singularly effective
in protecting fortunes which have been the fruits of these
crimes.

Rockefeller, at once the richest and the most despised of
the whole population, has long been the chief beneficiary of
this corruption, and his fortune is the chief monument of its
extent. [Applause.] Unfortunately he stands not alone; he
is but the type of a band growing ever more numerous and
more dangerous. These men have established themselves as
a privileged class. They are so far above and beyond the law
that they plead the magnitude of their crimes as a reason for
arresting the pursuit of justice. Have we not seen within a
few days the adoption of a resolution by this very House
propounding an inquiry concerning the relations between two
great railway systems, which it was our duty to formulate,
create a disturbance in the market which almost amounted to
a panic? Do we not hear it urged as a reason against pressing
the inquiry, which the law enjoins upon us, that to persist in
it will uncover extensive violations of the law which can result
only in a profitless scandal, since the community would prefer
submission to these crimes rather than pay the frightful cost of
redressing them? Is not this a cynical admission that this
Government, organized to establish justice, cannot afford to
do justice, even when injustice is palpable—that under the
protection of laws intended to foster industry criminals have
grown so powerful that instead of submitting to the law they
can treat with the law—nay, defy and command it?

It is no exaggeration to say that in all those great States
the debates and contentions which on the surface appear to
be the competition of politicians for leadership are usually but
screens behind which different financiers contend for the control
of some political machine which they consider a useful instrument in the prosecution of their enterprises. No man can be

considered an eminent financier nowadays unless he counts the leader of a political machine among his followers, his clients, his retainers, his dependents. [Applause.]

Sir, do I exaggerate the influence, the powers which these men wield? Am I extravagant when I describe them as a privileged class enjoying immunities unknown to the law, exercising powers above the law and in spite of it? Must we submit to the domination of this class, or should we make an effort at least to bring it within subjection to the laws?

The gentleman from Maine [Mr. Littlefield] says the courts can afford redress for all these evils by simply enforcing existing law. If the courts had held uniformly that all men were entitled to service by railways on equal terms and if they had used their processes and all their powers to facilitate discovery so that any man who had reason to believe himself aggrieved could ascertain the terms on which all other men were served— the rates they were charged—these abuses would never have arisen and the demand for this legislation would never have been heard. But, as a matter of fact, the courts have not prevented these abuses. When have the courts undertaken to prevent, much less to punish, any financial exploit by which railway managers have enriched themselves enormously at the expense of the stockholders who intrusted them with their property and of the community who depended upon their capacity and fidelity? What feat of spoliation by syndicates or financiers has been interrupted by judicial process?

Doubtless the case of the Northern Securities Company occurs to some gentlemen. Doubtless they are asking themselves now if the judgment declaring the organization of that company to be a conspiracy did not constitute a judicial interference with the consummation of an illegal financial operation. Sir, there can be no stronger proof that a privileged class exists among us, no more striking illustration of the extent to which these privileges are tacitly recognized by the courts themselves, than this very case, so often quoted as an evidence that the law is still capable of regulating and governing the conduct of all citizens, even of men mighty in finance.

You will remember that the Northern Securities Company was organized avowedly for the purpose of placing control of several railroads in the hands of two groups of financiers. The Attorney-General of the United States, by direction of the President, instituted proceedings in the courts praying that this attempt to reduce control of several railways to such a narrow compass that it could be held by two groups of financiers

be adjudged a conspiracy in restraint of trade under the
Sherman anti-trust law.

In rendering judgment on this suit the Supreme Court declared:

> In our judgment the evidence fully sustains the material allegations
> of the bill and shows a violation of the act of Congress, in so far as it
> declares illegal every combination or conspiracy in restraint of com-
> merce among the several States and with foreign nations and forbids
> attempts to monopolize such commerce or any part of it.

Here, then, we find the organization of the Northern Securities Company declared a conspiracy by solemn judgment of the
court, and the persons who promoted it were therefore conspirators—criminals—specifically denounced as such by the law.
Yet, what was the actual outcome of this decision?

The court directed that the stock held by the Northern
Securities Company be distributed, but the method of distribution was so ordered that when the judgment was put in actual
force the Harriman group was found to have been eliminated
and the Morgan group was left in supreme control. The attempt
to reduce control of these companies to two groups was pronounced a conspiracy, and the actual result of the decision
was to reduce the control of them to one group. The object
of the conspiracy instead of being defeated was more effectually
accomplished. And that was not all. The stock of the company, which was selling at about 100 when the suit began,
sold at 160 when the adverse decision was rendered. Its
capital stock was $400,000,000, and therefore, this decision, that
is generally supposed to have destroyed the corporation, enriched its promoters by $240,000,000. Conspiracy was found
by the court; the conspirators were identified by name in its
decision, but the object of the conspiracy, instead of being
defeated, is more completely effected by the decision itself,
and the authors of the scheme, instead of being punished or
even questioned, walked out of court, not weighed down by
its fetters, nor staggering under its sentence, but joyfully
bearing a golden burden of $240,000,000, perfectly satisfied that
the court which pronounced their conduct to be a conspiracy
would use all its powers to protect them in holding and enjoying
the fruits of their crime. [Applause.]

Now contrast this enrichment of men found guilty under
the Sherman law with the treatment of Eugene V. Debs, who
was not even accused of transgressing a criminal statute. The
violation of an injunction order was the head and front of

his offending. At most, he committed a civil offence. Although, when we contrast the penalty which followed it with the rewards heaped on these men whom the decision of the Supreme Court adjudged to be criminals, we must conclude that if his offence was civil his treatment was decidedly uncivil. [Laughter and applause.] There is no doubt about what happened to him. He was not punished by mere animadversion or judicial denunciation. He was committed to jail. His body was taken into custody. He was confined in a cell; the bolts were turned on him. He ate the prison fare. Prison wardens controlled his movements. He expiated to the last moment by confinement and discredit—so far as imprisonment can inflict discredit—the violation of an injunction order. Tell me that Debs stands equal before the law with Messrs. Morgan, Harriman, Hill, *et al.*, and you say that which mocks common experience and common sense. [Applause.]

Now, what objections have been offered to this bill aside from the suggestion that the courts can of themselves accomplish the object at which it aims without any further legislation?

The gentleman from Maine [Mr. Littlefield] tells us that he is opposed to this measure because the Interstate Commerce Commission might become dominated by populists, by socialists, by enemies of property, who, incapable of appreciating the rather delicately balanced rights of the community and the stockholders in railway enterprises, would pervert the powers conferred upon them to the oppression of all right and the injury of all property. But, surely, sir, if that objection have any weight, it is an argument against all government. Are we to abolish courts because judicial decisions have been sometimes bought and sold, and that by the most learned and accomplished judges? Are we to abolish the Presidency because its powers may be perverted by some incumbent to an ignoble purpose?

Why, sir, it is the argument of anarchy itself. It is based upon precisely the same premises and is marked by the same *non sequitur.* The anarchist argues that, because all governmental powers may be abused, therefore they will be abused—because government is a potential source, therefore it is an inevitable source of tyranny and demoralization. Sir, this argument of anarchy, as we have heard it here, is new in nothing except in the theater of its delivery. When we consider the place in which it has been put forth with such dialetical skill and rhetorical brilliancy, we cannot help feeling that from this moment it must assume a new weight and force in the estimation of mankind. It has acquired the enormous advantage of having been delivered, not to a motley throng of long-haired enthusiasts by some nameless, hare-brained rhetorician in the back room of some obscure café, but by a conspicuous ornament of American citizenship on the floor of the American Congress to the sanest and most conservative legislative body in Christendom. [Applause.]

The gentleman from Massachusetts [Mr. McCall] tells us he will go as far as anyone in attempting to punish rebates. But, while his disposition and his capacity are inspiring, while he is willing of purpose, sound of mind, and vigorous of muscle, eager to go any distance in pursuit of this wrong, there is an insuperable difficulty in the way of utilizing for the public weal his eminent capacity and excellent disposition—we cannot get him to start. [Laughter.]

Sir, if his contentions were sound; if it be true that, under our present system of transportation, government is incapable of affording a remedy for oppressive exactions or unequal rates, then we must change the system. There is no other alternative. For the American people to remain helpless and submissive under injustice would be intolerable and inconceivable. [Applause.]

I know it has already occurred to some on this floor and to many throughout the country that public ownership, or rather public operation, of railways is the only adequate remedy against this form of oppression. And, here, sir, I deem it proper to say that I am not one of those who believe the operation of public utilities by government is always and necessarily socialism. I entreat gentlemen to mark that word *"necessarily."* I say it is not *necessarily* socialism, because, while the direct operation by government of any enterprise essentially public is not necessarily socialistic, the grounds on which this policy is urged are nearly always distinctly socialistic. Bearing in mind that a railway is always a public function, whether it be administered by government through its own officers, or by a private agency empowered and employed by government for that purpose, it must be perfectly clear that, what government can empower an agent or corporation to do, government can do itself. Nay more, government would be bound to perform the public service itself if a private agency could not be found to perform it. The only ground on which the employment of a private agency to administer a function essentially public can be justified at all is that the private agency can administer it better, that is to say, it can give better, cheaper, and more efficient service than the government through its own officers.

I am opposed to public operation of railways for the very simple reason that in the nature of things it is not possible for governments to administer them as efficiently as they are administered now by private agencies—even though the service actually rendered to the people is far below the standard of efficiency to which they are entitled. The reasons for this belief are, in my judgment, conclusive, but the time now at my disposal will not permit a full statement of them. At this moment I can do no more than point out that there is not on record a single instance in which a public utility administered by government has resulted in as good service as where it has been administered by private agencies. The post-office is often cited as a striking instance of efficient service by government. What improvement in transportation or business methods has ever been developed by a post-office through its own operations? Where has a single invention or discovery been added to the resources of civilization by the administration of a postal system?

In many countries the railways are a feature of the public service administered by public officers.

When has any important device for improvement in travel been developed in the administration of a railway by government?

All improvements in travel, in transportation, in the transmission of intelligence, have been developed by private agencies authorized to operate public franchises by some government— most of them by this Government. If the control of transportation were transferred now from private agencies to public officers, the effect would be to impair its efficiency, and at the same time increase the cost of it. If this were understood by the people, proposals for public operation of railways would be robbed of all popularity. Nobody would be found advocating a policy of poorer service at higher rates. Why, then, are these proposals popular, or supposed to be? Because they are always accompanied by a promise or suggestion—a covert hint —that if the railways of the country be operated by Government the rates charged for transportation will be reduced, no matter what the service may actually cost. Now, if anybody be given a service for less than it cost, as we have already seen, the deficiency must be made up by excessive charges in other directions. Some men must be compelled to contribute from the fruits of their industry to the expenses of others, and that is socialistic, it is undemocratic, it is un-American, unjust, intolerable, among a people where equality is the universal aspiration and justice the universal passion. [Applause.] Thus it is that public ownership, while not essentially or necessarily socialistic, is always conveyed with a suggestion of socialism, and that suggestion is the sole source of its popularity. [Applause.]

If public operation of railways, far from redressing the evils of which we complain, would aggravate them, is there no remedy? Are we helpless before these wrongs—their perpetrators and beneficiaries? Must we submit to these discriminations and inequalities which have created a privileged class— which have corrupted our whole industrial system, so that finance, as I said here some weeks ago, has become synonymous with piracy in the minds of the people? [Applause.] No, Mr. Chairman, we are not helpless or even feeble. Redress—ample and complete redress—is within our power. This bill, in my judgment, affords an important measure of it. The gentleman from Massachusetts assigns as one of his reasons for opposing it that not one line of it specifically prohibits rebates. But, sir, a moment's reflection must satisfy the gentleman that, if no single line of it expressly prohibits rebates, every line of it tends to make rebates impossible. The most effective feature of the bill is the popular determination it embodies; the overwhelming—practically unanimous—popular determination that this evil shall stop, now that its magnitude is understood. [Applause.]

This bill, sir, aims at nothing but justice—to establish justice between a great public function and the people whom it is organized to serve. Its provisions can only become operative where injustice is attempted. It will remain a dead letter while justice is respected and obeyed. Those who are likely to be affected by its operation, and who doubt its policy, who distrust its provisions, who fear that the making of rates by any public body may lead to confusion—contention—and possibly to socialism, can obviate all the possibilities which they apprehend by simply doing justice. For my part I regard the practically unanimous passage of this bill as the most inspiring event since the war of secession, because it registers the inflexible determination of the American people that, whether by the voluntary action of the railroads or by the intervention of Government, justice shall be enthroned in our railway system and in our whole industrial system as it is supposed to be enthroned in our political system, for it is only by extending and maintaining the dominion of justice wherever any function of government is exercised that peace can be permanent in this land and prosperity general among its people. [Prolonged applause.]

James R. Mann [Ill.] supported the bill. He summarized his position as follows:

The fixing of railroad tariffs is the most complex and delicate work now carried on in our country. The interests, the localities, the commodities, the persons interested are as diversified as our land, our productions, and our people. No one set of men ever have or ever can manipulate the delicate mechanism of railway tariffs for all parts of our country, for all commodities produced by us, and for all interests which may be destroyed or upbuilt.

But government must exercise some control. It is as necessary for government to be the judge in the last resort between shipper and carrier as to the rate to be charged as it is for government to determine the right to any other class of property.

The railroad officials fear that it is dangerous to confer, to any extent, rate-making power upon a governmental agency. Let us admit it. There is some danger. No one can tell how dangerous it might become if fully exercised. But no new legislation is ever enacted without some element of danger in its possibilities. The best guaranty is that the pending measure is conservative. It protects the interests of the shipping community and does not permit the confiscation of the railway properties. The present bill is a compromise measure. It probably does not meet the full views of anyone. But the subject is a great one. It is the most stupendous subject in its many ramifications which has ever come before this body. In a sense, we grope in the dark.

This measure is an advance in the complexity of our internal affairs and in the progress of Government paternalism. The necessities of the case require us to take this step. We cannot avoid it. If properly used in the future, it will be a great advantage to both shippers and railroads. If improperly used in the future, we must trust the people to correct its abuse as we must at all times trust the people to provide safe government and to observe the safeguards of government. [Great applause.]

John Sharp Williams [Miss.], the leader of the Democratic minority, spoke in favor of the bill.

I congratulate the Democratic party, because, although in the minority, by constant driving and constant reiteration, a very much cherished Democratic policy is about to triumph under a Republican Administration. [Applause on the Democratic side.]

I need not run over the bill introduced by the Democratic floor leader for the purpose of bringing about this result before any other bill was introduced; the utterance of the last Democratic platform; the utterances of the temporary chairman of the St. Louis convention, calling upon the Republican party to know whether they were going to stand pat or not upon the then impotent condition and the now impotent condition of the Interstate Commerce Commission, as the tribunal to which these questions have been relegated by Congress.

I congratulate the Republican party upon the all-familiar principle that, "as long as the lamp holds out to burn, the vilest sinner may return." [Applause and laughter on the Democratic side.]

I congratulate the President of the United States because although this is not his child in the sense of being blood of his blood and bone of his bone and sinew of his sinew, for all of its blood and bone and sinew are Democratic, it is, at least, his adopted child. [Laughter.] I congratulate the President, because having seen the light on his way to Damascus he has become sincerely and honestly converted.

Mr. Williams then addressed himself to answering objections to the bill.

The gentleman from Maine [Mr. Littlefield], a man of magnificent individuality and courage, who has more than once stood athwart the pathway of a public gust, more than once stood against his own party in the Chamber, made a speech the other day which was, like every speech he has ever made, powerful of its sort, but after you analyze it, Mr. Chairman, you find that it meant but two things:

First, an impassioned appeal to the Congress of the United States to regard as vested rights certain discriminations which, in his opinion, have built up certain New England cities. He based his argument altogether, almost, upon the fact that if these unjust discriminations, if these "preferentials," as he calls them, were done away with, a great many industries in New England would be injured.

Now, Mr. Chairman, the question comes—if such preferentials exist, are they just, are they nondiscriminatory, are they fair? If they are such, then this bill will not interfere with them; if they are unreasonable, unjust, unfair, or discriminatory, will he stand up before the American people and tell them that he wants cities in New England made prosperous and kept prosperous by unjust, unfair, and unreasonable transportation regulations? [Applause.]

Mr. Chairman, there is no vested right in discriminations made by Government-chartered corporations in favor of one person against another, or in favor of one locality against another. There may be a vested wrong, and, if there be, it ought to be done away with just as soon as possible. Ah, Mr. Chairman, it is not without significance that the main opposition to this bill comes from the Northeast. The shareholders, directors, and presidents of the great railroad companies come thence, and they have so fixed so-called "preferentials" and other things—that they call by still more polite names, but the plain English of which is unjust discrimination—as to build up that part of the country in which they are interested at the expense of that part of the country in which they are not interested.

Mr. Chairman, if discriminations, rebates, and unjust preferentials went to the railroad treasury and through the railroad office to the shareholders as dividends, it would not be so bad, but they do not go that way. There are rings within rings in the management of a railroad company just as we have lately ascertained that there are rings within rings in the management of life insurance companies. When the traffic managers of great systems meet in a private room to arrange joint traffic rates, they are not so much guided by the interests of the railroads which they represent as they are guided by the interests of the ring within the ring where management is concentrated and in the places in which they have investments.

The gentleman from Massachusetts [Mr. McCall] talked about the dangerous power to be lodged in these seven men. Why, of course, the power is dangerous. All power is dangerous. The power lodged in twelve men to determine whether I shall be hanged or not is dangerous. [Laughter.]

But power has to be lodged somewhere, and in the ultimate analysis you have to determine where it is safest to lodge it.

To which would you rather give the "power to crush"—to a public tribunal exercising its functions in public, subject to be visited with public indignation, to be removed, or somebody who is doing the crushing act when you do not know when they are doing it, where they are doing it, nor when done know who did it?

I know what a perfect natural-born conservative dread my friend from Massachusetts [Mr. McCall] has of the Government doing too much. I share it with him, but I can assure him that within five years from now he will not know that this legislation was ever passed, except that he will find out that whenever unfair and unreasonable preferentials or discriminations exist they have been terminated. He will find that the railroads will not have many lawsuits, because with this law on the statute books they will themselves correct culpable discriminations between persons or places for the purpose of avoiding being brought up before the Interstate Commerce Commission and being made subject to all this expense.

Now, Mr. Chairman, as to the Federal Government taking too much authority upon itself in the regulation of interstate commerce, I want to say this to Democrats: They seem to forget one side of what old Thomas Jefferson said years ago. He believed in preserving inviolate the reserved rights of the State as the sheet anchor of local self-government and individual liberty, but he added to it, "and the delegated powers of the Federal Government in their full integrity as the only safeguard of national independence."

Now there are two sorts of States rights. The States right to insist that its reserved rights shall not be usurped by the Federal Government, and generally that is all men think about when they think about States rights, but there is a coördinate and coequal States right which exists in this: the right of the State to insist that the Federal Government shall perform the duty delegated to it by the Federal Government for the protection of the State and of the people. [Applause.] That is the States right for which I stand here.

Mr. Chairman, we on this side of the Chamber have dreamed for years that some time we might get into power, and when we did one of the things we were going to do was to pass a bill like this. Now, I think I see this bill take its way out of this Chamber northward, and as it goes northward it shall go as a catapult, overcoming every possible obstruction in its pathway. Oh, it may receive a few stabs over there under the fifth rib in the shape of amendments coming from the enemy acting as nurses to the bill for the time being, while they pretend they are friends of it; a few little railroad jokers may be put in it, but when it comes back let us all, Democrats and Republicans, make up our minds right here to stay here until the next session of Congress comes before we in conference cede one single essential principle in this bill or adopt as an amendment upon it one single thing that will devitalize it in the slightest degree or deprive the commission of that power which it ought to have. [Applause.]

What are we? The American House of Commons. Who are our allies? The man in the White House for one, and he is no contemptible ally either, and I am glad he is with us; the people of the United States, greater than he or we both put together and multiplied by ten. Let us find out who governs America—the President and the House of Commons and the people all added together, or somebody else somewhere else. As for my part, I would be willing to stay here and make it a condition *sine qua non* to the passage of ordinary appropriation bills that this bill should come back from whencesoever it may go—virtually as it now is, or at any rate not rendered impotent of operation by amendment.

Mr. Hepburn closed the debate.

Mr. Chairman, I regret somewhat that some gentlemen participating in this debate should have used the occasion for taking the credit to themselves and to organizations with which they are connected for the present state of legislation upon this great question. This is a matter that ought to rise higher than party. I do not choose to follow any of those who have spoken on these lines further than to suggest that the law that we have was written by Republican hands and pressed through Congress by the arguments and efforts of members of the Republican organization. I want to remind them that the amendments to that law adopted two years later were written by a distinguished Republican, and it was Republican zeal that secured them as part of the law of the land. I want to remind gentlemen that the act of 1890—the Sherman Act—was written by a distinguished Republican Senator; and, further, I want to remind gentlemen that the act of 1903—the Elkins Act—was the work of a distinguished Republican member of the Senate, and that, if there have been shortcomings in the way of declarations in national platforms upon the part of the Republican party, there has been no failure when work was to be done and things were to be accomplished. [Loud applause on the Republican side.]

Mr. Chairman, this is a great question. One-twelfth of all

X—31

the wealth in the United States is involved in greater or less degree in this bill. But even this does not mark fairly the importance of this subject to the American people. Think how dependent we are for our prosperity, for the comforts of life even, upon the common carriers of the land. Think of the infinitude of the transactions between the carriers and those they serve—millions and millions of transactions.

And yet, Mr. Chairman, the gentleman from Massachusetts [Mr. McCall] announced the astonishing doctrine that in all of these multiplied transactions there shall be no practical arbiter, no one to settle disputes except one of the parties in interest.

MR. McCALL.—And the courts.

MR. HEPBURN.—And the courts! Ah, yes, the courts. But we have had the courts during all these years.

I am not like the gentleman from New York [Mr. Cockran], disposed to decry the power, or honor, or necessity for preserving respect for the courts. [Applause.] I recognize they are a necessary agency in the preservation of everything that is dear to the American citizen, and I reprobate, at least, the good taste of any gentleman who undertakes to disparage them in the minds of the people. [Applause.]

I tell you, Mr. Chairman, that whenever that evil day comes, should it ever come, when the people of the United States feel that in the courts they cannot hope for justice, that in the courts they cannot find an agency that will protect them in their rights and punish their offenders—whenever that day comes, and that other spirit "of righting oneself"—when that evil spirit takes possession of the public mind, there is an end to our institutions and to our boasted liberty. [Applause.]

The gentleman from Massachusetts says the remedies by courts are ample. Experience teaches that they are not. Not because of the fault of the courts, but because of the peculiar character of the transactions involved and because of the disparity in individual power of the contestants in the courts.

MR. COCKRAN.—Mr. Chairman, I am sure the gentleman wants to be fair. I would like to know how the statement of the gentleman differs in the slightest degree from the statement that I made. I have not criticised the courts any more than has the gentleman from Iowa [Mr. Hepburn].

MR. HEPBURN.—The remarks of the gentleman from New York seemed to me, if not intended for the purpose, to have the result of inflaming one man's mind against the courts, because that man was taught that, being poor, he lacked the power and could not have that efficient justice, that quick disposal of his business that another man with wealth behind him and station to aid him could have, and it was that spirit that I found in the gentleman's language that seemed to me ought not to pass unrebuked.

MR. COCKRAN.—Mr. Chairman, I would like to ask the gentleman how his statement now differs from mine. It is undisputed that the one person whose imprisonment I took occasion to mention—and I do not at all criticise the justice of that decision—was committed to jail for violation of an injunction, while others, although pronounced guilty of a crime by the decision of that same court, had not been actually incarcerated or even prosecuted.

MR. HEPBURN.—If I misunderstood the character and purpose of the gentleman's remarks, I am sorry.

MR. COCKRAN.—Well, I want to congratulate the committee on this contribution to the discussion, as I understand the gentleman now corroborates me by stating that, so far as the courts are concerned, they are inadequate, and therefore a more efficient agency to effect a remedy must be established.

MR. HEPBURN.—With that portion of the gentleman's remarks I am in entire accord.

It is the carrier that fixes the rate. He imposes upon the other party the necessity of accepting his rate. He may pay the charge and then the common law, says the gentleman from Maine [Mr. Littlefield], gives him a remedy and allows him to recover for the overcharge. Ah, how barren is that remedy! It is a known fact that, though the cases where such suits might be instituted are counted by millions, none is ever brought because of the expense, because of the delay, because of the inability to secure the proof whereby a judgment is within the limits of possibility. Therefore it is futile to talk about the courts as they are constituted furnishing that remedy that ought to be somewhere existent.

Now, what do we do by this bill? The gentlemen who oppose it have discussed it as though it conferred upon the railway commission the power to establish schedules and rates. They have, I think, sometimes purposely set up this bogy for the purpose of combating it. No one has proposed that. The jurisdiction of the commission is limited, as is its power limited, by this law. They cannot at pleasure establish a rate. Before their jurisdiction attaches it must be ascertained that a wrong has been done, an overcharge has been made, a wrong in an extravagant, unreasonable rate, because the law to-day and the common law provide that the carrier's charge shall be just and reasonable. That is the limit to which he is permitted to go in fixing his tariff of schedules.

Now, under the operation of this bill, if it should become a law, it is necessary for some one to allege a violation of the statute—in other words—that a crime has been done. Investigation follows and, if it is ascertained that the carrier is in violation of the law, then the jurisdiction of the commission attaches, and it is permitted to do what? Fix a rate? Oh, no; oh, no. It is permitted to establish a just, reasonable, and fairly remunerative rate that shall be the maximum rate that the carrier shall charge. That is all. Can you think of any legislative effort in the direction of control more conservative than this? One gentleman complains of this bill because the words "unreasonable" or "reasonable" have no accurate judicial determination. There are some words, I think, that cannot be defined, and yet we use them every day, and the courts use them. Is it probable that any two of the critics of this bill would agree as to the legal definition of the word "fraud"? And yet the courts have been industriously at work upon that for centuries, trying to find out what constitutes fraud. There is no definition that would be satisfactory to any lawyer that ever read a law book. There are proximations, and yet you will find after the study of the most carefully prepared definitions that in your own experience you have had cases that do not come within that definition.

I could not define the word "reasonable" in a way satisfactory to myself. I doubt whether any gentleman could do that, but he could in a series of cases, exercising his best discretion, looking at all the facts that may be brought to bear upon a given case, arrive at a conclusion that will be in harmony with the demands of justice and will be right in all of its bearings upon all of the parties. It is a very difficult thing, a very difficult thing, to use words of our English language that are not susceptible of varying interpretations. The gentleman from Ohio [Mr. Grosvenor] was exercised the other day because there was not sufficient definiteness in the language used. I do not know that I see before me one individual whom I believe can write an English sentence of twenty words that I cannot give more than one meaning to. He has undoubtedly heard the story of the little Kentucky girl who at her prayers in the morning said, "Good-by, God; we are going to move to Missouri!" [Laughter.] Her wicked brother, who happened to overhear her, and who was jubilant at the idea of the journey, used the very same sentence, but he said, "Good! By God, we are going to move to Missouri!" [Renewed laughter and applause.]

The gentleman from New York [Mr. Sulzer] told us that this bill did not provide dire and certain punishments behind the bars of the penitentiary for the criminal classes—those whom gentlemen here will agree are violating the provisions of this law or engaged in conduct now that if continued after the proposed law would become criminal—and that it was because of these two defects that the law was fundamentally and radically deficient. He told us with much elation that he had prepared a bill—No. 8414. Those figures impressed themselves upon my memory, and I never will forget them [applause] as the file number of a bill embodying all wisdom upon this subject.

But here is the provision of bill No. 8414 on the subject of punishments. The gentleman wanted Rockefeller and all those gentlemen he named behind the bars, so that he could enjoy the sight of them as prison convicts.

That any person, association, or corporation violating any of the provisions of this act shall be deemed guilty of a misdemeanor—

[Laughter.]
The penitentiary is "suspended." [Laughter and applause.]

And on conviction thereof shall be punished in the manner provided by the act approved February 19, 1903, entitled "An act to further regulate interstate commerce."

You may recollect, gentlemen, that the act of 1903 repealed the prison penalty of the interstate commerce act. [Laughter and applause.]

MR. SULZER.—If I made an error in regard to the extent of the punishment, why did not the gentleman from Iowa; as chairman of the committee, in the interest of the people, amend my bill and make the punishment fit the crime?

MR. HEPBURN.—There is no trouble about answering that question at all, sir. We had an act passed in 1887 that provided vigorous, severe prison penalties for the violation of many provisions of the interstate commerce act.

Up to 1903, sixteen years, no conviction had been had under that act. It was said here upon this floor and elsewhere that the reason was obvious—that the men who knew the facts by which convictions before juries could be made possible were

all of them railroad men. They were the men familiar with
conditions, familiar with facts, the only ones whose testimony
would be adequate to secure convictions, and that there was
that *esprit du corps* among them that they would not testify
where it meant going to prison on the part of their fellows and
that if the punishment were by fine largely increased convictions could be had.

Mr. Hepburn concluded as follows:

I regard this as the most important single question which we
now have to deal with. I do not believe that we will be able
by this legislation or any other to prevent rebates in some
instances being given, to prevent preferences being shown to
some locality, to some person, or to some character of traffic,
but it will aid toward minifying a number of wrongs; it will
give greater contentment to all the people in the belief that
they are not being made the puppet and the football of carriers.
I would be glad if certain other enactments might have been a
part of this bill, but I contented myself in omitting them with
the hope that we could unite upon this measure in the committee
with unanimity and secure its passage through this House without amendment, believing that in other places there might be a
moral effect from that action that would aid in the completion
of the legislation. I thank the members. [Prolonged applause.]

A number of amendments to the bill were offered
and rejected. It was passed on February 8 by a vote
of 346 to 7.

The Senate referred the bill to the Committee on
Interstate Commerce, which reported it on February 26.
It was debated at great length, the chief opponents being
Joseph B. Foraker [O.], John T. Morgan [Ala.], and
Edmund W. Pettus [Ala.], and, after amendment, was
passed on May 18 by a vote of 71 to 3 (the Senators
above mentioned).

Robert M. La Follette [Wis.] took a leading part
in the discussion. In an exhaustive speech thrice continued, beginning on April 19 and ending on April 23,
he advanced a number of propositions, which, on the
day of the vote (May 18), he enumerated, closing with
an appeal for the

Physical Valuation of Railroads

Senator La Follette

I offered several amendments to this bill. I offered no amendment upon which any political question ought to have been raised or any party vote cast. Every amendment which I offered would have strengthened its provisions and made it more just to the shippers, the consumers, and yet not one of those amendments was unfair to the carriers of this country.

I proposed the following amendments to this bill:

1. To restore the penalty of imprisonment for violations of the interstate commerce law.

This amendment was defeated by a vote of 49 nays to 27 ayes, forty-seven of the negative votes being those of Republican and two of Democratic Senators; of the votes for the amendment, twenty-six of the Senators voting were Democrats.

2. To strike out the two-year limitation, by the terms of which orders of the commission expire two years from the time when such orders go into effect.

This amendment was rejected without a roll call, the votes in opposition thereto coming from Republican Senators.

3. To provide that, when testimony is offered upon trial different from the testimony upon which the order of the commission is based, testimony shall be taken by the trial court, the action suspended for fifteen days, the evidence certified back to the commission, and the commission given an opportunity to modify or revoke its former order.

This amendment was defeated—ayes 26, nays 49. Twenty-five Democratic Senators voted for the amendment; forty-eight Republican Senators voted against the amendment.

4. Substitute to section 15 providing for—

(a) Authority for the commission to issue orders upon its own motion.

(b) To fix a maximum rate.

(c) To fix a differential, and to prescribe both a maximum and a minimum rate.

(d) To change the classification of any article.

(e) To determine what regulation or practice in respect to transportation is just and reasonable.

All Republican Senators who voted, excepting myself, voting against the amendment.

5. To forbid every Federal judge who owns shares of stock or bonds of a common carrier subject to the provisions of this

act, or who uses a free pass or procures for the use of others free passes over such railroads, from hearing or deciding any proceeding or presiding at any trial under the provisions of this act.

Laid upon the table by a vote of 40 to 27—forty Republican Senators voting in the affirmative, twenty-five Democratic Senators voting in the negative.

6. That upon the trial of any action brought to set aside or modify any order made by the commission a copy of the evidence introduced by the plaintiff shall, upon motion made on behalf of the commission, be transmitted to the commission, and the court shall stay further proceedings in such action for fifteen days from the date of such transmission that the commission upon receipt of such evidence may alter, modify, or amend the same. The amended order shall take the place of the original order, as though made by the commission in the first instance.

The amendment was laid upon the table without debate— ayes 41, nays 30. Forty Republican Senators voted to lay the motion on the table. All Senators voting in the negative were Democrats except four.

7. That the commission shall estimate and ascertain the fair value of the property of every railroad engaged in interstate commerce, as defined in this act, and used by it for the convenience of the public.

Motion to lay on the table rejected by a *viva voce* vote. Motion later renewed, and amendment laid on the table—ayes 40, nays 27. Thirty-nine Republican Senators voted to lay the amendment on the table. All votes against laying the amendment on the table were recorded by Democratic Senators except six.

8. To adopt the block system, insuring greater safety to the traveling public. Amendment rejected without roll call. All votes against the amendment came from the Republican side of the Chamber.

9. For the railway employers' liability amendment for the relief of railway employees.

Defeated—ayes 28, nays 45. Those who voted in the affirmative were all Democrats except four. Of those voting against the amendment all were Republicans except three.

There cannot be offered here or before the country any satisfactory argument or reason against the amendments which I proposed. No arguments have been made or reasons offered against their adoption. My Republican colleagues, under the leadership of a few New England Senators, lined up to vote down those amendments in nearly every instance without explanation or justification.

This bill, when it becomes a law, will not put this question at rest. It cannot. When Congress merely clothes the commission with power to ascertain whether rates are relatively equal and withholds from it all authority and all means of determining whether those rates are just and reasonable, it cannot be expected that such inadequate legislation will solve this great problem and satisfy the public demand for not only equal, but also just and reasonable rates.

The question which this bill should settle, but does not settle, will be a live issue in the next campaign for the election of men to both branches of Congress who will stand for a full measure of relief from oppressive transportation abuses.

So long as the legislation relative to the common carriers of this country permits these corporations to increase their capital stock without limit, increase it without adding anything of value to their properties, and increase it solely with the purpose of fixing rates upon that inflated capitalization, in order to pay profits and dividends to those holding the stocks and bonds, in which they have no real investment, just so long this question will be a vital issue before the American people.

There is to-day in the stock and bond valuation of the railroads of this country upward of seven billions of water. If the American people are expected to continue to pay transportation charges that will make a return upon that valuation, the temper of the people of this country is not understood here. Until there is invested in this commission or some other authoritative body the power to determine the real, true valuation of the railroads of this country and the authority to fix rates so that they shall bear only a fair return upon that fair value, Senators may as well understand now that you will have this question constantly before you. It will not be possible to suppress it or keep it within the closed doors of committees for nine years to come. At every session, until an adequate measure is adopted, while I remain a member of this body the demand will be made here for legislation that will insure to the people of every State fair treatment at the hands of the common carriers of the country.

On May 25 the House disagreed to the Senate amendments, and the bill went to conference. This was abortive, and a second conference was ordered which also ended in disagreement. The third conference was successful. It reported a compromise bill on June 28. The compromise provisions were thus explained by James S. Sherman [N. Y.] of the committee:

The new bill incorporated generally the Senate amendment forbidding passes except to certain classes of passengers such as railroad employees, charity agents and objects of charity, inmates of soldiers' homes, etc.;

It ordered the installation of switch connections where the commission thought advisable;

It receded from the Senate amendment forbidding discrimination between passengers (e. g., as against negroes, thus permitting "Jim Crow" cars);

It forbade "rebating" in the fullest and most explicit fashion;

It changed the House provision requiring that the order of the commission shall take effect thirty days after notice to the carrier to the Senate amendment that, except in the case of money payment, the order shall take effect "within a reasonable time—not less than thirty days";

It provided for appeals from orders to the Supreme Court;

It made the "original carrier," i. e., the railroad taking the shipment, responsible for the same.

The bill was passed on June 29, and signed by President Roosevelt on June 30, 1906.

DATE DUE

GAYLORD			PRINTED IN U.S.A.